COME & GET IT!

MCDONALDIZATION AND THE DISAPPEARANCE OF LOCAL FOOD FROM A CENTRAL ILLINOIS COMMUNITY

Robert Dirks

Published by
McLean County Historical Society
200 N. Main St.
Bloomington, Illinois

MᶜLEAN COUNTY
MUSEUM
ᴼᶠ**HISTORY**

For Deborah

CONTENTS

McLean County in Illinois

WI

IA

IN

MO

Scale
50mi

KY

INTRODUCTION

This book surveys the history of eating and drinking in McLean County, Illinois from pioneer days in the 1820s through the final years of the twentieth century. I began writing it as the master text for a museum exhibit initiated by Greg Koos, Executive Director of the McLean County Museum of History (MCMH). He wanted to assemble a show that told the story of food in Central Illinois. The exhibit, which he later dubbed "Come & Get It!" would recount the foodways of past generations with ample illustrations drawn from the museum's rich collection of food-related objects.[1]

Greg offered me the job of writing the script. I had some experience having worked on the museum's permanent exhibit many years before. I also lived in the area for more than 30 years and was busy writing about the diet and nutrition of American immigrants. I saw Greg's offer as a fine opportunity. It would give me a chance to acquire a better understanding of local foodways, including some of the traditions and tastes I have enjoyed over the years, not to mention others I have abhorred, but better yet, I would be able to complement my historical grasp of American diet and nutrition nationwide by taking a detailed look at the food history of a particular community, a place that in many ways has been typical of the country as a whole and the Midwest in particular. Best of all, the project would break new ground. To my knowledge, never before has a comprehensive, holistic culinary history been written at a community level. There have been studies of regional foodways – plenty of them – but never an account at the level of a town, a city, or a particular county. As an anthropologist, I am inclined to take little communities as microcosms, so the prospect of writing a food history at ground level struck me as a meaningful challenge.

Greg assured me that I would have a free hand to tell the story the way I wanted to, but I knew the exhibit had to be something more than a pleasant trip down memory lane. The museum takes local history seriously. Substantial intellectual frameworks invariably inform its exhibits and help the public make holistic sense of the objects on display. With this in mind, I suggested that Come & Get It! revolve around several kitchens, each representative of a particular historical period.[2] The objects in these kitchens and the ancillary materials connecting them to the food economy beyond the kitchen door would serve as a kind of case study showing the effects of rationalization and delocalization on our food system.

RATIONALIZATION

Rationalization refers to the application of a business model to the processes of manufacture, distribution, and consumption. Applied to food, the model has been called "McDonaldization" after the restaurant giant that has so aggressively applied it.[3] But, the principles involved in rationalization pre-existed McDonald's and, for that matter, fast-food joints and chain restaurants generally. The principle of efficiency, the cornerstone of rationalization, was the focus of a late nineteenth century social movement that postulated the existence of one best way to get something done. A second principle, the notion of calculability, insists that "best" be determined quantitatively – the shorter distance, the least amount of time, the biggest bang for the buck, etc. The third principle of McDonaldization has to do with replication and tolerates no surprises. Never must a procedure deviate from its defined course. That demands control, a fourth principle. To stay on course and be perfectly predictable, everyone must do as directed.

Today, these principles appear inexorable, sweeping through every industry and every institution from agriculture to religion the world over. So pervasive is rationalization that it is easy to forget that it is not a natural process but rather a cultural contrivance, an invention based on a set of beliefs and practices international in their appeal.

DELOCALIZATION

Delocalization refers to the backside of globalization. The latter describes an ongoing process by which regional societies become integrated through a worldwide network of communication and economic activity. The process begins with rational approaches to modernization and results in progressive centralization and standardization. Local economies become parts of a national economy and go on from there to become constituents in international systems of exchange. Delocalization refers to a concomitant loss of integrity at regional and community levels and to the disappearance of locally distinctive products and activities.

The delocalization of food and drink is an old story, universal in scope. It began in ancient times with incipient urbanization and still goes on throughout most of the world. In parts of China and India recently exposed to intense economic development, delocalization proceeds at a dizzying pace. Peoples who less than a generation ago ate nothing but foods raised close to home now consume supermarket diets consisting primarily of imported foods. Most regions of the industrial West began experiencing such changes many years ago, though usually at a slower pace than that experienced in developing areas nowadays.

THE CASE OF MCLEAN COUNTY

McLean County, Illinois, the largest county in Illinois, has a population of somewhat over 173,000 persons. Bloomington-Normal, its metropolitan center, sits about half way between Chicago and St. Louis, adjacent to the interchanges linking Interstate Highways 39, 55, and 74. The metropolitan area's population totals approximately 165,000. Employment is largely white collar and concentrated heavily in insurance and finance (e.g., State Farm Insurance, Country Financial) and education (e.g., Illinois State and Illinois Wesleyan Universities).

Tracing the course of rationalization and delocalization in McLean County and the Bloomington-Normal area takes us back 180 years. Early settlers from the Southern states and parts of the Northeast brought with them divergent tastes, but irrespective of their culinary leanings they generally made do with foods they either raised or collected themselves. Later on, newcomers from Ireland and Continental Europe established homes in various parts of the county. As a result, area foodways increased in complexity, and a variety of new food-related industries developed. Residents made beer, candy, ice cream, pickles, sausages, soda water, and vinegar. They manufactured stoves and refrigerators, milled flour, baked various types of bread, packed pork, and canned tomatoes. Bloomington companies distributed produce and groceries throughout Central Illinois. Still, many families beyond the city limits produced and processed nearly everything they ate and only occasionally visited a grocery store. By the end of the second millennium it was hard to find locally produced food in McLean County, let alone people with many food-related skills. The area's telephone directories listed no cheese shops or fishmongers. Skilled butchers and bread bakers barely existed. A couple of artisanal confectioners still had shops in Bloomington, but you could forget it if you wanted to buy milk from a local dairy. Finding groceries and fresh produce outside of a chain supermarket was a challenge, not to mention locating a chef-owned restaurant.

The McDonaldization of eating and drinking in McLean County has been across the board and patently extreme. Other parts of the Midwest have their eccentric foods and unique dishes, items that somehow have never been appropriated by chains and featured on franchise menus. Southeastern Wisconsin has its brats and other wursts, Upper Michigan the pasty, Southern Indiana its persimmon dishes and turtle suppers. Some places in Illinois celebrate burgoo as enthusiastically as folks do in Kentucky. Chicago has its special hot dog and deep-dish pizza, and Springfield has its horseshoe sandwich. McLean County, however, has nothing distinctive. Its residents eat as America eats, and generally speaking they are proud of it. Boosters in the 1990s chuckled and took obvious satisfaction in learning that few other places in the country had as many fast-food outlets per capita as Bloomington-Normal. Citizens throughout the county take pride in the more than 325,000 acres covered in corn and nearly 310,000 acres devoted to soybeans and the fact no other place in the United States funnels as much corn and soy into the nation's industrial food system.[4] Fruits and vegetables amount to no more than an afterthought. McLean County farmers according to recent figures maintain just 56 acres of orchard and cultivate a mere 52 acres of garden vegetables.[5] Livestock and dairy production barely exist. All of this means that McLean County comes nowhere close to feeding itself. Nearly every food and beverage consumed in the area bears a UPC stamp and arrives by tractor-trailer. Indeed, probably less than four percent of the food consumed in McLean County even comes from within the State of Illinois.[6]

WHAT MAKES FOOD HABITS CHANGE

What explains delocalization and rationalization? The short answer is profitability. A longer answer involves some economics and conversations about comparative advantage, economies of scale, and how people make effective choices. When it comes to explaining eating and drinking, however, economic thinking takes us only so far. This is because cultural inertia – commonly referred to as "custom" or "tradition" – often gets in the way, and overcoming it can be difficult and sometimes chaotic.

Simply stated, decisions about what to put on the table and how to eat it are never determined by economy alone. Cost is important, and inexpensive may be good, but for something cheap to be regarded as eatable also requires a certain mentality or cultural complicity. A vegetarian has no interest in a fine looking beefsteak, no matter how low the butcher prices it. The very expression "eating habit" indicates some resistance to change. Habits have a history, and their persistence often defies reason. American nutritionists a century ago worried that Italian immigrants behaved irrationally. They generally had little money, yet in spite of their poverty they purchased costly cheeses, fruits, and olive oils and ignored cheaper alternatives. Experts called for re-education. As nutritionists and economists saw it, the Italians needed to be assimilated. As consumers and aspiring Americans, they had yet to learn that cheap is good, irrespective of tastes and traditions. Assimilation meant getting immigrants to accept new paradigms. It required making newcomers see things and think about them in previously unfamiliar yet locally acceptable ways. The process never met with total success among Italian Americans, at least as far as food was concerned. They continued and continue to this day to spend more than most Americans on groceries, and customary eating habits remain a defining characteristic of Italian-American identity.

None of this is to say that economy does not have a powerful influence but merely that foodways carry a great deal of cultural and historical baggage. This often makes them difficult to overturn. Pressures – in some instances ecological, in others economic or political – build and build. A social crisis develops. People find themselves in a predicament, conflicted between habit and novelty, torn between old ways of thinking and completely new attitudes. Suddenly, a tipping point is reached and rapid change ensues.

This image of how culinary history works compels me to think about McDonaldization and delocalization against a background of sometimes-thorny turning points in the history of the region and the nation. These began in McLean County with overhunting and the collapse of a frontier way of life and culminated with the consumerism of the late twentieth century that reduced the role of homemaker to part-time work. In between, local foodways were shaken up by anti-saloon and nativist agitation, World War I and the rise of Home Economics, the Great Depression, World War II, and the automotive revolution. I consider each of these predicaments and their effects over the course of six chapters with a final chapter devoted in part to the contradictions that currently afflict our culinary culture and threaten established ways.

ACKNOWLEDGEMENTS

A great number of people help me research and write *Come & Get It!* I have already credited Greg Koos for the original idea, but I would be remiss were I not to add an expression of thanks for the expertise he lavished on this project. Greg's readiness to share his knowledge of McLean County's history proved as ample as his mastery of the subject. Susan Hartzold, curator of the Come & Get It! exhibit, was no less generous. Her questions and reminders about effective communication have resulted in more improvements in this narrative than I can count. Bill Kemp, the museum's multi-talented Librarian and Archivist, extended countless courtesies, guided me through collections, and kept me supplied with source materials. I also received substantial assistance from the museum's Registrar, Terri Clemens, and Director of Education, Candace Summers. Rachael Kramp, Education Program Coordinator, graciously found time in her schedule to draw the maps that accompany this text. Other members of the staff who contributed to the project include Graham Cowger, Manager of Development Operations; his predecessor, Scott Callan; George Perkins, Assistant Librarian; Jeffery Woodard, Director of Marketing and Community Relations; and Mary Anne Schierman, Director of Volunteers and Interns. Mary Ann helped recruit a very capable set of student assistants. These included Illinois State University (ISU) graduate students in Historic Archaeology Meredith Hawkins, the late Melissa Khojamova, and Stephanie Lechert; ISU undergraduates Derek Koshinski , Betsy Ludewig, and Bryan Alverez; and Rachel Shulman, an Illinois Wesleyan University history major. Additional help came from museum volunteer Jose Sacaridiz.

Long conversations with members of the Come & Get It! Exhibit Advisory Committee, including Julie Dobski, Margaret Esposito, Sandy McGhee Yanzy, Michael Pullin, Terri Ryburn-Lamonte, and Elsie Schalk, got the project off on the right foot by helping to define key issues and to identify potentially useful sources of information. I also received helpful suggestions from committee members Nancy Steele Brokaw, Robert Cullen, and Connie Mueller as well as from Robin Bagwell at University of Illinois Extension - McLean County.

An especially valuable service rendered by members of the Exhibit Advisory Committee was to identify well-informed members of the community I might tap as expert informants. I am grateful to Margaret Esposito who identified herself and her friend Marian Harris as candidates. Both women provided pages of information about kitchens and cooking back in the days before modern appliances. Nancy Steele Brokaw volunteered for an extended and wide-ranging interview about places to eat in Bloomington-Normal in decades past, and I owe her an extra thank-you for sharing with me drafts of the many historically informed restaurant reviews she wrote for *The Pantagraph*. My thanks go out as well to Michael Pullin, who suggested I interview Dorothy Bushnell, a veteran kitchenware retailer, and then took time to sit in on that conversation and contribute to it. I am obliged to Dan Barringer; Henry and Terra Brockman; Jack Capodice; Bill Case; Ike Chiu; Ruthie Cobb; Steve and Glaida Funk; Dennis Gieseke; Myra Gordon; Bob and Sandy Knapp; Arden Nowers; Ray, Alice, and Casey Lartz; Jackie Pope-Ganser; Sally Pyne; Tony Robbins; Don and Ruthie Roth; Marty Travis; Ed and Anna Marie Ulbrich; Marilyn and Larry Wettstein; and Mabel Wu, all of whom gave me permission to record their recollections and ideas about aspects of local food history, not only for the benefit of this book, but for the museum's archives and posterity generally.[7] My appreciation extends to Marcia Young, Site Superintendent of the David Davis Mansion State Historic Site, and Rebecca Landau, former Executive Director of the Ewing Property at Illinois State University, for helping me understand what I needed to know about Sarah and David Davis, their Clover Lawn estate, and the people who worked there. Other readers of the many drafts that went into the making of this book included Deborah Dirks, Kathryn Dirks, Mike Dougherty, Julie Hendricks, Bob Hathway, Mike Matejka, Charlie Schlenker, and Mark Wyman. Their ideas inspired me to enrich the content of this work, improve its style, and in the end, produce a more comprehensive history of the way we ate than I originally planned.

Finally, I want to express my gratitude to museum publications volunteer William P. LaBounty and Ruthie Cobb, editor *extraordinaire*. William generously took on the task of preparing the manuscript to go to press and helped make last minute changes. Ruthie, who impressed me with her tireless proficiency in whipping the final draft of this book into shape, turned out to be a font of knowledge about many of the people and places that populated McLean County's food scene over the years. Thanks to Ruthie, I was able to add more to the story even as it was being edited.

CHAPTER 1 – FRONTIER APPETITES

The settlement of Central Illinois by Euro-Americans began in the 1820s, and almost from the start there were disagreements about foods and eating habits. The first settlers, folks from Southern Appalachia, saw the way Indians ate as vile, and the New Englanders and New Yorkers who arrived a short time after the Southerners insulted their cookery and table manners.[1] The feeling was mutual. Each group had its own tastes, its own style of cooking, its own notions about the proper way to eat and drink. This made the Illinois frontier a kind of microcosm of early nineteenth-century America where there was no single food tradition that engaged the entire nation. Typical diets and food habits varied by region, proximity to ports, ethnic group, and occupation. Wealth and social class also came into play.

Still, there were certain conditions in common. Most people, for instance, ate foods produced close to home, and furthermore nearly everyone's diet changed with the seasons. Fresh fruits and vegetables generally disappeared from the table after the first frost.[2] Cabbage, onions, turnips, and a few other species could be stored for a time, but if they ran out families had to make do until spring with various sorts of pickles and fruits either dried or preserved in thick syrups. Bread was usually more constant. In most places, it was more likely to be made of corn than wheat because the latter could be difficult to grow and expensive to purchase. Barley, oats, and rye were popular in certain areas as well.[3] With their bread, Americans ate meat and usually a lot of it. Adults consumed on average around 300 pounds of flesh per year.[4] Most of it was pork, and usually it was cured. People ate hardly any poultry so as not to depress egg production.[5] Dishes tended to be well spiced, at least in well-to-do households, and everyone developed a sweet tooth – no doubt because sugars and syrups were commonly used as preservatives.[6] As for beverages, the Central Illinois frontier existed during the golden age of the fermented and the distilled. Whiskey and cider accompanied meals, and no gathering outside of church took place without copious amounts of alcohol – no surprise then that the average annual rate of consumption in 1830 amounted to around four gallons per capita.[7]

EARLY SETTLERS

The first wave of European Americans to settle McLean County consisted of self-styled "White Folks" from the mountains of Kentucky, Tennessee, Virginia, and other parts of the South.[8] Many came to the region after spending a few years in Southern Illinois, Indiana, or Ohio. Other Americans often saw these largely unlettered rustics as particularly rude and uncivilized. Men wore their hair long and walked around barefoot. When it turned cold, they slipped on moccasins and buckskin shirts and britches, donned homespun overcoats, and covered their heads with wolf-skin caps. A man dressed in a buckskin outfit dyed green might strut about and reckon himself very stylish. Such garb appeared vulgar to those who subscribed to metropolitan fashion, but White Folks did not genuflect toward the metropolis. They embraced a decidedly parochial worldview in which a person made the most of life by relying on whatever resources came most easily to hand. For their material needs, people depended heavily on local plant and animal species. As for human resources, all anybody needed, the local community provided.

Among the first White Folks to venture into Central Illinois were John Hendrix and John Dawson, two young men who met in Ohio and became inseparable. They set out for Illinois with their families in 1821. After spending the winter in Sangamon County, the two headed north. When they came upon Keg Grove, later called "Blooming Grove," in what was to become McLean County, they liked the look of the place and decided to settle. Others soon joined them.

The first to show up were brothers William and Thomas Orendorff. They set out from Sangamon County in 1823, and after considerable scouting south and east of the Illinois River they encountered nothing more to their liking than Keg Grove. William, who was born in Georgia, and Thomas, a native of South Carolina, had moved to Illinois in 1817 and settled in St. Clair County. After a short time, they resettled in Sangamon County but to their dismay on land too soggy to cultivate properly. Keg Grove looked more promising.[9] However, no sooner did the Orendorffs set to work clearing timber than Machina, a Kickapoo chief, came to their cabin and ordered them to leave. His manner was threatening and caused the brothers considerable concern. Aside from Hendrixes and Dawsons and a handful of men who had a salt works near Danville they knew of no other White Folks on the Grand Prairie.[10] A few lead miners worked around Galena to the northwest, but the Indians in that direction were rumored hostile. The Orendorffs, however, refused to be intimidated, and nothing further came of the incident.

Soon more settlers began to arrive. One of them, Elijah Walden, built a cabin in middle of Keg Grove by a small clearing the Indians had cut for their gardens a year or so before. There he found plenty of building material and fuel, and a superabundance of mast (fodder) for pigs. Most pioneers preferred to live near the edge of the woods where the land was easier to clear and game proved more abundant. A nearby creek was ideal. Otherwise, water had to be not far below ground. Walden dug a well and drew water from it with a sweep, a long pole pivoted on a stump located some distance away. To the well-end of the sweep, he fastened a bucket using vines. When he lowered the bucket into the well, the sweep gave him the leverage to raise it with little effort.

DWELLINGS AND FIREPLACES

Because White Folks generally arrived with few possessions, their household goods were generally as makeshift as Walden's waterworks. All the Hendrixes and Dawsons brought with them aside from some livestock were several bags of corn and wheat flour, a few tools and farm implements, some kitchen utensils, a couple of bedsteads, a table, and several chairs. Robert and Dorothy Stubblefield, who settled at Funks Grove in 1824, carried even less. Robert, a Virginian by birth, enlisted as a soldier during the War of 1812, and after surviving a case of near-fatal yellow fever, he followed his brother, Edward, to Ohio. There he wed Dorothy, and 10 years later took out after his brothers-in-law for Central Illinois. The Stubblefields built a house measuring just 18 by 20 feet. They crammed into it a bed, several frame chairs, and six old-fashioned homemade chairs. Robert crafted a table by cutting a puncheon from a tree limb and fitting it with four-foot legs.

Cabins like the Stubblefield's were typically made of logs and generally over-crowded from the start because in addition to providing shelter they served as primary storage space. Eliza Farnham, a visitor from New York, put up for the night in a two-room cabin in Tazewell County.[11] There she found her sleeping place crowded with three beds, two chairs, four barrels of flour, bundles of old clothing, and a cast-off fireplace oven. Settlers usually built a little smokehouse adjacent to their cabin, and when not being used to cure meat it helped temporarily relieve some of the congestion. The long-term solution was a larger dwelling. One example, the "Old Orendorff Brick" located in Tazewell County, survived well into the twentieth century. It was built by Aaron Orendorff (unrelated to William and Thomas) who emigrated from Kentucky in 1827. He originally constructed a typical cabin but soon longed for a house like "his old Kentucky home." In 1832, he baked the necessary bricks and built one. It measured 18 by 32 feet, stood one and a half stories tall, and had two rooms on each floor. On the ground floor, Orendorff fitted one of them with two doors and five windows to create a cooking space far more open than that of the typical log cabin. However, a great fireplace still dominated the room, leaving the Old Orendorff Brick, in spite its relatively spacious kitchen, firmly planted in the log cabin era.

McLean County's earliest fireplaces were not nearly as large and substantial as those Ordendorff built. Jesse Funk, the first to settle Funks Grove, constructed his out of wooden puncheons and plastered them with clay. The chimney was nothing more than sticks and mud. Folks used such fireplaces to cook by extending two or three chains across them for positioning pots and kettles.

The cooking vessels themselves were typically large but few in number. The Dawsons arrived at Keg Grove with a Dutch oven, a skillet, a pot, and a teakettle. The Stubblefields brought only a Dutch oven and a skillet. The Dutch oven, which was made of cast iron, had a capacity of six gallons. Legs three inches long enabled it to stand up in ashes. The Stubblefields baked bread in it. Others made do with homemade clay ovens. The Stubblefield's cast iron skillet had a handle about a foot long and held about four or five gallons of liquid. The family used it as a frying pan and to boil meat and cabbage. Some households used "spiders," pans equipped with legs, for the same purposes. These vessels were all very heavy, and the bending and lifting required positioning them over the fire made cooking strenuous and tiresome work. With the added hazard of open flames and the danger of losing one's balance, burns ranked as one of the leading causes of death among women on the frontier.

Cooking in the nineteenth century called for considerable physical activity. Substances were chopped, churned, mixed and pounded by hand. Spices had to be ground. Coffee needed to be roasted first and then ground.

LOCAL SUBSISTENCE

White Folks, specifically the men, made no secret about being more interested in hunting than in farming. The Dawsons, Hendrixes, Orendorffs, Waldens and the rest embarked on a mixed subsistence, but all across Central Illinois the first settlers showed less enthusiasm for planting crops than they showed for hunting, fishing, and foraging. Not that anyone could afford to neglect farming from a practical standpoint, but frontiersmen were no more deeply dedicated to raising corn than the Kickapoo and other Indians they drove off. Rather than stalwart peasants committed to ax and hoe, frontiersmen above all valued their rifles and the skills it took to bring game to the family table. Hunting provided deer, turkey, prairie chicken (grouse), quail, squirrel, goose, and duck, and men looked forward each year to autumn when they could leave their corn standing in the field and set off after game fulltime. In this way, the pioneers' way of life was not entirely unlike the Kickapoo's. Men hunted and did some of the heavy agricultural work, but women produced most of the cultivated foods. Pioneer women raised sweet corn, pumpkins, beans, potatoes, and a variety of greens in their gardens. They tended flocks of chickens and geese, collected eggs, killed roosters, milked cows, and churned butter. They made pickles, cider, dried fruits, fruit butters, and jams and in addition assumed much of the responsibility for grains and fodder.

HUNTING

Old settlers, thinking back to wilderness days, recalled nothing more enjoyable than hunting. Certainly it was not difficult. Clearing land and planting crops was backbreaking labor, but game on the Illinois prairie was plentiful and at first almost tame. The quality of hunting as White Folks saw it gave value to the land, and good hunting spelled easy living. Corn planting attracted deer and made hunting nearly effortless. Men could simply lie in wait at night next to a field and shoot the animals as they approached. John Dawson shot deer out the front door of his cabin. Men in the Springfield area found that half a day's hunting produced a week's supply of meat. Fishing proved worthwhile, but hunting fowl, primarily turkey and prairie chicken was perhaps the most rewarding of all. Hunters killed the greatest number of turkeys during the spring "gobbling season." By chirping through a quill to make a sound resembling the call of a female turkey, William Wilcox of Money Creek could kill as many as a dozen turkeys a day. The prairie chicken was more ubiquitous than turkey and even easier to kill. Admittedly indifferent hunters, like Samuel Richardson of LeRoy, had no difficulty shooting prairie chickens. Abraham Carlock, a mountaineer from Virginia and a resident of White Oak Grove, remembered his boys catching upwards of twenty or thirty prairie chickens in a single trap, some of which they set no more than 30 yards from the Carlock house . The birds were then "dried and hung on strings to be preserved." John and Cassandra Smith's boys trapped 750 prairie chickens during the winter of 1834. This harvest, taken during their first winter in the Mackinaw Timber near present-day Lexington, was salted away in barrels and proved sufficient to last the family well into the following summer.

Avid and indiscriminate hunting and trapping resulted in regional extinctions even before agriculture completely transformed the character of Central Illinois's environment. Beaver, otter, valued for their furs, disappeared first. Next to go were the brown bear, the panther, and the gray wolf. As predator populations declined, rabbits and squirrels increased. Deer and the prairie chicken, in spite of terrific pressure from hunters, also resisted extinction, primarily because the pioneer landscape of mixed farming and virgin prairie created an environment that favored them with increased carrying capacity. Toward the end of the frontier era, the state's prairie chicken population numbered in excess of 10 million birds. However, as the nineteenth century drew to a close, loss of habitat, unregulated hunting, and the introduction the ring-necked pheasant together brought about a catastrophic drop in numbers. Local extinction occurred about 1899 when Bloomington's *Daily Pantagraph* reported the prairie chicken so scarce that local hunters were returning home disappointed.

FOOD COLLECTING

Early settlers in addition to hunting and fishing gathered a considerable number of wild fruits, nuts, roots, and tubers. They also collected two very important sweet liquids, the honey of wild bees and the sap of the sugar maple. These products and their procurement received a significant amount of attention because when it came to sweetening and preserving other foods there were practically no alternatives. Cane sugar, especially white sugar, was exceedingly expensive and rarely used. A story went around for years about William Buckles of Buckles Grove. He was drinking coffee at a neighbor's house and had never laid eyes on granulated white sugar. His host, thinking Buckles might want to sweeten his cup, set a bowl of it in front of him. Buckles passed, declaring resolutely he never took salt in his coffee.

HONEY

Buckles and other McLean County folks normally used honey and plenty of it to sweeten their coffee as well as their tea. Honey, in fact, rated as one of the most important items in the frontier diet, and indicative of its importance collecting honey counted as a manly skill akin to stalking deer and shooting wolves. Indeed, people talked about "bee hunting," not about collecting honey or wax.

The bee hunters' quarry, the common honeybee (*Apis mellifera*), originally came to North America from England in 1622 as a domestic species. Subsequently, it moved westward independent of beekeepers through a process of periodic swarming and hive division. As a result, runaway colonies could be found all along the North American frontier and as far as 100 miles in advance of white settlement. When the first settlers arrived in McLean County they discovered colonies of honey bees already well established in the groves.

As an expeditionary activity, bee hunting, like deer and duck hunting, took place in the fall. However, men and boys watched for bees and throughout the summer followed them back to their hives. A hive was usually holed up in a so-called "bee tree." Hunters marked bee trees with their initials. Later that fall they returned to cut down the tree and rob the hive of honey and wax. A good bee hunter might find as many as 30 bee trees a season and collect as much as 50 gallons of honey and 60 pounds of beeswax.

Great bee hunters did substantially better. For example, one year William Stansberry of Cheney's Grove collected 300 pounds of honey, and at one point in the 1840s he had in his cabin a three-year supply. James Reyburn, a settler at Panther Creek, accumulated a trough of honey six feet long and 18 inches wide. He had comb piled up outside his cabin as high as two feet. Reyburn, who much preferred hunting over farming, left McLean County and moved on after just two years, but people remembered his prowess as a bee hunter.

Like Indians counting coup, bee hunters and their kin recounted quantities of honey and wax taken and related exploits. Take, for instance, John Benson, a man who grew up in Kentucky, served in the War of 1812, and settled early on at Keg Grove. Years later, his relatives and friends recalled Benson as "a great bee hunter." They recollected – no doubt because the story had been recited over and over again – that the first bee tree John found was on Salt Creek.

Out of it he obtained three gallons of honey. On the day following he found a tree, out of which he took six gallons of honey and eight pounds of beeswax, and after that he found many trees and much honey.[12]

Similarly, settlers remembered Jonathan Hodge, a Stout's Grove pioneer, as "a great hunter . . . very successful in his excursions after bees, wolves, deer, turkeys, etc." Hodge's reputation was further enhanced by the fact that he hunted bees with Sabena, a Potawatami chief. Ephraim Stout, founder of the Stout's Grove settlement (later renamed Danvers), hunted with the celebrated frontiersman Daniel Boone – and was reputed to be a better hunter than Boone. Stout once astonished a party of fellow hunters, who had collected more honey than their containers could hold, by cutting down a butternut tree and building a barrel on the spot.

Perhaps the most famous bee hunters in all of Central Illinois were the Newcoms. Ethan Newcom and his son, Joseph, left Ohio and in 1828 settled the Sangamon Timber some 40 miles from Blooming Grove. Later they moved to Cheney's Grove, but one warm September day before they relocated, the men found two bee trees. Having seen other bee hunters in the vicinity, the Newcoms needed to act fast. The men had no time for protective clothing or becalming smoke. They cut down the trees, endured the enraged bees' stings, and wound up terribly sore for weeks. Nonetheless, the two got away with about 20 gallons of honey.

Honey was exceedingly abundant in McLean County, so much so that nobody could sell it locally. Rest assured, however, that the Newcoms did not suffer the pain bees inflicted upon them for sake of reputation, or because they were especially fond of sweets. They had a pecuniary motive, but realizing it required carting their spoils far beyond McLean County. The Newcoms on one occasion hauled 1,000 pounds of honey and 60 pounds of beeswax to Chicago and returned 75 dollars richer. This was a large sum of money on the frontier, and men went to great lengths to cash in. Parties came up from Sangamon County to hunt bees in McLean County. Groups from McLean County hunted bees to the north along the Kankakee River. Isaiah Coon, an immigrant out of Ohio, freshly settled near Towanda, traveled west with two companions in the autumn of 1836. They ventured far beyond the frontier into Iowa and six weeks later returned with six barrels of honey and 150 pounds of beeswax.

MAPLE TAPPING

Although today one thinks of maple syrup as the chief product of the hard maple, early settlers tapped the trees primarily to make sugar. Indeed, *Acer saccharum*, which continues to thrive in McLean County's remaining woodlands, is still referred to popularly as the "sugar maple." Several stands were once well-maintained groves or so-called "sugarbushes." Some of them pre-existed white settlement. Pioneers found them cleared of underbrush and competing trees, presumed them abandoned, and claimed ownership.

Indians husbanded the sugar maple because its sap constituted an essential source of nourishment. It flowed and could be harvested in great quantities toward the end of winter, a fortuitous time just when supplies of other foods usually were running low and people face imminent starvation. Hunting did not answer to caloric needs at this point on the calendar given the exceedingly lean quality of late-winter game. However, the two percent solution of sucrose in the rising sap of the sugar maple filled the bill perfectly, and when the "sugar moon" appeared in February and a run of warm days punctuated with cold nights caused the sap to rise, it came like a godsend.

Bands of hunters and their families promptly established sugaring camps. Men cut wood, built huge fires, and heated a large number of stones. Women prepared the maples by cutting horizontally across their trunks. Sap flowed from these wounds through wooden spiles and into birch-bark buckets. The women emptied full buckets into big wooden troughs where the sap met the hot stones, came to a boil, and soon granulated. The Indians stored granulated sugar in bark envelops and used it to season foods, but before they made a single crystal of sugar everyone drank large quantities of the thickening, energy-rich sap. This syrupy drink had a remarkably revitalizing affect, and what with high spirits all around, life in a sugar camp invariably proved more festive than laborious. Sugaring had the same effect on White Folks. Neighbors got together and camped in the groves, sometimes for weeks on end. Nancy Howell Conger, a resident of Stout's Grove, told her son, Robert, that she looked forward to sugaring as "great sport."

In the settlers' sugar camps, women tended the trees and the boiling. Men fueled the fires and hunted game. Hilda Deems remembered her father getting his sugar camp ready in February. He first built a wall of mud and brick about three feet high and placed his great iron kettle between the walls. He then cut and stacked plenty of wood. Brush and limbs went into neat piles, ready to burn for the amusement of those who found themselves boiling sap late at night. Deems next readied his troughs and spiles. He made troughs by sawing logs about two feet long, splitting them in half, and hollowing out the centers. The spiles he fashioned from sumac. He bored holes into his maples with an auger, placed a short length of sumac stem in each hole, and removed the pith from inside the stem so the sap could run through. Once the sap began to flow, someone always kept a horse, sled, and barrel going from tree to tree, collecting it. Kettles were filled with the rich liquid, and huge fires kept their contents boiling. Hilda remembered that her father scooped finished maple sugar into large wooden boxes fitted with legs and stored it in these containers throughout the year.

COMMERCIALIZATION OF MAPLE SUGAR

The French, who had learned to tap maples from the Indians more than a century before White Folks began to show up in Illinois, introduced copper and brass kettles and the processes of straining and refining to sugar-making. They also moved the process indoors. As a consequence, the French manufactured a maple sugar as white and fine as sugar produced from cane. Nevertheless, to Native Americans it had no appeal. They complained that white sugar lacked flavor; it no longer tasted of the forest. As the French said, it had no *terroir*. It did, however, have commercial value because nineteenth-century folks needed it to cure meats and preserve fruits. Maple sugar sold for a good price and all the more if it was refined. Moreover, as a relatively durable commodity, maple sugar served as a kind of tender, widely accepted as payment for debts.

The first commercial maple sugar in Central Illinois may have been manufactured by Indians. In the timber close to an Indian trading house near present-day Urbana, John Smith, who would later move to Haven's Grove near Hudson, saw two sugar camps operated by indigenous groups.[13] Huge troughs capable of holding from six to eight barrels of sap stood in the center of both camps. When the Newcoms, the famous bee hunters, moved to Cheney's Grove they too became sugar makers on a grand scale. One spring they manufactured a full ton of sugar plus a barrel of syrup. Over a span of seven days and nights they produced 1,100 pounds of sugar, boiling up to eight kettles of sap at once. That same spring, their neighbors, the Cheney family, made 1,500 pounds of sugar, which they sold for 10 cents a pound.

East of Cheney's Grove near Ellsworth sugaring continued as an industry into the twentieth century. Six producers had groves in the area as late as 1901. A.L. Bullta alone tapped 500 trees. A neighbor, Henry English, once bought 300 galvanized pails in which to catch sap.

FUNKS GROVE MAPLE "SIRUP"

Today Steve and Glaida Funk preside over the only commercial sugar grove left in McLean County. Their home, located in Funks Grove, Central Illinois's largest remaining forest, sits not far from Timber Creek, amidst mighty oaks and sugar maples. Tapping them and producing maple sirup (deliberately spelled the old-fashioned way with an "i" instead of a "y") has been central to the Funks' livelihood for some 60 years.[14]

Steve got into the business after World War II. When he returned from service in the Air Corps, his cousin, Hazel Funk Holmes, approached him about opening a sugar camp. Hazel had been very close to Steve's father, a sugar-maker for many years. He and his brother had started in sugaring 1891, and although their camp had been in another part of Funks Grove, Hazel thought that her cousin should resurrect the business and situate it on her land. Hazel's tenants had tapped maples there prior to the war, but once hostilities broke out they could no longer recruit sufficient manpower to keep the enterprise going. Steve accepted Hazel's proposition, but knowing the job would be too big for one man he went a step further and volunteered as a partner his cousin, Duncan. Unfortunately, he was still in the army, so Steve brought a mutual friend, Gordon Kwasigroh, on board. It took a while, but by the spring of 1948, Steve, Duncan, and Gordon were producing sirup.

Tapping a maple in Funk's Grove, 1933. Courtesy of *The Pantagraph*.

Historic U.S. Route 66 cuts through Funks Grove, passing within a couple of hundred meters of Steve and Glaida's house. The highway, which once ran from Chicago to Los Angeles and was one of the busiest in the nation, supplied a steady stream of sirup customers over the years. Some came as regulars, many of them from Bloomington-Normal and the surrounding area, but many were motorists from other parts of Illinois out for a Sunday drive. Cars full of vacationers from all over the country saw signs announcing "Maple Sirup Just Ahead" and pulled into the Funks' driveway on an impulse. The construction of Interstate 55 just to the east reduced traffic past the Funks' place to a trickle, but devoted regulars continued to buy all of the sirup the Funks produced.

In recent years, promoters have developed Historic Route 66 into a tourist destination. It attracts a generation of motorists born too late to experience the original but intent on seeing some of the remnants of what writers now call the "Mother Road." The Funks' sugar camp with its boiling house and little shop has become part of the experience. Write-ups about it can be found in every Route 66 guidebook and on every Mother Road website. Alone and in groups, in automobiles and on motorcycles, hundreds of tourists, many of them foreign, stop by each week. Today, they are apt to be greeted by Steve and Glaida's son,

Michael, or his wife Debby. They took over when Steve and Glaida retired, but the emeritus couple is still happy to show visitors their operation.

The camp looks quaint nowadays, but it is a model of efficiency. Taps connected to miles of polyurethane tubing sprout from the sides of nearly every maple in the forest surrounding the Funks' sugar house. Pumps move the sap to storage tanks and into a modern gas-fired boiler equipped with a steam recovery unit. As the boiler concentrates the sap to 14 percent sucrose and makes sirup, the recovery unit assures that little escapes the system. Thus, modern methods produce a traditional food for which the Funks currently charge around fourteen dollars a quart. It is an expensive pancake topping compared to Log Cabin brand; still, each year's production is sold out by the end of August, some of it destined to go into recipes native to Funks Grove.

Funks Grove Maple Sirup Bars

INGREDIENTS – ½ cup butter, ¼ cup sugar, 1 cup flour, ¾ cup brown sugar, ⅓ cup maple sirup, 1 tablespoon. butter, 1 egg, ½ teaspoon vanilla, ⅓ cup chopped pecans. PREPARATION – To make shortbread: Cream butter and sugar in food processor. Add flour and process until just blended. Dough does not form ball. Pat into bottom of greased 9-inch square pan. Bake at 350° for 15 minutes or until lightly brown. To make topping: Beat brown sugar, sirup, and butter to blend. Beat in egg and vanilla.Pour over shortbread. Sprinkle with nuts. Bake 25 minutes or until set. Cool and cut into bars (makes 2 dozen).[15]

Will the next generation of consumers be as appreciative of Funks Grove Maple Sirup as the present one? A resident of the grove tells of serving a young house guest a breakfast of pancakes topped with Funks' sirup. He pointed out to the boy that the sirup came from "those trees just down the road." The youngster looked at the trees. He looked at his plate and again at the trees and pushed his plate aside with a disgusted, "Yuck! How gross!" The boy remained in an ill mood until his host replaced his pancakes with a Pop Tart fresh from the toaster.

NUTS

Illinois' nineteenth-century woodlands contained more species of edible nuts than any other forests in the world. Oaks produced heavy crops of acorns. Beeches, including the chestnut, yielded immense quantities of nuts, as did hickories, pecans, and various other members of the walnut family. The hickory nut, a food rich in oils, constituted an important source of fat for Native Americans whose diets otherwise tended to be almost too lean. People pounded the nuts to crack their shells and then placed them in boiling water. The heat caused the oils in the nut to separate and rise to the surface as cream-colored substance that was skimmed off, allowed to cool, and stored as a paste called "*pawcohiccora*" – in English, "hickory milk." Indians used *pawcohiccora* like butter and spread it on other foods. In addition, it was used as an ingredient in corn cakes and other dishes. The Illinois nut, known later as the pecan, was processed and used in a similar way. In McLean County, Indians and pioneers alike collected hazelnuts, hickory nuts, and walnuts for their meats. The primary domestic consumer, however, was the hog. While nuts are an especially labor-intensive food for humans to process, hogs have no trouble munching the hard shells, and converting nuts into readily accessible pork products.

WILD FRUITS, TUBERS AND ROOTS

In addition to nuts, Central Illinois's forests produced a variety of fruits. May apples, mulberries, raspberries, and wild strawberries became ripe in the spring. People collected blackberries during the summer. Crab apples, paw paws, persimmons, red and black haws, wild cherries, and wild grapes were ready to eat in the fall or early winter. Women made sport out of fruit collection. In the autumn when men set out in groups to hunt, their wives organized fruiting parties to gather haws and nuts. Eliza Farnham recalled these as delightful rambles of an hour or two and remembered returning "with baskets laden with delicious haw-berries," a feast for many days.[16] The Dawsons, who had a big thicket of wild crab apples near their cabin, collected and preserved them in maple sugar after the fruit had been mellowed by the year's first frost.[17] The Dawsons also preserved blackberries, raspberries, and wild strawberries, sometimes by drying them in the sun, at other times by mixing them with maple sugar.

Early settlers ate a number of wild species that few people nowadays have heard of, let alone sampled. One of these was the American wild plum (*Prunus americana*), a fruit once harvested by the wagonloads. Plum trees flourished along the edges of the prairie, producing a reddish or yellowish fruit with a thick skin and sweet flesh. They grow today along country roads and at the edge of open fields. Indians in various parts of the West maintain orchards of wild plum, but nobody has marketed the fruit on a large scale. This may never happen because trees at present produce less fruit than they did in the nineteenth century.

Another species commonly consumed by Central Illinois' pioneers but unfamiliar to most residents of the region today is the ramp or wild leek (*Allium tricoccum*). Native Americans knew the ramp well because it was the first green

edible to make an appearance in the spring. Just as the sap of the maple provided a timely source of calories, the ramp was a potent source of vitamin C,
a nutrient often lacking in native peoples' winter diets. The Menominee called
the ramp "*pikwute sikakushia*" (skunk plant), and they referred to the area near
the southern shore of Lake Michigan, where the ramps grew abundantly, as
"CicagaWuni" or "Shikako" (skunk place). The place became known in English
as "Chicago."

The ramp belongs to the same genus as onions, chives, and garlic, and has a
complex and assertive onion-garlic-woodsy taste. McLean County settler David
Cox described the ramps as tasting like an onions but prone to give a bad flavor
to cow's milk should the animal graze on them.[18] It may be for that reason the
ramp never developed a strong following in Central Illinois. Already in 1874,
local historian Edward Duis had no familiarity with the species and proceeded
to pronounce it extinct.[19]

Duis was wrong. Kris and Marty Travis currently dig more than 3,000
pounds of leeks from the timber on their property, a place called "Spence Farm."
Kris and Marty's land is located near Fairbury in Livingston County, just east of
Weston Cemetery, the last piece of unbroken prairie in McLean County.

Spence Farm has a long history.[20] It was settled by Marty's great, great, great
grandfather in 1830 and is the oldest family farm in Livingston County. It began
as 160 acres, but by the late 1800s the property had grown to nearly 1,000 acres
dotted with 36 buildings. Spence Farm back then produced horses for export. It
also produced sheep, hogs, cows, and chickens and gallons of maple syrup from
the sap of over 600 trees. By the 1970s, however, the farm had dwindled to its
original acreage, and the Spence family nearly lost it. Today, Kris and Marty have
resurrected it as an organic farm and education center where farmers and others
can learn about crop and animal diversity, heirloom crops and heritage breeds,
woodland management, and building restoration.[21]

Kris and Marty's ramp market begins at Dave's Supermarket down the road
in Fairbury, but extends to the gourmet restaurants of Chicago and beyond. In
Appalachia, the ramp is celebrated as a folk food. Every spring, people throughout the southern mountains consume it in great quantities. It is the featured
food at many hundreds of church and civic suppers. In Illinois, the ramp is high
cuisine. Represented as fugitive from the past, it sells at more than ten dollars per
pound, a price that effectively reserves it for the wealthy. Elite chefs use Spence
Farm ramps as an ingredient in soups, omelets, pesto lightly daubed on pasta,
and many other creative dishes. Chicago chef Paul Kahan makes ramp *kimchee*
and serves it with sturgeon and oxtail at around $30 a plate.

Bon Appétit's Seared Salmon with Linguine and Ramp Pesto
INGREDIENTS – 2 tablespoons plus ½ cup olive oil, divided; ⅔ cup thinly sliced trimmed ramp bulbs and slender stems; 1 cup freshly grated Asiago cheese; ⅓ cup Marcona almonds; 2 tablespoons chopped fresh tarragon; 12 ounces linguine; 6 6-ounce salmon fillets. PREPARATION – Heat 1 tablespoon oil in large nonstick skillet over medium heat. Add ⅔ cup ramp bulbs and stems to skillet and sauté just until soft but not browned, reducing heat if necessary to prevent browning, about 5 minutes. Transfer sautéed ramps to processor (do not clean skillet). Add green tops, cheese, almonds, and tarragon to processor; process until finely chopped. With machine running, gradually add ½ cup oil and puree until almost smooth. Transfer pesto to bowl. Season to taste with salt and pepper. Cook pasta in large pot of boiling salted water until just tender but still firm to bite, stirring occasionally. Meanwhile, heat remaining 1 tablespoon oil in same large skillet over medium-high heat. Drain pasta, reserving ¾ cup pasta cooking liquid. Return pasta to pot; add all but ¼ cup pesto and toss to coat, adding enough pasta cooking liquid by tablespoonfuls to moisten. Season with salt and pepper. Divide pasta among plates. Top with lightly grilled salmon (salted and peppered and cooked about 4 minutes each side. Spread remaining ¼ cup pesto over fish and serve (pesto can be prepared a day ahead).[22]

And then there was the hog potato, a species familiar to pioneers, but never very popular. It was just something folks ate when they had to. Albert Philips, his brother Calvin, and a companion named Andrew Barnard had to in 1832 while camping at Indian Grove, an old village abandoned by the Kickapoo.[23] The men had brought little to eat along with them because they expected to be joined by their families the next day. They and the food supplies they carried with them were detained, however, and did not show up for a week. In the meantime, Albert, Calvin, and Andrew subsisted on honey and hog potatoes, which grew wild on the bottomlands and along sloughs near their camp.

Albert subsequently described hog potatoes as "little black things about the size of an egg," but there is no telling for sure today what those "little black things" actually were. The problem is that the label "hog potato" or something similar has been applied to several different North American plants. To confound matters further, the name is no longer popularly applied to anything growing in McLean County. Nevertheless, judging from Albert's description – tubers, growing three to six inches apart, two or three potatoes per stem – McLean County's hog potato was very likely *Apios americana*, a legume with a nutritious root that resembles a tuber and was commonly eaten by Native Americans (and is sometimes referred to as the "Indian potato"). Whites generally ate hog potatoes roasted or boiled. Either way, their flavor was said to be very different from that of an Irish potato. Efforts currently are underway to domesticate *Apios americana*. Whether it has a future as a cultigen remains to be seen, but almost certainly the name "hog potato" will not be featured in marketing efforts.

HUSBANDRY

Early settlers came to Central Illinois with horses, some cattle, and in a few instances oxen. The Hendrixes brought twenty-four sheep in addition to three cows and their horses.[24] The cows were for milk, the sheep presumably for wool. The Dawsons had a yolk of oxen as well as a cow.[25] Central Illinois farmsteads generally did not have many cattle at first for want of pasture. However, right from the start fowls of all kinds were reared in abundance. The meat of ducks and geese gave families a welcome break from salt pork during the summer months, and folks ate hen's eggs in large quantities.

HOGS

The pioneers generally did not bring pigs with them because there were plenty of feral hogs roaming the woods. Why bother raising swine when you could hunt razorbacks and eat wild pork free of charge? The catch was that hunting wild pigs, descendants of domestic creatures brought to Peoria by the French, was not an occupation for the faint hearted. It could be quite dangerous. The animal had a vicious disposition, great speed, remarkable jumping ability, and awesome tusks. A boar could easily cut out the eye of a dog with one swipe. A few early settlers tried to redomesticate some of these fearsome "land sharks," as they were called, but on the Illinois frontier even well bred domestic pigs invariably went semi-feral and had to be shot like wild animals.

Nonetheless, settlers much preferred hogs over cattle, and long before wild pigs were hunted to extinction (which took about 10 or 15 years) farmers were traveling to Springfield to purchase Berkshires. They had good reason. Most White Folks had a Southerner's taste for pork, but generally speaking preference follows economics, and from the standpoint of economy no domestic animal prospered as well as the pig and with so little husbandry. A pig born in the spring required no pasture and put on weight far more rapidly than a calf or a lamb. Rooting through the forest or scavenging fields, pigs converted plant materials to meat approximately seven times more efficiently than ruminants.

Consequently, the pig became a part of almost everything on the pioneers' tables.[26] Lard, rendered from pig fat, went into corn breads as shortening. Cracklings – the bits of crisp flesh leftover from lard making – were mixed with cornmeal batter and baked into bread. Lard ranked as one of the two chief mediums of cooking. The other was water – which is to say, most dishes were either fried or boiled. Potatoes might be fried. Favorite vegetables such as cabbage and turnip greens were apt to be boiled but not without some salt pork (or "sow belly" as many referred to it) for added flavor. Settlers cured pork by packing parts of the pig covered with salt in a box for a month or more and then slowly smoking them. Meat processed in this way kept for many months.

EARLY HOG KILLS

Central Illinois's early settlers killed domestic hogs for both market and home consumption during an annual period beginning around Christmas and lasting until mid-January. The sustained cold weather at that time of year kept fresh uncured meat from spoiling quickly. Preparations for the slaughter began with the first hard freeze. It prevented the animals from rooting for food. Taking advantage of this, men constructed pens in the woods and baited them with corn. Hogs that entered these enclosures to feed were gated and kept pacified with additional corn. Of course, feeding corn also improved the quality of pork.

The killing and butchering was a community affair. First one household and then another announced a butchering day, each family expecting neighbors to come by and lend a hand. On the appointed day, the host family was up at dawn, setting roaring fires and heating water in iron kettles. Anxiety ran high until the neighborhood marksman arrived. Men known to be especially good shots were in high demand because pigs needed to be dispatched quickly and quietly. Ideally, a single rifle shot to the head dropped an animal in its tracks. A bullet off mark provoked a lot of squealing and tumult, upset the other hogs, and made them unmanageable. Distraught animals could break through fences and run off into the woods. At a botched slaughter witnessed by William Oliver about 1840, a herd of frightened pigs nearly killed an errant marksman and his assistants.[27]

Once the hogs were dispatched and the rifle put away, it was time to take out the knives and begin butchering.[28] First, each carcass needed to be bled. After that, the dead pigs were hoisted one at a time above a scalding kettle and lowered head first into the boiling water. This dunking prepared the carcass to have its bristles scraped off. That done, the carcass was hung up, gutted, and cut to pieces. Hams, shoulders, sides, and several other cuts went to the smokehouse. Other parts were sliced up, fried, placed in jars, and covered with lard. The settlers called these jarred pieces "fried down meat" and found them palatable for many months. Fried down meat, which might include shoulder, bacon, and sausage became a staple in Central Illinois and continued as such until refrigeration became widely available.

LATTER-DAY HOG KILLS

Hog butchering continued as an annual event on McLean County farms well into the twentieth century. It remained a red letter day on which neighbors gathered and the kids stayed home from school through the early 1930s, but by the late '30s the custom was disappearing. This prompted a nostalgic piece in a 1938 issue of Bloomington's *Daily Pantagraph* recounting a day of butchering hosted by A.C. Lanz and his wife on their farm near Kerrick, just north of Normal.[29]

For the Lanzes, butchering day began before dawn, and by the time men from nearby farms arrived two big kettles of steaming hot water were ready and waiting. The plan was to slaughter two animals, a year's supply of meat for the Lanzes, but the affair got off to a somewhat rocky start when it took three bullets to kill the first of the two big porkers. After that, things went more smoothly. The man nominated by Lanz as head butcher took great care and successfully removed the gall bladders from the livers. He then cut off the hams, fatback, leaf fat, bacon, ribs, bellies, shoulders, and jowls. The butchering completed, attention turned to cooking. By now, the women had assembled, prepared to make sausage. Hearts and livers went into the pot to be cooked and ground as liver sausage. What the Lanzes served for lunch went unreported, but Bertha Zehr said it was usually fried liver because the rest of the meat needed time to cool down.[30]

After lunch, the Lanzes and their neighbors returned to work making lard and stuffing sausage. The most experienced man in the group took charge of rendering the lard. He put fatback, leaf fat, and fat trimmings into a kettle, watching closely that it did not get too hot, burn the lard, and turn it dark. An expert, he explained, watched for little white blisters on the cracklings. When they appeared the lard was nearly done. The final test required dipping up some cracklings. If they fried themselves dry as soon as they were removed from the kettle, the lard was ready for pressing and straining. Lanz made sausage by jacking up his car and running shoulders, sides, and trimmings through a little mill attached to a rear wheel. The women scalded and scraped entrails for casings. Darkness fell as the final casings were being stuffed with ground meat, which the Lanzes made sure was approximately 75 percent lean. There was still some side meat to pack in sugar cure, and some salt cure to apply to the bacon, but otherwise the party, by now thoroughly exhausted, was through for the day.

Making pork sausage at the A.C. Lanz farm near Kerrick, Illinois in 1938.
Courtesy of *The Pantagraph*.

However, work remained for the days ahead. The Lanzes still had to slice the bacon once it was cured. They then would have to wrap it in two-pound packages and take it to the cold storage plant in town. In addition, hams needed to be cut into roasts and sliced for frying. Loins had to be cut into chops and roasts, and there were pigs' feet to be pickled. The Lanzes also wanted to pack a few jars of fried down meat, something they could keep on hand for an emergency or for when it simply was not convenient to pick up meat from the locker. Previous generations had set aside the entire day after butchering as "fry down day." It was spent cooking skillet after skillet of meat, which would be packed in jars and consumed over the next several months.

The Lanzes were among the last farmers in McLean County to butcher their hogs the traditional way. Some households stopped butchering because it involved too much work. Others cited too many losses of meat owing to curing mistakes. Some families responded to the introduction of home refrigeration by joining so-called "butchering rings." These consisted of several families, each taking a turn and killing a pig as the year progressed. The idea was to share the meat and store it at home in the freezer. For the Lanzes, who routinely presented a roast to those who helped them butcher and who normally received a roast when they took their turn, the meat itself was not what butchering was all about. The point was community. Practically speaking, there was work to be done, but as if by magic it became negligible thanks to the company of one's neighbors.

CORN CULTIVATION

William Oliver once described corn as the potato of Illinois's poor.[31] It afforded subsistence to everyone and everything, including the farmers' dogs and cats. Compared to wheat, corn produced four times as much grain per acre. The grower did not have to spend much time on field preparation, and he could let a mature crop stand during the winter, harvesting ears as needed. Besides that, stalks and leaves provided livestock with fodder. All in all, substantial returns from trifling amounts of seed and relatively little effort.

CRACKING CORN

Corn on the Illinois frontier was ready to eat "green" in about six weeks, but eating corn fresh off the cob was a new experience for some. Phebe Weeks, a newcomer to Hudson, wrote about her first encounter with fresh corn to her sister back in New York. "If you have any sweet corn, just put in butter and fry," Phebe instructed. "It's good eating I tell you."[32]

Dried out corn became hard work getting it ready for the table. First, the kernels had to be "cracked" or "brayed." At a minimum, this required a mortar and pestle, not to mention a pair of strong arms and considerable endurance. Nearly everyone in McLean County who lived through the exceptionally snowy winter of 1830-1831 needed a mortar and pestle. The Dawsons of Keg Grove and old John Patton who settled near Lexington owned hand-cranked mills, but otherwise folks without a mortar and pestle had to make a set in a hurry because the heavy snows prevented travel to grist mills.[33] Robert McClure, who settled his family at Stout's Grove in 1827, made a mortar from a log about three feet long and two feet in diameter.[34] He burned a hole 16 inches deep in one end and cleaned it out with an inshave (a woodworking tool). Grain was placed in the hole and pounded with a pole serving as the pestle. Fitting a piece of iron on the business end greatly improved its efficiency.

Instead of an ordinary mortar and pestle, some McLean County residents fashioned an arrangement that utilized a springy sapling to make cracking corn less exhausting. The heavy pestle was attached to a sweep, the opposite end of which was tied to a young hickory. It functioned like a spring, pulling the pestle upward on the rebound and negating the need to lift.

Pounded corn, no matter what sort of mortar and pestle households used, did not have a uniform texture. Consequently, when people sifted their meal to remove impurities, which was usually done using a perforated deer skin, they wound up with some relatively fine meal and a lot of coarse grits. Homemakers reserved the fine meal for bread. They boiled the grits and used them to make hominy.

EARLY GRIST MILLS

Grist mills were the first commercial food processing sites on the frontier, and to begin with they were few and far between. The Orendorff brothers hauled their corn back to Springfield to have it ground.[35] Others took their corn to a mill at Attica on the Wabash River, a distance of about 120 miles.[36] Later on, Green's Mill opened at Ottawa on the Illinois River and began attracting customers from McLean County.

People tried different mills hoping to find one that produced good quality meal. The first mill Robert Stubblefield visited was run by an old man known as Riggs.[37] He owned an animal-powered band mill, so called because the machinery used belts instead of cog wheels. Stubblefield felt that it did not grind meal sufficiently fine, so he visited another band mill at Twin Groves run by a man named Harber. The first watermill Stubblefield tried was the Eveland Mill on Kickapoo Creek. Eveland acquired its power from a tub wheel. DeWitt County had a similar mill, and a fellow by the name of Hampton opened one in McLean County at Randolph Grove.

The earliest corn mill in the McLean County began grinding in 1825 at Blooming Grove.[38] It was a so-called "nigger-head" mill built by millwright Ebenezer Rhodes and his son John. They began with a pair of granite stones found on the prairie, cut them to about 30 inch diameters, and fastened the end of a sweep to one of the stones. To the opposite end of the sweep, they hitched a pair of horses. As the horses plodded around the mill, one stone rotated atop the other crushing corn between them. A customer had to supply his own team or hire one. The milling charge was twelve and a half cents per bushel.

A second mill powered by horses was built in Blooming Grove on the farm of Seth Baker in 1831. It stood two stories tall, and an upright shaft and a set of gears transferred rotation from the sweep to the lower member of a pair of grind-stones, a fine, cone-shaped piece of granite about 13 inches in diameter at the base. The upper millstone remained stationary. It fit over the bottom cone, which the operator could raise or lower to produce fine or coarse meal. People regarded the Baker's Mill as a technical marvel, and they came from many miles around to see it work. Soon, similar mills sprang up elsewhere in the county. Moses Harner and Harrison Foster both built facilities near Selma (known then as Pleasant Hill or Poverty Hill). Moses Harbord constructed a similar mill in Dry Grove, and Ephraim Stout put one up at Stout's Grove.

Mills developed into popular social haunts because the wheels turned slowly, and customers had a lot of time on their hands. Millstones powered by horses could grind no more than three or four bushels of corn per day, which meant hanging around for days at busy times of the year. Samuel Lewis once waited three weeks at Crocker's Mill and had to work for his board. Some millers took advantage of the waits by opening dram shops and selling whisky to those killing time. Customers mingled, discussed the news of the day, and enjoyed a variety of sports. Stout's mill became an especially popular meeting place for those in the western part of the county. Ortogrul Covell's trio of mills in Bloomington – a lumber mill, a fabric mill, and the town's first dedicated flour mill – became known as good spots for keeping up with the politics of the day.

Windmills worked much faster than horse-powered mills. Indians under Jesuit tutelage were using them at Kaskaskia as early as the eighteenth century. Still, for some reason settlers never mastered the windmill. In the 1830s, Wilson Allin built one in Bloomington and invited all of his friends to come and witness its maiden run. A stiff wind blew on the appointed day, and the mill at first ran fine. Soon, however, the machinery began whirling around at breakneck speed. The grindstones spun out of control, twisting the frame, and sending the entire contraption crashing to the ground. One run and Allin's windmill wound up a total wreck.

The last operating mill in the county was Moore's Mill located in Johnson's Grove on Sugar Creek in Mt. Hope Township.[39] John Caton built it with the help of his neighbors as a water-powered lumber mill about 1840. Unable to make it run properly, he sold the mill the next year to Jacob Moore, a jovial miller, who operated it until his death in 1887. Moore made the mill work by installing millstones, carving his own shaft and cog wheels from oak logs, and attaching a more efficient waterwheel. Early millers like Moore usually had more resources than the ordinary frontiersman. Frontier millers were typically the sons of hard-working millers back east, and as such they were thought of as a "better class" than most of their neighbors. Central Illinois's settlers generally regarded the miller as a community leader. He enjoyed a relatively steady income – a portion of every bushel of grain that passed between his grindstones – and if his mill proved popular he stood to become relatively affluent.

Moore's Mill, where the "toll" amounted to a one-eighth share, experienced great success. Grist arrived at Moore's in quantities ranging from wagonloads to a single bag, and capacity in general was about six bushels per hour. During harvest season, business backed up, and customers might have to wait several days to get their grinding done. No matter; those in line pitched camp and might hunt or fish as they waited their turn.

At the height of its popularity, Moore's Mill served large areas of McLean, Tazewell, Logan, and DeWitt Counties, but eventually it lost out to steam mills. These began appearing and taking away business during the 1850s shortly after the Chicago and Alton (C & A) Railroad built its mainline through McLean County. By 1860, they had taken away so much business that Moore discontinued milling flour. In 1876, he turned production over to his son David. He enlarged the facility and modernized operations by installing steel machinery. The old millstones, however, remained in place. These monsters, 46 inches in diameter, one of them weighing 1,600 pounds, were still grinding corn when Lee Moore inherited the mill in 1909, and they continued to function smoothly until he went out of business in 1914.

The closure of Moore's Mill caused sorrow throughout the area. People talked about the unbeatable quality of its flour and the mill's picturesque setting. They regretted the loss of community, the group of people that lingered about the premises, sharing stories and expressing views on any and every topic imaginable. As late as 1926, old settlers from the area held regular reunions at site of the old mill, although by then it was no more than a ruin.

OTHER CROPS

McLean County's pioneers did not limit their cultivations to corn. Buckwheat and wheat were harvested in such quantities that Moore's Mill reserved Fridays for grinding the former and Saturdays for the latter. Settlers regarded apples and peaches nearly as important as grain and regarded planting an apple orchard a top priority. James Coon, a resident of Gridley Township, had apple trees planted and bearing fruit before he even occupied his land.[40] Late maturing apple varieties kept most of the winter, and others could be preserved by slicing them and drying them in the sun or by tossing them into a pot and reducing them to apple butter. Illinois's peaches, although small by world standards, met with universal approval from the standpoint of taste. Peach trees grew like weeds in Illinois, and after three or four years every farmstead had more than enough. Fruit needed for the winter was split in half and dehydrated. Surplus peaches either went to the distillery to be made into brandy or got fed to the hogs.

FOOD AND THE SOCIAL ECONOMY

Economic transactions on the Illinois frontier depended on social relationships. Cash never exchanged hands among friends and rarely was there any direct barter. Goods and services flowed back and forth as reciprocities, following the dictum "friends make gifts, and gifts make friends."[41]

This does not mean that the frontier economy was any less self-interested than the commercial economy to come later. Quite the contrary: People eagerly saw to the neighbors' needs with the implicit understanding that personal well-being depended on the generosity of neighbors. The idea was to create obligations. McLean County's settlers lived in a web of mutual obligations and involving favors of many sorts. Take David Gilmore for example. Every autumn, Gilmore's neighbors willingly carted his surplus wheat all the way to Chicago while he remained comfortably at home.[42] His neighbors never asked Gilmore for compensation, but then Gilmore, who happened to be a skilled blacksmith as well as a farmer, never asked anything from any one of them who needed him to do some smithing.

NEIGHBORHOOD FROLICS

The institution people back East referred to as "bees," folks in Central Illinois commonly called "frolics." The frolic embodied reciprocity in a practical, work-related event. The idea was simple: a neighbor invited everyone living in the vicinity to help him complete a certain project on a particular day and in return for their help he promised plenty to eat and a whacking good time. The subtle part was that the food and drink and the various sports a host offered in no way repaid his guests for their labor. Indeed, there was no repaying because today's guest would surely become tomorrow's host just as a current host could count on an invitation to the next frolic. The net result was a maze of expectations in which personal indebtedness became indistinguishable from community obligation.

As an event, a proper frolic had three basic components: a labor-intensive project to complete, a sport such as a dance or an athletic contest to entertain participants, and a banquet featuring more than enough food to satisfy even the most voracious appetite. A fourth component, waived when the occasional teetotaler played host, was an ample supply of strong drink, particularly for the men in attendance.

People organized frolics to accomplish time-consuming tasks. These included moving logs, building houses, butchering hogs, cutting wheat, and husking corn. Men held a frolic when they wanted to exterminate wolves in the neighborhood. A woman might put one together when she had a lot of sewing or quilting to do. Communities sponsored frolics to build and repair churches, schools, and roads.

The sports were often multiple and occasionally spontaneous. A frolic might include foot races, wrestling matches, or weight lifting. Many concluded with a dance. Men often tortured animals for amusement. At log-rollings, they liked to catch a chipmunk or some other small animal, force him into a pile of brush, set it alight, and then watch the critter burn to death. The main event at a corn-shucking frolic attended by William Oliver involved a contest to see who could finish the quickest.[43] After everyone breakfasted from a table piled high with food, the guests divided the unhusked corn into two equal piles. Captains were chosen, and they called sides. The teams in place, there commenced an uproarious battle to see which side could finish husking its pile of corn first.

When the competition finished and the work was over the feasting began, and in preparing for it the woman of the house spared no trouble. She and her neighbors usually began a day or two in advance, cooking a multitude of dishes and then arranging them as a grand display. The food at a typical frolic included Johnnycake and hoecake, pone bread and dodger, salt bread and milk bread, pumpkin and other pies, and several fanciful pastries. All of this was accompanied by a never-failing supply of coffee. When they could eat no more, the guests lounged about and talked about the news of the day until it was time to go home. Should a fiddler be on hand, he might strike up a tune that beckoned everyone to remain and dance.

Men drank heavily at frolics. At a house-raising, while everyone else worked under the direction of a local raising master, the host kept busy treating one and all to swigs of corn whiskey or peach brandy. Although men did not necessarily get drunk at such affairs, drinking was fashionable, and people considered it essential to conviviality. A pious few abstained, but typically most men looked at an acre of corn and saw a year's supply of whiskey. Folks were known to put off house raisings and other such undertakings until they could raise enough money for the whiskey. Some Illinois homesteaders added distilleries to their farms just so they could make their own "currency."[44]

OTHER COMMUNITY EVENTS

In addition to frolics, pioneers participated in a number of other events that all involved eating, drinking, or both. Political and religious meetings were formulaic. First came the speech-making or preaching, frequently punctuated with interludes of singing. Then, everyone got up, walked outside, and sat down to a big spread of breads and meats set out on temporary tables. Camp meetings held in late summer before harvest, attracted hundreds of families. In McLean County, these amounted to annual reunions, once-a-year opportunities to see people living dozens of miles away and otherwise encountered very infrequently. Unbridled hospitality turned camp meetings into enormous picnics.

Camp meetings and church suppers were among the venues at which men expected to indulge in whisky and other ardent spirits. The drinking at these gatherings took place out of the sight of women and children, but not because anyone regarded it as shameful. Rather, the attitude was like that of a secret fraternity. The whiskey jug stood for masculinity. Uncorking it and passing it around enacted a kind of rough-and-ready communion. The sharing engendered a sense of camaraderie and community while the intoxication perhaps counteracted the inevitable anxieties that hovered about a newly settled place where everyone lived as more or less a stranger among strangers.

At militia musters and on Election Day, men again consumed copious amounts of alcohol, and again there were few women and children present to witness the antics. These were exclusively male holidays. At muster, officers customarily treated their subordinates to whiskey. As a result, fighting among volunteers broke out regularly at the assemblies of the McLean County's militia.[45] Election Day amounted to a drunken revel from start to finish. Tavern keepers in Springfield set out bottles and kegs in front of the courthouse. Indians and "darkies" had no right to vote, but nevertheless they got as drunk as those enfranchised. With every candidate treating voters to whiskey, the Indians and Blacks dancing, and the White Folks singing, the day played out as a bacchanal. The Fourth of July was much the same in some communities, and every week Saturday get-togethers could get out of hand.

On Saturdays men loitered around the general store (which often doubled as a dram shop) or public house drinking sour mash or brandy with their neighbors.[46] Occasionally, they rode to a neighboring town to amuse themselves, or they might organize a squirrel hunt.[47] Other options were to stage a shooting match, a cock fight, or a horse race; the latter almost guaranteed to end in a fight. Another popular sport was the gander pull.[48] Before the game began, someone greased a gander's neck and hung the creature upside down from a tree limb. Then, everyone mounted his horse and raced to the tree. The person who pulled the gander's head off won the carcass.

Early settlers celebrated weddings with particular intensity.[49] Typically, a wedding day began with the groom and his friends, half-drunk, carousing about the neighborhood, inviting folks to the ceremony. The nuptials usually took place at the home of the bride's parents. They set a table – often no more than a large door laid across a couple of benches – with the best food available. Wedding tables frequently featured wild turkey, venison, a variety of corn and wheat breads, maple sugar donuts, and pumpkin pies. Guests were invited to eat their fill after the exchange of vows, and then came the drinking and dancing. The festivities continued far into the night. Indeed, it took little encouragement for guests to stay the night and resume eating, drinking, and dancing the next day.

RURAL HOSPITALITY

Hospitality was another aspect of frontier culture informed by the principle of reciprocity. Wayfarers, who had little hope of encountering an inn or other commercial lodging along the trail, either camped under the stars or approached a homestead and requested lodging. Early settlers generally honored such requests and almost never charged for their hospitality. Based on her experience in Tazewell County, Eliza Farnham described the hospitality of "Westerners" as "inexhaustible."[50] In her experience, folks with no more than a one room cabin welcomed travelers and whatever food there was on the table was free to anyone who happened by. Later on, especially along well-traveled roads where open-handed hospitality began to impose a substantial burden, residents began levying charges and offering poor accommodations "in self-defense."[51] The first time the Stubblefields charged anyone for food and lodging their guest was an itinerant peddler, a class of merchant for which Robert Stubblefield harbored a general dislike.[52]

COMMERCE ON THE FRONTIER

Commercial transactions on the frontier often involved direct exchange. Settlers bartered with peddlers and merchants and for services rendered gladly accepted goods in trade. Only transactions involving unknown passersby definitely called for money.

BARTER

Barter and trade prevailed as the preferred ways of doing business in Central Illinois well into the 1840s. George Dietrich, a tinsmith who opened a shop in Bloomington in 1839, made his living repairing pails, teakettles, butter churns, and rain gutters. He received in return chickens, pigs, cuts of beef, bushels of apples and coal, and cords of wood.[53] Bloomington's first school teacher, Amasa Washburn, accepted chickens and calves in exchange for tutoring.[54] As Clerk of County Commissioners' Court, Isaac Baker traded wedding licenses for wolf scalps and maple syrup.[55]

COMMODITIES AND MARKETPLACES

The Orendorff brothers and others who came to McLean County from the Springfield area periodically returned there to trade for necessities.[56] Springfield was well populated and served by reliable transportation by the early 1830s, and its merchants eagerly bartered their goods for hogs, which they promptly turned into cured pork.[57] The meat, packed into barrels, was loaded onto flat boats and sent down river to St. Louis where it was exchanged for new inventory.

Early settlers traveled to other markets as well. Some drove their hogs to packers at Vincennes. Others went to Vandalia. A few headed north to Galena or Chicago. When Alfred Moore Stringfield of Randolph's Grove undertook a drive to Galena in the fall of 1831 he followed a trail marked by no more than stakes and poles placed in the ground as far apart as could be seen from one to the next.[58] Reaching Chicago entailed a long push and occasionally some serious delays owing to high water or heavy snow. Nevertheless, some folks figured the prices Chicago buyers paid more than compensated for the difficulties a drover might encounter. The same went for produce. When Robert Stubblefield and his son George set out for Chicago in 1836 with a wagonload of sweet potatoes and a barrel of eggs they expected to be on the trail for two weeks.[59] No matter, there were those who made the journey regularly. John Gregory of Gridley Township, who began hauling grain to Chicago in the 1840s, often took his wife, Mary Ann, along for the ride.[60] She later claimed that she got to know Chicago every bit as well as she knew Bloomington.

For the most part, however, McLean County's pioneers oriented south and looked to St. Louis as the best place to do business. Its status as the region's metropolis received a huge boost in 1828 with the initiation of steamboat service to Pekin (or Peking), a port on the Illinois River less than forty miles from Bloomington. This opened the prospect of traveling to St. Louis via Pekin in just a few days, a week at most. By 1832, several packet boats were calling regularly at Pekin bringing shipments addressed to families living as far as 70 or 80 miles from the river.[61] A few years later a dozen such vessels served the port.

A good road to Bloomington gave Pekin an immense advantage over the ports at Beardstown, Copperas Creek, Frederick, LaSalle, and Peoria. By the mid-1830s, it developed into a busy thoroughfare with wagonloads of manufactured items and imported goods, including groceries, kitchen utensils, and tableware, moving in the direction of Bloomington, and livestock, grain, and other commodities traveling the opposite way. Traffic was especially heavy during the spring and early summer when the river was high.[62] Pekin's merchants purchased large numbers of hogs during the winter and employed scores of men and boys as butchers, meat cutters, coopers, packers, teamsters, and boatmen to insure the meat was ready to go down river in the spring. Honey and maple syrup arrived from the countryside. Buyers began traveling from one farm to the next, making offers to purchase eggs, poultry, and butter and procuring grain by the ton. Henry Welch, a Bloomington teamster, hauled corn to Pekin's wharfs behind four powerful oxen yoked to wagons with capacities of up to one and a half tons.[63] As its business expanded, Pekin attracted a crowd of receivers, forwarders, and freight handlers. A large collection of warehouses lined the riverfront, and for the benefit of travelers the city added amenities, including City Hotel on Court Street and the Mansion House, a popular tavern that doubled as a stagecoach stop. Vessels serving New Orleans began to call. Packets to LaSalle connected with Illinois-Michigan canal barges and provided passage to Chicago beginning in 1848. Major shippers with accounts in McLean County included Henry Meyers and Company, Daniel Thompson and Company, and the firm of Wagenseller and Chain.

About the time steamboats began to call at Pekin. Bloomington had seven general stores stocked with the essentials of frontier life.[64] The basics included three groceries: coffee, tea, and salt. Even the town's residents were largely self-sufficient and needed little else. Samuel Hayes, recently wedded and writing to his sisters in Connecticut, listed the provisions he and his bride began married life with.[65] The couple purchased one dressed pig weighing 155 pounds, 250 pounds of flour, two bushels of cornmeal, five or six bushels of potatoes, and two venison hams. They had a supply of beans, peas, cucumbers, squashes, and new potatoes, all of them very likely from their own garden. The Hayeses also had 150 pounds of maple sugar that William himself had made the previous season. In addition, they owned a cow and her calf, six hogs, three chickens, and two hens, the latter a gift from a neighbor, and all kept around and about their residence to assure a supply of meat, butter, and eggs for months to come.

Groceries first came to Central Illinois stashed on the back of peddlers' wagons along with farm tools, clocks, crockery, and other house wares. Peddlers needed approximately 150 dollars to assemble an inventory. Just as importantly, they had to know settlers' wants and how much they were willing to pay for this or that item. A successful peddler usually invested his profits in a general store. A store in town held potential for enormous earnings, due in large part to interest charges of 10 to 15 percent on credit accounts.

Ezekiel Greenman, who moved from Ohio to Illinois in 1829 with his parents, went from peddler to store owner in little more than a year.[66] After knocking about Wisconsin and Iowa for awhile, Greenman met Isaac Baker, at the time Bloomington's postmaster. Baker saw Greenman's talent for business and offered to set him up as a peddler. Greenman accepted and proved himself a good investment. After just a few months traveling around the southeastern quarter of McLean County, Greenman received an invitation from the citizens of LeRoy to set up permanent shop. He accepted but not before he persuaded the townsfolk to agree to two conditions. First off, they consented to rent Greenman ample floor space at a cost of no more than one dollar per month. Secondly, they agreed to provide his meals at the price of just one dollar per week. His conditions met, Greenman opened a shop and experienced immediate success. The very next year he had accumulated enough money to build his own store, and needing help he brought Isaac Baker's son, Sydney, into the business.

TAVERNS

Two basic types of commercial eating places, boarding houses and taverns (alternatively referred to as "inns"), existed in early nineteenth-century America. Boarding houses offered food and a place to sleep but nothing alcoholic to drink. Some such establishments catered to unmarried factory laborers. Others accommodated travelers, especially those in need of a place to stay for more than a day or two. Taverns and inns offered victuals and a bed usually at one inclusive price (later known as the "American plan"). They also sold beer, whiskey, and other intoxicating beverages.

McLean County had taverns (the term "inn" was not often heard in Illinois) but in the early days no boarding houses. Local tavern keepers prepared simple dishes, such as boiled pork and turnip greens, usually accompanied by bread and coffee. At night, customers often found themselves assigned several to a bed. Ethan and Joseph Newcom, who for awhile operated a tavern at Newcom's Ford on the Sangamon River, charged patrons 18¾ cents per meal and 50 cents for overnight accommodations (including fodder and bedding a guest's horse).[67] Business was very brisk during the fall when as many as 30 or 40 grain wagons could be seen at once parked adjacent to Newcoms'. The first tavern license in Bloomington was issued to Greenbury Larison. He came to Illinois in 1830 after some years as a flatboat man, took up residence in Bloomington about 1832, and purchased a saloon.[68] He kept it lively thanks to his considerable skill as a fiddler. He became a constable in 1835 and was later elected sheriff. Gaylord's Tavern in Bloomington opened for business shortly after the Blackhawk War.[69] Old settlers recalled the proprietor as an exceeding hospitable man who provided his guests with slippers to wear to their rooms. When Jonathan Bond Warlow and his family arrived at Bloomington in 1834, they rented a room at Caleb's, the town's other tavern.[70] Caleb's rude call to breakfast – a servant girl making a great racket by beating a pot hook against a steel bar suspended adjacent to their window – remained etched in their memories for years.

Just a stone's throw from Caleb's, Peter Withers built a huge tavern, completely out of proportion to Bloomington's size and importance.[71] The two-storied structure, erected in 1832, consisted of 30 rooms opening onto spacious verandas and cost Withers $30,000 to construct. To the west of the building (some called it a "hotel" rather than a tavern) was a stable yard. A guest passed through its gate, turned his horse or team over to Withers' hostler, and repaired to the tavern for refreshment. Supper, bed, breakfast, and feed for one horse cost guests 50 cents a night.

Withers sold his place to John Ewing in 1844. Bloomington by that time had grown into a sizable town, and it was Ewing's Tavern that regularly hosted Abraham Lincoln and Central Illinois's other political luminaries as they held court and saw to other matters in and around the county seat.

FRONTIER KITCHENS

Kitchens on the Illinois frontier began changing in the mid-1830s. The hand-hewn wooden bowl was still commonplace, as was the dipper fashioned from a gourd, but the battery of cooking implements was expanding. In addition to Dutch ovens and skillets, there were now cake pans, chafing dishes, dripping pans, saucepans, skimmers, stew pans, toasters, reflector ovens, and waffle irons. Soon the typical household had multiple kettles and other sorts of vessels in various sizes and made from a variety of metals, including brass, copper, and tin. Cooking itself became less fatiguing and much safer thanks to brick fireplaces equipped with cranes. The crane enabled housewives to hang a pot of stew in the fireplace and without much effort raise or lower it to regulate how rapidly it cooked. Moreover, there was no need to work directly over flames; the crane swung in and out of the fireplace as needed. Other cooking accessories included jacks rigged to turn a spit set across a pair of heavy andirons and ovens built directly into the side of the fireplace. Gauging temperature in one of these was tricky, but a women able to hold her arm inside for no more than a count of twenty had a very hot oven indeed. A count of forty indicated sufficient heat to bake a fruit pie.

MEAL PATTERNS

Fireplace cooking dictated the settlers' meal pattern.[72] The time it took to get a good fire going in the morning and cook a pot of victuals left no opportunity to fix more than one substantial meal each day. Consequently, homemakers cooked in large quantities for a mid-day repast, assuring sufficient leftovers for supper that evening. Breakfast (and on occasion the evening meal as well) consisted of quick and easy dishes such as mush or pancakes. McLean County bachelors John and Hiram Havens who resided near Hudson always had cornmeal mush for breakfast.[73] John fed the oxen in the morning while Hiram cracked corn. The brothers occasionally shot a deer and had venison alongside their mush. Once, Hiram, stranded on the far side of the Mackinaw River by a flood, spent alternate days having breakfast with two neighbors. He later reported that while one family ate much the same as he did at home, the other had nothing more than a plate of parched corn.

Coffee or tea normally accompanied a frontier breakfast, and one or the other was commonly served at other meals as well. The earliest pioneers, however, did not have access to imported products; hence they had to make do with ersatz coffees brewed from parched corn or wheat and teas prepared from sage or wild sassafras.[74] To make a gallon of sassafras tea required four average-sized roots. They could be gathered at any time during the growing season, but really good tea required young, tender roots. These were washed, scraped, and chopped into pieces. These could be dried and saved for later use. The next step in any case was to boil the pieces in water. The longer they boiled, the stronger the tea, but in general between 15 or 20 minutes was sufficient. The tea was strained before serving and consumed hot or cold. Either way it was ordinarily sweetened with honey or sugar.

Mid-day meals depended on the season. Late fall and winter were usually the only times folks ate fresh meat. Once cold temperatures set in, most fruits and vegetables disappeared from the table and cool weather species like cabbage, onion, and turnip appeared. These were stored, often in pit cellars, for winter meals, but by early spring many families had nothing left other than pickles and a few dehydrated fruits and vegetables. The most popular pickled foods were cabbage (sauerkraut), cucumbers, and green melons. Pickled pig's feet and pickled eggs were favorites as well. Apple and peach topped the list of dried fruits. Families preserved large quantities of peaches and other fruits by cooking them in heavy syrup and storing them in crocks. During the growing season, European vegetables, primarily turnips, parsnips, cabbage, onions, carrots, beans, and peas, could be found in kitchen gardens. Samuel Hill's vegetable patch at New Salem, not far from Springfield, contained beets, turnips, potatoes, sweet potatoes, tomatoes, and cabbage.[75] In general, however, White Folks were not much for vegetables. This can be seen in a series of nineteenth-century Appalachian dietaries collected during late summer at Crooked Creek in Eastern Tennessee.[76] Households there consumed on average just four items over the course of one week – typically, cornmeal, lard, salt pork, and potatoes or cabbage. In McLean County, the Stubblefields normally consumed just three vegetables – white potatoes, turnips, and parsnips.[77]

BURGOO

White Folks like the Stubblefields often combined roots and other vegetables with meat to make a soup or stew. Typically this was something like a succotash or Brunswick stew, but in Illinois folks called it "burgoo." The name originated in Kentucky where the dish is as time-honored as gumbo is in Louisiana. Among Illinois's Upland Southerners a pot simmered in nearly every cabin.[78]

Burgoo survives to this day in several Illinois towns, including Arenzville, a West Central Illinois village of little more than 400 people. Properly speaking, it more than survives; the town proudly proclaims itself the home of the world's best burgoo, and every September it hosts a two-day burgoo festival for the benefit of community organizations.[79] The festival has a history of more than 100 years, and back in the early days the burgoo was made as it was in Kentucky using rabbit, squirrel, venison, and other kinds of wild meat. Illinois law currently forbids selling dishes containing game, so nowadays the meat consists of chicken and beef. Recipes for burgoo abound in cookbooks and on the Internet, but few call for venison or "varmint meat." An heirloom recipe for "Company Stew" posted anonymously as part of a discussion of the annual burgoo festival held in Utica, Illinois represents one of the few. The recipe is described as a dish "our great-grandmothers served . . . from the old iron pot which hung from the crane over the hearth, using any wild game brought home by her 'man.' "

Squirrel Burgoo
INGREDIENTS – 1 stewing hen, 5-6 pounds; 1 squirrel or rabbit or hunk of beef, veal, or pork weighing about 3 pounds; 5 or 6 large potatoes, peeled and cubed; 1 quart lima beans; 1 quart whole kernel corn; 5 or 6 carrots, peeled and sliced; 2 or 3 onions, chopped coarsely; 6 or 7 tomatoes, peeled and quartered; salt; black pepper; Cayenne pepper. PREPARATION – Cut chicken into serving-size pieces. Treat squirrel or rabbit likewise. If using other meat, cut into 2-inch cubes. Place in heavy kettle, cover with water, and simmer until very tender, about 1 to 1½ hours. Remove chicken and squirrel or rabbit bones. Return boned meat to broth, add vegetables, season to taste,

and simmer until done, about 45 minutes (serves 6 generously). Note: Variations are in order, to suit your fancy and the garden's offering. Avoid cabbage, turnips, and such; they are a bit strong-flavored for this dish. Use cabbage for slaw, if you wish. This stew is particularly satisfying made with almost any meat available today. Serve with a green salad and a slab of homemade bread.[80]

STAPLE FOODS

Meat and cornbread were co-staples on the Illinois frontier. Nineteenth-century Americans consumed on average about 300 pounds of meat per year. In Central Illinois, settlers preferred game over domestic species, though archeological evidence indicates they actually ate more of the latter.

Domestically, pork was favored over beef. Away from the coasts, Americans generally ate little fresh fish, and nowhere in the country did people eat much poultry. People raised chickens in profusion, but at the time it took a hen more than two hundred days to mature. This long maturation made birds more valuable as egg producers than as a sources of food and virtually guaranteed that the only chicken settlers tasted were cocks or old hens boiled to make soup or stew.

If cornbread had any rival as the popular accompaniment to meat it had to be cornmeal mush. The key was convenience. Corn in any form was no great trouble to put on the table. People boiled it or roasted it and ate it directly off the cob. Some cut it off the cob and fried it. Dried corn was ground into meal and made into a variety of breads or cakes. The simplest consisted of just meal and water, perhaps some salt. A common recipe at New Salem called for pouring two quarts of corn meal, cold water, and salt into a greased skillet. These ingredients were mixed by hand. Once the dough was ready, the homemaker impressed it with her handprint and then situated the skillet amidst the coals. To enrich their cornbread, some homemakers added baking soda, milk, buttermilk, lard, or eggs. The batter went into a pre-heated Dutch oven that had been greased with a piece of pork rind and dusted with bit of cornmeal to prevent the bread from sticking. A Dutch oven buried in hot coals turned out nicely baked bread in about 20 minutes.

Early settlers seldom ate wheat bread, mainly because flour was relatively expensive. When folks had flour they used it to make "rusk" (a flat, hard, cracker), various cracker-like biscuits, and dough for tarts and pies. Early on, McLean County residents had to go to Peoria or Springfield to have wheat milled. On the Dawson farmstead, a horse trampled the wheat on a dirt floor.[81] The Stubblefields also used horses and then winnowed by tossing the wheat into the air.[82] The wheat was then run through a hand mill and sifted using a box made for that purpose, but still the flour came out brown and produced a bread of the same color.

EARLY TABLEWARE

Tableware among the earliest settlers of McLean County was as scant as kitchenware. The Dawsons arrived at Keg Grove with a small number of plates and hardly any knives and forks. The Stubblefields brought with them some pewter plates and bowls and a few cups and saucers.[83] For sites predating 1835, archaeology has turned up a remarkably narrow range of ceramic vessels, and pieces are generally limited to small and medium capacity pots, jugs, and multi-purpose kitchen bowls. Excavators rarely uncover refined tableware of any sort.[84]

Later on, beginning about 1835, tables on the Illinois frontier were increasingly likely to be set with queensware instead of pewter or wooden dishes.[85] The label "queensware" applied originally to a cream-colored ceramic invented by Josiah Wedgewood in the 1760s, but over the years the term was extended to encompass most types of inexpensive English earthenware. Most of it in Illinois came up river from St. Louis. Wholesalers there began plugging cheap ceramics in the 1820s suitable "for the country trade." Peddlers and shopkeepers purchased crated assortments specially selected to appeal to rural customers. These pieces usually had edges painted blue or green.

ATTRACTIVE TABLES AND TEA PARTIES

Queensware at first probably appealed more to settlers from the East than native Southerners. More so than folks like the Dawsons and Stubblefields, Easterners concerned themselves with the aesthetics of the table. When Eliza Farnham arrived in Tazewell County, for example, she felt gladdened by the sight of shining plates atop a snowy tablecloth.[86] The sound of the bubbling tea-kettle and the sight of a reflector oven filled with tender biscuits glittering upon the hearth she savored as much as the meal itself. New Englanders bristled at the casual table manners of Southerners and the way they ate with such dispatch. Oddly, men ate first, and then the women followed by the youngsters.[87] To Eastern sensibilities, Southern words and phrases like "dinnertime" and "heap o' vittles" were utterly vulgar.[88] To turn matters around, Farnham discovered that she could not eat in private without being taken as uncouth by neighbors from the South.[89] Southerners could not endure the New England boiled dinner. Good cooks, in their estimation, did not boil potatoes in their jackets, nor did they boil cabbage, turnips, or what have you together with meats. White Folks put a bit of fat into a pot of cooking vegetables to flavor them, but otherwise a proper cook boiled meat and vegetables separately. Soups or stews such as burgoo counted as an exception because they were much reduced.

Frontier women, irrespective of where they originated, occasionally hosted and attended teas. Eliza Farnham saw them as odd affairs, quite unlike anything she had experienced back East, and after a party at which the hostess served corn dodger, a "salt risin" loaf of bread, milk, butter, fruit preserves, fried bacon, and "a chicken full of pinfeathers" she reported on the proceedings at length.[90]

The affair commenced in the early afternoon. Those with invitations left home shortly after their mid-day meal since etiquette demanded they arrive at their hostesses home around one o'clock. After an exchange of greetings, the hostess seated her guests at a table near the fireplace and began preparing several dishes. To begin with, she hung a kettle of dried pumpkin over the fire and placed a teakettle on the hearth. About an hour later, she situated an oven full of gingerbread next to the fire and removed the pumpkin. This she then mixed with eggs, milk, ginger, and molasses to make a pie filling. The gingerbread was removed from the oven about four o'clock and replaced with a pan of biscuits. Where the pumpkin pot had hung, the hostess placed a teakettle. At half past four, it was time to move the tea table to the center of the room and cover it with a white tablecloth. The hostess then proceeded to set the table with dishes of many different colors and styles. She removed the biscuits from fireplace at five o'clock and wrapped them in a cloth. She next set the pumpkin pie to bake. A plate of dried beef and pickles arrived at the table at six o'clock, along with a saucer of honey and a dish of plum preserves. The teapot commenced boiling at about half past six, and 15 minutes later the gingerbread and biscuits arrived on the table. If the pie refused to bake, a common occurrence, it might not be served until nearly eight, the time at which guests usually took their leave.

BEGINNING TO APPEAR MORE DOMESTICATED

By the 1840s, McLean County's landscape was beginning to appear more domesticated than wild and its eating habits starting to lose their frontier character. Jonathan Maxson, whose family settled at Stout's Grove around 1830 and who never saw candy as a boy, had his first taste of it at age eighteen. The Hayeses began married life cooking on a stove rather than in a fireplace, and in Tremont Eliza Farnham bought a set of flatware and ordered several pieces of hollowware for her table.[91] What with mushrooming markets and new foods, new appliances, and new utensils arriving from the East, the area's culinary history was entering a new era.

CHAPTER 2 – FOOD, CLASS, AND ETHNICITY

Innovations in transportation and food processing and waves of immigration in the 1840s and '50s changed American foodways profoundly. The introduction of steamboats, canals, and railways made it possible to move products great distances. Oyster-eating became a craze and swept the country almost as soon as trains connected the Midwest to producing regions along the eastern seaboard. More fundamentally, improved transportation made it possible to move wheat economically from producing areas to consumers in other parts of the country. This propelled the assent of wheat flour over corn meal in areas outside of the South. The subsequent replacement of grindstones with much more efficient but expensive steel rollers caused thousands of local and regional flour mills to go out of business. This left a handful of large firms and created the first instance of centralization within the food industry. In the meantime, the cast-iron stove transformed the American kitchen, and a huge influx of European immigrants affected American tastes.

In McLean County, both the popularization of the kitchen stove and the flood of immigrants depended on railroads. Lines running both north and south and east and west brought rapid population growth and a slew of new hotels, boarding houses, and other eating places to the area. Even before the railroads arrived some people grew rich buying and selling land, but with Bloomington's development as a railway center there emerged a set of *uber* wealthy families that immediately distinguished themselves by constructing ornate mansions, staffing them with servants, and entertaining lavishly. Tastes and standards of hospitality echoed those of Eastern elites and reflected notions of conspicuous consumption. Irish newcomers, many of them as conspicuously poor as they had been in their famine-ravaged homeland, stood on the lowest rung of the social order. Most worked as common laborers, but it was not long before a significant number found places as cooks, servants, waiters, grocers, bar keepers, and hoteliers.[1] In the meantime, German-speaking immigrants fleeing the consequences of the failed European Revolutions of 1848, brought continental manners and customs to America's shores while introducing such varied fare as potato salad, sauerkraut, wieners, three bean salad, lentil soup, liver dumplings, *Wiener schnitzel*, steak tartar, *sauerbraten*, potato pancakes, red cabbage, *rouladen, knackwurst* (or *knockwurst*), bratwurst, liverwurst, *hasenpfeffer*, Black Forest cake, *lebkuchen*, *schnecken*, and strudel.

IMMIGRANTS FROM THE EAST

America's frontiers disappeared when "men of capital and enterprise" arrived, bought up pioneers' farms, and started developing towns and cities.[2] This began in McLean County about 1830.[3] That year James Allin, formerly of Fayette County, Illinois, arrived at Blooming Grove, purchased land, and agitated for establishing a new county. He convinced state officials to situate its seat on his property, a piece of real estate close to where he happened to have a general store. The next year Asahel Gridley, a native of New York, showed up. He purchased a lot from Allin, opened another store, and began acquiring land as fast as he could from pioneers eager to move west. Gridley with Allin's help purchased a printing press and recruited a couple of newspaper editors. They set up shop in Bloomington and began publishing articles promoting the area as an immigrant destination.

People from New England, the Mid-Atlantic States, and Ohio liked what they read in the newspaper about McLean County, and in 1836 they began arriving in large numbers. Gridley and his partners had the towns of LeRoy and Lexington laid out in advance with plenty of lots available for sale. That same year a group of investors from Hudson, New York formed a company and sold shares to prospective immigrants. The new organization purchased land and established Hudson, Illinois at Haven's Grove, a few miles north of Blooming Grove. Similarly, the Mt. Hope Company, chartered in Rhode Island, purchased land in the southwestern part of the county and built the village of Mt. Hope. The towns of Concord (later renamed Danvers), Clarksville, and Lytleville (both abandoned later) were developed at about the same time.

Housing in these places consisted chiefly of frame and clapboard cottages. These were built in a number of styles, but in typical New England fashion, a kitchen usually occupied the back of the residence, often spanning its entire width. Alternatively, the kitchen might jut out of the rear of the house as part of a "succession of annexed outbuildings" that could perhaps include a dairy, a washroom, a woodshed, and a privy.[4] Many backyards contained a stand-alone kitchen, a dedicated "summer kitchen," built away from the house. This was to avoid afflicting residents with even more heat on hot summer days. Among common households – those unable to afford servants – family members spent a great deal of time in the kitchen. It doubled as a dining room, tripled as a laundry room, and on and on – washroom, sewing room, or sitting room, depending on time of day and season of the year. As a general rule, the colder it got outside, the busier the kitchen inside. It was often the only heated room in the house.

COMMON KITCHENS OF
THE NINETEENTH CENTURY

The furnishings of mid-to-late nineteenth-century farmhouse kitchens reflected the great variety of activities that took place in them. On Monday, kitchens commonly contained a clutter of vessels and other paraphernalia for washing clothes. Tuesday was ironing day, and another battery of equipment appeared. On Saturday, out came the bathtub. Universal fixtures consisted of a table and chairs flanked by such auxiliary items as rockers, work stands, desks, and shelving.[5] Some kitchens, particularly those having fireplaces, contained a high-backed bench called a "settle" or "settee." It was placed in front of the fire to shield the backs of those who sat there from the chilly drafts that blew in around doors and windows. Homemakers covered the cold floors with rag carpeting during the winter, and around the cooking stove or fireplace they laid down a section of oilcloth or canvas to catch grease. Whitewashed walls gave the kitchen a bright look. In season, they were frequently hung with dried or drying fruits, vegetables, and sausages. Nails driven into studs and beams held bunches of dried herbs, tools of various kinds, different sorts and sizes of bags, not to mention hats and coats and an assortment of other personal belongings. Plates often were placed on a rack suspended from a wall. In addition, there were wall-mounted or free-standing dressers. These contained upper shelves with rails for holding plates and other pieces of tableware so they leaned forward and did not accumulate dust. Lower shelves held pots and pans and perhaps a cupboard. Many kitchens had one or more closets, again either nailed to a wall or free standing. These held various pieces of cookware, lamps, lanterns, and foot and bed warmers. Closets and cupboards provided space for grocery items and the many cooking utensils a homemaker needed, including scales, measuring spoons and cups, whisks, rolling pins, a chopping knife and board, cleaver, coffee pot, knives and forks, salt box, pepper box, sugar nippers, sugar box, and a table-top mortar and pestle. A sink set with a pitcher and bowl for washing face and hands was usually found in the kitchen or directly adjacent. The roller towel hung on the wall next to the sink was ordinarily changed twice a week.

COOKING STOVES

Newcomers to McLean County from the eastern states, in contrast to those from the South, favored abandoning the fireplace in favor of cast iron cooking stoves and ranges. When Eliza Farnham, a native of Rensselaerville, New York, traveled west in 1836 to visit her sister and brother-in-law, cooking throughout much of New England already had gravitated toward these appliances. After Eliza married and moved to Tremont, the new seat of Tazewell County, she found herself keeping house in a two-room cottage with a presentable front room and a Franklin stove in the back.[6] To Eliza, seeing the Franklin was like running into an old acquaintance lately arrived from some pleasant sitting room in New York. It was a venerable device, but here on the fringe of civilization Eliza intended to do more with the stove than heat the room.

Cooking was not what Benjamin Franklin had in mind when he invented what he called a "Pennsylvania fireplace" back in 1744. What he envisioned actually was a portable heating element fabricated from cast iron plates. A proper stove is fully enclosed; Franklin's device had an opening in front. It stood away from the wall and had a built-in box for warming air before it circulated through the room. The Pennsylvania fireplace's chief selling point was economy; a Franklin used much less fuel than a conventional fireplace.[7]

Franklin admitted his fireplace could be used for cooking in a pinch.[8] Certainly it could heat a teakettle, warm a fireplace oven, and keep a dish hot. It could even roast meat suspended by a string above the fire, but unfortunately the Farnhams' little Franklin was really not suited to such clever cookery. It had a grate, but Eliza's teakettle barely fit through the fireplace opening, and multiple burns on her hands and fingers attested to the difficulty of removing the kettle once it was boiling. The biggest cooking vessel she could place over the fire was a three-pint saucepan. As result, she had to use it for everything from fricasseeing chicken to boiling corned beef and cabbage. She owned a good oven designed to bake bread when placed in front of a fireplace, but the appliance was too big to sit on the ledge of her stove. Eliza cobbled together several contraptions to support the oven, but none worked very well. Yet, she persisted, fortified perhaps by the knowledge that modern thinkers condemned fireplace cooking as wasteful and old-fashioned.

A TRIUMPH OF YANKEE INGENUITY

Dedicated cooking stoves came on the market about the beginning of the nineteenth century and almost immediately were a commercial success, particularly in areas of the East where firewood had become scarce.[9] Elsewhere the public was hesitant. Some feared the device could explode. Others worried about the emission of poisonous fumes. Nevertheless, once one household in a neighborhood purchased a stove, the rest followed. This was particularly true after 1834 when Philo Penfield Stewart of Oberlin College patented a new stove. The "Oberlin Stove," as it was popularly known, contained a firebox with slanting sides. These had the effect of concentrating a fire as it burned down, thereby creating more heat from less wood. The ineluctable fact was that diminishing wood supplies and the need to transport wood from increasingly distant locations made feeding a fireplace prohibitively expensive. In short, the cost of firewood forced an increasing number of Americans to come to the same conclusion most Europeans had reached decades earlier – it was time to buy a stove.

Food habits usually tend to be conservative, and there was greater hesitance to cook on a stove than there was to heat a room with one. As a result, heating stoves outsold cooking stoves by a wide margin. To help overcome the inertia in the kitchen and assuage qualms about giving up fireplace cookery, manufacturers portrayed the cooking stove as the smart, contemporary way to prepare a meal. An 1837 ditty (to be sung to the tune of Yankee Doodle) published by New Hampshire stove merchants Kimball and Page celebrated the Moore cooking stove as a triumph of Yankee ingenuity:

Johnny Moore

One Johnny Moore of Yankee blood,

A cute and cunning fellow,

He made himself a Cooking Stove –

By gosh! It was a whaler.

Four holes upon its top it had,

And rims both big and little,

So he could boil his dinner in

Most any kind of kettle.

A darn'd great oven, too, it had,

As big as Granny's apron,

In which he always baked his bread,

While Molly fried the bacon.

It took but mighty little fire

To cook a rousing dinner;

'Twould bake his bread and boil his pot,

And warm a chilly sinner.[10]

Between 1835 and 1840, 102 cooking stoves received U.S. patents, and as competition for sales heated up, freight rates fell, making stoves more affordable in western markets such as Illinois. Amelia Boggs recalled that her mother owned one of the first cooking stoves in McLean County.[11] This appears to have been sometime in the 1840s. Amelia remembered her mother using the stove to fry chicken, brown homemade sausages, and boil fresh vegetables. Its oven baked the best cornbread, light biscuits, salt-rising bread, and spongy cake. By 1850, a total of 54 foundries in 13 states were manufacturing cooking stoves, and many households considered the cooking stove a "must have" item. Phebe Weeks, freshly installed in Hudson, wrote in 1850 to her sister back home on Long Island that her stove had arrived safely.[12]

About this time, advertisements for cooking stoves began to appear in McLean County's *Weekly Pantagraph*. D. D. Haggard took out an advertisement in 1849 announcing that he had for sale Roots' patented cooking stove.[13] Two years later George Dietrich, the hardware store owner, opened the "Cincinnati Stove Store" in a new brick building on Bloomington's Main Street. Dietrich's advertisements assured readers that he personally selected his stock from the best foundries in Cincinnati.[14] Sawyer and Bunn about the same time trumpeted a variety of St. Louis brands.[15]

Manufacturers in both Cincinnati and St. Louis had an advantage selling stoves in McLean County because their products could be shipped by river as far as Pekin. Nationally, however, the cities of Albany and Troy, New York dominated the industry and did so throughout most of the nineteenth century.[16] The Hudson River provided both towns with a direct route south to New York City, and the Erie Canal opened the way to the Great Lakes. By the 1850s, Albany and Troy hosted a total of seven foundries and together employed 1,700 people in the stove industry, and that was just the beginning. By 1875, the two cities boasted a total of 32 foundries. Once McLean County was connected by rail to Lake Michigan, George Hazelton, a Chicago wholesaler, began touting Albany stoves, particularly the Eagle brand, in *The Weekly Pantagraph*.[17]

STOVES MADE IN BLOOMINGTON

Stove making came to McLean County with the founding of the Bloomington Stove Works in 1870. By this time, stoves were a source of national pride, and American brands such as Black Diamond, Clipper, Express, Governor, Mayflower, New Eagle, Prairie Flower, Ruler, and Western Star bore romantic and powerful names. Consumers everywhere regarded these and other models manufactured in the United States as among the most efficient and beautiful stoves in the world.[18]

Such had not always been the case. American-made stoves at first tended to be small and low to the ground, and they lacked sufficient capacity to cook for a big family. Manufacturers, however, eventually enlarged their models, put legs on them, and elevated cooking surfaces to waist height. Soon even the cheapest stove generally had four pot holes or "rims" on the cooking surface and one oven underneath. Expensive models had more expansive cooking surfaces, more rims, multiple ovens, and one or more tanks for heating water, and elaborate decorative elements, including fanciful figures molded in the cast iron. The quest for new and improved designs developed into a national mania. Inventors came up with novel grates, flues, warming ovens, and vents.

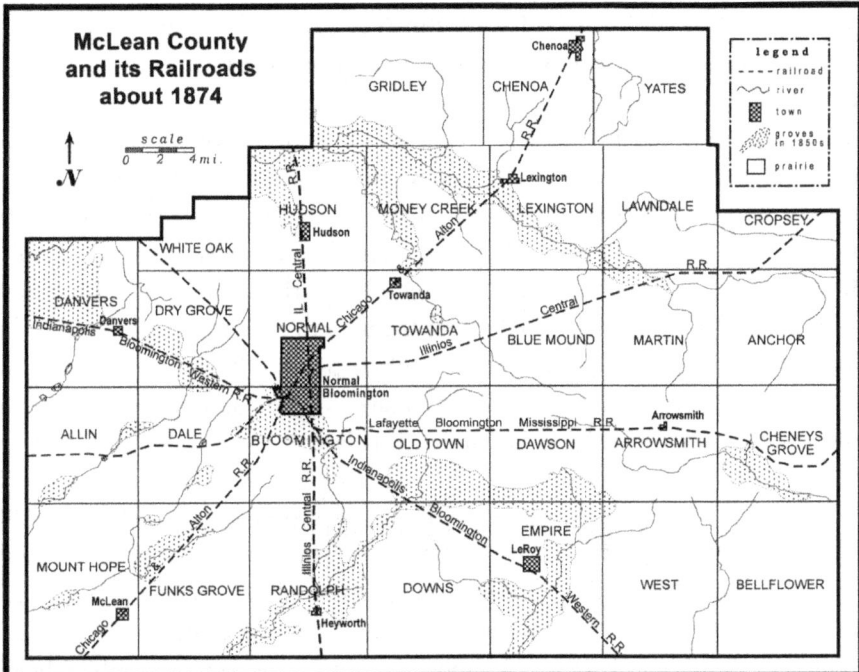

McLean County about 1874. Four railroads carried food and food-related products to and from markets nationwide. The railways also brought in foreign immigrants with a variety of different tastes.

Bloomington Stove Works joined the innovation derby by offering models with detachable water tanks. The idea, the brainchild of Maurice Seward, a company superintendent, was to create more oven space.[19] Nearly every manufacturer sold stoves mounted with tanks for heating water; only a Bloomington Stove would be equipped with removable tanks to free up compartments for baking.

Seward's invention helped sales, but without question, railroads were the key to Bloomington Stove's success. Two major lines, the Illinois Central and the Chicago, Alton, and St. Louis, ran through town north and south. Two other routes, the Lafayette, Bloomington, and Mississippi and the Indianapolis, Bloomington, and Western connected to points east and west. These railways enabled Bloomington Stove to import pig iron from Missouri and the Great Lakes and to ship and sell its products at very competitive prices in Illinois and Iowa.[20]

McLean County acquired a second stove manufacturer in 1887 when a group of disgruntled molders left Bloomington Stove Works, organized the Cooperative Stove Company, and opened a foundry in Normal. Cooperative Stove's leading product became the Normal Steel Range, a creation later promoted as "the most durable steel range manufactured."[21]

The Cooperative Stove Company underwent several reorganizations, moves, and name changes over the years.[22] Sometime in the mid-'20s, it became the Hayes-Custer Stove Company. Hayes-Custer started out fabricating wood and coal-burning stoves, but eventually switched to producing gas ranges. A gasoline unit called the "Safe-T-Gas" was also assembled at the plant. Fire destroyed the facility in 1929. Other towns tried to get the firm to relocate, but Bloomington's Association of Commerce and Industry raised $100,000 to keep the company where it was. Housed in a new factory, Hayes-Custer manufactured and sold 28,000 stoves nationwide in 1935.[23] Two years later it went out of business.

SIGNIFICANCE OF THE KITCHEN STOVE

Meal preparation in a nineteenth-century household was far and away the most time-consuming task confronting a homemaker. In many homes, her work actually began out back in the kitchen garden Cultivating vegetables helped defray food costs that typically amounted to 40 or 50 percent of the average household income. Inside the kitchen, housewives ground their own spices. They roasted and ground the coffee, sifted flour for breads, cakes, and pies, and baked two or three times a week. Granulated sugar did not exist. Sugar came in cones as hard as stone and weighing several pounds. These needed to be cut and hammered and rolled until reduced to powder. Homemakers bought poultry and other small animals live at the market and killed and cleaned them at home. Fish needed to be scaled. Shelling nuts, seeding raisins and drying herbs were all part of the kitchen routine. Just fueling and removing ashes from a wood-burning kitchen stove took as much as an hour every day.[24]

Compared to a fireplace, stoves were quick and easy to start, and many home-makers regarded them as a blessing.[25] A little wood was placed on the grate inside the firebox and ignited – making sure, of course, to get started well in advance of actual cooking so the cast iron would have time to get good and hot. Damper adjustments controlled heat flow. An open damper in the smoke stack created a strong draft and got a fire going quickly. A partially closed damper caused hot air and smoke to flow through passages that warmed the oven. Vents controlled oxygen flow to the fire, allowing the user to increase or reduce the flames. An experienced cook with a few sticks of wood could take a stove from stone cold to ready to boil water for tea in about 20 minutes. A person could have the oven ready to bake biscuits within 40 minutes.

Although cooking stoves seemed to make life easier, they actually made greater demands on householders' time than the old fireplace did.[26] Installing a stove was not quick and easy. It had to be positioned carefully to create a proper draft and to avoid setting fire to woodwork. There were problems year after year in many homes when the stove had to be disassembled, moved to and from its summer location, and then reassembled. Drafts, flues, and pipes had to be cleaned often, and frequently the cleaning left such a mess that the entire kitchen had to be washed. Monthly scrubbings with a stiff brush and "blackings" with black lead or British Lustre kept the stove from rusting. Stove wood had to be cut into small, uniform lengths, carried into the kitchen, and stacked. After a range had gone cold came the task of ash removal, and in the case of coal stoves someone had to get rid of the heavy "clinkers."

The most insidious demand exacted by the cooking stove had nothing to do with either installation or upkeep. It had to do with the kind of meal a cook with a modern stove was expected to prepare. Straight to the point, the new appliance effectively killed the traditional one-pot-a-day routine of fireplace cookery.[27] Newspaper and magazine writers around the middle of the nineteenth century began insisting that a healthy meal consisted of a variety of dishes. Fixing multi-course meals on a modern cast-iron stove was supposed to be effortless. Magazine writers declared that every family ought to have three freshly prepared meals a day. A breakfast of coffee and mush was a thing of the past. The contemporary homemaker looked after her family's well-being by fixing a breakfast of cooked or fresh fruit, fried or baked potatoes, fried beef, ham, or fish, fresh bread or biscuits, and coffee.

Given this added work, was the quality of stove-cooked food superior to food prepared over an open hearth? Not in everyone's opinion. Roasted meats, accord-ing to some, were not nearly as good out of the oven as they were cooked over an open fire. Furthermore, there were those who argued that brick ovens baked bread better an iron range. Stove sellers admitted to problems, but invariably blamed the trouble on competing brands. "Don't be annoyed with half baked bread or a scolding wife . . . ," advised Bloomington stove merchant G. H. Read. "BUY A DICTATOR and remove that great impediment to domestic felicity – the poor cook stove."[28]

ELITE FOOD HABITS

Wealthy nineteenth-century men and women celebrated their good fortune by eating immense amounts of rich food and were not the least bit ashamed of becoming more than a bit fat. Less fortunate people, who often had little to eat, admired them for it. The public during the Gilded Age loved to read about high society's magnificent dinner parties, featuring fantastic dishes prepared by French chefs.[29] The newspapers told of waiters setting tables with enormous spreads. The rich and famous tucked them away enthusiastically. No one imagined it shameful to look overstuffed. After dinner photographs showed brandy and cigars and men's bellies protruding from their waistcoats. Female fashion favored ample bosoms, sturdy hips, and strapping buttocks, all testifying to a healthy appetite. Holding one's own at a splendidly appointed table was for the fortunate few an important validation of status.

The lean, hard-looking body so much admired today represented poverty or serious illness. In the eyes of late nineteenth- and early twentieth-century Americans, slimness was an embarrassing affliction. Just as young women in recent times have become enslaved to fashion and made to feel at fault for being full-figured, many women back then struggled mightily to avoid appearing too thin. Everyone from college coeds to shop girls wanted their bodies to have a certain "florid plumpness," epitomized most famously in the soft, broad-breasted body of Lillian Russell, an American singer and actress who weighed about 200 pounds (91 kg).[30]

To achieve the Lillian Russell look, many women had to watch their diet. At Western Reserve University in Cleveland, Ohio, Professor O. F. Tower discovered that women consumed disproportionately large amounts of fat, chiefly in the form of butter and cream.[31] He also found they were far more attentive to cleaning their plates and wasted significantly less food than their male classmates. For those who were having trouble achieving a fashionable figure, bookshops throughout the country sold T.C. Duncan's self-help guide, *How to be Plump: Or Talks on Physiological Feeding*.[32] Duncan was a Chicago physician. His advice to the young woman unhappy with her slender body was to eat right. That meant having a plain but substantial breakfast of potatoes, meat, fried mush, oatmeal, bread, butter, and well-milked tea or coffee. A hearty dinner was to follow no more than five hours later. The doctor advised beginning with a first course consisting of a light, moderately seasoned soup. The main course was to be built around plenty of vegetables, again lightly spiced, and with no condiments. Duncan did not permit drinking water with the meal, believing it was better for the woman desirous of a voluptuous figure to have milk or a chocolate drink instead. Only in the evening did Duncan permit a light meal. Bread or oatmeal and milk, in the doctor's opinion, were almost too substantial at this time of day because they might interfere with sleep, and plenty of sleep was important if one wished to become more robust.

Bloomington's newspapers advertised products to help people gain weight. For example, there was Deveroux's Medicated Cordial Gin, a drink that purportedly stimulated the appetite.[33] For men worried about being underweight and looking scrawny, there was Henrietta Water. Its exclusive Bloomington distributor, Cuyler's Restaurant, touted it "as the greatest water on earth, the only water known to increase a man's weight twenty pounds in one month."[34]

THE DAVISES AND THE BEECHER SISTERS

The foremost representatives of society's upper crust to take up residence in McLean County were David Davis and his wife Sarah. David Davis, a native of Maryland, had the Gilded Age look of eminence. He was a large man who continued to put on weight until he eventually tipped the scales in excess of 300 pounds. He was not the state's wealthiest man, but he owned an immense amount of land, and as a landlord he presided over more acreage than anyone else in Illinois. After moving to Bloomington in 1836, practicing law, and accumulating a small fortune, Davis married the beautiful and talented Sarah Walker of Lenox, Massachusetts and moved her to his home on the Illinois frontier. With Sarah's help, Davis's star continued to rise. He got himself elected Judge of Illinois' Eighth Judicial Circuit, successfully managed Abraham Lincoln's first presidential campaign, and became his candidate's appointee to the United States Supreme Court. He left the court in 1877 after being elected to United States Senate by the Illinois legislature. Two years later, his wife, Sarah, died. Davis retired from the Senate in 1882, remarried, and returned to his home in Bloomington. He died there in 1886.

Sarah Davis was a woman of considerable education who reveled in the business of running a prominent household. Her schooling, which included a stint at Hartford Female Seminary where she studied under Catharine and Harriet Beecher, prepared her for exactly that kind of work. The Beecher sisters pioneered domestic science and can be regarded in a sense as home economists before the invention of home economics. Catharine Beecher's book, *Treatise on Domestic Economy*, and Catharine and Harriet's *The American Woman's Home* took household management as a topic for serious study years before the idea caught hold in conventional academic circles.[35] The sisters argued that homemaking was a profession like any other. Housewives needed to think about efficiency and to work always with the best tools available.

The Beechers' message, its novelty notwithstanding, rested on a traditional worldview. Women, they believed, were inherently more nurturing than men. Consequently, females assumed the role as homemaker by design. Working within the home complimented the male role of breadwinner outside the home. Just as men strived for success in business and industry, a woman needed to do her utmost to uphold domestic life and to assure her family's health and happiness.[36] Reflecting her husband's achievements by decorating, dressing, and entertaining appropriately, comprised part of the challenge. The Beechers' writings advocated the development of expertise across such mundane topics as cellar care, kitchen routines, table settings, and servant training. Everything about the house demanded attention to detail, and without question Sarah Davis became imbued with this attitude.

CLOVER LAWN

Sarah Davis had the good fortune to be able to apply some of what she learned from the Beechers to the construction of a lavish new three-story home on the eastern edge of Bloomington. The 36-room, yellow-bricked structure, dubbed "Clover Lawn," was designed by Alfred Piquenard and completed in 1872. It fused elements of Italianate style with Second Empire while incorporating a number of advanced features. These included central heating, modern gas lighting, indoor plumbing, hot and cold running water, and several in-house communication systems.

The interior layout of the Davis mansion was typical of the era in most respects.[37] The front vestibule opened into a central hall, an important nineteenth-century indicator of middle to upper-class status. Lower class homes, including the cottages and bungalows of skilled workers and managers, did not have entry halls. A hall afforded better-off families with an in-between space, a transition between outside and inside, as well as passage to other rooms of the house. The more public of these, the parlor and the dining room, perhaps a library, were located toward the front of the building and richly decorated. The more functional rooms, the kitchen, the pantries, in some instances a sewing room, were situated at the back of the house. The hall of the Davis Mansion helped separate as well as connect front and back.

PARLOR

At the front of the Davis's hall, double doors opened to rooms on both the right and the left. The room on the left as one entered was the parlor, the room where members of the family received guests and Sarah Davis served tea. The room on the right was the sitting room. It provided a place for family and very close friends to meet informally and to read and write at their leisure. Some private meals may have been served in the Davis's sitting room.

Not all of America's better homes had sitting rooms, but from the early years of the nineteenth century through much of the twentieth a parlor was deemed essential. It was supposed to be the best room in the house and can be regarded it as a kind of formal showplace reflecting a family's wealth and good taste. Ostensibly, its sole purpose was to entertain guests. This typically occurred several times each week and involved a period of polite conversation accompanied by tea. Although men participated in parlor visits from time to time, women assumed primary responsibility. Late afternoon was the proper time to call in many parts of the country, but Bloomington's high society visited in the early afternoon. The food served with tea (usually green tea with sugar and milk) was normally lighter and easier to manage than dishes served at regular mealtimes. Favorite tea-time foods included thin sandwiches of cucumber or tomato, cake slices, and cookies.

DINING ROOM

The Davis's parlor opened directly into their dining room. This allowed Sarah to move her guests easily between the two rooms, as she had to do, for example, after a dinner when it was time for ladies to withdraw to the parlor. This left the men in the dining room where they could drink, smoke and talk among themselves. The Davises could accommodate up to 12 guests in their dining room, and when not entertaining they regularly ate there themselves.

The notion of a dedicated dining room had originated in France. The English adopted it during the eighteenth century. In America, having a dining room became an upper-class marker. Those without social aspirations did without; they continued to eat in the kitchen and used the parlor to fete guests. Some homeowners built dining rooms, but they used them only on special occasions. Homebuilders usually situated dining rooms on the ground floor. Ideally, they were constructed on the north side of the house to avoid the direct rays of the sun. To prevent heat build-up, householders used inner and outer curtains, painted shades, and Venetian blinds. These were drawn during the summer months until the sun went down and candles were lit.

Dining room furnishings were ideally plain and simple. From about 1750 through most of the nineteenth century, furniture included the dining table and chairs, a sideboard, and a china closet. Some families added mirrors, lamps, polished fireplace tools, portraits, and perhaps a clock to the room.

People considered the sideboard the most important piece of dining room furniture. A sideboard typically consisted of a set of cabinets, or cupboards, and one or more drawers, topped by a flat surface at waist level. Furniture makers built sideboards in a range of decorative styles, frequently using costly woods and veneers such as mahogany and walnut. In wealthy homes such as the Davis's, two sideboards in the dining room were commonplace.

Sideboards served several purposes. They were convenient places to store liquor bottles and prepare drinks. Some sideboards contained built-in liquor cases. Others held wine coolers lined with zinc. Often there were drawers for keeping flatware and carving knives. A sideboard also presented a convenient surface for creating a display. Hosts and hostesses used it to show off their finest china, glassware, and silver.

Dining tables were also arranged to create a grand impression. Guests admired the tablecloth, the silverware, and the cut glass. Nineteenth-century conventions called for covering the table with a white cloth and placing every piece of cutlery, glass, and plate in perfectly straight lines. So-called "Russian service" became fashionable at dinner parties in the 1850s. Russian service prevails today and entails serving every course of the meal to each guest individually. Earlier, French service prevailed, and dinner came to the table in two or more parts, the serving dishes for each part coming all at once. By custom, the cloth was removed from the table after dessert but prior to the arrival of the final nuts, fruit, and wine. That changed during the second half of the nineteenth century when it became fashionable to leave the tablecloth in place until everyone had left the room. About the same time, table napkins became universal in polite society.

PANTRIES AND THE DAVIS'S CHINA CLOSET

Middle- and upper-class nineteenth-century homes had one or two pantries or special rooms for the storage of food, kitchen utensils, tableware, and related items. In homes with two pantries, one usually was located off the kitchen toward the back of the house. The other, sometimes called the "butler's pantry," was situated between the kitchen and the dining room. It contained drawers and cupboards intended for cutlery, dishes, and glassware.

The Davis house possessed an unusually ample amount of pantry space divided among three rooms. The smallest was the kitchen pantry. It stood adjacent to a very large cold-storage pantry that opened onto the back hall. The butler's pantry, referred to as a "China closet" by Sarah Davis, contained the usual cupboards for serving dishes and tableware. However, instead of having a doorway between it and the kitchen, its only connection to the kitchen consisted of a small window. The intent was to wall off food preparation. When Sarah Davis held dinner parties, not the slightest sound or accidental glimpse of the kitchen disturbed the ambiance of her dining room. Guests did not so much as see Sarah summons servants to the table. Whenever needed, they appeared as if by magic, an illusion facilitated by a small pedal concealed under the table at Sarah's place and connected to a little bell in the China closet.

SARAH'S KITCHEN

Sarah Davis had a perfect kitchen by the standards of her day. It was located in the servants' wing of the mansion and contained a large cast-iron stove and a big icebox. It was a workroom with nothing decorative about it. Except for the bricks under the stove, bare wood, thoroughly oiled, covered the floor. Green paint and calcimine whitewash covered the otherwise unadorned walls.

The Davises' kitchen stove was a coal-burner of exceptional quality. Sarah considered its purchase at length and searched carefully for the right model. When a friend told her the Gridleys owned the best stove in Bloomington, Sarah went to see it. She finally decided on a model manufactured by the Magee Furnace Company of Chelsea, Massachusetts. It featured two warming ovens set above two baking ovens and six pot holes. To facilitate ash removal, the Magee came with a chute that connected directly to a receptacle in the basement.

The Davises' icebox, which in the vernacular of their day was referred to as a "refrigerator," had two compartments, one in which to place food, the other large enough to accommodate a two hundred pound block of ice. The icebox was old technology by the time the Davises built Clover Lawn, but it had yet to become commonplace in American homes.[38]

The cost of ice was one reason most homes lacked an icebox. Artificial ice production began in the 1870s, but until about 1900 most ice in United States was harvested from streams and lakes, stored in icehouses, and delivered to homes and businesses as needed. Most households used ice only occasionally to cool drinks and make ice cream. The Davises used ice in great quantities. An 1877 receipt reveals that their supplier, Monroe Brothers of Bloomington, delivered ice to Clover Lawn eleven times a month from June through September.[39] From May 17 through November 5 that year, the Davises purchased 3,855 pounds.

IDEAS ABOUT FOOD

Sarah Davis's food-related concerns can be detected in her surviving correspondence, which for the most part includes letters sent to and from her husband, brother, sister, and niece.[40] The earliest surviving letter was penned in 1839. The last was sent in 1879. The majority of letters containing passages about food and related matters were put to paper between 1871 and 1874. Most were authored during the autumn, especially the month of November. The Davis's correspondence contains few letters written during the summer because they usually resided together at that time of year.

In her communications, Sarah often referred to food. She wrote about species that she and her staff had recently planted or harvested and described the various dishes they had prepared, served, or eaten over the past several days. The foods mentioned most frequently in Sarah's correspondence were: dairy products (22 references), turkey (19 references), cake (18 references), apples (15 references), eggs (10 references), pears (10 references), oysters (9 references), and lard (8 references).

DAIRY PRODUCTS

Sarah Davis had a special fondness for the dairy. Clover Lawn under her management always had at least one milk cow and sometimes as many as four. These animals produced milk and cream sufficient to meet household needs.

Sarah exercised considerable care in preparing her milk products. She was very much "hands on," in part because her servants did not always measure up to her standards of cleanliness and good order. From a technical standpoint, she took pleasure in applying the lessons of Mrs. Clesson, a former instructor. Nevertheless, Sarah's love of the dairy may have resided less in the discipline of milk handling and butter making than in a deep nostalgia or melancholy. She once confessed as much to her niece. The sound of a dasher in a butter churn always recalled to Sarah those bygone days ". . . when good old Jenny sang, 'Peter stands at the gate, waiting for Butter Cake. Come butter, come. Churn butter, churn." Here it is appropriate to note that in Sarah's day the main point to milking a cow was to make butter. Milk at this point in history was rarely taken as a beverage except by infants and children.

TURKEY

Sarah Davis loved turkey. She had her first taste, a bite of wild turkey, not long after she moved to Illinois. Later on, she raised turkeys, and they became a mainstay on her table. Once in 1856, after her cook served roast turkey two days in a row, Sarah seemed more amused than perturbed. She never tired of turkey, but she was forever fussy. When a servant came home on one occasion after buying a turkey that did not meet her specifications, Sarah herself hastened to town, returned it to the store where it had been purchased, and visited several other shops before finding a suitable specimen.

Sarah Davis served turkey at her Thanksgiving Day dinner parties, just as many Americans do today. In her day, however, Thanksgiving had yet to be established as a national holiday, and roast turkey was not reserved for special occasions, as it tends to be nowadays. It was rather a seasonal dish frequently served during the fall and winter months. Thus, a little more than a week before the Thanksgiving of 1871, Sarah dined on turkey. Ten days prior to that, she had a cold-turkey supper, suggesting another encounter with roast turkey the day before. Sarah served turkey at a dinner party just two days in advance of Thanksgiving in 1873 (She feared the bird, which had been received as a gift, would spoil if she kept it until the Thanksgiving meal).

CAKES AND HOSPITALITY

Sarah Davis liked to bake cakes, and she often helped her servants prepare them. People in her day baked cakes for visitors. A cake embodied the notion of hospitality, and by serving it a hostess paid tribute to her guests.

Inhospitable individuals made bad cakes. Sarah wrote to her young niece in 1845 about the proprietor of the Globe Hotel in Springfield, perhaps as a kind of object lesson. You will find, Sarah declared, no gingerbread on the Globe's tables. Its miserly owner, unlike other hoteliers, deemed gingerbread (properly speaking a type of cake) too dear for daily consumption. Worse yet, the cake the Globe did serve was made light and airy on the cheap by adding a great deal of Saleratus (baking soda). This, according to Sarah, turned the cake yellow. It also conferred upon everyone who ate it a nasty case of gas.

APPLES

In her letters, Sarah Davis brought up apples in many different contexts. She frequently worried about the condition of the trees in her orchard, and in one instance she told of putting men to work cutting fresh grafts on specimens that had been yielding poorly. She testified to fine yields, such as a crop of baking apples her workmen picked in 1859. She also wrote about big disappointments – for instance, the great number of specked apples that ripened in 1874 (though she figured she could dispose of them to someone who wanted to make applesauce). Sarah kept her husband abreast of her staff's efforts to press cider and ferment cider vinegar. Her interest in such prosaic issues as market price and keeping a barrel of apples through the winter attests to the fruit's importance in nineteenth-century diets and Sarah's attention to the details of management. As far as apples were concerned, there was little to differentiate Sarah Davis from the common farmer.

EGGS

With regard to eggs, Sarah Davis occasionally reported how her hens were laying, but her chief concern was egg preservation during the winter when the birds stopped laying. David Davis worried about this too, and on one occasion he mailed his wife a recipe for keeping eggs.

The instructions sent by the judge have been lost, but Isabella Beeton, a contemporary cookbook author, wrote about a number of techniques in her text on household management.[41] The best time to preserve eggs, in Beeton's estimation, was from July through September.[42] Collect the eggs in good weather, she admonished, and see to their preservation within 24 hours. Her primary method of preservation required boiling a saucepan of water, putting about 20 eggs into a net, and lowering the entire batch into the water for 20 seconds. After that, the eggs were to be packed in sawdust until needed.

Egg preservation was never entirely reliable, and purchasers could never count on eggs being fresh. Consequently, buyers needed to exercise great care. Before purchasing an egg, Beeton recommended touching one's tongue to the large end.[43] If it felt warm, the egg was fresh. Another test was to hold the egg up to a lighted candle. If the egg appeared clear, it was good. If not, the purchaser was to consider it stale. When candling revealed a black spot, the egg was spoiled.

PEARS AND PRESERVES

Sarah Davis enjoyed pears. Her orchard contained two types, a dwarf and a standard variety, and she also purchased pears by the box.[44] Sarah ate pears fresh, served baked pears to her guests, made pear preserves, and gave gifts of fresh and preserved pears to her friends. Precisely how Sarah made pear preserves is unknown. However, it seems a safe bet that she followed Catherine Beecher's formula, if not in every detail, at least in general outline.

Pear Preserves

Take out the cores, cut off the stems, and pare them. Boil the pears in water, till they are tender. Watch them, that they do not break. Lay them separately on a platter as you take them out. To each pound of fruit, take a pound of sugar. Make the syrup, and boil the fruit in the syrup till clear.[45] (Place fruit and syrup in pots or jars) Lay brandy papers over the top (of the containers), cover them tight, and seal them, or, what is best of all, soak a split bladder and tie it tight over them. In drying, it will shrink so as to be perfectly air-tight. Keep them in a dry, but not warm place.[46]

Combining the fruit and sugar and allowing them to stand together for a period of time drew the water from the fruit and assured it would retain a fairly firm texture while cooking. The cooking generally took place in a shallow brass or enameled iron pan; direct contact with iron darkened the fruit. Finished preserves kept well in stoneware pots or glass jars.

ATTITUDES TOWARD PORK

"Good sweet lard" was another product Sarah Davis wrote about. She became intensely concerned with it every November about the time her hogs were butchered. Lard rendering, as well as the sausage making, at the Davis mansion took place in the kitchen. The slaughtering Sarah had done commercially.

Sarah never mentioned in her letters who did the slaughtering. During the first decade or so of her residence in McLean County, it was probably a neighbor or one of the itinerant butchers who frequented the Bloomington area. For instance, it may have been J. Shough and Company, an outfit that sold pork products and beef tallow on the street outside the National Hotel every Wednesday morning. By the mid-1850s butchers began establishing shops open at regular hours. Rankin and Allin launched one on Front Street in 1856, and the following year David White opened a stand nearby. A dozen or so years later there were 33 individual butchers and at least eight companies selling meat in the Bloomington area.

The era of industrial butchery arrived during the 1870s. The number of butchers and meat cutters in Bloomington declined immediately as small shops were replaced by big outfits slaughtering scores if not hundreds of animals daily. The largest plant was William Van Schoick's packing company (later Bloomington

Pork Packing).[47] Van Schoick's, located near the Indianapolis, Bloomington, and Western Railroad yards, opened for business in 1873 after tearing out vineyards planted by Herman Schroeder (see Chapter 3) and replacing them with a stockyard and slaughterhouse. That season the company butchered 3,000 hogs. White and Daniels, a competing firm, slaughtered 800. Smaller packers butchered and packed hundreds more. Van Schoick's holding pens at the start of the 1874 slaughter contained approximately 700 animals. Workers began the season by slaughtering 40 of them in 40 minutes, but they had to stop after that because of rising temperatures. By 1889, Van Schoick's was known as Bloomington Packing, and employed 75 men, who butchered up to 15,000 hogs over the course of a three-month season. The company shipped lard to New York, Baltimore, and other Eastern cities. It sold fresh meat to buyers in New Orleans, Memphis, and other places in the South and marketed hams in Illinois, Indiana, Kentucky, and Missouri. International Packing Company, a Chicago firm, took control of Bloomington Packing in 1890.

Packing by then had become economically important to Bloomington, and many residents eyed the fortunes being made in Chicago and hoped the industry would continue to flourish locally. A letter to *The Daily Pantagraph* complaining about the smell emanating from Bloomington Packing prompted the newspaper to investigate.[48] Its reporter found the facility generally neat and clean. His article about the plant concluded that the significance of pork packing to the city warranted tolerance of occasional nuisances such as unpleasant odors. The press in the village of McLean expressed nothing but pleasure when Fred Leach, proprietor of a local meat, grocery, clothing, and shoe store, enlarged his slaughterhouse. Leach installed a gasoline engine and reportedly modeled ". . . his new facility after the big plants of Armour and Swift in Chicago."[49] This, the paper enthused, meant that Fred now could kill, hang, and dress carcasses just as efficiently as any of the giant packers.

Pork may have been good for business, but by the time Bloomington became a packing center, middle- and upper-class Americans had developed a remarkably negative attitude toward eating it, particularly in its fresh or uncured forms. This dislike or avoidance, which continued well into the twentieth century, was most pronounced in the urban areas of the Northeast and Midwest and was remarkably stronger among women than among men. Early nutrition studies conducted on elite college campuses disclosed little, if any, consumption of uncured pork among coeds. Men appeared more inclined to consume fresh pork, though it was generally absent from the athletes' table. More than a decade before Upton Sinclair published his exposé of the packing industry, *Good Housekeeping Magazine* had already declared pork an anathema to hygienists and something that anyone with a scrap of intelligence would shun.[50] Such warnings helped beef sales, but the entire packing industry suffered a loss of public confidence on account of investigations and repeated stories of filthy conditions. President Theodore Roosevelt commissioned two trusted advisors, Charles Neill and James Reynolds, to visit and objectively report on Chicago's meat-packing facilities in the wake of the uproar created by Sinclair's book. Neill and Reynolds came away from their visit disgusted with what they saw and heard, and following their report Roosevelt came out in favor of regulating the industry. As a result, the Federal Meat Inspection Act, requiring the U.S. Department of Agriculture to inspect meat processing plants, passed Congress in 1906.[51] The Pure Food and Drug Act, a statute meant to assure food safety, received Congressional approval the same day.[52]

IRISH IMMIGRANTS

Irishmen first came to Illinois as laborers hired to build canals and railroads. The Illinois Central Railroad, having launched the largest construction project in U.S. history, worked through the Irish Emigration Society and recruited at all of the ports on the Eastern Seaboard.[53] When the Illinois Central's grading and bridge-building work reached McLean County in 1852, a wave of these recruits arrived in Bloomington.[54] A second bunch came the next year when the Chicago and Alton Railroad built shops on the city's west side. By 1860, the county had 2,670 Irish-born residents, 1,769 of them living in Bloomington.[55] Among these residents were the city's first Irish businessmen, Luke Nevin and William Condon, both of them grocers.[56]

Irish customers required nothing of Nevin and Condon that other grocers did not carry, nor did Irishmen demand anything special from Bloomington's butchers and bakers. The items purchased were much the same as those bought by the city's other residents. Irish immigrant cooking tended to be simple. Ideally, some form of meat, poultry, or fish needed to be present at every meal. However, eggs or cheese could be substituted. On average, approximately 45 percent of the Irish immigrants' diet derived from animal products. Late eighteenth- and early nineteenth-century dietaries collected from Irish immigrants revealed diets exceptionally rich in energy, containing more fat and considerably less protein than the diets of other European immigrants.[57] Fruit and vegetable consumption tended to be limited to certain cool climate varieties, including cabbage, carrots, turnips, and potatoes. The latter, a dietary mainstay, were found in stews such as *stobhach Gaelach* (Irish stew) and were the principal ingredient of side dishes such as boxty, a pancake, and colcannon, a potato casserole.

Colcannon

INGREDIENTS – 1 medium cabbage, quartered and cored; 1 teaspoon salt; 3 large red (waxy) potatoes, scrubbed and sliced; 2 medium leeks, whites only, halved; 1 cup milk; ½ teaspoon mace; salt and pepper to taste; 8 tablespoon butter, unsalted. PREPARATION – Fill a large saucepan with enough water to cover cabbage and bring to boil. Add salt and cabbage. Reduce heat to medium high and cook until tender (about 10 to 12 minutes). Drain and chop cabbage, set aside. Add more water to pot, bring to boil, and cook potatoes until tender (about 10 minutes). Drain potatoes, set aside. Put milk in sauce pan, add leeks, and heat over medium high flame until simmering (but not boiling). Cook leeks until tender. Set aside pot with milk and leeks. In large bowl, mash potatoes with mace, salt, and pepper until smooth. Carefully mix in milk and leeks. Add cabbage and butter. Mash lightly to achieve thick, velvety potato mixture with bits of leek and cabbage, adding additional milk if needed. Place mixture in oven-proof casserole and brown under broiler. Serves 6.[58]

Beverages consisted chiefly of tea, beer, and whiskey. Strong black tea served with milk or cream and sugar was preferred. Among the beers, top-fermented varieties, the so-called "ales," prevailed. This latter preference faded, however, as the nineteenth century progressed and Irish Americans adjusted their taste to the milder, bottom-fermented beers favored by Germans.

CLOVER LAWN'S IRISH SERVANTS

The Davises, like other wealthy Bloomingtonians, regularly employed Irish servants and handymen. City households in 1860 provided work for 132 Irish domestics, the vast majority of them women in their twenties. At Clover Lawn, the staff included Bridget Kelley, Katie Walsh, and brothers Willie and Joe Fitzgerald. These were employees with considerable tenure, and the Davises in many ways treated them like junior members of the household. They regularly received presents of food and clothing and extra money, and on occasion Sarah Davis took time to help entertain their guests.

The Davises' generosity helped compensate their staff for the long hours they put in. Most urban employees at the time worked ten hours a day, five and a half days a week. House servants were generally on call, if not actually working, from the time they woke up in the morning until the time they went to bed that

night. Time off was generally limited to one evening a week. It became customary in the 1880s to allow a few hours off on Sunday as well. The Davises granted
their domestics a day off every other Sunday and rarely denied a request for an
evening out.

The Davises employed Bridget as their primary cook, and given a little tutoring she had no difficulty satisfying the family's tastes. Not that this was particularly difficult seeing as the family desired nothing more than basic American
cookery and inclined to be quite malleable in matters pertaining to food and
drink.[59] American eating and drinking habits generally have been susceptible
to immigrant influences, and in this respect Clover Lawn represented a kind of
microcosm. For instance, with over half of her residence inhabited by Catholics
from the Emerald Isle, Sarah found herself eating fish on Friday. Bridget, Katie,
the Fitzgeralds did so as a matter of religious discipline. For Sarah, a Protestant,
it was probably a matter of economy – no sense preparing separate dishes for dining table and kitchen table. But what about the spare ribs, a cut of pork popularly
associated with Blacks and Irish immigrants?[60] Sarah once gave spare ribs away to
the poor. Some years later they were being served in her dining room.

BEEF FRESH AND CORNED

Sarah Davis did not mention red meats in her correspondence as often as
she referred to turkey and fish. Her surviving letters contain just five references
to beef and even fewer to pork. Many Americans in Sarah's day avoided fresh
beef because (prior to feedlots) it was generally stringy and too difficult to chew.
The rich to some extent were an exception because they could afford to purchase tender pieces cut from young animals. Wealthy consumers bought sirloin
steaks, rump roasts, and rib roasts. Bloomington's best restaurants served only
veal steaks or steaks from young, fat beeves. After reading in the newspaper that
Jake Stout had killed a fat heifer, Sarah arranged immediately to purchase a steak
from him. Another time she bought a quarter of beef because the butcher assured
her it would be long time before he would have such a tender animal again.

Butchers sold the tougher and more commonly available cuts of beef to
working class customers like the Irish laborers laying track across Central Illinois.
John Busher advertised in the Springfield Daily Journal in 1852 that he had
corned beef available for daily delivery "at any of the shanties for twenty miles
along the line."[61] The Irish ate beef flank, round, brisket, and plate, all of which
needed long cooking times to render them edible and most of which wound up in

stews or soups. Brisket and plate were also made into corned beef through a wet curing process similar to that used to manufacture barreled pork.

Corned beef in Irish history goes as far back as the eleventh century.[62] In ancient times, it was primarily a holiday dish. Easter Sunday, the most important festival of the year, occasioned feasting on lamb, veal, and chicken, but the meal people took greatest pleasure from was corned beef, cabbage, and floury potatoes. Refugees from the Great Famine carried this tradition with them to America where they promptly transferred it to Saint Patrick's Day. The city of Cork produced immense quantities of corned beef for export from the late seventeenth to the early nineteenth century, much of it shipped to Great Britain and continental Europe. Other ethnic groups, however, never took to corned beef as much as the Irish. In addition to eating it on Saint Patrick's Day, Irish Americans made it a core item in their regular diet. The meat was nowhere near as popular with other Americans except perhaps Jews. Oddly, however, corned beef appeared regularly on the nineteenth-century menus of grand hotels. It was served regularly at Clover Lawn where David Davis claimed a heaping plate of corned beef hash as his favorite meal. He may have been especially fond of Catharine Beecher's version, which, while quite unusual by today's standards, surely Sarah would have been familiar with.

Catharine Beecher's Corned Beef Hash
INGREDIENTS – 1 corned beef brisket; 6 large tomatoes, peeled; 1 onion, sliced; 1 teaspoon sugar; 2 teaspoons flour; butter (piece about the size of a hen's egg); ½ pint cold water; salt and pepper to taste. PREPARATION – Combine tomatoes and onion. Add water, butter, sugar, salt and pepper. Shave up the meat into small bits as thin as thick pasteboard. Dredge flour over the meat. Simmer meat in tomato and onion mixture for 1 hour. Serve immediately.[63]

Residents of Bloomington to this day generally share Judge Davis's affection for corned beef. On rye bread, it is the centerpiece of the Moses Montefiore Temple's Food Fair (see Chapter 7). For others, it is a matter of Irish heritage and a fondness that stems from corned beef's association with Saint Patrick's Day and the carousing that takes place. Whatever the association, in 1957 on the day before Saint Patrick's Day, many undoubtedly were pleased to learn that Marcel Comte, one of America's foremost corned beef experts, had recently decided to call Bloomington home.[64] Comte, a native of France who grew up in New Orleans, gained attention through a rave review of a corned beef dinner he cooked for a local "stag affair." He catered such gatherings as a representative of "corned beef king" John P. Harding of Chicago. Harding sold his product through advertisements that frankly invoked pro-Irish political sentiments.

The famous corned beef of John P

Is a succulent delicacy . . .

Why, it's England's belief

It was Harding's corned beef

That practically set Ireland free.

That Harding's top chef, a man who once made eleven corned beef sandwiches in one minute, was French may not have set well with some. The idea, however, was to sell corned beef. Comte would serve impressive dinners, using these occasions to teach consumers how best to cook Harding's product. An admiring *Pantagraph* reporter took notes.

Marcel Comte and John P. Harding's Corned Beef

Submerge a choice brisket of corned beef in cold water. Heat the water close to boiling, but do not allow it to gallop. Water temperature should be about 212 degrees F. Cook for 5 to 6 hours or until a fork easily penetrates thickest part of the brisket. Place cooked brisket in container of cold water, fat side down. Allow to stand for 15 to 20 minutes to seal in juices. Remove from water and slice thin against the grain. Do not trim fat as it has an unusually delicate and desirable flavor.[65]

DIET, POVERTY, AND SEASONAL HUNGER

By 1860, a number of destitute people lived in the Bloomington area. Helen Ross Hall, an impoverished Irish woman with a husband often out of work and seven children, described how neighbors worked together baking and canning and doing their best to survive difficult times.[66] The extent to which the poor received assistance from local government and churches is difficult to estimate, but during the nineteenth century the well-to-do and the impoverished often met face-to-face and a great deal of charity was dispensed personally. Sarah Davis's letters make it clear that much of her charity was person-to-person and unmediated by cash. She wrote in 1860 about seeing to her annual hog butchering, and afterward dividing the heads and spare ribs among the "needy." She gave out surplus eggs to the destitute, and when a vagabond showed up at her window, she gave him meat and bread – never any mention from her or the vagabond about money to buy a sandwich.

Much of the food Sarah gave out went to penniless neighbors. Poor Mrs. Flauherty, who Sarah considered a friend, received a pie at Thanksgiving. She gave a turkey to Mrs. Werty. Once Sarah met a little boy walking up the lane and recalled that he had been coming to Clover Lawn to beg for milk. The boy handed her a note from an acquaintance, Mrs. Grim, soliciting bread for her children's supper. Mrs. Flauherty paid a call after tea and requested milk to have with the rice Sarah had sent to her the day before. Sarah learned from Mrs. Flauherty that families, especially those out in the country, were in the midst of a pneumonia epidemic. James Liston's little girl had just died from the disease.

Ironically, a few months earlier Sarah had written about a mild winter and how the moderate conditions came as a great blessing to the poor. She observed how the price of apples had fallen, making them more affordable, but what Sarah failed to realize was that spring tended to be considerably more dangerous than winter, especially for people living at a subsistence level. Beginning in November or December, families in McLean County, like families throughout most of the United States, had to live on stored tubers, root vegetables (beets, carrots, turnips, potatoes, parsnips, etc.), winter squashes, celery, and cabbages, supplemented by whatever meat they could afford. Root cellars by early spring became depleted, particularly among the poor who had little put away to begin with. As store prices rose and the new growing season had yet to begin, the only solution for those caught short was to tighten their belts and do without. Adults withstood this, but undernourished children proved especially vulnerable to protein-calorie undernutrition. This opened the door to a variety of diseases, including pneumonia, and death rates increased appreciably. Seasonal hunger and its associated ills continued to plague both the rural and urban America poor throughout the nineteenth century and well into the twentieth.[67]

COMMERCIAL DINING ROOMS AND KITCHENS

Large numbers of passengers holding one-way tickets got off trains in McLean County during the latter half of the nineteenth century. In 1850, just prior to railroad construction, the county had a little over 6,500 residents. Ten years later the total came to nearly 29,000. In another decade, with both north-south and east-west rail lines operating, the county's population jumped to almost 54,000. Bloomington's population went from 700 residents in 1837 to more than 1,500 in 1850. By 1860, Bloomington was a full-fledged railroad town with over 7,000 residents. The 1890 census registered a population of around 20,000.

A raft of new residents called for a large number of new businesses to serve their needs. From a newcomer's perspective, boarding houses, hotels, and restaurants were especially crucial. More farmers created a need for more grist mills, and with the arrival of European immigrants, many unaccustomed to baking their own bread, a demand for professional bakers developed.

HOTEL DINING ROOMS

During the land rush of 1837, McLean County had Withers and a few other taverns plus a handful of inns. When immigrants began arriving in large numbers, they had to sleep several to a bed or spend the night in wagons or tents. People ate as best they could, often relying on foods they had brought with them.

Taverns were still found in Central Illinois's small towns in the 1850s and for the most part were unchanged. Ezra Prince and Abraham Lincoln, traveling from Bloomington to Peoria in 1856, took a room for the night at Micken's in Stout's Grove. Prince described the accommodations as "primitive and poor."[68] He and Lincoln shared a bed. Their breakfast consisted of muddy coffee and yellow biscuits. Prince recalled Judge Davis, staying at Barnett's in Clinton, about 30 miles south of Bloomington; he had to make a dinner entirely out of boiled cabbage because everything else on the table appeared too vile to eat.

Bloomington, as a burgeoning railroad center, no longer had old-fashioned taverns. No sooner had a railroad arrived than the town sprouted eight hotels. At least three of them, the Railroad Hotel at the Chicago, Alton and St. Louis Depot, the American House on Front Street, and Pike House at North and Center, boasted dining rooms and professional cooks. For nearly a century to come select hotels would reign as the finest places to eat in the city.

By 1900, the number of hotel dining rooms in Bloomington increased to eight, and the city directory listed no less than 47 employees involved in the preparation and service of food. That number included two African American cooks, both employed by the Hills Hotel. A decade later the much larger and stylish Illinois Hotel employed 25 people in food-related capacities, including two black chefs, five black cooks, and at least a dozen black waiters. Fashion dictated that dining rooms throughout the country emulate the elegance of a railroad dining car replete with cooks and waiters of the proper color. Ten years later, fashion changed, and there were no longer any African American cooks and waiters, but the Illinois Hotel continued to be regarded as the most elegant place in the city to eat. A 1927 dinner menu offered patrons consommé Julienne, queen olives, roast prime rib, baked young Texas turkey with cranberry sauce, roast Watertown goose with baked apple, roast suckling pig with apple sauce, and

Nesselrode ice cream.[69] A 1929 menu presented for consideration fruit cocktail, chicken a la Neopolitan, consommé clear, sweet pickles, mammoth ripe olives, roast prime rib, broiled lamb chops, fried calves sweetbreads on toast, lemon ice, one half cantaloupe a la mode, and fresh red raspberries par fait.[70]

BOARDING HOUSES

American boarding houses had a reputation for bad food and discourteous behavior.[71] People still joke about the "boarding house reach." Supposedly, it was every man for himself; a boarder had to spear his own portion from a serving plate, no matter where it was on the table, or risk going without. This and other negative images developed during the Great Depression, inspired it would seem by the rude behavior seen in establishments operated under contract on behalf of large firms.[72]

McLean County's nineteenth-century boarding houses were by no means contract operations. They were cast instead in the more traditional mould of a family-like place where people from the country working in the city lived and ate before they were able to marry and set up a household of their own. Boarders in such residences often found themselves drawn into the host family and treated more like a distant relatives than a paying guest.

A considerable number of boarding house keepers in McLean County were women. In 1855, they operated six of the 15 boarding houses situated in Bloomington. By 1880, the city had 22 boarding houses, 14 of them kept by women. Such a high percentage of female proprietorship was typical across the country because keeping a boarding house was one of the few occupations that women could undertake without fear of censure from other members of the community. This made the boarding house an important safety net. Widows and other women in difficult financial circumstances could earn a living using skills honed as homemakers. So long as the prospective businesswoman owned a house, she needed little additional capital.

Boarding houses generally offered guests three meals a day, and from all indications these were usually quite ample.[73] In 1900, H.S. Grindley studied food consumption in a typical Urbana, Illinois boarding house for a period of two weeks during the month of June.[74] He found the residents' diet evenly split between animal and vegetable foods from the standpoint of energy intake. Animal foods consisted mainly of veal roasts and various beefsteaks, but pork (mainly bacon and roasts), eggs, butter, and milk (mostly whole) were also central to the boarders' diet.[75] Cereals were consumed primarily in the form of wheat breads, rolls, dumplings, pies, and cakes, most of which were homemade. Among the vegetables, potatoes, cabbage, roasted sweet corn, peas, and celery predominated.[76] Blackberries, apples, and peaches outweighed other fruits.[77]

Grindley calculated energy values and found an average consumption of 3,390 kilocalories (kcals, popularly referred to as "Calories") per day. Protein consumption amounted to 117 grams per day (g/d). Fat intake averaged 146 g/d, nearly all of it coming from animal sources. These values, especially those pertaining to fat and energy intakes, appear excessively high by today's standards. However, when considering the amount of animal fat consumed, bear in mind that concentrated vegetable fat products such as Crisco had yet to appear on the market. It should also be noted that the 2,500 or so kcals consumed by the average adult man nowadays may be adequate in a twenty-first-century environment, but generations ago when people walked just about everywhere they went, engaged in a lot of manual work, and did not have central heating, 2,500 kcals would have amounted to a starvation diet. The U.S.D.A. around the beginning of the twentieth century figured the average 150-pound man needed approximately 3,500 kcals/d to keep active and stay healthy. By that standard, the average energy intake of the boarders Grindley surveyed appeared sufficient given their work as locomotive engineers and railroad mechanics.

OTHER EATING PLACES

Late nineteenth-century America had three kinds of stand-alone eating places: coffee houses, oyster parlors, and restaurants. All three types originated in the late eighteenth century and became ever more popular over the next one hundred years.

COFFEE HOUSES

Coffee houses traditionally attracted businessmen and other middle-class patrons, but during the nineteenth century the genre never took hold in Central Illinois. John Stetzner's bakery and coffee house made a brief appearance on North Main in Bloomington in the early 1880s, but otherwise the stock and trade of the coffee house – coffee, conversation, and a bite to eat – fell to the restaurant and later to that particular type of restaurant known as the "café" (see Chapter 3).

OYSTER SALOONS

Oyster houses, oyster parlors, or "oyster saloons," as they were often referred to in Central Illinois, became an enormously popular American institution.

Oysters were harvested in immense quantities along North America's coasts and were readily served up as a tasty snack or a filling meal at a very low price. Middle- and upper-class oyster-eaters had their own establishments. Thomas Downing's, a New York City oyster house, was famous nationwide for its elegance. Its specialties included scalloped oysters and various game items accompanied by oyster dressings. Many Americans preferred to eat them raw, but fried and stewed oysters had great numbers of devotees as well. By mid century, oyster places existed for every taste and pocketbook throughout the United States. In a country where virtually every other dish was regional, ethnic, or specific to a social class, the oyster became its first truly national food.

Oysters were already on their way to becoming nineteenth-century America's favorite food about the time the first settlers arrived in Central Illinois.[78] By 1840, annual shipments from Chesapeake Bay to Philadelphia reached 4,000, and an oyster craze was in the making.[79] Some 20 years later, New York City residents spent more on oysters than they did on meat. America's keenness for oysters spread westward as the bivalves themselves were shipped inland by barge and railroad. In Bloomington, David Davis was ahead of the curve. As a native of the Chesapeake Bay area, oysters on the prairie must have tasted like home to him, so imagine his delight when in 1850 he was able purchase cans by the dozen in Springfield. Davis carried them back to Bloomington with him, but that soon became unnecessary. In 1853, Kellog and Holmes Family Supply Store in Bloomington began advertising fresh oysters, and two years later W.M. Reeves' Headquarters store was receiving oysters by train from Baltimore on a daily basis.[80] In 1858, M'Millan and Wilmeth, a purveyor of "family groceries" with a kitchen that prepared meals "at all Hours of the Day," advertised "Oysters served up in every style at short notice, and warranted to give satisfaction in all cases."[81]

Commercial eateries and in particular specialty houses played a leading role in whetting America's appetite for oysters. One of the first dedicated oyster places in McLean County was Bloomington's Tawawah Oyster Saloon. Proprietor George Holcomb took advantage of express deliveries from Baltimore and capitalized on a growing demand by adding the Tawawah to his existing restaurant. Holcomb assured prospective patrons in an 1858 advertisement that his was a first-class venue suitable for both "ladies and gents."[82] This distinguished the Tawawah from drinking places such as Gilliland's Billiards and Oyster Saloon. Respectable women did not patronize places like Gilliland's or any other establishment without special facilities. Hough's Oyster and Eating Saloons catered to women by setting aside a dedicated "ladies room." There women and their companions could order a plate of oysters or a dish of ice cream, depending on the season. [83]

The juxtaposition of oysters and ice cream may seem peculiar, but from a business standpoint, oysters – best eaten during the "r" months – needed a summertime replacement. Ice cream filled the bill. Oysters and ice cream both qualified as entertainment foods. Thus, the principal offerings at Stanton's Fine Confectionery, Ice Cream, and Oyster Parlors in Bloomington went together hand in glove.

Oysters during the latter half of the nineteenth century, like pizza during the latter half of the twentieth century, appeared everywhere. Bloomington's Presbyterian Church Club dished them out free – raw, stewed, or fried – to any stranger off the street willing to attend its meetings.[84] At the same time, the Ashley House, a posh hotel, could lay out a house-warming supper for guests representing "the beauty and fashion of Bloomington" that tempted the taste buds with oyster soup, raw oysters, fried oysters, oyster pie, and sliced chicken or sliced turkey with oyster dressing.[85] Sarah Davis organized an exclusive supper of scalloped oysters, accompanied by chicken salad, cold ham, bread, butter, and cakes, for a society dance, and the Davises often served fried or stewed oysters to their dinner guests. That fried oysters were a favorite among the servants, so much the better. Sarah Davis more than once praised both Bridget and Katie for their skill with a frying pan full of oysters. When Sarah treated her servants and their friends to a Halloween party, the supper featured fried oysters and, of course, roast turkey.

RESTAURANTS

Restaurants – known originally under such names as "victualing houses," "dining rooms," and "eating houses" – first appeared in Old World market-places where cooks prepared meals for buyers and sellers alike. In America, the earliest and most common source of prepared food for working people was the street vendor.[86] As time passed, street vendors on foot gave way to those with horse carts. These yielded in time to sellers with regular stands who catered to low-income customers on short work breaks. The essential concept, a business purveying a variety of foods for consumption on site, spread to indoor venues motivated primarily by the need to feed laborers unable to go home for their noonday meal. The food itself did not differ much from the dishes served at home in that the bulk of the meal consisted of bread and meat. However, these were ordinarily unaccompanied by any vegetables or fruits.

Commercial dining rooms and eating establishments received a great boost about 1850 when hotels and lodging houses began dropping the American Plan for accommodating guests (meals included with the room) in favor of the

European Plan (room only).[87] This forced workers living in rented rooms that previously came with board to look elsewhere for a place to eat. In Bloomington, Probasco and Scott, proprietors of the Burch House, took advantage of the situation by advertising non-resident board at two dollars per day.[88] Once Bloomington acquired restaurants, they offered additional options for "day boarders."

A generally overlooked but important impetus to the development of restaurants in Central Illinois was the prospect of feeding farmers visiting town for the day. By custom, saloons treated patrons to a free lunch, and no doubt many farmers paid for a beer or a shot of whiskey and got a sandwich on the house to go with it. However, the temperance movement was growing. A saloon lunch was often no more than a cold buffet. Restaurants dished out the kind of hot food farmers normally ate at mid-day. Conant's Eating House announced to readers of the *Weekly National Flag* that "Warm Meals furnished to order" awaited them at the corner of Oak and Mulberry in Bloomington.[89] Houghton and Brigham's Eating House and Bakery advertised in *The Weekly Pantagraph*, a newspaper aimed primarily at rural residents. The postscript to its ads regularly assured readers that Houghton and Brigham's paid the highest prices in town for chickens, eggs, and butter.[90] Hunter's, located across from the Bloomington post office, portrayed itself as "the great resort to farmers," a place to eat with "prices as low as the lowest."[91] W. D. Hallett's, located on Bloomington's Courthouse Square and one of the first establishments in McLean County to explicitly label itself a restaurant, offered clientele a "farmers lunch" consisting of a slice of roast beef, rusk, butter, and coffee for twenty-five cents.[92]

From 1855 through 1900, the number of restaurants in Bloomington steadily increased. As the number grew, proprietors addressed every concern about eating out a person might imagine. Worried about price? Go to Mrs. Clark's where patrons were promised a good meal for just 15 cents.[93] What about hygiene? Shade's Dining Hall billed itself as "the neatest and nicest place . . . to get your meals."[94] Want respect? People's Restaurant promised "first-class meals, fine lunches, and good treatment."[95]

The Bloomington area may have been a frontier dominated by a parochial Southern culture at first, but by the second half of the nineteenth century its population was becoming progressively Europeanized. By 1870, Germans alone made up 13 percent of the city's population. Many of them had emigrated from towns and cities with large French, Hungarian, Latvian, Lithuanian, Polish, or Romanian populations and were thus familiar with other ways of life and possessed of an uncommon degree of cultural sophistication. Their own German tradition prescribed a big breakfast and included a taste for the foods mentioned at the outset of this chapter.

Naturally enough, Bloomington's restaurants catered to these and other European predilections. In the 1890s, city residents had Cuyler's European Hotel, Restaurant, and Café as well as French's Chop House, an eating place "dispensing every dish known to the culinary art." As early as the mid-1860s, Dr. Hiram Bateman offered his guests at Bateman's European Restaurant a choice of coffees – either Mocha or Java – and a menu that featured beef steaks, ham and eggs, homemade bread, pies and cakes.[96] Bateman originally opened for business on Front Street in downtown Bloomington but moved later on to Union Depot on the far west side. Sarah Davis patronized Bateman's and once wrote to her husband about purchasing quails there "at a rather high figure" to roast in her own kitchen.

Otto Kadgihn's Sebastopol Saloon was another highly regarded Bloomington dining spot.[97] It opened as an "eating saloon" featuring English, French, and German cuisines, and in its original location in a basement on Courthouse Square the Sebastopol looked very much like a *rathskeller*.[98] Kadgihn later rechristened the Sebastopol as Kadgihn's Model Chop House and Ladies Restaurant, to imply a less rowdy, more genteel character than might be suggested by the term "saloon." To attract American women unfamiliar with the domestic character of a German restaurant, the new facility featured a separate ladies' entrance to the dining room, allowing women access to it without having to pass through the bar room.

Kadgihn appears to have had no background in food or cooking. He was born somewhere in Eastern Europe and educated in Tilsit (now the Russian city of Sovetsk). A Prussian flag flew over the town in Otto's day, but culturally it was a center of Lithuanian language and learning. His schooling completed, Otto moved to Riga, Latvia where he married Hedwig Ruttenberg. The couple immigrated to the United States in 1851 and settled in Bloomington. There Otto found work as a day laborer. He opened the Sebastopol in 1858. His son, Otto Jr., joined the business around 1875. Another son, Herman, became involved ten years later, around the time Otto Sr. retired. The restaurant then became Kadgihn Brothers'.

Under all its names and in each location, Kadgihn's was known for its good food and Otto for his showmanship. His culinary specialty was wild game, the height of gastronomic fashion in the 1860s and early '70s. Other restaurants also highlighted wild game dishes, including Bateman's and the St. Nicholas Hotel, whose manager promoted a series of wild game dinners. Perhaps Otto wanted to gain a competitive edge when he let it be known that the famous Buffalo Bill Cody stopped by the Sebastopol whenever he came through town. Otto made sure that whenever he had something novel to cook up the newspapers heard about it. An 1871 article in *The Daily Pantagraph*, for instance, announced that Otto that very morning at precisely ten o'clock intended to offer his customers a soup made from turtles shipped fresh from the Gulf of Mexico.[99] This, according to the newspaper, was a special occasion that nobody would want to miss.

Just Opened !!---New Eating Rooms !!
AT THE
SEBASTOPOL SALOON.

OTTO KADGIHN.   -   PROPRIETOR.

HAVING ENGAGED THE services of an excellent cook, customers will be provided with dishes served in the best English, French or German styles,

At all hours of the Day & Evening.

Meals prepared to order at all hours.
FRESH OYSTERS received Daily per Express, together with other dainties of the season.
MILWAUKEE LAGER BEER, the best ever brought to Bloomington, continually on hand.
Don't forget the SEBASTOPOL SALOON, south side of the Public Square.
Bloomington, Sept. 21. 1858.   d1y

Advertisement in the September 8, 1858 *Daily Pantagraph* for the Sebastopol Saloon.

Otto's son, Henry, married Ottilia Stautz, daughter of Jake Stautz, a Bloomington butcher. Although neither she nor Henry appear to have joined Otto, Jr. and Herman in the restaurant business, Ottilia carried on the Kadgihn tradition by earning her own reputation for excellence in the kitchen. Several of her recipes have been preserved, and although intended for home use, a number of them represent the German classics the Kadgihns must have had on their menus[100] Ottilia's favorites included stuffed turkey, sauerbraten, sour veal kidneys, potato pancakes, and hot potato salad prepared according to the following recipe.

The Kadgihn Family's Hot Potato Salad
INGREDIENTS – 6 or 7 boiled potatoes, 3 strips diced bacon, 1 tablespoon flour, 1 tablespoon sugar, 1 tablespoon mayonnaise, 1 teaspoon mustard, ¼ cup vinegar, ½ cup cream, 2 hard boiled eggs, diced celery, onion, and parsley, salt and pepper. PREPARATION – Fry out bacon. Combine flour, seasonings, vinegar, mayonnaise, and

cream. Add to fried bacon and grease, pour over hot potatoes. Add eggs (sliced) and diced celery, onion, and parsley.[101]

MILLING AND BAKING

Milling, though not often thought of as a kitchen activity, was actually the first aspect of food processing homemakers turned over to operatives outside the home – a fact not very surprising given the arduousness of the task. A primitive grist mill was never more than two hundred miles behind the leading edge of the Illinois frontier. A mill capable of producing reasonably white wheat flour followed initial settlement by about twenty years. Baking as an American industry did not exist when McLean County was first settled. A generation later the industry was still in its infancy. This explains why the number of bakeries in the United States in 1850 totaled less than two thousand. [102]

LOCAL MILLERS

People in Central Illinois may have consumed a lot of corn bread and other corn meal dishes to begin with, but by 1900 the market for corn meal was more or less limited to areas of the South. Elsewhere wheat bread predominated, in no small part because the cost of wheat flour had declined to just 20 percent of what it had cost in 1800. No less relevant was the arrival of great numbers of European immigrants, who were accustomed to wheat and, for the most part, were unfamiliar with corn.[103]

McLean County had no shortage of millers eager to grind wheat and sell flour. Ortogrul Covell assembled Bloomington's first facility on South Main about 1838.[104] It was a small, two storied building located on the north side of the big slough that cut through town. John Mayers took over from Covel and added another story to the structure. The firm, which became Mayers and Brown and later Mayers and DePew, dissolved in the 1850s. These men and the three or four other millers doing business in Bloomington at the time were important persons in the community. Most came to the area with money and were regarded as men a cut above ordinary settlers. When Elihu Rogers, who began milling about 1850, moved to Bloomington, he already owned 1,190 acres of fine land. Rogers went into the lumber business partnered with his cousin, James Robinson, and began milling with Esekial Folsom. When his mill burned to the ground in 1864, Rogers continued as a grain dealer. Later he opened another mill in Normal, which he operated until 1874.

Nearly every farm in the county by that time raised some wheat and nearly every place had a flour mill. In Chenoa, there was Dehner and Zeigler; in Danvers, Danvers Flouring Mill; in Dry Grove, Joseph W. King's; and at Ellsworth, Hitch and Company. Heyworth had William H. Kinney's, and Hudson had William Hasenwinkel's. Farmers had their wheat ground at Bruner, Barnum, and Keenan's in LeRoy, and near Saybrook they went to Peabody and Rankin. Bloomington had seventeen mills by 1868, several of them sizable enterprises, including Eagle Mills, Jacob Mayers and Company, L.D. Haines and Company, Red Mills, S.D. Barber and Company, and Union Mills. Eagle Mills, situated at the west end of Jefferson Street next to the Chicago and Alton Railroad tracks, regularly placed advertisements in *The Weekly Pantagraph* under the eye-catching headline, "Bread for the Millions."[105] These promoted Eagle's brand-name product, Extra Family Flour, and at the same time announced to wheat growers that they were welcome to either sell their grain to the mill or to exchange it directly for flour.

Eagle Mills operated under the proprietorship of Thomas Cox and P.W. Becker. Little is known about Becker, but Thomas Cox, whose father was among McLean County's early settlers, became an eminent local businessman.[106] He began his career in Bloomington selling carpets in his father-in-law's store. He entered the grocery business after that but sold out and went into dry goods. Later, he switched to construction. Cox bought Eagle Mills during the Civil War and went on to run it for twenty years, all the while expanding and acquiring additional facilities. In 1875, he purchased Union Mills, located in Bloomington at East Taylor, adjacent to the Illinois Central line. Cox also bought the McLean County Mills, the former S.D. Barber and Company facility, situated at Clinton and Taylor streets. Later, he sold McLean County Mills to his brother George Cox, general manager (and later co-owner) of both Eagle and Union Mills. George passed McLean County Mills on to Thomas' son-in-law, Gustave Gehlert, who turned the facility into the Bloomington Vinegar Factory (see Chapter 3).

The Eagle and Union Mills were modern steam-driven facilities yet bound to ancient tradition in their dealings with farmers. In keeping with custom, the Coxes never actually purchased any of the wheat they processed. Instead, like millers of old, the Coxes charged farmers a toll by taking a percent of the flour. Until it was sold, nobody received a cent.

The 1880s and '90s witnessed a terrific attrition among flour mills. By 1889, Bloomington was down to two. By 1893, there were just eight mills in the entire county.[107] Forcing the closure of little mills throughout the country was a revolution in milling that brought in iron rollers and made grinding stones obsolete. Although the roller mill technology originated in Hungary, John Stevens of Wisconsin received a U.S. patent for an improved version in 1880. Large-volume millers adopted the Stevens machine immediately. For small companies it suddenly became a matter of doing the same or closing down. Rollers produced much finer and whiter flour, a product far more attractive to consumers than stone-ground wheat. Besides that, rollers greatly sped up the process. This paid off with lower prices at the store, not to mention greater profits for millers. By 1890, seventy-five percent of the flour produced in the United States was processed by rollers, and two Minneapolis millers, C.C. Washburn and C.A. Pillsbury, dominated the industry nationwide.

George Cox, who succeeded Thomas as company president, retooled Bloomington's Eagle Mills and renamed it "Hungarian Roller Mill" in celebration of the firm's newly installed steel machinery.[108] Hungarian Roller Mill produced and aggressively promoted Kossuth brand general purpose flour and Germania brand cake flour.[109] Branding occurred early in the flour industry because grocers' unmarked barrels were all-too-often found to contain adjuncts such as ground rice, sand, plaster of Paris, lime, alum, and potato starch. Producers addressed consumers' apprehensions with assurances that their company's brand name stood as a testament to quality.

Hungarian Roller Mill and its brand names were sold to J.G. Heberling and E.F. MacKenzie in 1913. Four years later the company went out of business. Its demise may have been due in part to the wheat shortage brought on by World War I, but it was fundamentally a matter of location. There simply was no competing with mills in places like Minneapolis and Omaha given their barge and rail connections to the great wheat terminals of the West.

LOCAL BAKERIES

The stock and trade of most early bakers was wheat bread, but just how popular wheat bread was during the nineteenth century is a matter of some disagreement. Culinary historian Andrew Smith argues that after the Civil War commercial bakers began opening shops in increasing numbers, especially in places with significant numbers of immigrants.[110] He finds that by the end of the nineteenth century, about 75 percent of all bread was commercially baked. U.S.D.A. dietary studies, on the other hand, indicated that before World War I most people avoided commercially baked bread. Purchased bread aroused suspicion. What exactly was in it? Granted, it cost more to bake at home than to buy bread from the baker on account of the price of fuel. But if one could afford it, no sense taking a chance. From the working class on up, people left bakers' bread to the poor.

One of the earliest bakers in Bloomington, Joseph Ankerbeck, may have been an immigrant with a distinctively German surname, but his competitors for the most part were men with Anglo-Irish monikers. Among the first to set up shop were partners Haines and Eyre (Christian names unknown). An advertisement for their store – a combination bakery and grocery – made no mention of bread. Instead, it boasted of Eyre's talent for baking cakes of all kinds on short notice.[111] Several months later Doughty and Coleman opened "New Bakery," a store in "the western part of town" intended to furnish families "with bread, cake, rusk, pies, etc."[112] Houghton and Brigham's Eating House and Bakery followed in 1856. Here the proprietors stood "determined to spare no pains to give entire satisfaction" while promising "to supply families and parties with the best bread, cakes, pies, crackers, etc."[113] The bill of fare included "pound, sponge, jelly, gold, lady, and cocco-nut cakes" as well as "lady fingers, jellies, *blancmange*, ices, and pyramids." At Denison and Mitchell's, another new bake shop, it was all "Bread! Bread! Bread!" and at a price in keeping with "the tightness of the times."[114]

The number of bakers in Bloomington expanded after the Civil War. This may have reflected the increasing number of poor residing in the city – folks who could not afford to bake their own bread. More likely it testified to an increasing European presence. Many immigrants would have been familiar with and indeed dependent upon professional bakers before coming to the United States. Bloomington had 16 bakeries by 1867, nearly all of them one-person shops and two of them belonging to "colored" bakers. As the century progressed, directories listed as many as 12 bakeries serving the Bloomington-Normal area, most of them owned by individuals with German surnames. The biggest shops in the city were Gerkin's on East Front Street and J.A. Schneider's on South Center.[115] German bakers supplied the city with such Teutonic specialties such as cinnamon buns, coffee cake, German Chocolate Cake, hard rolls, jelly doughnuts, pepper nuts (spice cookies), sticky buns, and strudel. They also trained and developed a subsequent generation of master bakers. Charles Kammerman, for example, came to the U.S. at age 16 from Switzerland and learned his craft under the guidance of William Gerkin.[116] Afterward he went to work for J. A. Schneider and became his foreman. Kammerman opened his own store in 1907, and in 1915 he and his wife, Annabelle, added a restaurant, which they continued to run until 1924. Later on the Kammermans opened a grocery store and no longer sold hand-crafted baked goods.

Jennie MacDonald Wickizer was one of the few native English-speakers in the business. She came to the United States as a child from Nightswood, Scotland in 1852 and married William W. Wickizer of Minonk, Illinois in 1875. The couple moved to Bloomington in 1879, and within a few years they opened a bakery and confectionary on North Main.[117] Their shop specialized in "home-made breads and pies." The 1893 county directory listed Jennie as owner and her husband as business manager. Wickizer's by this time had become one of Bloomington's biggest bakeries with five bakers manning its ovens on a regular basis. Every other shop in town was a one- or two-man operation.

Inside Jennie Wickizer's bakery, an undated photo.

Wickizer's went out of business around 1917, a dozen or so years after William died and less than a decade after Jennie gave up control of the company. Exactly why the company closed its doors at this time, practically in the midst of World War I, is unclear. The war generally benefited commercial baking. During the conflict, when private citizens found it difficult to purchase flour and were being asked by officials to bake wheatless breads, professional bakers had the advantage of normal supplies. On account of government policy, most Americans by the end of conflict were buying bread rather than baking it at home.

CHAPTER 3 – OLD TRADITIONS AND PROGRESSIVE IDEAS

In McLean County, certain dissimilarities in what folks ate and drank coincided with differences in affiliation. Mennonites and other Anabaptists introduced Pennsylvania Dutch cooking. Catholics and Lutherans from the German Empire and Austria-Hungary arrived with the somewhat more cosmopolitan cuisine described in the preceding chapter. Members of these liturgical churches as well as the Anabaptists harbored traditions involving beer, wine, and spirits. These set them apart from certain American Protestants and fomented a political tumult that lasted nearly a century. In the end, the jingoistic hysteria of World War I and National Prohibition drove German food and continental dining out of public places. Large Midwestern cities such as Chicago, Milwaukee, and St. Louis avoided this, but the problem in Bloomington was numbers; the percentage of German-Americans in the city's population was substantial but just too small to resist those who wanted the culture to disappear.

Nationally, fulminations against saloons provided convenient cover for folks who feared that Uncle Sam was being emasculated by foreigners. Toward the end of the nineteenth century, this fear and the anxiety about drinking spread to eating habits, and social reformers launched an effort to standardize diet and impose a particularly austere version of New England cooking on the rest of the nation.[1] Their campaign never really took off. What America got instead was a jumble of cafes, cafeterias, coffee shops, diners, grills, lunch rooms, tearooms, and restaurant chains and a nearly ubiquitous cuisine affectionately dubbed "greasy spoon." In Bloomington, immigrant restaurant owners carried on by calling their places cafes or grills, Americanizing their menus, and quietly blending into the newly homogenized culinary culture.

ANTI-SALOON MOVEMENT

Back when Central Illinois was a frontier region, Americans were far from united when it came to matters of food. Typical diets differed from region to region and from one population to the next, but for most part no one was especially bothered by the diversity. With drinking habits, however, it was a different story. Public drunkenness, whiskey drinking on the Sabbath, wife and child at the table with papa in the saloon – such things upset people, particularly if they belonged to an Anglo-Protestant church. Church-goers concerns inspired a temperance movement, which began as a moderate, progressive coalition worried primarily about what we currently call "alcohol abuse."[2] Between 1830 and 1840, some began to reason the only way to prevent excessive drinking was to eliminate the consumption of alcohol altogether.[3] Their argument caught on. The Temperance Society became the Abstinence Society, and soon the Anti-Saloon League, the National Prohibition Party, and a number of other organizations appeared and began enlisting ardent teetotalers. All of these organizations counted heavily on women alarmed by alcohol-inspired domestic violence and exasperated by how much their husbands spent on liquor. Methodist preachers spearheaded the movement, proclaiming that drinking, even at moderate levels, impeded spiritual growth. Additional church support came from Baptists, Presbyterians, Disciples, Congregationalists, Quakers, and Scandinavian Lutherans. From a secular perspective, saloons were represented as barriers to material progress. Drinking in the eyes of modernists and reformists was a waste of time and money, and to make matters worse, drinking establishments functioned as agencies for the kind of corrupt politics that made any semblance of rational government impossible.

Opposition to prohibition came from elements of the Democratic Party and liturgical Christians, including both Catholics and many Lutherans. The Democrats' antagonism stemmed back then from a general opposition to government regulation. Moreover, the Democratic Party represented farmers who worried about the price of corn and what would happen to it if everyone stopped drinking. Liturgical Christians, many of them first and second generation Americans, rejected the idea that government should define morality. Matters of right and wrong, from their perspective, did not change. Brewed, fermented, and distilled beverages, made by clergy as well as laity, had been enjoyed throughout the ages. The mantle of tradition enveloped beer, wine and certain spirits and in effect made them sacrosanct. As for the character of those adverse to alcohol, German-Americans had an aphorism: "Who does not love wine, wife, and song will be a fool for his lifelong!"

ANABAPTIST FOOD AND DRINK

Expert whiskey makers were among the first Anabaptists to establish homes in Central Illinois. Amish, Apostolic Christian, Mennonite, and other Anabaptists generally abstain from alcohol these days, but congregations in the past simply did not worry about it. No matter if Pa had a mug of beer at his favorite saloon on Saturday while Ma sold the produce and bought supplies.[4] Church members possessed a strong collective consciousness. Folks may have shared a taste for Old Grand Dad, a brand known as "the Mennonites' whiskey," but rarely did they drink to excess.[5]

Anabaptists began immigrating to North America prior to the Revolutionary War.[6] They came as individuals and families and contributed to the growth of the Pennsylvania Dutch population. A second wave began to arrive after the Napoleonic Wars, settling parts of Canada and areas of the United States beyond the Appalachians, including the banks of the Illinois River and its tributaries. Apostolic Christians traveled to Illinois's Anabaptist communities as missionaries and subsequently established their own churches.

John Strubhar, the first Anabaptist to take up residence in McLean County, left Lorraine, France in 1826 to investigate immigration opportunities on behalf of his family. He worked at a distillery for two and a half years in Hamilton, Ohio. In 1830, he quit and began hiking toward the Illinois frontier. He stopped in what was soon to become McLean County and purchased eighty acres and a house four miles northwest of Danvers. Amish settlements were emerging about the same time in the timberlands along the Mackinaw River and two of its tributaries, Dillon and Rock Creeks. Soon Mennonite families began to turn up, and shortly thereafter folks known as Hessian Amish found their way into the area. Peter Donner and his family, the first Hessians to settle in McLean County, took up residence in Dry Grove Township in 1837. Their sect differed from the others by keeping in closer touch with mainstream society. Women dressed in up-to-date fashions, and unlike other Anabaptists men grew moustaches instead of just beards. Hessians sewed buttons on their clothes, danced, played musical instruments, and did a number of other things Amish folks generally disapproved of.

Bloomington's first professional distiller, Michael Kinsinger, a native of Marburg, Germany, was Hessian Amish, but the first large-scale still in the region was built in 1834 by French immigrants Christian and Peter Farnis, brothers of a more orthodox persuasion than Kinsinger. Located on the south bank of the Mackinaw River, the Farnis's distillery and adjacent grist mill spawned the development a frontier town popularly known as "Farnisville." Together with Slabtown (or Fredericksburg) on the opposite side of the river, Farnisville became a magnet for Anabaptist immigrants and a staging point for area settlement.

Christian and John Nafziger, brothers who settled in northern Tazewell County and later moved to Hopedale, would have spent time in Farnisville. They arrived in Central Illinois with few possessions and little money but in good health, thanks to (or perhaps in spite of) a steady diet of *zwieback*, ginger cookies and sausage.[7] The Nafzigers, who embarked at Habre, France in 1846, prepared these provisions in advance, carried them aboard ship, and ate little else during their voyage. The *zwieback* and the cookies, which were none too soft to begin with, became as hard as rocks during the voyage and had to be dunked into coffee to soften them and make them edible. Christian and John eventually landed in New Orleans, and from there they walked to Central Illinois. The Nafzigers' descendants saved the recipes for the provisions that sustained the young men during their journey.

The Nafzigers' *Zwieback*
INGREDIENTS – 1 cup scalded milk, ¾ cup lard, 1 yeast cake, ½ cup sugar, 2 tablespoons salt, flour (enough to make dough slightly softer than bread dough). PREPARATION – Mix ingredients and let rise to double in bulk. Make small walnut-size balls. Let rise 1 hour. Bake at 420 for 20-25 minutes. To store, cut roll in half, and place in low oven to dry.[8]

The Nafzigers' Ginger Cookies
INGREDIENTS – 1 tin cup molasses, 1 tin cup sour milk, 1 tin cup lard, 1 teaspoon soda, 1 heaping tablespoon ginger, flour to make soft dough. PREPARATION—Mix ingredients and bake.[9]

When the Nafzigers finally arrived in Central Illinois they found earlier Amish settlers housed in log cabins and living mainly on cornmeal supplemented with milk and game. Otherwise, conventions were much the same as in Europe. Women wore black dresses and white caps. Men grew beards but no moustaches. Those who fastened their clothing with buttons received a reprimand, and nobody wore jewelry, fine clothes or any other adornment.

Things began to change in the 1860s. Distinctive dress became less common, German was heard less often, and congregation members started participating in civil affairs. This acculturation proved inexorable in some ways, but still community life revolved around the church. After church, members of the congregation sorted out who was going where for dinner, and sometimes half of the congregation went home with the other half.[10] Quilting bees, barn and house raisings, weddings, funerals, and a variety of other events provided men with ample opportunity to talk about farming and women with plenty of time to exchange recipes.

Changes may have been afoot in other areas of life but Amish and Mennonite women persisted in using a distinctive set of recipes referred to nowadays as "Pennsylvania Dutch." Never mind that most of Central Illinois's Anabaptists had neither any connection with Pennsylvania nor even the slightest bit of Dutch ancestry. The label simply refers to a style of cooking that emerged when traditional German cooking encountered the material conditions of backwoods America. Several generations of women passed around the resulting recipes, adding personal touches, and the Pennsylvania Dutch style was born.[11]

The original flavor principle underlying Pennsylvania Dutch consisted of a combination of tart and salty. Cooks achieved this by combining fruit with smoked meat, such as in *Schnitz un Knepp*, a stew of dried apples, smoked ham, and dumplings. Mary Emma Showalter, in her *Mennonite Community Cookbook*, published a definitive recipe for this old-fashioned favorite.[12]

Showalter's *Schnitz un Knepp*
INGREDIENTS – 1½ pounds cured ham or 1 ham hock, 2 cups dried apples, 2 tablespoons brown sugar. PREPARATION – Wash dried apples, cover with water, soak overnight; cover ham with cold water, cook slowly for 3 hours; add apples and water in which they soaked; add brown sugar, cook 1 hour. INGREDIENTS (for the knepp or dumplings) – 2 cups flour, 3½ teaspoons baking powder, ½ teaspoon salt, 1 egg beaten, 2 tablespoons butter, ⅓ to ½ cup milk. PREPARATION – Sift together dry ingredients; stir in beaten egg and melted butter; add milk to make batter stiff enough to drop from spoon; cover pot tightly and cook dumplings 10 to 12 minutes with ham and *schnitz*; do not lift cover until ready to serve.

Tastes have changed, and Showalter has met some Mennonites who now prefer a meatless *Schnitz un Knepp* over the genuine dish. However, in days gone by it was meat three times a day. Showalter's own grandfather ate scrapple for breakfast, a beef or chicken pot pie for dinner, and fried ham for supper.[13] Many meat dishes used tough and undesirable cuts. Organ tissues, including tripe, liver, and pig stomach, were popular, if for no other reason than to demonstrate a household's dedication to thrift. Traditional meat recipes included Lebanon bologna, summer sausage, beef stew with dumplings, breaded oxtail, creamed dried beef, beef with sour gravy, ham loaf, headcheese, pickled pigs feet, roasted pig's stomach (hog maw), liver and gravy, minced meat pie, and chicken and noodles.

Housewives usually baked bread twice a week, the loaves more apt to be rye than wheat, especially before the Civil War. Bread pudding rated as a virtual staple because it turned stale leftovers into an appetizing desert. Wheat flour went into noodles and dumplings, which were omnipresent as thickeners for soups and stews. A soup dumpling sometimes contained bits of meat blend into it. Flour pudding, basically a large dumpling sliced and served as a main course, often contained dried fruit.

The Pennsylvania Dutch culinary tradition has evolved and people's tastes have changed. Rye-bread eaters turned increasingly to wheat bread, as the price of wheat flour came down. Similarly, as sugar prices fell and Americans generally began to use more of it, Pennsylvania Dutch cooks followed suit. The classic sour pickle became sweet and sour.[14] The traditions of the "sweet and sour table" and the "seven sweets and seven sours" were born, fabricated from charity cookbooks and cobbled together by commercial "family style" restaurants. Showalter recalls the novel, *Tillie the Mennonite Maid*, in which grandmother is said never to have dinner without including the proverbial "seven sours."[15] The author, Helen Reimensnyder Martin, made no mention of seven sweets because when she published the book in 1904 they did not exist.[16] Testifying further to the relatively recent genesis of sweet and sour, Showalter's modern pickle recipes generally call for considerable sugar. Early recipes, in contrast, produce sharp, salty flavors without the slightest hint of sweet. The sweet and sour pickles sold today as traditionally Pennsylvania Dutch or Amish are actually typical of commercial products which were developed in various parts of the United States about the beginning of the twentieth century.[17]

The principal sweet condiment in old-fashioned Pennsylvania Dutch cuisine was apple butter. Family and friends made apple butter collectively sharing large copper kettles. Cooked right, it would keep for a month stored in a gallon jar. Applesauce, on the other hand, required canning. Verna Nafziger of Hopedale recalled canning parties in the 1930s, attended by women with children in tow and paring knives in hand.[18] Grandma brought her big canning kettles and a bone-handled knife. Verna once attended a canning party that put up one hundred quarts of applesauce in a single day. The companionship of her friends and neighbors made the experience more fun than work, and the next day everyone moved on to another house and another round of canning.

VINES AND WINE GARDENS

Wine was a considerably more popular beverage than whiskey among McLean County's German speakers because it could be enjoyed by the entire family. Many houses had several grape vines out back and every year households throughout the county made wine for the family table.

Dr. Herman Schroeder, a man who had been active in the German Revolution of 1848 and who enjoyed telling about how he narrowly escaped execution, developed a vine nursery business that catered to back-yard vintners.[19] He and his wife, like thousands of other Germans, made their way to Cincinnati in 1849. From there, they moved to El Paso, Illinois and then on to Bloomington. Herman made his living as a physician at first. Later, he tried to raise silkworms commercially and failed. All the while, he could not help noticing a great scarcity of the kind of inexpensive wine he and his countrymen were accustomed to drinking with dinner. He decided to capitalize on this observation by nurturing a variety of young vines and selling them to folks eager to make wine at home.

Schroeder experienced his first success about 1860 at the Illinois State Fair. He took a wagon full of grapes and cuttings to the exhibition, which was held in Decatur, and filled display cases with vines in fruit. His exhibit attracted a lot of attention, and he quickly sold out of his entire stock. Customers bought several pounds of vines on the spot, men carrying them away in their hats, women stuffing them into their shawls. Schroeder made so much money at the fair that he had to tuck his trousers into his boot tops and stuff the legs with currency. The next year, he traveled to a fair in Chicago where he sold four tons of grapes and grape vines and once again came home with his trousers filled with cash. Over the next 40 years or so, Schroeder sold over 20 million grape vines and became one of America's leading exponents of grape culture. His catalog for 1890 listed 67 varieties of grapes, most of them intended for wine making.[20]

Wine making on the farm was not a complicated process. On their property near Eureka, Robert Yoder's parents had a large arbor of Concord grapes.[21] Turning them into wine began with young Robert being allowed to stomp the grapes. He washed his feet, put on clean socks, and tramped about in a big washtub. Dad and mom added a little sugar to the juice, barreled it, and then placed it in the cellar to ferment. The wine would be siphoned into another barrel after a few months for safekeeping and eventually tapped.

Although primarily a viticulturalist himself, Schroeder hoped that someday a wine-making industry would develop in the Bloomington area. With that in mind, he sold grapes to a handful of other commercial vintners and produced some wine for sale himself. It retailed at a popular price, and he envisioned the day it would challenge the popularity of beer and whiskey. Such was the case in areas of Germany, and in places like George Miller's Wein and Bier Salon in Bloomington where wine, indeed, received top billing. William Schmidt, an educated gentleman, attracted local wine lovers by building a German wine garden, *Williamschoehe*, just west of Bloomington. The garden, which was crosscut by a small stream, encompassed a vineyard, flowerbeds, a small pond, and a dance floor. Customers gathered on summer evenings and Sunday afternoons, purchased wine – probably some of it made by the proprietor himself, and drank in the "little chapel," an arbor romantically situated under a wild apple tree. Although a popular venue, *Williamschoehe* went out of business following Schmidt's death in 1891.

Schmidt and other McLean County wine makers likely produced the typically low-alcohol white varieties prized to this day by German drinkers. J. Brechbeller and Company, a Bloomington wine and liquor distributor, specialized in domestic and imported Rhine wines.[22] Such beverages had a reputation for being exceptionally healthful, which was why judges at the Illinois State Fair could credibly declare one prize-winning example more efficacious than "anything the doctors can furnish from their laboratories." Druggists sold vintage wines throughout McLean County. At Wakefield and Thompson's, a wholesale and retail drug store established in 1850, Bloomington residents could buy for medicinal purposes, "pure native Catawba wine and brandy from the grape," as well as other wines and spirits, both foreign and domestic.[23] Kendrick and Company, although primarily a grocery and cookware vendor, also advertised "the best foreign wines and liquors warranted pure for medicinal purposes."[24] As with wine, so with beer; druggists Paist and Marmon of Bloomington offered Scotch Ale and London Porter because "in many cases pure malt liquors are superior to all others as a tonic."[25]

CIDER AND VINEGAR

In addition to his wine-related enterprises, Schroeder produced apple cider and vinegar as a joint venture with William Rahn. Their company, called "Bloomington Cider Mills and Vinegar Works," commenced operations in 1880 out of a factory located in the 300 block of South Main in Bloomington with Rahn acting as production manager.

Cider in most parts of the English-speaking world refers to alcoholic beverages made from apples or pears. In North America, however, it applies to unfermented apple juice, and the phrase "hard cider" is reserved for the alcoholic drink. Schroeder and Rahn's cider was hard, the type Germans call *"Apfelwein"* (apple wine). Producing it simply extended Schroeder's engagement with grape wine to another fruit.

Vinegar, that all-important ingredient in German cooking, is essentially "sour wine" (from *vin aigre* in Old French). Bloomington Cider Mills and Vinegar Works manufactured cider vinegar – the product of fermented apple juice naturally infected or deliberately inoculated with acetic bacteria. The company thrived and remained in business for more than twenty years. Earlier Bloomington vinegar makers, including Leake and Somes, founded about 1868, and John H. Neuerburg, established around 1875, were short-lived ventures.

Gustave Gehlert of Detroit came to Bloomington to help run Bloomington Cider and Vinegar, and changed the company's focus from apples to cucumbers.[26] He bought out Schroeder's share of the company in 1883. The next year Gehlert and his new partner, Rahn, acquired McLean County Mill on the corner of Clinton and Taylor and converted it to a vinegar factory. At this point, if not before, Bloomington Cider and Vinegar began manufacturing vinegar from corn and malts. Gehlert purchased Rahn's half of the business in 1885, and four years later the company began pickling cucumbers.

The pickling business proved lucrative, and as it expanded, Gehlert persuaded McLean County farmers to devote increasing acreage to cucumbers. He provided seed and offered growers attractive contracts to deliver cucumbers no more than four inches in length.[27] Pickling at the factory began in July. Bottling got underway in October and ended by the first of May. Seven thousand barrels of pickles left the loading dock in 1893. At the time, most were sour pickles, although the market for sweet pickles was expanding.[28] A cooker explosion in 1894 injured several employees and curtailed production. Vinegar output continued apace, however, averaging 15,000 barrels annually and supplying markets that extended from Pennsylvania as far west as Nebraska. In addition to cucumbers, Gehlert's company produced chow-chow, a relish made from locally-grown pickled onions, beans, green tomatoes, and imported cauliflower.

Bloomington Cider and Vinegar became Bloomington Pickle in 1904. Gustave Gehlert was already retired because of poor health, but his successors continued to contract for cucumbers.[29] That ended in 1907 when the company went out of business. Vinegar continued to be made in Bloomington at Keeran-Lafferty, a small company with five employees. It opened in 1905 but shut down just few years later.

LOCAL BREWERS

William Hay brought the first barrel of lager beer to Bloomington in 1854.[30] It soured on its way from St. Louis, but local enthusiasts wanted a taste anyway. Hay sold out at 10 cents a glass and decided to start a local brewery. Unable to find a cellar suitable for aging beer, he reluctantly gave up on the idea.

Christian Markgraff dug his own cellar and opened Bloomington's first brewery on the southern edge of the city in 1859. The inaugural event featured music and speeches and an enormous quantity of beer. Some celebrants, unaccustomed to the beverage, drank a little too much and became "glorious o'er a' the ills o' life victorious."[31] Once the celebration was over, Markgraff got down to work and began producing around five hundred barrels of lager beer annually.

Markgraff sold his brew house in 1862 to Anson Meyer. Francis Wochner, Anson's brother-in-law, joined him in the business a few months later. Both men had roots in Germany. Meyer came from Baden Baden at age nineteen with experience as a brewer's apprentice.[32] He settled first in New York City, continued his career in St. Louis, and eventually became foreman at one of that city's many breweries. His next move was to Rock Island where he joined another beer maker and stayed for three years. He then took a job in Springfield where he remained for four years before moving to Bloomington to take over from Markgraff. Wochner landed on American soil at age eight. He married in Springfield in 1856, and after his sister wed Anson Meyer, Wochner and his new bride followed them to Bloomington and into the business of making beer.[33]

The two men wasted no time putting Meyer and Wochner Brewery Company on a sound financial basis.[34] They christened their newly acquired brewing facility "Gambrinus," and punched its annual production up to ten thousand barrels. For awhile, they also used the name "Evergreen City Brewery," a reference to Bloomington's then current nickname. Gambrinus referred to King Gambrinus, the fabled patron saint of beer. Statues of Gambrinus, "the King of Beer," decorated beer halls throughout Europe.

Meyer and Wochner were the biggest brewers in Bloomington from day one, and their company kept growing until it occupied eight buildings and several sheds on 125 acres of land.[35] Louis Stein built a much smaller brewery along a creek on the city's west side around 1861.[36] The property, situated on Springfield Road, consisted of nineteen acres of land under which Stein dug an aging vault for his beer. A beer garden was laid out on the rolling landscape and equipped with a bandstand and dance floor. These amenities made Stein's a popular gathering place among members of the German community. Nevertheless, the brewery was closed for some time before Meyer and Wochner purchased it and converted its brew house into a malting facility. The new owners used Stein's beer cave for additional storage and erected a new, three-story icehouse on the property.

Another little brewery patronized by Bloomington's German immigrants was built by William Frederick on Market Street at Sugar Creek.[37] It too appears to have had a beer garden. Frederick began brewing there about 1862. He continued for several years but was out of business before the end of the decade.

Other brewers to come and go during the 1860s were W.T. Ragland and Lyman Pankhurst. Ragland, proprietor of the Bloomington Steam Brewery, produced cream and stock ales. Pankhurst worked as maltster, yeast merchant, and ale brewer. Apparently, he sold his malt and yeast to home brewers, who at this point in time would have produced much if not most of the beer consumed in McLean County. Brewing, until some point in the 1860s or early '70s, was like wine making; a big share of it took place at home, intended for household consumption. The problem was that lager beer, the kind of beer Germans preferred, required cold fermentation and conditioning – in other words, cellars and a considerable amount of ice. This made it exceedingly difficult, if not impossible, to brew at home. Hence, the excitement when a keg of lager first arrived in Bloomington.

Lager, a refreshing, low-alcohol brew, was very popular in Europe and captured the fancy of many Americans in the urban areas of the Northeast not long after it was first introduced to the United States in the 1840s. Valentin Busch and Michael Brand began producing it in Chicago in 1854. Previously they had brewed ale, a far more ancient beer than lager and America's favorite from colonial times. The biggest brewer in Chicago, Lill and Diversey, produced immense amounts of ale, including both porter and stout.[38] The company advertised heavily in Bloomington, and with the city's growing Irish population, local agents McMillan and Tator must have found a ready market for the Lill and Diversey line. Samuel Waddle bought out McMillan and Tator about 1864 and began promoting Joliet's Eagle Brewery and its selection of ales. However, by this point brewers everywhere were shifting to lager in response to consumer demand. As for Lill and Diversey, they continued to produce ales, but their market declined, and after the Great Chicago Fire destroyed its facilities the company did not rebuild.

Meyer and Wochner profited from lager's popularity and needed to do little to promote their beer around Bloomington prior to 1880. By then, however, advances in pasteurization and refrigeration made it possible to sell beers hundreds of miles from where they were produced, and lagers brewed in other cities started appearing in Bloomington. Meyer and Wochner responded by running newspaper ads boasting of their beer's wholesome, hometown quality. As one ad put it:

> If you would quaff a good, healthful drink of beer, patronize home manufacture; drink a pure, fresh unadulterated article, drink Meyer & Wochner's beer for health and pleasure.[39]

For the next twenty years, Meyer and Wochner repeatedly urged beer-drinkers in the area to buy local, its ads questioning the wholesomeness of products from distant cities and asking consumers to consider how purchasing beer made in Milwaukee or St. Louis affected the economic well-being of Bloomington and its workforce.[40]

The competition, however, was brutal, and Meyer and Wochner suffered a heavy blow in 1883 at the hands of saloon-owner Louis Lowentrout. This occurred when two of Lowentrout's bars, the Bouquet and the Tivoli, which had been major outlets for Meyer and Wochner, discontinued selling the company's product, replacing it with brands brewed in St. Louis and Cincinnati.[41] As Green Tree, a St. Louis beer, began attracting a considerable local following. Meyer and Wochner retaliated by opening a new saloon at Market and Oak near the Tivoli. Lowentrout's sales suffered, and he countered by contacting Green Tree about establishing a brewery in Bloomington. As encouragement, he offered the company land on which to build. Nothing came of his offer except more intense efforts on the part of Meyer and Wochner to improve their brewing methods and to strengthen loyalty to their brand among area beer drinkers.

By this point, Meyer and Wochner counted as a big brewer with statewide distribution. The company received and processed during one week in 1883 no less than 34 carloads of barley and a full carload of hops. Gambrinus, running at full capacity, turned out approximately one hundred barrels of beer per day. Still, its brewmasters insisted on aging all of the beer produced at the facility for six to eight months. Company officials affirmed repeatedly that Meyer and Wochner beer contained no other ingredients than water, malted barley, yeast, and hops. Francis Wochner, who ran the company with his son, Ed, after Anson Meyer died in 1883, was fond of implying that brewers located in big cities like Cincinnati, Milwaukee, and St. Louis routinely adulterated their products.[42] This could mean that they brewed beer using wheat, corn, or rice instead of, or in addition to barley. These grains are commonly used in brewing American beers today, but under the Bavarian or German *Reinheitsgebot* (purity law), were forbidden in beers for many centuries.

Improvements at Gambrinus primarily involved infrastructure. The physical plant in 1889 consisted of a brew house, an office building, two large icehouses, two malt houses, a cooperage, a well house, and stock sheds. A new brick building replaced the old brew house in 1890, and at about the same time a mechanical refrigeration unit was installed. However, the beer continued to be aged in two, naturally cool subterranean vaults containing a total of 300 wooden casks, each with a capacity of 40 barrels. To send beer to the cellars more efficiently and to bring well water up from 400 feet underground, the company installed a 100 horsepower steam engine. It powered pumps throughout the complex and sent steam to the huge copper kettles in which the brew master boiled his wort (malt extract).

On the public relations front, Meyer and Wochner courted several segments of the community. Advertisements assured workers that the brewery relied exclusively on union labor. The company wooed sports enthusiasts by constructing a first-rate baseball park on its property. At the ground breaking in 1881, the field was designated the future home of the "brewery nine." Officials praised the company as a good citizen, pointing out that the new diamond was far enough removed from the nearest residences to avoid disturbing any churchgoers opposed to Sunday baseball.[43] Before long, The Bloomingtons, the city's municipal baseball team, made the new ball park its home.

Competition for a share of Bloomington's beer market intensified, and by the 1890s seven of the biggest brewers in the United States owned cold storage facilities in the city. All summer beer from such giants as American Brewing (Baltimore), Anheuser-Busch (St. Louis), Val Blatz (Milwaukee), Indianapolis Brewing, Isaac Leisy (Cleveland), Miller (Milwaukee), Pabst (Milwaukee), Schlitz (Milwaukee), Schoenhofen (Chicago), Terre Haute Brewing, and Union Brewing (Peoria) arrived at the rail yards in refrigerated cars containing eighths, quarters, halves, and full kegs. Each car carried nearly one hundred barrels plus sufficient ice to keep them cool. These same cars arrived packed with straw or hay to keep the kegs from freezing during the winter.

Brewers generally had no interest in bottling beer until 1878. This created an opportunity for local bottlers, like John Lasswell, agent for the Miller Brewing Company. Lasswell bottled the contents of some of the barrels he received and delivered the bottles to customers' homes. George Koch bottled ABC Steam Export Beer and delivered it free of charge. Independent bottlers purchased kegs of beer from various distributors and did the same. Frank's Bank, a Front Street saloon owned by Meyer and Wochner, bottled its beer for home delivery at no extra charge. The first brewer to ship bottled beer was Isaac Leisy & Company of Cleveland. Leisy's agent in Bloomington, Louis Wollrab, must have conducted a brisk business in the 1890s when pouring from bottles was becoming the most stylish way to drink beer. Meyer and Wochner began bottling at the brewery about 1897. They labeled their bottled beer "American Eagle."[44]

After Francis Wochner passed away in 1898, his heirs sold their shares in the business, and the firm changed its name to the Meyer Brewing Company. It developed new brands over the next several years, including Blue Label, "brewed exclusively for hotel and club service," and Extra Select, "brewed especially for home use."

The company went out of business in 1914 when Bloomington voted itself "dry" and banned the sale of all alcoholic beverages within its boundaries.[45] The city purchased the property in 1922 to construct Highland Park golf course. Two of the old brewery buildings, one now serving as a maintenance facility and the other remodeled as a pro shop, have survived.

SALOONS

As the taverns took on the character of hotels, people of limited means found themselves excluded. Hotel barrooms decorated with fancy woodwork, ornate furniture, large mirrors, and ornamental carpets assumed a posh character. The American cocktail originated in fancy hotel bars. In the meantime, grog shops and "sample rooms" where wholesalers courted prospective buyers with trial tastings, as well as general stores and groceries devoted more to selling alcohol than anything else. The term "saloon" began to be attached to such businesses during the 1850s.[46] Subsequently they evolved into workingmen's havens and flourished nearly everywhere in the country until 1920 when Prohibition went into effect nationwide.

McLean County's drinking establishments adopted the saloon label in the late 1860s. Calvin Jenkins's of Towanda, a place listed in the 1866 *McLean County Gazetteer*, appears to have been the first. Two years later Bloomington had at least 33 such establishments.[47] The number of saloons in Bloomington climbed to 44 in 1893, but this amounted to a slight decline relative to population size (from 442 residents per saloon to 465). Entries in the 1902 city directory pointed to a reverse trend (a ratio of 431:1), and indeed by 1912 there was one saloon for every 379 city residents.

One reason why the number of drinking places relative to population increased had to do with how easy it became to set one up. All a person needed to do was rent a storefront, make a small down payment, and a brewing company did the rest.[48] Anheuser-Busch, Blatz, or any of the others gladly installed the back bar, front bar, work board, cigar case, bottle case, icebox, lunch counter, steam table, customer tables and chairs, swinging doors, and everything else an establishment needed. A mortgage guaranteed payment for these articles at so much per month. Brewers' agents went so far as to procure licenses for their clients and take reimbursement as small weekly payments. For his part, the saloonkeeper agreed to buy only the beer his agent represented and to purchase it at an undiscounted price.

With such easy terms available from the brewing giants, independent saloonists became increasingly rare, replaced by proprietors under contract and operating a "tied-house."[49] These saloonkeepers frequently operated on a shoestring and drew their patrons from no further away than the immediate neighborhood, but every brewer also contracted with one or more showcase saloons boasting regulars from all parts of the city. In Bloomington during the later nineteenth century, such places included George Koch's (American Brewing), the Sevilla (Anheuser-Busch), Costello's, Frank's Bank, and the Gem (Meyer and Wochner), Schmitt's (Blatz), Shausten's (Muerline), John Feicht's Union Bar and Christian Riebsame's (Pabst Brewing), and Michael Foley's (Union Brewing).

Saloonkeepers and bartenders at these premier establishments, as well as lesser places, worked long hours. Many bars opened at six o'clock in the morning and did not close until midnight. The Illinois Department of Labor in 1900 reported an average wage of $25 per month for bartenders.[50] Chefs by comparison earned between $50 and $80 a month. Janitors took in between $20 and $70, and bookkeepers earned a minimum of $40 a month. Many saloonkeepers in the neighborhoods paid no wages at all. In family-operated places, the owner poured drinks, his wife prepared lunches and filled in behind the bar, and the kids cleaned up.

Beyond Bloomington's city limits, McLean County refused to license saloons, but this did not stop other incorporated areas from doing so. The 1893 county directory listed 17 drinking places located in various municipalities, including one in Arrowsmith, two in Colfax, three apiece in Chenoa and LeRoy, and four each in Danvers and Gridley. In Towanda and several other places, saloons came and went. A few towns – McLean and Normal, for example – remained steadfastly dry.

KINDS OF DRINKING PLACES

Saloons in Central Illinois fell into two basic categories. On one hand, there were the German-style saloons such as Otto Kadgihn's (see previous chapter). These were well-lit with airy rooms where wives and children were welcome and in which food was every bit as important as drink. On the other hand, there were the American saloons. These celebrated beer and liquor and acquired early on some of the dark, club-like, male-only character of the Irish *shebeen*.

Beer gardens, *ratskellers* (also spelled *rathskellers*), and taverns have been central to German community life for centuries. Typically, such places were furnished with large tables where groups of men, women, and children could sit together and eat pickled herrings, sausages, sauerkraut, rye bread, and other traditional foods.[51] The children had root beer to drink. The adults consumed mostly lager and usually at a leisurely pace. Proprietors discouraged intoxication and never tolerated base language or fighting. Ideally, a feeling of *gemütlichkeit* or comfortable familiarity filled the room. Germans never felt this in the typical American saloon.

The proprietors of German saloons in Bloomington went to considerable lengths to make their establishments attractive to women and families. Robert Lander, a schoolteacher in Germany before he immigrated, founded Bloomington's first beer garden in 1862 on the northeast corner of Grove and Clinton.[52] It was supposed to be a romantic place. Beer gardens ideally harkened back to the sacred grove of European myth. Lander's indoor facility opened onto manicured grounds containing intimate booths, pretty arbors, and a small bandstand. After Lander raised a company of German-speaking soldiers for the Union Army and left for the war, others kept his place going. Lander survived the war but never returned to the business, and by 1880 the much cherished beer garden closed for good. Peter Engelken's beer garden adjacent to his saloon on

South Main near the edge of town opened about 1875 and continued to entertain patrons until around 1890.

Elsewhere, particularly in big cities, beer gardens moved indoors.[53] Owners decked huge halls with potted trees and plants and outfitted them with diversions such as bowling alleys and shooting galleries. Places like the Schlitz Palm Gardens in Milwaukee hosted Wild West shows and fabulous menageries.

Bloomington's German saloonkeepers never installed such elaborate entertainments, but they did create garden-like settings. Shausten's on Center Street, for example, occupied "a room 22x189 feet deep, fitted up in elegant style, with a flowing font in the center, making it a pleasant and desirable place to rest."[54] At Schmitt's Oyster and Chop House, the first floor barroom of antique oak, mirrors, and brass fixtures glistened with "grandeur and beauty." An elevator took patrons to a second floor dining room where a selection of dishes prepared by French caterer Mr. Miller awaited.[55] Otto Kadgihn's Sebastopol Saloon also attracted patrons with promises of good food.[56] The Sevilla, a Front Street "drinking emporium" and one of the most popular early twentieth-century saloons in Bloomington, did the same.[57] Owner John Moebus acted as agent for the Anheuser-Busch Brewing Company of St. Louis. His bartenders served "the lovely Budweiser," Faust, and other Anheuser-Busch brands exclusively. Customers could call for Rhine wines and old whiskeys, but in Bloomington's German-language newspaper, *Dem Bloomington Journal*, the Sevilla billed itself, as first and foremost a restaurant (*Deutsche Gastwirtschaft*).[58]

American-style saloons countenanced hard drinking, but they were by no means simply places for imbibing alcohol. Many were in effect working-class men's clubs.[59] They served lunch, often had variety of newspapers on hand, and frequently rented bathing facilities. In many cases, they hosted games of chance, sponsored sports, and bankrolled small loans. Some had prostitutes available. Political organizers found voters, and employers found employees in saloons. Fraternal organizations met upstairs or in a back room. Saloons on skid row were spots where derelicts found respite and where transients could orient themselves.

Saloonists generally did their utmost to accommodate customers because of the ruthless competition among establishments.[60] Operating a bar may have been the easiest business to get into, but it was just as easy to go broke should customers decide to drink elsewhere. To keep the swinging doors swinging, proprietors had to remain on their toes and forever helpful – perhaps by passing along useful information, perhaps by helping a customer solve some problem. Bigheartedness made for good business. Extra generous shots of whiskey, beers on the house, bar snacks, and souvenirs such as advertising calendars and serving trays demonstrated concern for regulars. In addition, there was the free lunch.

THE FREE LUNCH

The free lunch in Chicago is supposed to have originated after the Great Fire of 1871.[61] Saloonkeeper Joseph Chesterfield Macklin had tried a number of things to attract more customers but to no avail. In desperation, he began serving a hot oyster free with every drink. That did the trick, and soon his bar became one of the most popular places in the city. Soon, everyone in the business began copying Macklin's ploy, things escalated, and soon the free snack had swelled into a free lunch.

In Bloomington, a free lunch was served at Gilliland's Billiard and Oyster Saloon as early as 1864.[62] However, to eat without charge a patron needed to stop by between 10 and 11 in the morning.[63] At other times, the bartender needed to be paid for the oysters, pigs feet, tripe, and tongue listed on the menu. At Christian Riebsame's elegant "gentlemen's resort," in downtown Bloomington, where wife Bertha (a professional baker) oversaw the kitchen, the free lunch may have been more attractive. Much of the time Riebsame was in the saloon business the spread offered by premier establishments consisted of dozens of different dishes and enough "to kill a horse."[64] Typically, cold, pickled items dominated, but The Gem on Bloomington's Courthouse Square set out an array of hot dishes every day at lunch hour and again on Saturday evenings.[65] The Two Williams, a bar on West Grove, distinguished itself by extending free lunch from the standard one hour to two hours daily.[66] On special occasions and holidays, some saloonkeepers went all out. Christmas at John Moebus's Sevilla brought out ". . . an immense feast throughout the day, consisting of turkey, toothsome meats, egg nog, Tom and Jerry, and all the tempting accompaniments of the holiday." One year, Moebus proclaimed Christmas lunch ". . . worth going many blocks to see, without considering the privilege of participating in it."[67] In an advertisement for The Relay Saloon, Esek Day and John Mayer, its two "jovial caterers," declared their recent Christmas lunch "a grand hit." New Year's Day, they promised a spread "fit for the gods."[68] A planned lunch to celebrate the opening of the Jefferson House saloon on West Chestnut Street was heralded as so magnificent that "delegations from neighboring towns" were planning to attend the feast.[69]

BILLIARD PARLORS AND SPORTS CELEBRITIES

Saloon owners sought advantage from every imaginable angle. There were unique décors and distinctive atmospheres. Riebsame's in Bloomington, for instance, had a kind of formal elegance, imitating the ambiance of the elegant European spas and baths the proprietor and his wife often visited. Billiards went from being a barroom novelty intended to hold patrons during slack hours to a major accompaniment to drinking.[70] Around 1910, approximately 50 percent of Chicago's 7,600 saloons had at least one billiard table. Captain Riebsame devoted the entire second floor of his establishment to the "finest billiard room in the city."[71] Each of Meyer and Wochner's houses billed itself as "saloon and billiard parlor."

Other sports also found their way into drinking places. In Chicago, one could play handball or watch bicycle racing at a saloon.[72] Sports celebrities, mainly prizefighters, hosted several bars. In Bloomington, two former baseball stars, Charles Gardner "Old Hoss" Radbourn and William Darnbrough, opened bars.

"Old Hoss" entertained patrons at the Diamond Saloon on West Washington with baseball commentary and tales about his famous exploits.[73] Radbourn played in the major leagues, and as a pitcher he became the sport's first curve-ball artist. He won the National League's Triple Crown in pitching with the Boston Red Sox in 1884. After he retired, he teamed up with James Carroll and opened the Diamond where he poured drinks until his death in 1897.

William Darnbrough, proprietor of the Bouquet Café, played baseball as a boy in Normal and developed into an outstanding pitcher. He was on his way to Denver in 1889 to join a professional team when he was arrested in Belleville, Illinois on a paternity charge. He returned to Normal in 1891 to pitch a benefit game. Two years later he was running Bloomington's Bouquet Café where he traded on a reputation as a successful sportsman and as a man who demanded excellence in everything. Chef Hamilton, a specialist in wild game, presided over Darnbrough's kitchen.[74] An 1894 advertisement in the *Sunday Bulletin* carried the headline, "An Ex-Base Ballist: What He Has to Say as to Diet and the Diamond."

> Will Darnbrough says when you eat you should eat the best and when you drink you should drink the best; and it's just as cheap to eat and drink at the Bouquet chop house, west side of the square, where they keep the good old Anheuser-Busch beer, Faust and Pilsener, and the best and smoothest whiskies. Fine dinner everyday for 15 cents. Meals to order as high as you please.[75]

Darnbrough's barroom, a proto-typical sports bar, entertained patrons with up-to-the-minute game reports as they were telegraphed across the country. Darnbrough himself announced game highlights and scores, but sometime around 1895 he left the Bouquet Café behind and became a professional gambler. As such, he traveled to Alaska's gold fields and later to Monte Carlo where he purportedly "broke the bank." He was last heard from selling automobiles in London, England.

WRECKING OF THE BUENA VISTA

The war of words about the sale of alcohol heated up in the 1850s all across the country, and the prohibitionists gained the upper hand. Their growing strength became evident when Maine imposed a total ban on the manufacture and sale of liquor in 1851, and twelve other states followed suit. In Illinois, becoming "dry" or remaining "wet" was a local option. This permitted Bloomington, which was wet from its inception, to license saloons in the midst of a county that had voted itself dry.

Bloomington's first attempt to emulate the county was spearheaded by Mayor Frank Price and was intended to corral the city's Irish population. Price, a member of the anti-immigrant American Party, took his lead from several Protestant congregations that held rallies protesting an alleged desecration of the Sabbath by members of the Catholic working class.[76] Events turned violent in 1853 when a mob broke into three stores run by Irishmen and smashed barrels of whiskey.[77] When Price took office in 1855, Bloomington's City Council passed ordinances prohibiting the sale of alcoholic beverages. This enabled the police to go after the Irish and emboldened vigilantes, including a band of women who "created a mild riot by their assaults on saloons and publically dumping stocks of liquor into the sewers."[78]

Nevertheless, prohibition lacked popular support. Indeed, the public's disregard for the city's anti-liquor laws proved so pervasive that the number of drinking places in town actually increased.[79] When authorities attempted to prosecute a prohibition violator, witnesses swore the beverage at issue was dispensed as a temperance bitter – i.e., a genuine patent medicine.[80]

Advertisements in the newspapers propagated confusion. Gin and other liquors were described as tonic medicines. Among the most heavily promoted were Bininger's Old London Dock Gin, "an agreeable tonic, designed especially as a safe and reliable medicine for family use," and Deveroux's Medicated Cordial Gin, a tonic mentioned in Chapter 2 as good for stimulating the appetite. Deveroux's was also supposedly effective for curing dyspepsia, fever and ague, debility, gout, gravel (kidney stones), diseases of the bladder, diseases of the kidneys, etc. maker also represented it as a diet drink, claiming that it cured loss of appetite. All in all, Deveroux's was sold as a versatile swallow, ready to be taken either as a beverage or as a medicine, whichever way the consumer preferred.[81] Not so with Dr. Hoofland's German Bitters, however. Hoofland's manufacturer insisted it was "not a Bar Room Drink or an Intoxicating Beverage."[82] Nevertheless, it probably resembled Jaegermeister, a heavily promoted barroom liqueur that became especially popular among college students in the 1990s.

How Bloomington's first bout with prohibition formally ended is not clear, but patently the authorities' failure to successfully enforce it did not deter local anti-liquor advocates. Perhaps out of frustration with the law's impotence, a posse of women in the village of Towanda, a short distance northeast of the city, took matters into their own hands.[83] One evening in 1858, they walked into the Buena Vista Saloon, one of three bars in the vicinity, and completely wrecked it. The women, said to be incensed by the amount of money their husbands spent on liquor, had rendezvoused at sundown.[84] Their first stop was the hardware store where they purchased hatchets. With these implements in hand, they strode down Main Street and without a word pushed aside the Buena Vista's swinging doors and stepped inside. Four men playing cards looked up in astonishment, saw trouble, and fled. A man at the bar raised his glass. A hatchet flashed and cut his mock salutation short by removing the drink from his hand. As the man dashed out of the barroom, the previously routed card players returned to fetch their hats but did nothing to interfere. The bartender offered no resistance. He instead pushed his backside up on the bar and sat there swinging his heels while the women hacked away at everything on the premises. Bottles were tossed out the window where a member of the party, Susan Baylor, waited to smash those that did not break when they hit the ground. Liquor puddles on the barroom floor from demolished barrels soaked several petticoats and ruined Rebecca Haterman's new pair of kid-leather shoes. Once the interior of the Buena Vista lay in ruins, the women caught a train to Bloomington and surrendered to authorities. Several of the saloon-wreckers received a one-dollar fine. All of them were treated to dinner at one of the city's best hotels courtesy of local prohibitionists.

Towanda voted itself dry after the incident and remained so until 1991. By then every business in town had closed, and residents found themselves having to choose between acquiring a gasoline station and convenience store or remaining dry. A liquor license, the prospective store owner argued, spelled the difference between profit and loss. As he saw it, selling alcoholic beverages was a prerequisite to doing business in the community. Towanda residents bought the argument and voted the town once more wet.[85]

BLOOMINGTON'S ON-AGAIN, OFF-AGAIN PROHIBITION

After its first attempt to go dry, Bloomington wavered on the issue of prohibition for years. The wets gained the upper hand during the Civil War, and the prohibition movement seemed to vanish. However, the issue had merely been shoved to the back burner. The movement revived after the war and steadily

voters again lowered the boom on alcohol sales they put Meyer Brewing out of business. Also closed and never re-opened were John Moebus's Sevilla, the big Budweiser eating and drinking emporium, and Edward Fahey's Metropole, a downtown European hotel, saloon, and dining room, which in continental fashion welcomed both "ladies and gentlemen."

A few of the city's saloons converted to restaurants, including Chris Glowe's, Philip Wollrab's, and Charles Johnson's. The latter was the immediate successor of The Fish Club, a popular East Market Street saloon presided over by W.F. Lemme, who unabashedly proclaimed his bar the home of Bloomington's "triple alliance," Germans, Irishmen, and Swedes, members of the city's largest immigrant communities.[97]

The food at The Fish Club became Swedish about 1912 when it began offering a daily smorgasbord christened "The Swede's Buffet."[98] Bloomington's Swedes, who first came to the city as coal miners, ate simple and hearty meals without much meat. Back home in Sweden it had been exceedingly dear, forcing those of limited means to look elsewhere for flesh-foods and to stretch those that they were fortunate enough to lay hands on.[99] The Swedish meatball, an American buffet staple, is authentically made from a blend of ground beef, veal, and pork mixed with bread, egg, and seasonings, a recipe developed to conserve meat; the same for two other Swedish standards, stuffed cabbage and stuffed onions. For Swedes, fish – usually dried, pickled or smoked – constituted a major source of protein. They cooked with dairy products for fat and for vegetables they preferred cold weather species, including beets, rutabagas and turnips. The rye bread, the yellow pea soup, and all of the pickled dishes on the Swede's Buffet can be viewed as culinary adaptations to northerly conditions.

Of course, none of this mattered to Charles Johnson, who at the time was Lemme's bartender and the Swede behind the Swede's Buffet. Most important to him was the success of his smorgasbord. It proved so popular that within a year he bought Lemme out and transformed The Fish Club into Johnson's Café and Buffet. Customers at first descended on Johnson's, especially at night after the theaters closed. Unfortunately for the proprietor, within a year or two of going dry Bloomington's self-styled "headquarters for theatrical people" lost its appeal and was forced to close.

In rural areas, Mennonites and other Anabaptists came under increasingly intense pressure from other Protestants, including missionaries from the Moody Bible Institute of Chicago, to renounce alcohol. Robert Yoder, who was a just a small boy living near Eureka in the 1920s, recollected that back then his parents kept a big barrel of homemade wine in their basement.[100] The barrel had a wooden spigot from which dad and mom filled small wine glasses. Family members, including little Robert, took a glass before meals, but always in the basement, never at the table. This curious practice could be taken as an artifact of Prohibition and the need to be discrete, but actually there was nothing illegal about homemade wine. Drinking wine in the basement probably was more indicative of acculturative pressures and ambivalence toward tradition rather than worry about the law. Yoder remembered the wine barrel becoming a vinegar barrel about the time Bible Institute supporters finally succeeded in getting his church to insert a temperance lesson into its teachings.

If Prohibition and the closure of Meyer Brewing and Bloomington's European-styled saloons and restaurants were not enough to erase ethnic diversity from the city's dining scene, the anti-German hysteria touched off by America's entry into World War I sealed the deal. With the declaration of war, McLean County's nativists – persons opposed to immigration and any expressions of immigrants' native cultures – took license to fully express themselves. Unidentified parties attacked *The Bloomington Journal* and the Gummerman print shop, two German-language businesses. The McLean County Council on Defense, a self-appointed body of regulators, demanded cessation of the German-language classes at Bloomington High School. Sauerkraut was renamed "liberty cabbage."[101] Howard Humphreys, a local grocer and Federal District Food Administrator, wrote a piece for *The Daily Pantagraph* in which he called any woman who failed to heed the wartime proscription on wheat "a bungling housewife" and "a pro-German influence."[102] German religious congregations came under assault. St. Mary's Catholic Church in Bloomington received threats. A mob approached St. John's Lutheran Church in Anchor and threatened to burn the congregation's prayer books if services continued to be conducted in German. Vandals in Gridley despoiled the Apostolic Christian Church with yellow paint because of members' anti-war beliefs. Anabaptist men throughout Central Illinois went to prison for the same reason.

RESTAURANTS

Before World War I, Bloomington's German Americans had their eating-saloons and businessmen patronized cafés and hotel dining rooms. There were oyster parlors and other restaurants, but for most people the prospect of eating out scarcely existed. Many working-class families had no concept of going out to eat as a form of entertainment, and many farmers entered a restaurant only as a last resort. Bertha Zehr, who was born in 1906, ate in a restaurant just once as a child. As she recalled,

> My family had gone to Ohio to visit relatives. On the way home our
> car broke down and we had to ride home on the train. In Chicago we
> had to change trains, and our wait was so long that we ordered a bowl

of tomato soup. It was likely the cheapest food on the menu, but it tasted delicious to us.[103]

When traveling Bertha's mother usually packed sandwiches, hardboiled eggs, and cookies for the family. Otherwise, eating away from home was limited to church suppers and occasional visits to see relatives and friends.

Restaurants gained popularity in the 1920s and '30s. Chains developed into regional and national systems. The saloons and their free lunches were gone, but chains kept the cost of eating out within reach of wage workers. Other sorts of dining spots, including mom-and-pop places, served low cost meals as well. Many of them offered "short orders" (menu items that required little preparation time) to customers in a hurry to eat and be on their way. Short orders would eventually evolve into fast food, and by the 1930s the restaurant most instrumental in the development of fast food, the drive-in, was fast becoming a popular alternative to the sit-down restaurant.

EARLY MODERN RESTAURANTS

The first step toward the popularization of restaurants came in the late nineteenth century when standardization and mass production reduced the cost of eating out. Factory-built facilities, carefully rationalized organizational models, and new technologies facilitating quick and efficient service led to the development of new kinds of eating places, including the diner, the lunch room, and the cafeteria. All three developed at a time when most Americans depended on public transportation. Consequently, the new restaurants located near railroad depots and trolley stops or other districts with considerable foot traffic. The coffee shop or café, a long-standing institution in many parts of the United States, emerged somewhat later than the diner but offered a similar menu.

THE DINER

The American diner originated in the Northeast where it was produced in factories and sold as a fully-equipped business.[104] Its history began around 1873 when Walter Scott, a street vendor in Providence, Rhode Island, grew tired of running home to refill the hand basket from which he sold lunch items. Scott bought a wagon, cut a window on one side, and began selling hardboiled eggs with buttered bread, frankfurters, sliced chicken, and chicken salad sandwiches to walk-up customers. His lunch wagon drew crowds, and other vendors copied it. Soon, lunch wagons clogged the streets prompting the enactment of a statute requiring vendors to find off-street parking. This led to the development of semi-permanent locations and finally the emergence of diners at the beginning of the twentieth century. Essentially, these were manufactured sandwich shops with long, narrow dimensions intentionally recalling the lunch wagon. Some manufacturers, rather than building from scratch, made diners out of old railroad cars.

The diner in its classic form barely penetrated the Midwest. None opened in McLean County, although a couple of lunch wagons clattered up and down the streets of Bloomington for a few years beginning in 1912.

COFFEE SHOPS, CAFÉS, AND GRILLS

The Midwestern coffee shop, commonly called a "grill" or "café" in Central Illinois, originated in the early twentieth century. The word "café" had been bandied about in the 1890s, but back then it referred to a saloon. Examples included Cuyler's European Hotel, Restaurant and Café, William Darnbrough's Bouquet Café, and James Costello's Café Saloon located in the splendidly christened "New Grand Opera House." The first dedicated restaurant in Bloomington to call itself a café was Greider's about 1912. By 1917, several additional establishments had taken to styling themselves as cafés, including the Boston, the Grand Inn (noted in the city directory as a chop suey restaurant), and the New Home.[105] In the years that followed, the genre grew in popularity, and cafés proliferated in various locations, including hotels, office buildings, storefronts, and service stations.

Café cuisine developed along the same lines as the diner's. Both revolve around a menu of fried or grilled items, including eggs, omelets, bacon, sausages, pancakes, waffles, hash browns, French fries, hamburgers, hot dogs, and chicken. This constellation over the years has become commonly known as "Greasy Spoon." The Federal Café, a downtown eatery that opened around 1922, served classic Greasy Spoon for many years.[106] In addition to eggs and pancakes, breakfast included various skillets, typically a mélange of fried potatoes; bacon, ham, or sausage; onions; and peppers, mixed with cheese or other ingredients. The Federal's lunch menu listed hamburgers and other hot and cold sandwiches. It offered in addition soups, salads, French fries, breaded mushrooms, onion rings, cheese balls, cheese sticks, cole slaw, cottage cheese, applesauce, and garlic bread. Beverages included sodas (Pepsi, Diet Pepsi, Mountain Dew, Dr. Pepper, and Mug Root Beer), iced tea, lemonade, coffee, milk, and hot chocolate. Fruit pie, a cream pie, chocolate cake, and cheesecake could be ordered for dessert, and in typical café fashion waitresses poured coffee for customers throughout the meal.

The Federal kept typical café hours. It opened for breakfast in the morning, served through mid-day, and closed at three in the afternoon. These hours suited business people, most of whom went home to eat in the evening. Café hours made good sense in rural areas too. Most farmers ate a big breakfast and took their main meal at mid-day. There was little point in staying open after that.

On highways with late-night traffic or in neighborhoods frequented by "night owls," cafés extended their hours and in that respect became more diner-like. However, what has defined the café more than its hours, and even more than its menu, is an atmosphere of congeniality. Perhaps from the very beginning, the café has been a community institution, a place frequented by regulars who come in expecting to find friends as well as something to eat. The result is a kind of familiarity not unlike *gemütlichkeit*, but without the beer and wine. The dining room, or perhaps just a corner of the dining room, effuses a hearty amiability or clubbiness. Regulars, including various sets of local businessmen, farmers, retirees, sportsmen, and church-goers, often have their own tables. Some groups show up at the same time every week "to shoot the bull," others come in every day. At the Village Inn in downtown Bloomington, a long table was always reserved for bachelors and other men who dropped in alone.[107] Customers stopped by each other's tables to say, "hello," and there was always a lot of casual back-and-forth banter about family and friends and "what's new?"

In McLean County, the relationship between regulars and their cafés has become downright proprietary. When Kathy's Kitchen in Lexington burned down in 1970, no sooner was the fire out than members of community began rebuilding the facility.[108] Owner Kathy Phinney was back on her feet and behind the counter pouring coffee in a matter of weeks. Chief among her benefactors were 20 or so members of "the Coffee Club," a set of men who had grown so accustomed to going in and out of Kathy's all day, every day to discuss local events they were not about to let the restaurant close. Some had been regulars for more than 20 years.

Café regulars rarely tolerate criticism. Attempts during the 1980s by *Daily Pantagraph* critics to review local restaurants resulted in blizzards of unappreciative letters from habitués denouncing reviewer and publisher alike.[109] Restaurant reviews after that amounted to little more than unpaid advertising. The problem, a former reviewer confided, was that nothing negative could be said about a restaurant without it being interpreted by the regulars as a personal attack.

THE TEAROOM

The tearoom made its first appearance in the United States in the 1890s. Its popularity peaked in the 1920s when tearooms existed throughout the country and could be found in such diverse venues as fine hotels and dingy service stations.[110] In its initial conception, however, the tearoom was a downtown business intended to serve meals to the swelling ranks of young, working women who otherwise had few respectable places to eat. Most cities had WCTU dining rooms, but too few to meet the needs of the increasing number of women employed in the central city. Dairy lunch rooms, created to dish up quick meals at rock-bottom prices, took up some of the slack but were exceedingly Spartan. Tearooms appeared as somewhat upscale equivalents.

Ella Graham's Women's Exchange and Tea Room appears to have been the first in Bloomington. However, the most famous and enduring was Roland's, a department store tearoom, located on the Jefferson Street side of Courthouse Square, four floors above street level. Department store tearooms were already commonplace by the time Roland's opened in 1909 as a women's clothing shop. Its tearoom – billed as "the tea room of refinement" – opened two years after Roland's expanded to a full-service department store in 1918.[111] In 1935, amidst the Great Depression, it offered a "business girls" lunch for 25 cents. Other "dainty, delicious luncheons" were also available, with the added attraction of witnessing a thirty-minute remote radio broadcast presented by station WJBC every Tuesday, Thursday and Saturday at noon.

Beginning around 1922, Roland's tearoom transformed itself every Sunday from a lunch spot into a fine dining room. An advertisement urged *Daily Pantagraph* readers to take the elevator to the fourth floor tearoom and enjoy a delicious Sunday dinner at the "Coolest place in town to dine" (a boast made possible by the restaurant's air conditioning system rather than any particular demeanor).[112] The menu listed a complete meal with a choice of entrees, either roast beef and dressing or roast pork with brown gravy. Soup and wafers, new potatoes, beets, peas, radishes, onions, and a combination salad accompanied the entrees, and for dessert diners had their choice of strawberry shortcake, homemade cake, berries and cream, or ice cream. Roland's continued to advertise its Sunday dinners for nearly 20 years.

> Go to church - then come to Roland's for Sunday dinner!
>
> Special music every Sunday – open Sunday noon and evening. Sunday dinners 45 cents, 55 cents, 65 cents . . . . Get the Sunday habit of dining at Roland's . . . it gives Mother so much more time to enjoy the day![113]

The glory days of the tearoom ended, and by 1939 the "tea room of refinement" motto had to be ditched. No more dainty lunches. The Depression was nearly over, and to keep up with the times Roland's Tea Room became Roland's

Tea Room, Restaurant, and Lunch Counter, serving "milk shakes, hamburgers, chocolate sodas, malted milk. Anything you can think of."[114]

THE LUNCH ROOM

Lunch rooms, sometimes called "lunch counters," first appeared in the United States around 1870 and can be regarded as the forerunners of today's fast-food restaurants. Somewhat later, luncheonettes appeared and carved out a niche for themselves at the upper end of the genre. The idea, however, remained the same: Serve simple meals quickly and inexpensively to working people and others in too much of a hurry to sit down and enjoy something more leisurely.[115] Saloons and street vendors already were catering to those who had as little as thirty minutes to eat, but in the 1850s Chicago railroads introduced the quick-service counter. This was typically horseshoe shaped to reduce the distance among place settings. Shorter distances made for faster service and at the same time reduced the number of required waiters.

The lunch room concept took hold in McLean County during the 1890s. Bloomington's city directory for 1891 listed six lunch rooms, three of them situated in or adjacent to railway depots, well positioned to serve the more or less continuous stream of travelers coming and going and changing trains.[116] Two years later directory listings included 18 restaurants, three chophouses (establishments roughly equivalent to the modern steakhouse), and 15 lunch rooms, 11 of them in the city and one each in the towns of Arrowsmith, Heyworth, Lexington, and Saybrook.[117] Later directories merged restaurants and lunch rooms into a single listing, but it seems safe to assume that the number of lunch rooms in the area remained relatively high through the mid-twentieth century and until the arrival of the fast-food chains in the 1960s.[118] For the 1920s, it has been estimated that of all the restaurants opened nationwide approximately forty percent were lunch rooms.[119]

The luncheonette, which came to resemble the lunch room through a kind of convergent evolution, originated from the old-time soda shop.[120] Fountain operators began adding light lunches to their menus about 1900. As the lunches became more important to the bottom line, soda shops morphed into sandwich shops offering fountain treats and desserts in addition to typical lunch items. The Goodie Candy Company on West Washington Street operated the Goodie Garden, which styled itself as the sweetshop "Where Good Goodies Grow." In addition to sodas, ice creams, and a variety of other confections, it served hot dogs and sandwiches made with deviled ham, boiled ham, or ham salad. Olive butter, pimento cheese, pineapple marmalade, grape jelly, and peanut butter sandwiches were also available.[121]

Ike and Lue Sanders served lunches to miners and railroad workers in the Working Man's Club from 1909 to 1917.

Isaac "Ike" Sanders' lunch room, a fixture on South Main in Bloomington from about 1909 until 1917, existed a world apart from the Goodie Garden. Instead of selling peanut butter and jelly sandwiches, Ike's wife, Lue, ladled out bowls of beef stew and grabbed pig ears, feet, and neck bones out of a big lard can and tossed them on the skillet.[122] She cooked for working men – black, white, and Hispanic – employed as miners and railroad men. The city directory listed Sanders' restaurant as "colored," but his customers had no interest in soul food. The concept had yet to be invented. An interviewer once repeatedly asked Ike's widow if she fixed barbecue ribs, chitlins, greens, sweet potato pie, and the like for customers. Lue stopped the questioner cold. "No," she snapped, "I tell you we didn't have time for any fancy foods."[123]

At the other end of the spectrum were the lunch counters and luncheonettes in downtown Bloomington that thrived on the patronage of State Farm Insurance Company employees. When State Farm moved into its new office building in 1929, President George Mecherle considered a proposal to create an in-house lunch room, but having no desire to hurt nearby businesses he decided against it.[124] This sustained the flood of employees on downtown establishments, and it represented a gold mine during the Great Depression for places at which State Farm workers were able to redeem their employee lunch vouchers.

State Farm ventured into food service on its own premises shortly after Mecherle's death. In 1951, company executives ordered a kitchen and dining room built for their exclusive use.[125] The room contained seating space for the insurer's 42 top executives, and whenever one of them was away from the office the next in line received an invitation to lunch. State Farm opened in-house cafeterias for the rank and file in 1973. Corporate headquarters had moved to the eastern edge of the city where restaurants were few and far between, and employees needed a place to eat. Installing a cafeteria for those who remained in the downtown office was explained as a matter of equity. It resulted in the closure of most nearby restaurants, an extension of the general economic devastation of the downtown area caused by State Farm's move.

THE CAFETERIA

Cafeterias date back to the 1880s but received no publicity until one was built to serve the crowds attending Chicago's World Exposition in 1893.[126] The facility was called an "honor house" because guests declared what they had eaten and paid accordingly as they left. The honor house captured the themes of the industrial revolution – mass production, the interchangeability of items on the line, and rapid, uniform handling. Childs, a New York City restaurant, adopted the model and introduced tray service in 1898.

Outside of institutional settings such as hospitals and schools, there have been few cafeterias in McLean County. The Normal Cafeteria, the first cafeteria listed in a local directory, opened about 1922 and catered to Illinois State Normal University students. The Jefferson Cafeteria, which opened on North Main in downtown Bloomington in the mid '30s, is fondly remembered by many area residents to this day. It was a favorite hangout for Illinois Wesleyan University students in the 1960s.[127] Sunday mornings, however, it "belonged" to members of the nearby Second Presbyterian Church. Every week after the second service nearly the entire congregation ambled over for something to eat and a chance to visit.[128] Pastor Harold Martin worked his way from table to table, trying to greet everyone and keep abreast with their lives. All of this got disrupted during the spring while the annual Passion Play was in town at the Consistory a few blocks north on Main Street. Busloads of people descended on the Jefferson for something to eat before Sunday's performance, leaving second-service attendees scrambling to find somewhere else to meet. Often it was the Sinorak, a "smorgasbord" cafeteria on South Main near U.S. Route 66 (see Chapter Six).

CHAIN RESTAURANTS

America's first chain restaurants came into existence in the early nineteenth century, and then, as now, they attracted diners who wanted to know what to expect when they sat down and ordered a meal. A chain restaurant is predictable, and it feels familiar even though it may be far from home.

Fred Harvey Restaurants, fixtures at many of the passenger depots along the Atchison, Topeka, and Santa Fe Railroad, originated in 1876 and McDonaldized some 80 years before the establishment of McDonald's. Harvey insisted on uniformity and exercised strict control.[129] Most of his restaurants had a similar design, a Southwestern architectural style that made them recognizable at a glance. Employees wore uniforms, and every restaurant in the chain received supplies from a central commissary. Inspectors visited frequently, and they promptly fired managers whose venues did not measure up to Harvey's standards.

Owners of lunch rooms and cafeterias recognized the advantages of chains early, and several companies developed them during the 1920s. The Harvey group never exceeded 40 restaurants, but Waldorf Lunch managed to establish 75 stores in Boston, Buffalo, Philadelphia, and other cities in the region. Baltimore Dairy Lunch built more than 100 stores.[130] John R. Thompson put together a 104-unit chain in Chicago and nearby cities, including Bloomington.

SANDWICH SHOPS

The sandwich shop, a kind of blue-collar lunch room, did well as a chain. White Castle, an organization founded in 1916 in Wichita, Kansas, was one of the most successful. Its stores consisted of little square structures made of enameled metal with a crenellated facade meant represent a castle. The buildings could be put up and taken down quickly, almost like a diner. White Castle's most important technical feature was the heavy sheet-iron grill on which nearly all cooking took place.[131] This type of grill, which was especially commonplace in Belgium and the Netherlands, allowed many types of food to be cooked on the same surface. This, of course, excluded soups and stews and more or less restricted the menu to fried foods, the most popular of which was the hamburger.

White Castle's success inspired many imitators, including White Tower of Milwaukee; Little Tavern of Louisville; White Tavern of Shelbyville, Tennessee;

Toddle House of Houston; Krystal of Chattanooga; White Huts of Toledo; and several lesser brands. Industry insiders referred to them collectively as "white boxes."[132] All had streamlined menus, and together they helped create fast food. Steak 'n Shake (which originated in Normal and is currently America's second oldest hamburger chain) embodied a variation on the white-box theme (see Chapter 5).

IMMIGRANTS AND ETHNIC RESTAURANTS

Prohibitionist, nativist, and anti-German sentiments may have put an end to continental eating and drinking establishments in Bloomington, but immigrants persisted in their ways in their own homes and various private clubs (e.g., the Hungarian Club, see Chapter 7). Immigrants also continued to own and operate local restaurants. This did not present a problem so long as the proprietors Americanized their menus and conformed to mainstream conventions. Consequently, Chinese, German, Greek, and other immigrant restaurateurs called their places "cafés" or "grills" and quietly went about their business. The concept of an ethnic restaurant had yet to take shape. The public singled out Chinese and French places as special, but other eateries catering to foreign tastes failed to register. That began to change in the 1930s when Italian-American restaurants acquired a following among non-Italians.[133] In Bloomington, German cuisine surfaced again in a restaurant setting after World War II, probably on account of demand from the legions of men and women whose service during the occupation gave them an opportunity to savor Central European dishes.

QUALITY CAFÉ

When Carl J. Loeseke, born in Borbeck, Germany in 1884, opened the Quality Restaurant in 1918, nothing about it hinted of German culture. By the time it closed 42 years later, Germanic identity was no longer a liability, and his old place was happily serving *schnitzles*, *spaetzle*, and red cabbage.[134]

Loeseke's restaurant, which was renamed the Quality Café, began as a curious mixture of "greasy spoon" and superior cookery. In part, it emulated the American diner. Chili, a dish that was very much a part of the nation's Depression era food culture, was on the menu, just as it was at several other Bloomington cafés.[135] Like a number of other downtown eateries, Carl kept his place open late at night and offered a "late supper special" of bacon or sausage, eggs, toast, and fried potatoes and coffee. For breakfast, he had more of the same, but by lunchtime the menu presented an alternative track. Guests now had a choice of plain and fancy sandwiches, among which the fanciest of all was Carl's Special

Triple-Decker Club. By dinnertime, everything was upmarket. The menu promised nothing but excellence and described what amounted to a Midwestern high cuisine of steaks and chops prepared from the "the finest meat obtainable."

The Quality always retained a touch of the continental. Loeseke brought his nephew, Chef Henry Luetkemeyer over from Germany, and put him in kitchen. Carl and Henry kept a stockpot simmering perpetually on the back of the stove and prepared Old Country favorites like the Quality's Saturday night exclusive, Navy Bean Soup, without ever hinting at its continental origins.

Quality Café Navy Bean Soup
INGREDIENTS – 1 pint Great Northern beans soaked in water overnight, 1 ham hock, 1 pint potatoes diced in ½ inch cubes, 3 – 4 ounces chopped onion, 2 – 3 slices of bacon diced fine, 2 tablespoons butter, 1 quart beef stock, small quantity of ham stock, ¼ – ½ cup cream. PREPARATION – Soak the beans in water overnight. . Cook with ham hock until beans are just done. Cook diced potatoes separately until done. In another pan, combine onion, bacon, and butter. Cook slowly until browned. Add flour to pick up grease. Combine beans, potatoes, and onion mixture. Add beef stock in quantity desired for thickness. Add ham stock to flavor. Salt to taste. Simmer for about an hour but do not overcook. Just before serving, add cream to taste and to create rich creamy texture.[136]

Likewise, the breaded pork cutlet, the Midwest's deep-fried approximation of *Weiner schnitzel*, appeared on the lunch menu as the thoroughly Americanized tenderloin sandwich. It survives to this day in the historically German areas of Illinois, Indiana, and Iowa where aficionados like to dress it with yellow mustard, lettuce, onions, and pickles and accompany it with French fries on the side.[137] At the Quality Café, Carl dolled up his breaded pork for dinnertime guests by covering it with a rich cream sauce.

Classical music accompanied dinner on Tuesday nights. Each week Carl prepared a special menu and piped in critically acclaimed orchestral recordings for what he called "Symphonic Hour." One of the earliest Symphonic Hour dinners served in 1940 began with fresh grapefruit hearts followed by "home-canned spiced apple salad." Entrees included Roast Prime Rib of Beef Au Jus, Fried Ham Steak with Country Gravy, and Fried Spring Chicken. French Fried or Whipped Potatoes and Buttered Peas or Asparagus Tips attended the entrees, and to cap the evening off there was White Cake or a Butterscotch Sundae.

The critics approved. Duncan Hines, one of America's foremost dining authorities and author of *Adventures in Good Eating* (1936), gave the Quality his seal of approval. Carl also earned a listing in the American Automobile Association's well-regarded travel guide.

Loeseke retired and turned the restaurant over to his son, Carl W. in the late 1940s. He completely remodeled the building, added a bake shop, and reopened it in 1949 as Karl's Quality Café, a frankly German-American restaurant and the first seen in McLean County for well over a generation. Under the main dining room, Karl's featured a *Rathskeller* where patrons could order from a special menu that included *Sauerbraten*, *Rouladen*, and other German dishes.

The Loesekes closed the Quality Café in 1960. Steve Crifasi of Springfield leased the building and opened Stevie's Latin Village, part of a small chain of Italian steakhouses. It lasted three years. Once it closed, Jan Loeseke, Carl W.'s wife, jumped back into the restaurant business and with six members of her bridge club opened The Terrace. It featured a "gourmet style" that revolved around such dishes as Beef Stroganoff and Chicken Divan and epitomized gastronomic sophistication in parts of the Midwest through most of the 1960s.[138] The Terrace also served a salad topped with German Wilted Lettuce Dressing. It had been a favorite for many years at the Quality Café. Jan purportedly turned down a request for the recipe from *Gourmet Magazine* but "scooped" the recipe to *The Daily Pantagraph's* food editor Lolita Driver after The Terrace closed.

Loeseke's German Wilted Lettuce Dressing
INGREDIENTS – ⅔ cup sour cream, ⅓ cup vinegar, 3 or 4 tablespoons sugar (depending on taste), ½ teaspoon salt, 1 bunch green onions or one medium onion, chopped fine, 4 – 6 strips of bacon, cut up and fried crisp. PREPARATION – Place all except the bacon in blender and beat well. At time of serving, put dressing on lettuce and toss. Add crisp bacon piping hot. Eat at once (dresses one head of lettuce; keeps in refrigerator for one week).[139]

GREEN MILL CAFÉ

The Green Mill, established about 1919 at 212 West Washington, was operated by a number of individuals over the years, including at least two Greek Americans.[140] One of them, John Krikos, described his menu as "strictly American." The restaurant, open 24 hours a day, seven days a week, dished out eggs, pancakes, waffles, soups and sandwiches. In addition, there were all the usual beverages, including beer, sodas, ice cream soda, and milk shakes. Still, Krikos described the Green Mill as "Bloomington's Finest Restaurant for the Discriminating" and the place "Where Epicureans Meet." The front cover of a menu, circa 1940, carried an excerpt from the poem *"Lucile"* by Owen Meredith

> We may live without poetry, music and art;
>
> We may live without conscience, and live without heart;
>
> We may live without friends; we may live without books,
>
> But civilized men cannot live without cooks.
>
> He may live without books – what is knowledge but grieving?
>
> He may live without hope – what is hope but deceiving,
>
> He may live without love – what is passion but pining?
>
> But where is the man who can live without dining?

Although the slogans and verse seem pompous, the Green Mill was not high faluting. To the contrary, it was a student hangout, a businessman's coffee shop, a place to have a bite to eat after the show – it all depended on the time of day. A 1939 remodeling transformed the dining room into a stunning example of modern design. It featured streamlined booths covered in red Leatherette and trimmed in bleached oak. An oval ceiling illuminated by indirect lighting in various color combinations capped the room. Krikos presented his customers with a bill of fare listing all of the usual café items, but the grilled fish, fish salads and grilled lamb chops represented Greek influences. Krikos did his own baking, and on Sundays he prepared an elaborate *Table d'hôte* (a *prix fixe* menu).

Greek-American restaurants nationwide did wonderfully creative things with the old idea of the sandwich, and the Green Mill was no exception. Krikos's triple decked sandwiches – most of them on toast with mayonnaise and pickle – were a specialty. His repertoire consisted in part of the Wesleyan Special, peanut butter layered over ham salad; the Friday Sandwich, a layer of salmon salad topped with a layer of tuna fish salad; the Appetizing Sandwich, a layer of hardboiled egg overlaid by Russian caviar; and the Green Mill Special, combining sliced chicken, olive salad, and bacon.

THE GRAND CAFÉ

The Grand Café, a Chinese eatery, wears the mantle of oldest restaurant in the city. It opened as the Grand Inn Café on the second floor of North Center on Courthouse Square around 1917.[141] Lum Bing, who left China in 1918 and eventually found his way to Bloomington by way of Chicago, purchased it in 1921 from two partners in the midst of a feud and eager to sell out. Lum Americanized his name to "Charlie Lum," and after several years, his son, Peter, joined the business. Peter's wife, Jill, arrived later. When the restaurant expanded and moved to street level at West Front in 1948, Peter took over as manager.

The Lums lived and worked in the building.[142] Their apartment was above the restaurant, and in the basement below they grew the bean sprouts needed in many of the dishes they prepared. Jill spent much of her time baking fruit pies and custards. Her daughter, Mabel Wu, recalled how she and her sister pitched in whenever they were not busy with schoolwork.

> I remember even when we were little my father would have boiled potatoes and the potatoes would have to be peeled and he would give us little butter knives to peel the skin off the boiled potatoes. My sister Mary and I, we canned peppers, we washed the bean sprouts, and we rolled the egg rolls and made the won ton. The almond cookies as well; they were all homemade.[143]

And, Mabel will never forget how her grandfather worked relentlessly until the day he died.

> My grandfather . . . always made the bread for the restaurant. The night before he would prepare it and the next morning after the yeast would rise . . . he would punch it down . . . . In the morning that was his job, he would make the rolls that would be baked that day for the restaurant. We always would have homemade rolls at the restaurant . . . . It always was my grandfather's job, and he also made the noodles. Our Chow Mein noodles – my grandfather always fried the noodles and we would have these big baskets that after the noodles were fried he would put them in and we had our own fresh noodles.[144]

When Mabel was a child during the 1950s and '60s, the Grand Cafe's dining area, a long, narrow room with a little lamp on each table, was often crowded, especially at lunchtime. Customers, many of them from the State Farm Insurance Company building a couple of blocks away, could order from either a Western or a Chinese menu. Most patrons asked for the Western menu. During the noon rush, perhaps seventy-five percent of the lunches served were Western style (entrée, vegetable, dessert, and beverage). The most popular items on the Chinese menu were Chop Suey and Egg Foo Yung. Jeannie Breitweiser, a childhood friend of Peter and Jill Lum's daughter, Mary, recalled that a popular Grand Café snack among kids downtown on a shopping expedition was a plate of French Fries, an order of egg rolls, and a ten-cent bottle of Coke.[145]

Peter Lum growing sprouts at the Grand Café in 1946. Courtesy of
The Pantagraph.

The Grand Café remained at its Front Street location until 1972. That year the city cleared the south side of the street to make way for the McLean County Law and Justice Center. Lum, having decided he was too old to start over again, turned the business over to his wife's brother, Pong Chiu who had come from Hong Kong two years earlier to help with the business. Under Pong's direction, the Grand took up temporary quarters on North Main while building a new facility at the restaurant's present location on the southeast corner of Main and Locust streets. The Grand moved into its new quarters in 1976. Pong's son, Ike, a fourth generation proprietor, currently runs the business.

The Grand Café was not the first Chinese restaurant in the city. The Bloomington directory for 1908 listed the Fong Chinese Chop Suey Restaurant located above 208 West Front, and an undated program for the Majestic Theater advertised the Empress Inn situated at the same address. In 1909, yet another Chinese place, the Hong San, opened for business at 216½ East Front.[146]

If the name "Grand Café" does not sound particularly Chinese, Charlie Lum and his predecessors intended it that way. From the very beginning, menus in Chinese-owned eating places consisted primarily of American café foods – steaks, chops, ham and eggs, cream pies.[147] The reason almost certainly was prejudice. The Chinese knew Americans mistrusted Asian foods, and they were aware of rumors circulating about Chinese people eating rats. *The Daily Pantagraph* reported in 1896 that a local hooligan tossed a dead rat into a Chinese laundry.[148] The article described the ensuing fracas and noted with approval that it ended with the laundrymen getting their heads thumped.

The few Chinese dishes Charlie Lum carried on his menu were probably unlike anything he had eaten in China. He was, after all, a relatively inexperienced cook, and most of the ingredients he had to work with were not Asian. Very few Chinese who opened restaurants in the United States had any training in food preparation. Most were poor working-class men who, through trial and error, tried to recreate the tastes they remembered from home.[149] The dishes they prepared consisted mainly of rice or noodles supplemented with a few vegetables and a bit of meat. They quickly learned that Americans regarded meat as the centerpiece of a meal, and cooks responded by preparing meals containing much more animal protein than they themselves were accustomed to eating. The result was Chinese-American cooking or, if you will, American(ized)-Chinese cooking.[150]

Nowadays at the Grand Café, traditional American foods no longer dominate the menu, but the Chinese dishes on the list remain for the most part Americanized forms. Supposedly sophisticated restaurant goers usually fail to understand this. Having patronized Chinese restaurants in Chicago, New York, or San Francisco, or perhaps having visited China, they often scoff at mention of the Grand and denounce it as "unauthentic." Ike Chiu knows better. He has traveled the world and has resided in China and is familiar with Chinese cuisine of every denomination.[151] He has experimented with his own menu occasionally by adding *Kung Pao* and Szechwan dishes that Americans generally enjoy. However, adding new dishes has required subtracting old ones, and that has never sat well with the Grand's regulars. As Ike has come appreciate, his best customers are not interested in genuine Chinese cuisine. They savor food true to the Chinese-American tradition, dishes authentic to the style of the Lums. Ike calls it the "Midwestern version of Chinese food."

Old-school Chinese-American cuisine is no longer as commonplace as it once was. Occasionally, Ike hears customers complain that on a business trip or vacation they were unable to find dishes like those served at the Grand. This comes as no surprise; many of the recipes used today date back more than 80 years. Few Chinese restaurants founded before the federal Immigration Act of 1924 survive, and the vast majority reflects the Szechwan Chicken / Hunan Pork era of Chinese cooking that was ushered in by the Immigration Act of 1965. It encouraged a fresh influx of Chinese immigrants, which subsequently resulted in a proliferation of Asian restaurants and a demand for foods similar to those served in the Far East. Nowadays, one can hardly find American Chop Suey joints outside of the upper Midwest.

Ike still makes and sells a great deal of Chop Suey, especially to his lunchtime crowd. Regulars maintain a close watch on quality and are sensitive to any change. Ike once tried to make sweet and sour sauce, a job normally performed by his aunt. She was ready to retire, but the only recipe she had was in her head. Ike did his best to learn her formula, yet sometimes his sauce came out a shade darker than hers, and customers noticed immediately. Ike swears there was no flavor difference, but patrons complained anyway. Such conservatism tends to be the rule among the regular patrons of those very few Bloomington-area restaurants that have been around long enough to have served them as children.

THE LUCCA GRILL

Just as the Grand Café has maintained a kind of museum for the taste buds, the Lucca Grill on East Market in downtown Bloomington has preserved a barroom barely changed since its doors first opened in 1936.[152] Today's visitors delight in its ambiance. *The Washington Post* dubbed it "the world's most famous bar." A *New York Times* writer called it "a delightful old-time saloon." One reviewer described it as a relic from a by-gone age:

> Step into the Lucca Grill and step back in time. This is an old-style tavern where kids are welcome. The old-fashioned feeling comes from storefront windows, an ornate tin ceiling, a long, friendly bar, fourth-generation help and nearly seven decades worth of memorabilia on the walls. You couldn't reproduce this place if you tried. It's authentic, original and uniquely Bloomington.[153]

The Lucca, originally named Lucca Italian Restaurant, takes its name from the city in Italy where founders Fred and John Baldini grew up. Fred came to the United States in 1894 at age eighteen. He sold statuary and advertising specialties for several years. State Farm Insurance bought its first advertising materials, a supply of calendars, from Fred. His brother John lived in Somerset, Kentucky where he operated a confectionary. In the midst of the Depression, John moved himself and his equipment to Bloomington. He and Fred bought an old plumbing shop a short time later and used the confectioners gear to outfit the building as a restaurant.

The Lucca originated at a time when Italian restaurants were becoming popular nationwide. Nineteenth-century Italian restaurateurs, most of them from the north of Italy, had pretended to be French, an identity infinitely more fashionable than Italian.[154] Under French guise, they introduced spaghetti (e.g., Franco-American Spaghetti), tomato sauce (i.e., sauce Bolognese), and minestrone to American tables. Southern Italians appeared on the scene in large numbers early in the twentieth century. Some opened boarding houses for fellow immigrants and then became restaurateurs. Others graduated from the ranks of kitchen help or waiter. Their restaurants attracted "bohemians" from a variety of backgrounds. During the 1920s, for example, Gonfarone's Restaurant in New York City thrived on a clientele of artists, writers, and political radicals. They liked the food and wine, but Italian cafés were uniquely animated, and freethinkers were attracted to the gaiety and hedonism of Latin culture as much as the cuisine itself. Chefs in the meantime adjusted to the commercial realities of industrial life and reduced slow-paced, multi-course Italian meals to just a few plates offered in quick succession. This made the Italian restaurants Italian-American, and helps explain why they grew to be immensely popular well before pizza became a national sensation.

The Baldinis brought the first pizza oven to Central Illinois in 1953 and refashioned their menu, but this did nothing to dampen the atmosphere of conviviality that pervaded the Lucca from day one. Fred Baldini died in 1961, John in 1972, but a second generation, Fred's sons, Charles (better known as "Tot") and John, kept the ball rolling. Their unflagging involvement in community affairs, their charitable work, and their enthusiasm for sports helped turn the Lucca into a local institution. It continues to prosper to this day under the ownership of Chuck Williams.

Over the years, the Lucca has sold a lot of pizza. It has served many thousands of "Steak on Italian" sandwiches and tons of pasta made the way the Odorizzis, another Bloomington family, made it in their little shop many years ago. But still, very much in the tradition of the early twentieth-century Italian restaurant, people go to the Lucca for the local color as much as the food. Members of the Democratic Party, a sorely outnumbered but dogged minority in McLean County, have hung out there for many years. High school and college sport heroes of days gone by have been a fixture. Local barbershop quartets have dropped by after rehearsals for decades and have rarely failed to burst into song after taking a round or two of refreshments. Recalling the sentiments that prevailed in Bloomington's nineteenth-century German eating saloons, a wall plaque presented to the Baldini brothers in the 1940s by a group of businessmen reads, "This room is dedicated to Good Fellows, . . . who make drinking a pleasure and achieve contentment long before capacity . . . ."[155]

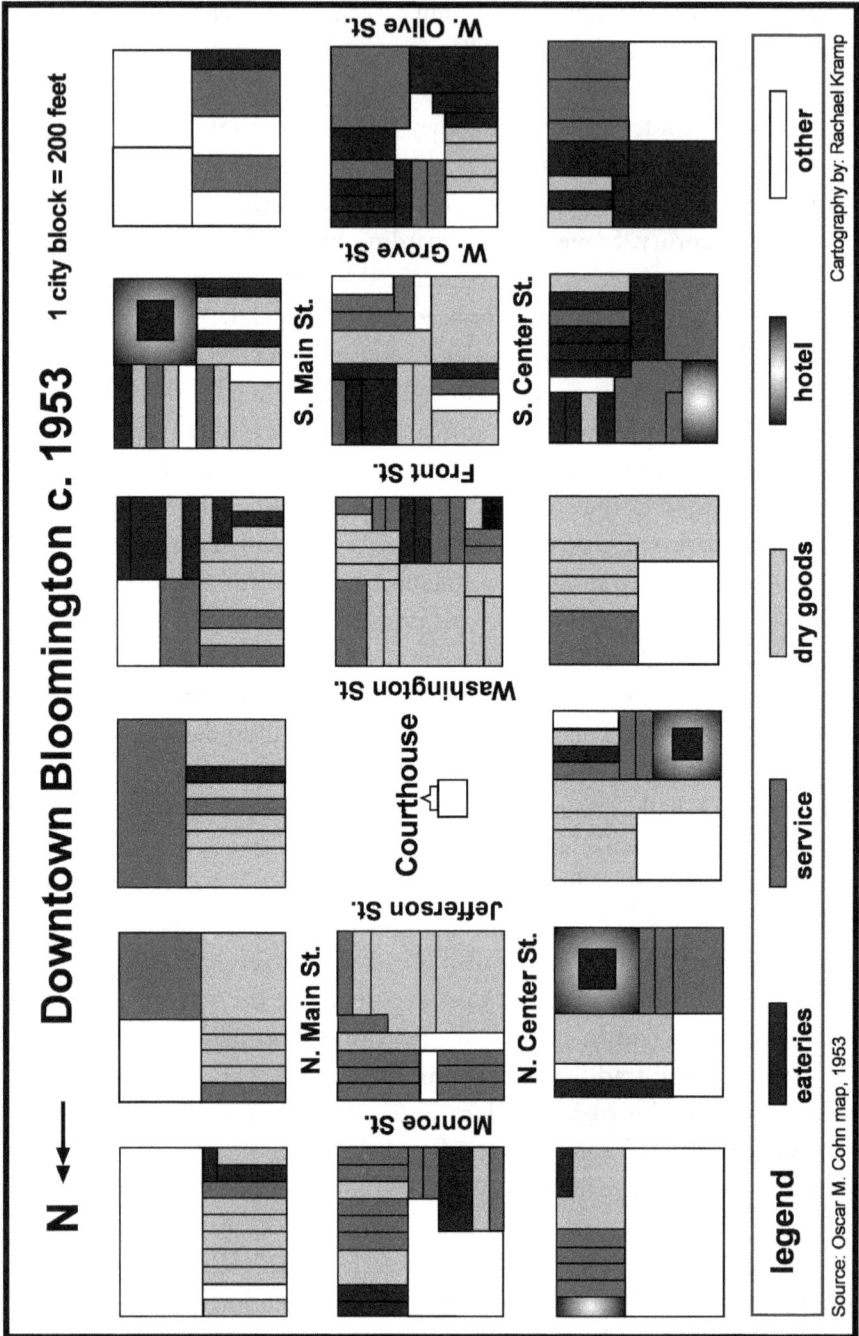

Map Key – Downtown Food and Beverage Places, c. 1953

Downtown Bloomington Food and Beverage Places, 1953

North Main Street
105 - Fannie May Candy Co.
207 - Grassfield Jefferson Cafeteria and Bakery
*314 - Sprengel's Fine Foods and Grocery
405 - The Copa Lounge Tavern
425 - Hoopey's Men's Grill and Restaurant
426 - Karl's Quality Café

South Main Street
105 - Miles Tavern
109 - Howard Kelley Food Shop and Restaurant
117 - Roy L. Wiley Tavern
201 - A. Brockhouse & Sons Grocery
203 - National Wine and Liquor Store
205 - Baker's Hamburger Inn
209 - Steak 'n Shake Restaurant
214 - Omar Bakery

North Center Street
*206 - Peter Frisch and Sons Tavern
208 - John R. Thompson Restaurant Co.
318 - The Alhambra Tavern
320 - M. Capodice & Sons Wholesale Produce

South Center Street
105 - Sweet Shoppe
107 - Eseki Day Tavern
109½ - Schultz Market Grocery
115 - Gene O. Lewis Tavern
*201 - Watkins Distributing Unit Food Products
203 - Senate Billiards and Tap Room
205 - Ryburn's Café Restaurant
218 - Darling & Co. Fish

West Monroe Street
102 - Midget Tavern
*201 - Century Club Tavern
216 - The Spot Tavern

East Monroe Street
*113 - Steak 'n Shake Restaurant

West Jefferson Street
201 - Illinois Hotel Dining Room

West Washington Street
*212 - Green Mill Café Restaurant
*213 - Hotel Tilden Hall Coffee Shop
*219 - Hotel Tilden Hall Tap Room

West Front Street
104 - Murphy's Buffet Tavern
105 - Federal Café
106 - Grand Café
*107 - The Empire Tavern
*108 - Circle Bar Tavern
115 - Duncan Wine and Liquor Store
202 - The Sweet Shop
204 - Blue Bell Tavern
208 - Schenk Bros. Tavern

East Front Street
101 - Eisner Food Stores No. 1 Grocery
106 - Twenty Grand Tap Rm. Tavern
108½ - Busy Bee Grill Restaurant
114 - 16 - Servrite Steak House Restaurant
*117 - Shierry's Grocery and Meats
118 - Pastry Shop Bakers

West Grove Street
106 - Connaway's Tavern
*207 - Mrs. Mimnie Bicknell Restaurant
209 - Bloomington Distillery

East Grove Street
112 - The Jolly Roger Tavern, Fiesta Room Restaurant

* = eatery not included in map

Downtown Bloomington's restaurants, bars, and other food-related businesses, c. 1953, about 20 years before State Farm's headquarters moved to the east side.

CHAPTER 4 – THE PAGEANT OF COOKERY MEETS THE GREAT DEPRESSION

When the United States entered the First World War its European allies desperately needed food.[1] To muster sufficient supplies, food consumption within American homes for the first time became a matter of government concern. Through the U.S. Food Administration (USFA), federal officials enlisted the help of home economists and charged them with teaching families how to conserve wheat, lard, sugar, and other essential commodities.[2] After the war, home economists acquired positions in education, agricultural research, and food-related industries and proceeded to address nearly every aspect of food and nutrition as an applied science.[3] Its efficacy was tested almost immediately in response to falling commodity prices and a federal policy that called for keeping white farm families on the land by improving their living conditions. At land-grant institutions such as the University of Illinois, home economists went into rural areas as Extension advisers (as the women who served in these roles were formally known) to teach homemakers about human nutrition, sanitation, food preservation, household budgeting, and the latest household appliances.[4]

Then came the Great Depression. It derailed expectations that rural women would soon be working in modern, scientific kitchens. Lack of income required farmers to minimize their dependence on costly commercial products, and townsfolk also had to stretch their dollars. The economy forced scores of independent grocers unable to match the low prices offered by the chains to go out of business.

Even before the Depression, packaged foods, brand names, and self-service had undermined the position of the local grocer. Through advertising, producers spoke directly to consumers about the virtues of their products.[5] As the twentieth century got underway, the press made Americans aware of how little they were being told and how dirty and adulterated industrial food products had become. Advertisers responded by inventing lovable characters like the Gerber Baby and the Jolly Green Giant and striving to make names like Kellogg, Kraft, and Heinz instantly recognized and trusted.[6] Smaller companies throughout the country followed suit to create successful regional brands.

WORLD WAR I

When the United States entered World War I early in 1917, the people of McLean County generally welcomed the move and wanted to become involved. Young men enlisted in the military. Others demonstrated their patriotism by contributing money. When officials in Washington declared dietary sacrifices essential to victory, everybody changed the way they ate.

FOOD CONSERVATION MEASURES

The argument, enthusiastically endorsed by editorial writers, insisted that as important as sending soldiers to Europe was, the United States played a no less critical role in shipping the commodities its allies needed to go on fighting. To keep food flowing to the troops and to feed civilians in war-torn regions, Americans had to reduce their consumption at home. The press portrayed it as an emergency, and conservation almost overnight became a patriotic duty.

The prospect of actively becoming involved in the struggle overseas by campaigning for conservation at home excited Lena Ewing, a Bloomington socialite married to local attorney Spencer Ewing. She volunteered her services to the McLean County Red Cross, and under her leadership it assumed a leading role in implementing federal food policy locally.[7]

Mrs. Ewing found no lack of cooperation. By the end of May, a month or so after she stepped forward, the Red Cross received pledges from no less than 45 civic and religious groups eager to assist in food conservation. This put the local Red Cross and its supporters well ahead of the USFA. Indeed, by the time the government program was ready to begin operating in July, Bloomington residents were already learning how to can fruits and vegetables in support of the war effort.[8] Mrs. Ewing brought in University of Illinois instructor Naomi Newburn, whose lectures about food preservation drew large audiences.[9] Later that summer, another instructor, Emma Wright, presented weekly demonstrations of wartime cookery and talked about how to comply with conservation edicts coming out of Washington.

Youngsters were especially keen about becoming involved. Ewing harnessed their enthusiasm by offering a prize for the best essay explaining why the county needed a full-time adviser to teach conservation in the kitchen. When she subsequently asked school children to write about conserving flour, Esther Farian, a Bloomington eighth-grader, responded with a paper listing 435 ways to prepare potatoes.[10] Earlier that year several high school and college groups prepared exhibits for the annual meeting of the Illinois Farmers' Institute in Bloomington.[11] Normal High School students arranged plates of meat and meat substitutes to illustrate conservation methods. Bloomington High School showed how to reduce sugar consumption. A group from Illinois Wesleyan exhibited alternatives to wheat, while Illinois State Normal University (ISNU) students demonstrated how use less fat in the kitchen.

By March, calls for economy from officials in Washington were becoming shrill, and directives calling for wheat conservation grew more stringent.[12] The Administration called upon homemakers to serve one wheatless meal a day and to refrain from using wheat altogether at least once a week. The Illinois State Council of Defense named Wednesday as the state's official day without wheat. The Council urged the use of alternative grains (barley, corn, oats, rice, and rye) and pushed for greater consumption of beans and potatoes. Almost overnight cookbooks appeared filled with instructions for preparing bean pots, potato breads, rice casseroles, and a variety of other no-wheat and reduced-wheat items. *Keep the War Foods Cooking*, published by the Illinois Farmers' Institute, provided advice for using leftovers and suggested such recipes as American Rice (white rice with green or red pepper, tomato, and ground cooked ham), Creole Rice with Chicken, Victory Mush, Scalloped Hominy, and Bean Croquettes.

Bean Croquettes

INGREDIENTS – 1 cup bean puree, 1 tablespoon onion or green pepper, 1 teaspoon fat, ½ cup milk, 1 cup bread crumbs, 1½ cups skimmed milk, salt, pepper. PREPARATION – Make into croquettes and fry in deep fat.[13]

The USFA addressed wheat conservation further by charging citizens to eat less cake and pastry. It also recommended that homemakers order any shop bread in advance so that each day their baker would know exactly how much dough to prepare.[14]

In addition to directives regarding wheat, the USFA issued instructions concerning meat, milk, fats, sugar, and fuel consumption. To spare meat, authorities cautioned consumers to eat beef, mutton, or pork no more than once a day. The Council of Defense designated Tuesday Illinois's official meatless day.[15] Indicative of its patriotic fervor, the Council went a step further and declared Saturday a day without pork. Poultry consumption escaped restriction because at the time it was difficult to ship great distances and, hence, was regarded as a local food. The Illinois Farmers' Institute called it the "meatless meat" and regarded dishes such as Goose Scalloped with Hominy as a suitable "war food."

Goose Scalloped with Hominy

INGREDIENTS – 2 cups cooked goose, 2 cups cooked hominy, ¼ cup bread crumbs browned in goose fat, 1½ cup gravy or white sauce, salt, pepper. PREPARATION – Cover bottom of baking dish with hominy. Add a layer of goose meat and half of the gravy, another layer of hominy, meat, and gravy. Put crumbs over the top and bake until they are brown.[16]

Milk conservation, in the view of the Administration, was more a matter of using every drop rather than cutting back consumption. For cooking, buttermilk and sour milk would do. With respect to fats, federal officials identified Americans as "the world's greatest wasters" and demanded that every household save at least one-third of an ounce of grease and other fatty substances per day.[17] Citizens were called upon to reduce their consumption of fried foods and to reserve butter for table use only. Saving sugar would be accomplished by consuming less candy and sweet drinks. To save fuel, government asked everyone to cook and heat with wood instead of coal whenever possible. Other suggestions included eating smaller portions, doing without "that fourth meal," and preaching to children the "Gospel of the clean plate." In addition, the USFA advised homemakers to use more perishable items, especially fruits and vegetables, and to reduce the strain on transportation by purchasing from local growers.

McLean County residents became more serious and less tolerant of grumbling as government's demands for sacrifice grew more insistent. The Red Cross opened a wartime kitchen on North Main in downtown Bloomington and had University of Illinois instructors demonstrating conservation cooking twice a day. Instructors showed how to use fish instead of meat, syrups instead of sugar, and vegetable fats instead of animal fats. They demonstrated how to make "liberty breads," using adjunct grains and flours instead of wheat. These programs drew overflow crowds, and for the most part, the administration's rules were obeyed without question.[18] As a result, sugar consumption locally was reduced to two pounds per person per month, wheat bread disappeared from local tables, and county residents wasted almost no fat.

Nevertheless, problems arose at harvest time when women had to cook for gangs of ravenous threshermen. These were often neighbors, accompanied by wives and children ready to help out and serve the noon meal. Preparations often began before daybreak. Breads, cakes, and pies normally went into the oven first. Beef roasts or meat loaves went in later in the morning. USFA rules created turmoil by prohibiting baking in advance. People argued. Were cakes made according to wartime recipes any good? Was it permissible to bake pies? Could meat be served to threshermen? The answers depended largely on the men involved and how much patriotism their hungry stomachs could tolerate, but watchful citizens reported few violations of official strictures.[19]

THE HOME IMPROVEMENT ASSOCIATION

Much of the work required to put conservation into practice in McLean County fell to Clara Brian, a young woman hired by Lena Ewing on behalf of the state. Isabel Bevier, nutritionist and home economist at the University of Illinois, had met with Lena and explained to her how Cooperative Extension, a new service offered by the university, could advance the cause of food savings by providing a dedicated home adviser to any county willing to pay a portion of the cost. Lena took the idea to Bloomington's Household Science Club and convinced its members to help her organize a Home Improvement Association.[20] Extension advisers were already working through Home Improvement Associations in several Illinois counties. Lena's goal was to institute one in McLean County and enroll a membership of least 50 women from each of its townships. The association would charge each member a fee of one dollar per year, and in that way acquire the money needed to pay for an adviser.

The plan ran into some resistance from prospective members who feared government surveillance and unfriendly criticism. As one housewife put it, "I don't want any strange women snooping 'round my kitchen, telling me what to do."[21] Such objections notwithstanding, the Home Improvement Association registered 1,500 members by April 1918, providing Ewing and her friends sufficient money to engage Clara Brian.

Brian, an Illinois native with a degree in home economics from Bloomington's Illinois Wesleyan University (IWU), began her work in June.[22] She started by addressing the difficulties experienced trying to make bread from flours other than wheat. Throughout the month, she visited one township after another conducting "Wheatless Bread" classes and providing demonstrations. These required getting out of bed before dawn, preparing dough, and assembling packets of ingredients for use later in the day. Clara traveled by car (a Ford Model T donated by the Rotary Club), and now and again she had to stop to punch down dough for a second rising. Once she arrived at her destination, everything needed to be unpacked, including her oven-ready dough. A demonstration ordinarily took one hour. Then, pack up, back into the car, and off to repeat the lesson in another township that afternoon. Clara hired a secretary, and she helped. The work went on six days a week and often into the evenings.

Potato War Bread

INGREDIENTS – ⅔ cup sweet milk, 1 cup potato, 2 cups flour, 1 teaspoon salt, 1 teaspoon sugar, ½ yeast cake. PREPARATION – Heat milk to boiling, then cool to lukewarm. Bake or boil potatoes, then mash or rice. Dissolve yeast in the milk. Make a sponge of the yeast, milk, salt, sugar, mashed or riced potatoes, and ⅓ of the flour. Beat well and let stand overnight to rise. In the morning, add the balance of flour. Let rise again until double in bulk, then mold into a loaf. Let rise again until double in bulk, then bake 40 minutes in moderate oven (a little more flour is required if potatoes are not mealy).[23]

Lessons changed monthly. In July, Clara turned from the topic of bread to the subject of "Meatless Dinners." She taught "Sugarless Desserts" in August. In September, she dealt with proper nutrition, lectured about the advantages of serving children a hot lunch at school, and demonstrated how to pack a wholesome cold lunch.[24]

All the while Brian was crisscrossing the countryside conducting demonstrations, the residents of Bloomington kept busy with a Municipal Canning Kitchen.[25] It opened in the Pantagraph Building in middle of June 1918 and closed at the end of August. During this period, approximately 1,200 people came to hear lectures and watch demonstrations. Local experts taught about canning and dehydrating fruits and vegetables, canning meat, pickle making, and the preparation of sauerkraut. Residents with surplus vegetables donated them for the demonstrations. Some donated jars. People who brought their own produce and jars received individual canning instructions. Alternatively, a person could send produce and jars ahead and have the canning done by volunteers who charged one-half of the goods they canned for the benefit of local charities. The Municipal Canning Kitchen, all told, put up over 1,100 jars and bottles of produce.

After the canning season ended, the kitchen sponsored demonstrations of wartime cooking. Grace Taylor, who for a time was Clara Brian's assistant, taught breadmaking. Mabel Sill of Normal made sugarless and wheatless cakes covered with sugarless icings. Her lessons drew especially big audiences because area residents were loath to give up cake, yet they feared being branded as unpatriotic if they served it.[26]

In October, the great influenza pandemic of 1918 descended on Central Illinois, and all war-related programming ceased. Clara Brian quit teaching and went to work as the dietitian for an improvised hospital set up at Bloomington Country Club.[27] Members of the Home Improvement Association helped care for thousands of flu victims at this emergency facility, laboring for two weeks and serving approximately 3,600 meals to patients and staff before the outbreak subsided.

THE HOME BUREAU

The influenza emergency ended in November about the same time the war ended. Homemakers gladly returned to baking wheat breads and serving meat to their families three times a day, and since nobody had the slightest interest anymore in hearing about sugarless cakes or cooking with a smaller amount of fat, the Home Improvement Association needed to shift gears or become irrelevant.

The staff at the Cooperative Extension barely missed a beat. With the influenza fresh in everyone's mind, lessons resumed in December with Clara Brian teaching "Food in Relation to Health." A few weeks later she received word that the Home Improvement Association henceforth would be called "the Home Bureau," and that as such, its mission was to be the historic mission of the Home Economics Movement, a nineteenth-century group of reformers with a deep faith in science and technology as the keys to a better society. Ellen Richards, a leading figure in the movement, believed improved diet was crucial to curing many of America's social ills, and given her credentials in the study of food adulteration and water contamination and the chemistry of cooking and digestion, policymakers listened.[28] Working in concert with home economists at the U.S. Department of Agriculture and in academia, university Extension advisers like Clara Brian would teach rural women the fundamentals of science and economy. This new knowledge would enable homemakers to work more effectively, manage budgets more effectively, and better navigate the pitfalls of consumer culture.

DIET AND NUTRITION

The progressive goals of home economists were difficult to discern in Home Bureau lesson titles like "Quick Breads," "The Cooking of Cereals and Other Starchy Foods," "Table Service," and "The How and Why of Candy Making," but when Clara Brian lectured about meal planning her audience received straight-forward instruction in the infant science of nutrition. It originated as a field of scientific investigation in the 1870s as scientists struggled to measure the carbohydrate, fat, and protein content of foods and to determine how much of these substances the body required. Such questions acquired strategic importance during World War I following the shocking admission by Lewis B. Hershey, head of the Draft Board, that approximately one-third of the men rejected for military service were turned away on account of physical conditions caused by malnutrition.[29]

Nutritional shortcomings among America's children about that time showed up in stunted growth, a high incidence of underweight bodies, and chronic illnesses. Seasonal hunger continued to be a problem in rural areas, including McLean County. Winter diets on farms in the early 1920s consisted largely of pork, wheat, and corn, insufficiently supplemented with cellared roots and tubers, dried beans, and various pickles and preserves. Clara Brian taught her

Home Bureau classes that the tired feeling at the end of winter popularly known as "spring fever" was due to diets lacking sufficient fruits and vegetables.[30] She insisted homemakers needed to provide them to their children not only when they were in season, but year around. Clara found herself repeatedly having to preach the virtues of cow's milk. Nutritionists recommended it, but many parents questioned its safety. Some simply did not think of milk as a fit beverage; others could not afford it. Brian discovered that for whatever reason, less than half of the McLean County children polled in 1919 drank milk regularly. Twenty-one percent did not drink milk at all.[31]

Brian made food and nutrition her chief concern during the years 1930 and '31. With the Depression worsening, her lectures titles included "Some Common Nutritional Problems" and asked such questions as "Am I Giving My Family the Right Kind and Amount of Food for Body Building?"[32] Clara taught her students how to score their own diets and in general she felt audiences took her lectures about diet and nutrition to heart. By 1940, she estimated that 97 percent of the children in the area were drinking milk.[33] A survey of 438 Home Bureau members conducted in February 1931 indicated many had come to recognize the nutritional importance of fresh produce.[34] When asked to list any fruits family members ate the previous day, 320 respondents listed apples, 203 listed oranges, and 157 listed grapefruits. Brian's survey showed that the most popular and almost universally served vegetable was the potato. After that came lettuce and tomatoes, both served the previous day in nearly half of the households she sampled.[35] One woman who had faithfully attended Brian's talks brought to her office a "Home Bureau Baby." The woman's previous children had been frail. This child was robust and rosy cheeked. The woman felt certain it was adherence to Brian's teachings that made the difference.[36]

THE SCIENTIFIC KITCHEN

In addition to teaching meal planning and preparation, Brian taught health and sanitation, accounting, textiles, and a course on household equipment and management.[37] The latter topics were her favorites, especially as they applied to the kitchen.

Efficiency in the kitchen had been a theme of Bloomington's Household Science Club, the group that helped Lena Ewing organize the Home Improvement Association. Whether the Household Science Club's fascination with domestic science was originally inspired by Sarah Davis remains to be established, but from a broader perspective the notion that domestic work warranted scientific scrutiny took shape nationally as a side effect of industrialization.[38] As factories proliferated, households became less concerned with producing things and more focused on purchase and consumption. Domestic science dawned as a field dedicated to addressing questions about homemaking in this new environment. The Morrill Act of 1862 prompted schools such as Illinois Industrial University (soon to become the University of Illinois) to offer courses in domestic arts and sciences. The idea, as explained in the previous chapter, was to make women's work the equal of men's in terms of its intellectual worth and dignity. Much of the reform revolved around cooking. The task was to bring a high level of intelligence to the kitchen and make meal preparation as rational as modern manufacturing.[39]

By the 1920s, the idea of the intelligent, progressive homemaker had captured the imagination of metropolitan America.[40] Popular design was all about simplicity and efficiency. Kitchen layout was modeled after a railroad dining car or a ship's galley and was informed by time-motion studies to minimize steps and eliminate wasted time. A powerful influence on design beginning around 1915 and continuing through the early 1920s was the germ theory of illness. Once domestic science became aware of germs, kitchens needed to be absolutely antiseptic and laboratory-like. Standards called for bright, well-vented rooms with ample, easy-to-clean work surfaces. Experts wanted everything white – white walls, white floors (ideally tile), white cabinets, and white appliances. Designers relented in the mid-1920s and allowed a return to color (e.g., yellow walls, green trim, a blue stove, all mixed with white accents), but hygienic concerns continued to be heard in demands for sanitary materials such as porcelain for sinks and stoves.

The most important thing about the modern, scientific kitchen in Clara Brian's estimation was its potential for social good. Her course entitled "Equipment and Household Management" showed Home Bureau members the latest household apparatus and reviewed the advantages of various gadgets. Its purpose was to make homemakers realize that modern appliances could save them significant chunks of time and labor. This would free women currently bogged down in drudgery to devote more of themselves to family and community. Far from being a selfish act, modernization was a woman's duty.[41] This made the kitchen something of a gender issue, especially on the farm, where men wanted the latest machinery working their fields and and out in the barn, but were unconcerned about out-of-date home appliances, no matter how poor their working condition.[42]

This award-winning kitchen, named "the most efficient" in the county in 1927, belonged to Mrs. Claude King of Carlock, Illinois. Photo by Clara Brian.

Brian addressed farmers' lack of interest in domestic conditions by putting together a number of special events. In 1919, she announced "Household Equipment Week." She asked appliance dealers and stores selling housewares to create special window displays for the week of June twenty-third. These displays would feature the newest labor-saving devices in their show rooms. Brian proclaimed in a series of concurrent lectures that no house in McLean County should be without running water, a power wash machine, a mangle or Simplex iron for pressing clothes, and a dish drier.[43] During the autumn of 1920, Brian organized five "equipment tours." The first four visited a total of 48 homes in 28 townships.[44] The fifth went straight to Champaign County and the home of Illinois State Senator Henry Dunlap, a new three-story brick mansion equipped with the very latest in home appliances. Nearly 500 people car-pooled on these jaunts, which altogether covered more than 450 miles. On each tour, participants inspected examples of modern lighting, home heating, hot water heaters, electric and gas mangles, washing machines, vacuum cleaners, chemical toilets, portable smoke houses, dumb waiters, and poultry houses. They looked at plumbing and plumbing fixtures, sinks, cabinets, shelving, stoves, and iceboxes. A letter to

The Daily Pantagraph criticized Brian's tours as crass exercises in consumerism and pointed out that Home Bureau members visited only the wealthiest homes.[45] The newspaper's editors, who had given the excursions ample and enthusiastic coverage, expressed no such concerns. For her part, Brian collected figures from appliance and houseware retailers and was pleased to find that the sale of certain labor-saving items, including "power machines" for home use (small electric generators), wash machines, steam pressure cookers, and fireless cookers, had increased sharply from 1919 through 1920.[46]

THE PAGEANT OF COOKERY

Brian carried on her modernization crusade for many years and continued to come up with fresh ideas for publicizing it. One of her most engaging was "The Pageant of Cookery," a three-day event staged in 1923 that drew 7,500 spectators.[47] The pageant took place in an empty Bloomington warehouse and was financed in part by the proceeds of cafeteria sales to those attending the event. The idea originated from conversations between Brian and Home Bureau members in various townships. Their discussions developed into a plan for all 26 units in the county to cooperate in putting together a colossal show about cooking and the history of food preparation from prehistoric times to the present day. Units would erect booths and exhibit materials that illustrated the eating habits of various times and places. The exhibits would show the foods people ate, the fuels they used to cook, the utensils and storage containers they employed, even the clothes that homemakers of the period wore around the house. The displays would represent water sources and transportation devices and their affects on diet and nutrition. Home Bureau officers got the ball rolling by visiting the Bloomington Public Library, consulting with its staff, and creating an exhibit outline. Library personnel helped unit members acquire the historical and ethnographic information they needed to flesh out their particular contribution to the pageant.

The plan was simple in outline. It divided all of human history into four periods: "Prehistoric," "Ancient," "Middle Ages," and "Modern." A number of cultures would represent each period. For example, the scriptwriters called for "Heidelberg man" and "Cave dwellers after the discovery of fire," to represent prehistory. Egypt, Judea, and Greece stood for ancient civilization. Rome, the "Monastic Period," "France at the time of Katherine di Medici," and "England at the time of Elizabeth" were to capture "the Middle Ages." To help represent these and other traditions, members staffing the booths clothed themselves or miniature figures in typical costumes. In the booth devoted to contemporary Chinese cooking, for instance, some women wore costumes emblematic of the ladies of the house while others donned servants' outfits. Food for the booth came from the Grand Café, Bloomington's Chinese restaurant. The display featuring the cookery of India differentiated between high-caste and low-caste diets and was staffed by Home Bureau members costumed in "Brahman" and "Mohammedan" attire.

Several booths represented American foodways historically and regionally. The members of one unit portrayed Puritan cookery; others demonstrated cooking during the American Revolution, the traditions of the Pennsylvania Dutch, and the way Kentuckians ate at the time of Lincoln. A booth covered mid-nineteenth-century Southern cookery and another displayed the American kitchen of the late nineteenth century. Finally, the pageant showed a modern kitchen containing a nicely set table attended by two women garbed in crisp white outfits.

The setting, intended as a model of efficiency, contained all of the latest appliances and gadgets. It featured a combination stove heated by both coal and electricity and an enameled icebox. The work area was equipped with a pressure cooker, a new device that could cook a chicken in a mere 20 minutes. The kitchen contained a bread mixer and a vacuum ice cream freezer, and included a sink placed high enough for comfort and within a step or two of the stove, just as home economists advised. The table at the center of the exhibit held dishes representing breakfast, dinner, and supper. Rolled oats, biscuits, fried potatoes, bacon, eggs, fruit, and coffee occupied the section of the table set for breakfast. The portion reserved for dinner held servings of bean soup, crackers, carrots, cabbage, slaw, sweet potatoes, mashed potatoes, pork, beef, beets, pickles, butter, jelly, bread, gooseberry pie, cream, and coffee. Supper's dishes included cold meat, baked potatoes, apple butter, canned peaches, two kinds of cake, bread, butter, and tea. Placards placed on the table displayed the number of daily Calories nutritionists prescribed for men, women, and children.

The almost clinical or scientific appearance of the modern kitchen contrasted sharply with the grayish, out-dated look of the adjacent booth where Home Bureau members reconstructed a late nineteenth-century kitchen. In it, they placed examples of iron skillets, enameled pots, and hand-cranked coffee mills, the kind of worn, old-fashioned items many pageant-goers still used at home but had to admit were obsolete. The modern American kitchen contrasted no less sharply with the Home Bureau's rendition of contemporary European cookery. The German, Dutch, Scandinavian, and Scots exhibits, for instance, showed traditional dishes situated in adjacent to quaint-looking fireplaces. The fact that modern stoves were more common in Europe at the time than they were in parts of the United States, mattered to no one.

Historical accuracy was beside the point. The Pageant of Cookery, its organizers' earnest intentions notwithstanding, little had to do with history or geography or even the study of food, except in the most superficial sense. From a historical perspective, it amounted to a celebration of modernity, a veritable salute to American efficiency and its embodiment in the scientific kitchen. As Brian and the Home Bureau would have it, all that existed before had been eclipsed. Local retailers like G.H. Read, Holder Hardware, and Mayer Livingston's Newmarket now offered the "perfect utensils" – teakettles, coffee pots, sauce pans, fry pans, cookware of all shapes and sizes and all available in light and shiny aluminum. Kitchen departments throughout the county stocked Pyrex bakeware, products that brought the lustrous look of glass to such otherwise dull items as baking pans and pie plates. There were spotless electric toasters, grills, percolators, and chafing dishes to be had, and by 1939 an array of Revere Ware pots and pans fitted with revolutionary heat-resistant plastic handles and combining copper, chrome, stainless steel and aluminum to create lightweight vessels with dazzling looks.[48]

The latest cookware in Brian's day was designed to place on top of a modern, clean-burning stove. Wood- and coal-burning models had no place in the scientific kitchen as soon as alternatives became available. In Bloomington, the gas stove was the obvious choice. It had been invented in 1854, but city gas pressures at the time were generally too low for effective operation.[49] High-pressure manufactured gas became available in some cities in the 1880s. When Bloomington's gas company initiated high-pressure delivery in the 1890s, dealers immediately began plugging gas cooking.[50]

The choice was between oil and gasoline in rural areas and towns without gas service.[51] Experts recognized oil as more precise and comfortable to work with than wood or coal, but oil-burners occasionally spewed black smoke and dirtied up the kitchen. Besides that, there was a safety issue; they could explode.[52] Gasoline stoves appeared more sanitary, but they were far more dangerous, especially if someone attempted to refuel while the appliance was still hot. Bloomington's My Store took out a newspaper ad for its leading brand of gasoline stove, which had the grimly ironic trade name, "Surprise."[53] The Golden Anvil assured readers of its advertisements that the gasoline stove it carried deserved the name "Insurance." "Why even a child could operate it safely," went the sales pitch.[54] Of course, neither the manufacturer nor the store offered a guarantee.

Electric stoves had yet to become practical. George Simpson had patented an "electro-heater" – basically a hotplate – in 1859, and Thomas Ahearn succeeded in actually cooking a meal in 1892 using an electric range he invented, but electricity was either unavailable or too expensive for most people to cook with well into the 1930s.[55] That, however, did not stop DeLoss Funk from electrifying the kitchen of his parents' home near the Town of Shirley, the Alton line's first passenger stop south of Bloomington.[56] DeLoss wired the kitchen in 1910, just after he graduated from the University of Illinois.[57] He assembled a gasoline-powered generator housed in a cellar-like structure next to the house, ran wiring under the kitchen floor, inserted outlets into a large table in the center of the room, and in effect created America's first electrified "kitchen island." It provided a platform for a variety of small electric appliances, including a chafing dish, a toaster, and a waffle iron. An electric stove stood by across the room as an alternative to the family's conventional cast-iron range.

ORGANIZING WOMEN

After serving as home adviser for more than seven years, Clara Brian listed what she believed were her 12 most important accomplishments.[58] Not surprisingly, five of them had to do with health and nutritional education. However, at the top of her list, Clara put her success as an organizer. Providing rural women with an opportunity to expand their horizons was, in her opinion, the most fundamental and important thing about her work. Through the Home Bureau, she was able to facilitate women's involvement in networks of people and ideas far more extensive than those that might otherwise engage them.

Not that farm women were ever entirely isolated, but from frontier days churches had functioned exclusively as the centers of community life. This kept rural communities sectarian and farm women in the company of others very much like themselves. The Home Bureau cut across denominations and created a broader identity. The churches brought their own congregations to communion on Sunday. Brian and the Home Bureau had farm families of every denomination all across the county sitting down to the same dinners prepared from recipes published in the newspaper the day before.[59] While church ministers discussed the spiritual side of life, Brian used the language of home economics to examine its material dimensions. She preached progress and measured it in terms of dollars and cents. She also taught accounting, enabling women to take charge of the books.

THE GREAT DEPRESSION

The Depression in effect began in Central Illinois in the early 1920s when its farm economy, like much of the nation's, fell into ruin. In rural McLean County, no one starved, but plans to modernize had to be put on hold, and children at an early age needed to learn about the importance of work and the meaning of frugality. The financial collapse of 1929 and the ensuing chaos affected working-class diets in Bloomington-Normal.

Undernourishment was typical. By 1930, the average American was eating less food than the average person took in before World War I.[60] People consumed less flour and cornmeal, fewer potatoes, and smaller quantities of red meat. Calorie intake dropped five percent on average. Vegetable and fruit consumption increased and so did milk consumption, but by the mid-'30s authorities believed that 40 percent of the population was to some degree underfed. The typical laid-off worker in Muncie, Indiana tried to feed a family of four on five dollars a week. Of that, two dollars went to cheap cuts of meat, the rest to bread, potatoes, and beans. Fruits, vegetables, and milk for the children were often out of reach.[61] The situation in Bloomington-Normal provoked anxiety and some antagonism, but for the most part it prompted sympathy and outpourings of generosity from those in better circumstances.

PRE-MODERN HOME KITCHENS

The Depression put the kibosh on many homemakers' dreams of fixing meals in the kind of well-outfitted kitchen Clara Brian talked about. With farmers having spent every spare penny on machinery and outbuildings for years and then having nothing to spare, the fact was that a great number of farmhouse kitchens – perhaps most – were basically the same as the one grandmother worked in shortly after the Civil War and would remain so throughout much of the 1930s.

Some McLean County residents can still picture such kitchens. Margaret Esposito and Marian Harris, both of whom worked and played in them, recall how big they were.[62] Margaret remembers her Aunt Helen's kitchen as the largest room in her house. Her family spent most of its time there, especially during the winter. Farm families typically "wintered" in the kitchen because usually a large and frequently hot wood-burning stove dominated the room. Nearby the stove stood a box or two containing kindling, corn cobs, and various sorts of wood. Marian remembers her grandmother selected the wood to burn in her stove based on the kind of cooking she had in mind. When she intended to bake bread, for example, she used hedge wood because it burned very hot. Aunt Helen's kitchen contained a small kerosene stove in addition to her big wood burner. The little stove was moved to the back porch at the beginning of summer when it became too warm to cook indoors.

A large table almost always occupied the middle of the kitchen. Marian recalls that her grandmother's kitchen table with all of its leaves in place accommodated more than a dozen men at one sitting. Family and farmhands took their meals at it, beginning with breakfast at five o'clock in the morning. With chairs moved back against the walls, the table served as a work surface. Bertha Zehr, a native of

Cullom, remembered that when she was growing up the kitchen table was ordinarily covered with an oilcloth.[63] It was replaced by a tablecloth when company was coming. Bertha's family always ate at the kitchen table. Some families ate in the dining room, though usually only on Sundays and holidays to avoid tracking dirt into it on workdays. The kitchen was a place where the folks could come in, clean up, and sit down to a meal without worrying about getting the floor dirty.

Many early twentieth-century farmhouse kitchens had linoleum floors. Marian remembers that in her grandmother's kitchen the floor boards remained uncovered and consequently had to be treated with linseed oil. Twice a year, grandmother heated the oil in a special pan. Then she got down on her hands and knees and applied the hot oil with a cloth. The wood glistened when she was finished. Marian's grandmother made throw rugs to place in front of the stove and elsewhere around the room. When something was baking in the oven, she left a hot pad on the floor as a reminder.

As late as the 1930s, many farmhouse kitchens still did not have running water. Margaret recollects that her aunt's kitchen did and that the plumbing included two faucets, one connected to a well, the other to a cistern. A large sink sat under the faucets, and over the sink hung a mirror so the men could comb their hair when they washed up to eat. Grandmother's kitchen, as Marian recalls, remained in the nineteenth century. It never had so much as a pump, and the washstand was no more than a shelf holding a basin between two walls across a corner of the room. Grandmother carried water in a bucket. A dipper hung on its side, and everyone used it to take a drink of water. A "slop bucket" sat behind the kitchen door and was used to collect all sorts of waste, including the dishwater. The slop bucket would be full by the end of the day. The next morning Marian's father would take it out and feed it to the hogs. Marian reminisced that her grandmother kept the slop bucket covered, but some less fastidious women did not.

Farm kitchens ordinarily had no wall cupboards, although some had open shelves on the walls. Margaret remembers her Aunt Helen had a Hoosier cabinet, a freestanding piece of furniture commonly used from around 1880 through the early 1900s. Hoosier cabinets were designed to keep all essential kitchen utensils in one place and were sold as labor-saving devices. Features included a pull-out work surface, a bread box, a flour sifter, and several tiers of shelving protected by doors. Some houses had pantries, small rooms for storage adjoining the kitchen. Pantries were typically long and narrow with counter space and wall cabinets both below and above for keeping staples, tableware, pots and pans, and various utensils.

As in the nineteenth century, the walls of kitchens in the 1920s and '30s were hung with utilitarian items. Marian cannot recall any empty space on the walls of her grandmother's kitchen. There were some pictures and a mirror above the washstand. Next to it hung a towel rack and a roller towel. Behind the kitchen door were big hooks for hats and coats. Above grandmother's worktable there were brackets for a kerosene lamp. A shield behind it reflected light onto the table and across the room. In addition, there was usually a kerosene lamp on top of the cabinet that held her dishes. Below the worktable were bins for flour and sugar. Grandmother also had a little cabinet behind the stove. The water bucket sat on top of the cabinet. Inside of it, she kept skillets and kettles. Other pieces of cookware hung from the wall behind the stove.

Farm kitchens back in the 1920s and '30s often were still not equipped to keep foods cool. Cooling took place out back in a spring house or in a cooling box lowered down a well. When excessively cold temperatures became a problem, a box built into the kitchen wall presented a solution. The box extended slightly beyond the outside wall of the house and was accessed through a small door in the inside wall. This device acted like a small refrigerator, and kept foods chilled but prevented them from freezing during the winter months.

Another common appliance in the pre-modern kitchen was the separator, a device for parting milk from cream by centrifugal force. Farmers generally sold milk and cream as distinct commodities, and regarded separating as women's work. For that reason, the separator was located in the kitchen.

The farm kitchens of Margaret and Marian's youth also served as places for bathing and washing laundry. Family members bathed in a large metal basin. It was large enough to accommodate small children, but adults had to sit with legs dangling over the sides. Some farmsteads had separate wash houses, but this was not common. A wash tub usually hung on the kitchen wall or sat on a bench next to it. On laundry day, traditionally Monday, the tub was placed on the floor and filled with soap and water.[64] Margaret's aunt did her laundry in the kitchen, washing her clothes by rubbing them on a scrub board which stood in the wash tub partially submerged on little legs. More up-to-date kitchens contained wash machines. When not in use, these were kept off to the side or out of sight under the stairs.

The farmhouse kitchen moved outdoors during the heat of the summer. Marian's grandmother had a summer kitchen and a screened-in porch for hot weather meals. It was located out back of the house in a little brick building near the well. The structure had two rooms, one with a loft, and originally may have been a house. It reminded Marian in a way of pictures she had seen of Abraham Lincoln's log cabin. Her dad eventually converted the back room into a smoke house for bacon and ham.

Later, when Marian moved to town her family had a summer kitchen connected to the house by a screen porch. Her father put a stove in and installed drains in the floor for both a laundry tub and a bath tub. Her mother did the laundry there and everyone took baths. The summer kitchen also provided space to store winter clothing.

Marian remembers kitchens in town as not very different from those on the farm apart from being smaller. Designers explained that smaller kitchens saved homemakers steps, not to mention construction costs.[65] Still, the town house kitchen was normally the biggest room in the house and, much like the farm-house kitchen, the busiest. The facilities could still be as primitive as those in the country. For instance, when Marian's parents moved to town their kitchen stove still burned wood and corncobs. It heated the whole house during the winter, and its reservoir was the family's only source of hot water. The kitchen itself had no running water. Drinking water was kept behind the stove in a bucket on a bench. Marian's husband, Russell, who grew up in Bloomington, also did without running water. He pumped water as a boy and continued to do so until the mid 1930s.

HOW FARM FAMILIES ATE

Ordinary farmers back in the 1920s and '30s were cash poor. Grain prices fell in 1921. Farm bankruptcies in the Midwest quadrupled in 1922 and doubled again in 1923.[66] The rest of the economy was in depression by 1930, and farm incomes went from bad to worse. To offset their meager earnings, farmers followed in the footsteps of the previous generations. They raised fruits, vegetables, and livestock in sufficient numbers to meet subsistence needs, traded for all but a few essential groceries, and expended a great deal of their own labor on food processing and preparation.

Everyone, including the children, had to pitch in and play a productive role. When Bertha Zehr was a youngster, she gathered eggs, pumped water, carried corncobs and coal up from the basement for the cooking stove, and helped her mother fix meals.[67] Marian Harris spent her summers working on her grandparents' farm. She recalls that once as a high school girl she helped feed 15 threshermen. It took until four o'clock in the afternoon to finish washing up, and afterward she helped her aunt pick and can green beans until nine that night.

Farm work tested a person's endurance, but with a big garden and some livestock nobody went hungry. Marian reminisces about times when there was nothing to spread on bread other than lard.

> We didn't like it, but you know you had to have something. But we always had some kind of fruit – most of the time apples and pears. We had a lot of apple trees and pear trees and my dad would pick those and

put them in the basement and we would have pears all year. They kept well and the apples did too. And in the fall we had grapes and plums. We had our own grapevines. And in summer we would have cherries and we always had a lot of rhubarb.[68]

In his youth, Robert Yoder lived on a farm near Eureka. His family tilled and planted a garden 100 feet long and 60 feet wide, but weeks before the spring vegetables were up he was out searching the ditches for dandelion leaves, the year's first edible greens.[69] His mother combined the tender leaves with hardboiled egg and dressed them with cream, vinegar, sugar, and salt to make a much-appreciated salad after a long winter without fresh vegetables. Bertha Zehr's recipe was similar but included bacon.

Dandelion Salad with Hot Bacon Dressing
INGREDIENTS – young dandelions; 4 slices of bacon; 2 eggs; ½ cup cream; 2 Tablespoons butter; 1 teaspoon salt; 1 Tablespoon sugar; 4 Tablespoons vinegar; paprika and pepper to taste. PREPARATION – Wash greens. Pat dry in a cloth. Place in salad bowl in a warm place. Add quickly fried and cubed bacon. Melt butter and cream over low heat. Beat eggs; add salt, pepper, sugar, paprika, and vinegar. Mix with warm cream mixture. Cook over high heat until dressing is thick. Pour over dandelions. Stir and Serve.[70]

The Yoders planted several kinds of lettuce, various radishes, spinach, and peas early in growing season. Beans and cucumbers went in the ground a few weeks later. Robert's grandmother planted by the moon and consulted *The Farmer's Almanac* for preferred dates. She planted potatoes on Good Friday in keeping with an old tradition, and Robert recalls that at least one-third of his family's garden was devoted to them. Cabbage, much of which was made into kraut, occupied another large section.[71]

Bill Linneman, who grew up during the Depression near Danvers, recalls that his family had two big gardens and an orchard, which together produced a wide variety of fruits and vegetables.[72] The family also kept chickens, ducks and a few cows. Bill collected eggs and his mother made cottage cheese and butter. The Linnemans traded the eggs and dairy products for sugar, salt, pepper, wheat flour, cornmeal, coffee, tea, and kerosene at Imhoff's Store in Danvers. When she was a girl, Evelyn Schwoerer and her family never ate chicken because they counted on trading hen's eggs for flour and sugar.[73] Robert Yoder's parents regularly traded eggs for flour, sugar, salt, and coffee at Mishler Brothers Grocery in Eureka, but every so often they came home with something extra.[74] Once they returned with some bananas cut from the stalk that hung in the Mishlers' window. On very special occasions, they purchased bread. Robert still remembers how he marveled at the soft crust and uniform slices back when the catchphrase "the greatest thing since sliced bread" was current.

Purchasing bread at the store denoted modernity, but most farm women continued to bake at home, usually twice a week, throughout the Depression. Preparations took a full 24 hours from the time the flour, water, sugar, and yeast were mixed until hot loaves emerged from the oven.[75] Marian Harris's mother baked for a family of six. On Tuesday, she made six to eight loaves of bread. On Saturday, she did the same and made several sugar, cinnamon, and cheese coffee cakes.

The perennial routines of cooking and baking, as well as seasonal canning, pickling, and other food preservation activities were essential to getting farm families through the winter without having to pay for additional groceries. Canning went on throughout the summer and fall as various species of fruits and vegetables ripened. Probably most of Central Illinois's peaches wound up canned in heavy syrup, and a considerable portion of its apple crop went into jars as homemade applesauce. Marian Harris made apple butter, grape jelly, and various preserves, including peach, pear, and strawberry-rhubarb. Although she did not own a pressure cooker until 1944, Marian put up bushels of green beans every summer. She also canned peas, lots of tomatoes and about 30 quarts of tomato juice a year. Tomatoes (some canned with salt and pepper and a little vinegar) were a winter staple in her house. Robert Yoder remembers his family's fruit cellar "as truly a sight to behold in the fall."[76] A whole summer's work was on display, neatly lined up on the shelves. Sauerkraut was preserved in large stoneware crocks and Mason jars, and there was a plentiful supply of pickled cucumbers and peppers. Robert's mother won particular praise for her cucumber dills.

Stella's Dill Pickles

INGREDIENTS – cucumbers 4 inches long and about 1 inch in diameter, dilute brine, fresh dill, cloves, cider vinegar, canning salt, black pepper, alum. PREPARATION – Wash and dry cucumbers. Wet them in brine. Place head of dill and clove of garlic in a boiled quart jar. Heat 3 quarts water with one quart vinegar. Add 1 cup canning salt and boil for 5 minutes. Place cucumbers in jar and pour in hot liquid. Add a dash of pepper and a lump of alum. Seal jar and allow pickling process to occur.[77]

Some fruits and fleshy vegetables were dehydrated or kept fresh in cellars. The Yoders sliced and dried a portion of their apple harvest and kept it in a large cloth sack in the washroom closet. When needed she needed apples to make a pie or father's favorite, *Schnitz un Knepp* (see Chapter 3), Robert's mother rehydrated the slices by soaking them in water. Bins in the cellar of Bill Linneman's boyhood home were filled with apples, potatoes, carrots, turnips, and other roots, most of which kept until March before beginning to spoil.[78] Marian Harris remembers keeping apples and pears fresh in the basement. Potatoes and carrots were also carried to the basement where they were placed in bins for the winter. Root vegetables kept especially well in her grandmother's cellar because it had a dirt floor.[79]

Depression-era famers conserved meat as their fathers and grandfathers had. They kept hams and bacon slabs hung from the joists in the smokehouse year round. Other pieces of pork were fried and put in large crocks, then covered with lard to preserve them. Robert Yoder recalls being sent to the basement to dig out pieces of lard-soaked meat from a crock. His mother put the meat toward the back of a warm stove where the lard melted off.[80] After that, she cooked the meat. Marian Harris's father canned beef as well as pork. He hung the beef in the corn crib and allowed it to get very cold. He then cut off thick steaks and cubed them for canning. Her mother packed the meat raw. Once the jars were filled, they were placed on a rack her father made and cooked inside a wash boiler.

HARD TIMES IN BLOOMINGTON-NORMAL

The extent of the Great Depression's impact on urban places depended on size. Unemployment averaged more than 20 percent in major cities such as Chicago and St. Louis.[81] In smaller cities such as Bloomington, it ran between 12 and 14 percent, but that was enough for things to get nasty. A series of fires set by arsonists in 1932 destroyed a school, a Catholic Church, and a park pavilion in Bloomington.[82] In Normal, by now contiguous with Bloomington, police and firemen fought with two hundred unemployed demonstrators.[83] The tension became palpable at workplaces like Paul F. Beich candy company and the central post office when those who could afford lunch ate outside in full view of those who could not. Worried managers subsequently asked employees with lunches to eat them inside.[84]

Local governments and other agencies sought to relieve workers' anxieties and some of the political pressure. Town of Normal leaders formed a Community Council to coordinate economic assistance. The council acquired 50 acres of land and dubbed it a community vegetable garden for the unemployed.[85] The local canning factory pitched in on behalf of the unemployed by putting up any fruits and vegetables they raised at no cost. Those with jobs paid nothing as well, but they were asked to donate half of their produce to relief agencies. Local donations helped St. Joseph's Hospital open a soup kitchen and allowed Bloomington's Home Sweet Home Mission to serve free meals to as many as 3,000 people a month.

Those who applied for emergency provisions were for the most part nearly destitute. As Evelyn Schwoerer remembers, the lines for food were very long.[86] From time to time, she and her family found it necessary to queue up, sometimes for cooked food, or on other occasions to obtain commodities. William "Willie" Tripp recalls that in Bloomington a great deal of food was stored at Brokaw Hospital, and many residents went there to get staples and a hot meal.[87] Sometimes Willie went with his mother to Union Baptist Church where she served bologna sandwiches to needy members of the congregation.

At State Farm Insurance Company in downtown Bloomington, employees deemed underweight were sent to the medical department where they received free milk.[88] Company officials worried mostly about the health of female personnel and whether they were up to working. Women, clericals for the most part, made up 70 percent of the company's employees. Many of them were single and helped support families back home. Many came from small towns, lived in rented rooms, and had neither transportation nor a telephone. Company nurses called on these women whenever they failed to show up for work. Those who appeared exceptionally skinny, received buttermilk at company expense. When managers started noticing a large number of employees skipping lunch, State Farm began subsidizing mid-day meals at nearby cafés.

HOUSEHOLD DIET

Diets in Bloomington-area households seriously affected by the Depression tended to be monotonous if not always scant. Carl "Bud" Ekstam recalls repeatedly eating beans and macaroni and cheese.[89] Willie Tripp remembers oatmeal; his mother fed him a lot of it. Marian Harris says she ate it nearly every day as a youngster.[90]

To relieve the monotony, children took jobs and foraged to get a little something extra. Bud Ekstam made money by going to Funk Seeds and filling gunny sacks with corn cobs, which he could sell for a nickel. He used his nickel to buy an ice cream cone. Walt Bittner combed the alleys for soda bottles so he could cash them in for the penny deposit. Other kids spent the money they made on refunds buying soda; Walt took his money home to help his mother pay the bills.[91] Willie Tripp did yard work for neighbors. He also spent much of his free time fishing.

Hunting and fishing made substantial contributions to the diet for some families. For laborers, this was true long before the Great Depression as a *Pantagraph* piece published in 1915 about railroad switchman John Kelly, who bagged 20 rabbits and a possum on a hunting trip and became the envy of his neighborhood aptly illustrates.[92] The Depression, however, made game animals even more important. At Kenneth Mann's house, rabbit, pheasant, and fish frequently appeared on the dinner table.[93] Florence Ekstam's father had his own business and earned decent money, yet he hunted regularly and brought home rabbit, raccoon, and opossum.[94]

The Depression turned urban lots into farm yards. Preston Ensign's family kept chickens and a cow.[95] There was a barn on the property and a cream separator in the basement. Preston's mother made butter and canned fruits and vegetables, so there was little need to go to the grocery store except for crackers and few other items she could not make at home. Florence Ekstam recollects neighbors who killed a pig in the fall, hung it in the attic, and ate pieces of it all winter just like countryfolks.[96]

Many households depended on backyard gardens. Kenneth Mann, recalling how important vegetables were at his house, says his parents canned as many as 200 quarts annually from their garden. They sold extra jars of pickles and sauerkraut to grocery stores all over town. Florence Ekstam's mother canned beans, peas, and tomatoes. She also made many jars of jams, jellies, and pickles. Florence's father made a crock of sauerkraut every winter. His other basement products included wine and beer as well as root beer for the kids.

At the store, families relied on credit. During the winter, Florence's father charged groceries and spent the following spring paying off his bills. Grocery stores, according to Florence, were the only places that offered extended credit. She remembers that when her father paid off his bill, the grocer showed his appreciation by telling the children to pick out some candy or a cookie on the house. Paul Penn's family also bought food on credit. He recalls milk, which some stores sold ladled from a bulk container, going bad because no one could afford to buy it.[97] Milk straight out of the cow, direct from the farm cost just a nickel a quart.[98]

In spite of social tensions in some quarters, conditions in McLean County never became desperate to the point that people ceased to care about their neighbors. Families borrowed food from one another throughout the Depression, and for the most part, they maintained an open-handed attitude toward the considerable number of destitute men who passed through town looking for work.[99] Hobo camps sprang up along railroad right-of-ways in Bloomington. Hobos called at homes asking to do chores in return for something to eat. At the Ekstam's house, they weeded the garden and picked bugs off the potato plants by hand.[100] Because hobos showed up almost every lunchtime and were never turned away, Florence Ekstam believed her family's house was secretly marked as a soft touch. Ruth Steele's mother took to leaving leftovers in a bin next to the kitchen door for passers-by in need of something to eat.[101]

As the 1930s progressed and business began to pick up a little, more and more people began patronizing Bloomington's restaurants. Popular spots for lunch downtown included The Village Inn and Roland's Tea Room. Walt Bittner landed a job at a "hamburger joint" where burgers were a nickel or six for a quarter.[102] Customers could have their hamburgers topped with onion, pickle, and mustard for another nickel. Florence Ekstam's father went out every Monday night to Baker's hamburger place and came home with three burgers for a dime. Preston Ensign and his parents occasionally ate at the Federal Café where they could get a plate lunch for nineteen cents.[103] For another dime, the Federal's guests could have soup and pie with their lunch. Preston saw poor Illinois State Normal University students at the café, and he knew one of them who lived mostly on milk and crackers. Such meager diets were not uncommon among college students at that time.

AN AFRICAN AMERICAN HOUSEHOLD

World War I and the employment opportunities it offered lured a great number of African Americans from the Deep South. Most moved to Chicago. Blacks from Mississippi and other plantation areas did not eat like they or their parents did back home. That was because the diet of sharecroppers and plantation laborers was extremely pernicious at certain times of the year, particularly late winter and early spring. At that time of year, Blacks in rural Alabama and Mississippi typically consumed no more than five commodities per week and in some cases just two or three – e.g., salt pork, cornmeal, and sugar or molasses.[104]

In Illinois, African Americans ate a far more varied diet. Oral histories recorded in Bloomington-Normal mention cheap cuts of pork like pig's feet and neck bones.[105] They do not hark back to collards or barbecue or chitlins or sweet potato pie, just to cite a few of the Soul Food staples that became popular during the latter part of the twentieth century. Wilbur Barton of Normal recalls his diet growing up in the 1920s and '30s as regional rather than particularly ethnic.

> My mother came from Kentucky. My father came from Southern Illinois and Missouri. My mother's cooking was representative of the cooking in those three states, not of the Deep South.

As Barton remembers, his parents were always able to provide three meals a day. These were taken as a family at the dinning room table. Wilbur's mother served breakfast at 7 a.m. and she normally baked two pans of (baking) powder biscuits, served with jelly, preserves, and butter, hand sliced back-slab bacon or salt pork, sliced fried potatoes and onion. Alternatively, she fried apples or tomatoes or made applesauce. Her preferred drink was coffee boiled in pan, but for her husband there was a cup of tea and for the children, a glass of milk. On school days, Wilbur and his brothers and sisters came home to a lunch of hand-sliced white bread with butter or margarine. There were also vegetables and perhaps some ham. Father took his lunch to work. For supper, the Bartons ordinarily had roast pork, chicken, beef, or fish accompanied by potatoes, green beans, creamed corn, a lettuce salad, and sliced pickles. The family dined on rabbit and squirrel in season. For desserts, Wilbur's mother made pies from fruit produced in the yard. There were also fruit cobblers, puddings, and cakes, and on occasion her coal-stove oven turned out cornbread, corn "ponies," crackling bread, muffins, and apple dumplings. The Bartons enjoyed homemade ice cream, sherbet, or tapioca pudding periodically. The ice cream was hand cranked. Wilbur says his family usually made ice cream in the back yard so the neighborhood kids would not see it, but usually they saw what was happening anyway had to receive a share.

The Bartons raised most of the food they ate. Wilbur recollects his father kept hogs in the back yard for while, and every year mother would get 300 chicks from the Bloomington Hatchery and raise them for meat. Some of the chickens were sold, but plenty of them wound up on the family table. The Bartons cultivated three vegetable gardens on their lot. These supplied white potatoes, peas, corn, onions, beets, beans, mustard, radishes, lettuce, Swiss chard, dock, turnips, cabbage, okra, lima beans, sassafras, pumpkins, and squash, but no sweet potatoes because they did not grow well in Normal. Wilbur's mother canned both spring and summer. She stored slaw and kraut in five-gallon crocks and canned the fruit in one quart and one-and-a-half-gallon Mason jars. In addition, she made fruit jellies, pear honey, and apple butter. Some of the fruit she bought from hucksters who came by the house with their wagons.[106]

The stage for the eventual introduction of Soul Food (i.e., Southern-style foods) to the urban North had yet to be set. That would require markets of sufficient size to attract entrepreneurs willing to produce or import typical products, and new attitudes toward ethnic identity. These requisites were finally in place by the late 1950s, making it possible for a city dweller to eat like an Alabama cotton farmer who could somehow put the foods of spring, summer, fall, and winter on the table everyday and never worry about a winter of unremitting bacon, corn bread, and molasses.[107]

THE MEALS AT SOLDIERS AND
SAILORS' CHILDREN'S SCHOOL

Allegations of misconduct on the part of employees at Illinois Soldiers and Sailors' Children's School (ISSCS), a state facility located in Normal, sparked public concern in the mid-1930s for the most vulnerable of McLean County's children. Could it be true, as a whistle-blower charged, that officers at the school were stealing food intended for the kids? ISSCS, after all, was an old and highly respected institution. It was founded in 1865 as Illinois Soldiers' Orphan's Home, intended to care for and to educate the indigent children of Union soldiers killed during the Civil War. The institution's mission expanded over the years to cover children of veterans of subsequent wars and for a time the children of non-veterans.

Life at ISSCS was closely regulated. Every day began with making beds. Students then dressed in identical clothes, washed up, and sat down on the floor in the hallway, arms and legs crossed and eyes closed. At the sound of a bell, they came to attention. A second bell cued entry into the dining room where everyone stood behind his or her assigned chair. A third bell signaled the children to be seated. A fourth bell rang, and eating commenced. Children were allowed to talk quietly during meals, but if a boy acted up his house mother was apt to come up from behind and rap the top of his head with her knuckles. House mothers expected students to eat whatever food was placed in front of them, and nobody left the table until his or her plate was empty. Gino Ullian, an ISSCS student from 1933 until 1942, detested buttered beets and vomited every time he ate them.[108] However, he discovered a sure-fire way to avoid that and come away with a clean plate was to offer his ice cream to anyone of his tablemates willing to take on a second helping of beets.

ISSCS divided its wards according to age and sex among various cottages, about twenty children to a cottage. The house mother in charge made oatmeal or bacon and eggs for the children in the morning. Other meals were prepared in a central kitchen, which from 1935 until 1962, was the domain of Joseph Pawlak, otherwise known as "Joe the Cook." The children adored him and relished many of his dishes. Some of them interacted with him every day when they were sent to his kitchen to pick up lunch or dinner and carry it back to their cottages. Secondary school students, who caught a school bus to University High School in Normal, returned home to lunch in the main dining room. They made their own way home again either by foot or city bus after school because many played sports and stayed late. No matter what time a boy or girl came home, supper was always waiting. Children went to the kitchen in the evening around nine or ten o'clock for milk and a peanut butter and jelly sandwich. Louis Williams, an ISSCS resident from 1942 through 1953, remembers the food as always excellent: "Big beef roasts, pork roasts, chicken, fish, you name it; we had plenty."[109]

Problems arose with the meals at ISSCS in 1935, at the height of the Great Depression. That year Paul Stepko, a former housefather at the school, swore under oath that residents of ISSCS were ill fed because staff members were consuming food intended for the children. His allegation was made during an investigation of conditions at the institution conducted by the Illinois Department of Public Welfare. Stepko testified that when he began working at the school meals were satisfactory. However, sometime in October 1934 their quality declined, and children went hungry. Stepko complained to school superintendent, J. Howard Russell, but testified that he was unreceptive. When Stepko insisted that youngsters needed some kind of meat at least four times a week, Russell replied that that was too much. Nevertheless, the superintendent made assurances that rations would improve, though according to Stepko, they never did. Stepko further stated that about the time he talked to Russell, breakfast in the cottages consisted of tomato juice, dry toast, and a cup of milk. When Stepko went to the officers' dining hall, he found ISSCS administrators partaking in a hearty breakfast of ham, bacon, and eggs. Superintendent Russell sought to discredit Stepko's testimony by referring to him as "a disgruntled employee." Nevertheless, his complaints prompted the Illinois Department of Public Welfare to conduct an audit. It found fault with neither the school's staff nor the children's diet.

Former students have no recollection of having been underfed. Eleanore "Sally" Zimmerman Wegener, an ISSCS student from 1932 to 1939, remembers nothing about the food other than the home-baked bread and being able to drink all of the milk she wanted. Before the Depression was over, however, meal planning at ISSCS became the responsibility of a registered dietitian. In 1956, a "Master Menu" went into effect. Officials said this was to make food services at all of Illinois's public institutions more cost effective, but the *Daily Pantagraph* assured its readers that ISSCS's dietitian, Ann Boylan, had some leeway in her budget.[110] Her commitment, the newspaper was convinced, remained with the kids and to seeing to it that they had as much as they wanted to eat.

GROCERIES

The Great Depression came as a terrible blow to small, independent grocers. Customers, strapped for cash and more price conscious than ever before, dispensed with long-standing loyalties. Increasingly the public shopped at chain stores owned by or affiliated with a handful of large companies. The larger groceries had little of the congeniality of the neighborhood shops, but were able to underprice them by as much as 12 percent. The number of grocers doing business in Bloomington-Normal declined sharply as a result. During the two decades immediately prior to the Depression, Bloomington-Normal supported as many as 126 groceries. In 1941, with the Depression practically over and supermarkets just beginning to appear, only 56 stores remained. Of these, 36 were independently owned. The other 20 belonged to three chains, A & P, Kroger, and Piggly Wiggly.[111]

GENERAL STORES

The story of the rise and fall of the independent grocery store in Central Illinois began about the middle of the nineteenth century. Prior to that, the early settlers traded for provisions in public markets, with neighbors or peddlers, and in general stores. The first men licensed to sell goods in McLean County, James Allin, M.L. Covell, Benjamin Haines, and the Durley brothers, John and Samuel, operated general stores stocked with a variety of merchandise intended to meet settlers' basic needs (see Chapter 1). The groceries found in these little frontier emporiums consisted of imported goods such as coffee and tea and items impossible to produce at home such as salt. By 1850, inventories expanded and folks stopping by to trade found loaves of cane sugar, a variety of syrups and spices, dried fruits, and wheat flour.

When storekeepers needed to replenish their stock, they took whatever money they were able to collect from unsettled accounts and visited their suppliers in Pekin or St. Louis.[112] Allin, Covell, and others waited until after harvest to settle up and restock. George Dietrich's books show that he extended credit to his customers for a year or more and charged no interest. That changed in 1850, but only for new accounts.[113] Dietrich was a tinsmith, not a general storekeeper, but levying little or no interest on credit accounts appears to have been common practice during the frontier era.

About the same time Dietrich began charging interest, a number of general stores began offering lower prices to cash customers. This was especially the case among merchants advertising groceries. Among the earliest was G.W. Sanford. He announced in an 1850 issue of *The Weekly Pantagraph* a "good stock of groceries" available at low prices for either cash or produce – butter and eggs especially welcome.[114] The next year D.D. Haggard, proprietor of the Old Corner, a general store with a large stock of groceries, began calling his establishment "The Cheap Cash Store."[115] A few weeks later a competitor, Babb and Company, made no bones about it, by taking out a newspaper ad headlined, "The Cash System Is Progressive and Will Prevail."[116] The advertisement went on to explain that by eliminating credit the company could offer its customers savings of 25 percent on everything it sold. Parke and Whitmer, "wholesaler and retailer of groceries, provisions, fruits, confections, and tableware," announced a switch to "the cash plan" in 1854, noting that zero losses owing to bad debts translated to low prices throughout the store.[117] Another merchant, J.F. Humphreys, announced in a somewhat ominous manner that his store would no longer offer credit because his profit margin was so narrow he could no longer "afford to trust anybody."[118]

The low-profit margin to which Humphreys attributed his cash-only policy arose from intense competition. General merchants-turned-grocery specialists found themselves joined by at least two dozen newcomers. By 1855, Bloomington, with population of little more than 5,000, had no less than 34 food stores, two specifically identified as "colored," one as Irish. Everyone struggled to carve out a niche, some insisting on cash and competing on price, most allowing customers to defer payment. Eventually, the cash-only policy succumbed to the railroads' monthly pay schedules. Men employed by the city's biggest employer, the Chicago and Alton Railroad Shops, got paid the first of the month, settled their bills, and charged until the end of the month.[119]

Some small-town merchants began to call themselves "grocers" not long after grocery stores appeared in Bloomington. Among the earliest were the Preble bothers, who opened a shop in Lexington about 1858. Wheelock and Wood's, a general store in McLean that sold a few food items in 1856, became Wheelock's grocery in 1866.[120] In Danvers, Charles Rowell went into the grocery business in 1863 after having clerked in Ira Abbott's general store for two years. By 1875, Mrs. Eliza Falkingham of Towanda, whose husband had owned one of that town's ill-fated saloons, was styling herself a grocer, as were brothers and former millers J. B. and R. E. Beckwith of Saybrook.

In the outlying areas of McLean County, there was little difference, practically speaking, between a grocery store and general store. For instance, R.E. Gifford regarded himself as a grocer, but his shop in McLean was described in 1879 as carrying "a general assortment of goods, (including) . . . queensware; china and glassware; fresh and canned fruits; sirups; oils; smoked, pickled, and dried meats; brushes; nails; salt; and garden seeds, and in fact everything pertaining to a well-stocked grocery and general assortment store." When Samuel Maurer opened his store in Carlock in 1888, he at first sold boots, shoes, dry goods, men's clothing, hats, caps, china, and hardware, but it was no more than a matter of months before he added groceries.[121] The business thrived. In 1898, Maurer moved it into a bigger building and took A.J. Schafer, a salesman for

Carson, Pirie, Scott of Chicago, as a partner. Schafer left the store in 1906, but not before deep discounts on merchandise from Carson's helped build an enviable reputation throughout the area. By the time William Ernst purchased the business in 1908, Maurer's was taking in so much produce in trade that the store needed a full-time teamster to haul it to Bloomington's wholesalers.

Bruce Hamilton acquired Maurer's some years later and put his 15-year-old daughter, Dorothy, to work as a clerk[122] She opened the store in the morning and waited on customers until her father arrived at noon. As Dorothy remembered it, customers typically entered the store with a list of items they needed. She took the list and scurried here and there, fetching goods and filling the order. Many of the items had to be weighed; even cookies were sold by the pound. Some of the items Dorothy sold came from area farmers, and when commodities like eggs were offered in trade she had to check to see none of them were spoiled. For a time, another store located across the street carried the same products as Hamilton stocked. Nevertheless, Carlock folks did not see the two establishments as competitors. People traded in one or the other depending on where their friends and family did business. The area had enough customers to support both stores and did so for many years.[123]

Maurer's had become a grocery store by then, but even at that late date some small-town groceries persisted in carrying certain dry goods, notions, and household items just like the old-time general stores. When Wilbur Taylor sold his grocery store in McLean to Bobby Snow in 1982, for example, the new owner found himself saddled with a considerable inventory of shoes, underwear, shirts, boots, and other merchandise unrelated to groceries.[124] Snow sold off such items, but by then the concept of a general store had come around again in the form of the so-called "superstore," and in Bloomington one of the originals, K-Mart, was doing a bang-up business.

My Store, a low-priced department store established in 1885, retained some of the character of a general store in downtown Bloomington until it fell victim to the Depression and went out of business in 1931. Under the proprietorship of Oscar Mandel and John Bachrach, it retailed everything from dry goods and fabrics to kitchenware and appliances, plus a full line of groceries, baked goods, and meats.[125] The store was refurbished and expanded from two to five floors in 1913, transforming it into what *The Daily Pantagraph* extolled as a "trade palace."[126] The Pantagraph's reporter took particular note of the grocery department and its sanitary standards.

> All the food products are kept in enclosed cases, either drawers or boxes, except the canned foods, which are of course dust and dirt proof. Cleanliness is the watchword of the grocery.

OLD-FASHIONED GROCERY STORES

Cleanliness in nineteenth-century food stores was unusual. Owners had chronic problems with dirt, dust, molds, and various contaminants, including those left by mice, rats, and other vermin. One Bloomington grocer admitted as much by contrasting his own well-kept stock of crackers with the stale and dirty examples sold at other stores.[127] Typically, grocers scooped commodities like flour and sugar from barrels and sacks kept on the floor. Packaged goods lined the walls on shelves that reached floor to ceiling. Products, like dried fruits and spices, might be stored in bins, but others, such as butter and cheese, sat out on the counter. Grocers displayed fruits and vegetables, purchased in season from area farmers, in open baskets. These were kept indoors at night but were typically displayed outdoors in front of the store during the day.

Inside the old-fashioned grocery, clerks stationed behind counters waited on customers, filled their orders, wrote up bills, and arranged for deliveries. The process remained much the same for more than two generations. Caribel Washington, who grew up in Bloomington on South Wright Street in the 1920s and '30s, remembers two stores in her neighborhood, Feicke Brothers' and Kumle's. According to Caribel,

> Kumle's was a very elite grocery store, which had quite an extensive meat market, and all the groceries that could be. This was the time when you went into the store and clerks waited on you. You didn't go pick up things and put them in a basket and go to the cashier. A clerk would wait on you for everything, and you could buy the crackers loose and the rice. And everything was in bins, and buckets, and barrels . . . . If you were going to buy meat you told the butcher what you wanted, and he would throw that big chunk of meat on the big block and cut off what you wanted.

Bloomington's earliest stores published partial inventories in *The Weekly Pantagraph*. In a December 1853 issue, H.M. Robinson's Grocery and Provision Store on Washington Street "at the sign of the China Man" drew particular attention to its peach, apple, quince, orange, grape, and current jellies; cucumber and mixed pickles; and No. 1 mackerel in kits and barrels.[128] Reynolds and Ely announced a stock of 450 barrels of N.O. (New Orleans) and Muscovy sugar, 500 barrels of refined sugar, 1,100 chests and half-chests of green and black teas, 1,250 bags of Rio, Maguayra, and Java coffees, 575 barrels of N.O. molasses, 300 barrels of Stuart's and other syrups, 100 casks of codfish (salted), 400 barrels of nuts of all kinds, 200 bags of pepper and pimento (dried), 1,600 boxes of (pickled) herring , as well as various quantities of mackerel, whitefish, ginger, nutmeg, ground spices, raisins, prunes, cloves, and woodware. Kellog & Holmes's goods included fresh oysters (constantly received), cider vinegar, fresh butter (constantly received), sugar (brown, clarified, and white), coffee (Rio and Java), teas (Hyson's, Imperial, and black), pepper, spice, cinnamon, cloves (ground or unground), mustard (French prepared, a splendid article). The store also stocked strawberries, pineapples, apricots, prunes, pears, etc., all preserved, as well as seedless raisins, prunes, and figs. Kellog and Holmes also sold clams, lobsters, pickled herring and sardines, tomato and walnut catsup and other sauces, and extra fine salt for the table, (baking) soda, and cream of tartar. In addition, candies (a large assortment), branded baking powder (Darkly's), and "very superior" chocolate and cocoa lined the shelves. The store sold cornstarch and offered Hecker's farina (for splendid puddings) and Baker's Broma (said to be an excellent article for invalids). The proprietors stocked fine flour and macaroni and vermicelli, and they boasted of peaches and "fresh tomatoes" in cans. Kellog and Holmes reminded *Weekly Pantagraph* readers of many of the goods they carried and bragged about their store with a piece of "Groce-ry Poet-ry" that might well have doubled as a shopping list.

Groce-ry Poet-ry

Good people, come out and buy things cheap,

All kinds of Groceries we intend to keep—

Pepper-sauce, pickles, and toilet soaps,

Fine sugars, codfish, and coils of rope.

Mouse-traps and coffee, teas of all brands,

And India Fruit for all demands,

Salt, mustard, pepper and new rice,

Good white oak cheese at any price!

Here's Durkey's baking powder, that's true and sure,

All sorts of traps for rich and poor,

Hams, candy, pails, and bars of lead,

Good flour, and pork, that's been well fed.

Hams, candles, tobacco, and snuff,

Cream tartar and butter that's good enough

Nice lemons, molasses, also fish,

Potatoes, onions, carrots, and more if you wish.

Peanuts, apples, large and fair,

Peaches, tomatoes, and wooden ware,

These nice new goods, and many more,

All cheap for cash, we have in store.

For cheerful smiles and yellow gold,

All kinds of goods are cheaply sold—

Folks of good sense we're sure to please

With precious goods and wares like these.

Come, now, we know you'll come—

Get all you want before it's gone;

Bring in your neighbors, if such you've got,

And Remember, — Kellog & Holmes is just the spot.[129]

Ever more items appeared on grocers' shelves as the years passed. Henry Stone's Tea and Coffee Store's price list for November 15, 1912 organized available goods into 24 categories. In addition to toilet articles and cleaning products, the store offered: coffees, teas, nuts, dried fruits, extracts, crackers and wafers, biscuits, candies, baking powders, chocolates, dessert products (e.g., cornstarch, tapioca, gelatin, cake flour, powdered sugar, loaf sugar, syrup), "favorites for salads" (e.g., olive oil, salad dressing, prepared mustard), canned meats and fish, spices, canned vegetables, canned fruits, olives and pickles and lunch favorites (e.g., peanut butter, chili sauce, Worcester sauce), breakfast foods and cereals, and "other grocer bargains" (e.g., beans, macaroni, spaghetti, toothpicks, soda, yeast foam, matches, salt).[130] All told, the Tea and Coffee Store offered approximately 250 different items, excluding fresh meats, fruits, and vegetables. Bloomington's Larkin Economy Stores in 1920 were handling over 800 articles.[131]

Neighborhood stores, however, generally kept smaller inventories, and many residents took the streetcar once a week to buy groceries at one of the big places downtown. The little market down the street was for daily needs. Neighborhood grocers thrived on small purchases and typically stocked fast moving items. A store might have a couple of aisles of basic canned and packaged items, perhaps a few fresh fruits and vegetables, and sometimes a small case of meat. Whenever school was out, children came running in, sent from home for bread or cream or whatever mother suddenly found herself in need of. Surviving bills presented in the 1890s to Mrs. Marton list a series of small purchases made every three or four days over a period of approximately one month. Freese Brothers grocery on Monroe Street in Bloomington billed Marton for the following purchases made in early summer, 1897.[132]

June 04th – Soap .25 St Berries .15 Onions .05

June 07th – St Berries .15 Sugar .50 Coffee .35

June 10th – Peas .05

June 14th – Berries .10 Potatoes .15

June 18th – Radish .05

June 21st – Peas .05 Tea .15 Butter .15

June 24th – Tomato .05 Butter .15 Berries .05

June 25th – Peas .05 Potatoes .10 Bread .05 Berries .10

July 01st – Tomato .05 Cereal .05 Eggs .10

SELF-SERVICE AND CHAIN GROCERIES

Henry Stone's Coffee and Tea Store became an A&P in 1930. It was Bloomington's second A&P and approximately the 16,000th store to join the chain. George Gilman and George Hartford started A&P as The Great American Tea Company, a business in New York City dedicated to purchasing tea directly from China.[133] When the transcontinental railroad was completed in 1869, Gilman and Hartford renamed their enterprise "The Great Atlantic and Pacific Tea Company" – A&P for short – and became general grocers. As such, they immediately went about setting up a number of so-called "Economy Stores," each with around 500 to 600 square feet of floor space and looking very much like independent groceries. A&P, however, consistently undercut the prices of independent grocers, in part because of a strict cash and carry policy instituted in 1912, but mainly because the chain bought all manner of food items the same way it bought tea – directly from the source and in large quantities. Independent grocers, unable to compete, went to court repeatedly to put a stop to A&P's way of doing business. They had no success.

Piggly Wiggly, the first grocery chain to enter the Bloomington market, opened a store at Front and Main Streets around 1918. This was just two years after Clarence Sanders built the very first Piggly Wiggly in Memphis and revolutionized the industry by installing self-service (shoppers went around the store and selected items themselves instead of having the store staff do so). Sander's cart and checkout system proved so successful that within three years more than 100 additional Piggly Wigglys were launched. Sanders accelerated the process by selling boxcars full of fixtures and inventory, essentially everything a prospective store owner needed except a building. Bloomington's second Piggly Wiggly held its grand opening in 1919. By 1941, Piggly Wiggly had seven markets in the Bloomington-Normal area, and nearly every food store in McLean County was self-service.[134]

The foundation for self-service was created by Quaker Oats in 1895 when the company began packing its product in the recently invented folding carton. By imprinting it with the Quaker Man logo and various bits of product information, Quaker turned its cereal's box into a kind of "silent salesman." Even more important from the grocers' perspective, the box made it possible to sell commodities in small quantities without having to scoop and weigh every purchase.

Pre-packaging made the grocers' work easier, but the public was not completely thrilled, particularly when it came to canned products. Canned fruits made their first appearance in the Bloomington market around 1855, and by 1865 they became quite popular. J.F. Humphreys regularly advertised a variety of canned fruits in *The Weekly Pantagraph*, including blackberries, strawberries, whortleberries, raspberries, cherries, pineapple, green corn, green peas, damsons, and tomatoes.[135] In the East, and especially in the big cities, the public showed less enthusiasm. The poor could not afford canned items, and the middle class had misgivings about purchasing comestibles the buyer could neither see, feel, nor smell, let alone taste, in advance.[136] How could a consumer judge the quality of a canned food? What about safety?

Such questions scarcely existed prior to the Civil War. Most people knew right well whence their food originated. It came from the farmer down the road, the miller on the edge of town, and the butcher across the street. Producers, processors, sellers, and customers generally did business with one another face to face. After the war, urban populations grew, and railroads extended their reach. The distances separating producers from consumers grew longer and more populated with middlemen.[137] As a result, the time elapsed between production and consumption increased, and food decomposition became an issue. Manufacturers responded with chemicals to retard spoilage, hide decay, restore colors, and change flavors. Companies packaged one thing and labeled it another, added an array of artificial ingredients, and saw their profits grow. By the end of the nineteenth century, most of the foods bottled, canned, or otherwise packaged in the United States were adulterated in one way or another.[138] Formaldehyde disguised rotten eggs; current jam was flavored with a coal tar derivative; flour contained ground rice, sand, or plaster of Paris; lard was doctored with lime, alum, and starch; Cayenne pepper contained lead, iron oxide, and rice flour; vinegar contained sulfuric, hydrochloric, and pyroligneous acids. None of these ingredients were listed on labels.[139] Canned meats achieved particular notoriety because, in addition to being adulterated, they were liable to be filthy. Tins often contained parasites and garbage. Deviled ham consisted of tripe colored with red dye. Potted chicken contained many ingredients, but no chicken.

Public awareness of this wholesale contamination of America's food supply was slow to develop, but a stream of scientific exhibits and published exposés eventually aroused the nation and its policymakers.[140] The U.S. Congress took action in 1906 and drafted the Pure Food and Drug Act, a federal statute that mandated the inspection of meat and forbade the manufacture and sale of adulterated food products. This paved the way for the creation of the Food and Drug Administration a few years later.

BRAND NAME FOODS

Even after the passage of the Pure Food and Drug Act, the public mistrusted packaged foods. Canned goods in particular were continuing to receive bad press as late as 1912, and many people looked askance at them.[141] Manufacturers responded with encouraging advertisements about the purity and wholesomeness of their brand-name foods. The term "pure" emerged as the earliest buzzword used in food advertising. Later on, associative ads appeared connecting products with images of trust like the kindly member of the Society of Friends portrayed on every box of Quaker Oats. Advertisers realized from the start that people needed to feel at ease with their food, and they needed reassurance that food from distant industrial centers was fit to eat.[142]

Branded foods originated in the 1860s as a way for a company to distinguish its particular product from the many others on the market that looked and tasted much the same. Before the invention of brand names, jobbers purchased products from processors and distributed them to local stores in bulk containers.[143] Grocers had no reason to insist on a barrel of oats or box of saltfish from one particular company. Branding represented an effort to by-pass retailers and impress customers with producers' names. The idea was to facilitate advertising and enable shoppers to ask their grocer for a particular manufacturer's product.[144]

Early evidence of insisting on a particular brand can be found in *The Bloomington Cookbook*, a collection of favorite recipes contributed by members of the Second Christian Church and published in 1902. The collection contained a number of recipes for making congealed salads. Several lists of ingredients specified a brand of gelatin, one calling for Cox's, another for Nelson's, and yet a third specifying the Plymouth Rock label. Mrs. Henry Spencer's recipe for a congealed fruit salad represents a prototype of the Jell-O salads popular to this to this day at Midwestern potlucks.

Mrs. Harry Spencer's Fruit Salad
INGREDIENTS – ½ box of Plymouth Rock brand gelatine (British spelling of the more familiar gelatin); ½ pint of cold water; 6 oranges, sliced or scooped; 1 can pineapple, diced; 1 pound of white grapes, skinned and seeded; a few maraschino cherries (optional). PREPARATION – Soak gelatine in cold water for 1 hour, the set on stove until thoroughly dissolved. Add oranges, pineapple, grapes, and cherries. Add sugar to taste. Place mixture in flat mould. Cut into squares (nice to serve with meat or for dessert).[145]

The Grace Church Cook Book, published in Bloomington in 1909, tendered a general soup-to-nuts collection in which every recipe for baked goods called for either Kossuth or Germania Cake Flour, the principal products of Bloomington's Hungarian Roller Mill. This represented an expression of gratitude for the company's sponsorship, but another recipe in the collection insisted on Karo Syrup, a brand with no local provenance. During the decade following the First World War, the names Karo, All-Bran, and Baker's Chocolate appeared with remarkable frequency in McLean County's fund-raiser cookbooks.

In addition to identifying certain brands, *The Bloomington Cookbook* also contained recipes that called for "N.O." or "New Orleans Molasses." Such geographic specification preceded the trade name, allowing a customer who enjoyed a particular coffee or tea to ask a grocer for it by region. Advertisements for Wait's grocery in Bloomington, for example, listed several specific sugars, including barrels imported from St. Croix, New Orleans, and Puerto Rico. Likewise, coffees bore labels indicating they came from Java, Rio, Maracaibo, and Laguayra.[146] Another identifier commonly used by grocers was grade. Bloomington's Chisholm Brothers advertised sugar varieties that included Coffee A, Extra C, Extra Golden C, Best Puerto Rican, Extra Cuba, Prime Rio, Good Rio, and Prime Rio Browned.

Many of the earliest brand-name groceries consisted of highly refined products rendered virtually indistinguishable from their competitors by milling and various other processes. Baking ingredients were prime examples, and such products as Popple's Flour, Stratton's Yeast, Dooley's Yeast Powder, and Pyle's OK Saleratus and Baking Soda were among the first branded foodstuffs to be advertised in McLean County. Perhaps the earliest brand-name food product manufactured in Bloomington was Tilton's Baking Powder, a product made by

W.H. Tilton and L.T. Danthutt, proprietors of the Quaker Store, a North Center Street grocery.[147]

WHOLESALE GROCERS

Several Bloomington grocers began selling wholesale as soon as the city acquired a railroad. McMillan and Roush, one of the first, advertised itself as "the oldest wholesale house in Central Illinois." It sent drummers (sales representatives) out to rural areas to search for prospective grocers. Candidates were promised every assistance; the company could outfit them with a complete store in practically no time.[148]

Brown and Gray Groceries was located at 113 W. Front Street in Bloomington in 1878.

McMillan and Roush almost certainly sold supplies to Benjamin Hoopes, a retail grocer who ventured into wholesale after the Civil War. Hoopes learned the grocery business working for Peter Whitmer and the Parke brothers, proprietors of one of Bloomington's largest general stores. By 1834, the Parkes were doing a substantial grocery business and needed an additional clerk. They sent word to Chester County, Pennsylvania, offering the position to Hoopes, a young man they had befriended before moving west. Benjamin accepted and worked in the store until 1857. Two of the Parkes, John and Samuel, had left by then, and Whitmer wanted out. Hoopes purchased his share, and together with George Parke opened Parke and Hoopes, a full-fledged grocery store on the North Center side of Public Square. Hoopes quit the business and moved to Springfield when the Civil War broke out. He returned to Bloomington and the food business after the war. A few years later, around 1870, Martha Smith, also known as Widow Garret, entered his life. With her help, Hoopes began selling groceries wholesale and added yet another business to his interests, Bloomington Coffee, Spice, and Hominy Mills. Widow Garret became Martha Hoopes in 1874. When Benjamin and Martha's son, Albert, joined the company around 1887, Hoopes's grocery concern became B.F. Hoopes and Son and remained so until it closed for good around 1900.[149]

John "J.F." Humphreys, whose name became almost synonymous with groceries throughout Central Illinois, came with his parents from Kentucky to the Peoria area in 1839. Almost immediately he was sent to reside with Dr. Thomas Rogers in the nearby village of Washington. John was just eight years old at the time, but 11 years later he accompanied Rogers to Bloomington as his business partner and helped him open Sampson and Rogers, a general store on Courthouse Square. After Sampson and Rogers burned down in 1853, Humphreys married Dr. Rogers' daughter, Laura. He rebuilt the store as a dedicated grocery, but two years later fire destroyed it again. Once more Humphreys rebuilt, this time in the 100 block of East Front. He later sold groceries at a number of other locations in the city and in conjunction with various partners, beginning with Robert Gustin. Subsequent deals involved John Roush (Roush and Humphreys), Mark Newton and Charles Barber (Humphreys, Newton and Company), and Robert Evans (Humphreys, Evans and Company). Humphreys' career culminated in 1889 with the incorporation of J.F. Humphreys and Company.

Humphreys turned the company over to his son, Howard, following incorporation. Howard plunged into wholesale and the distribution side of the business and soon met with considerable success. An aggressive expansion policy led to a merger with Springfield distributor John W. Bunn and Company in 1928. Bunn and Humphreys began operations in Bloomington but began moving them to Springfield in 1930.[150] Howard Humphreys died in 1932, but at the height of his company's success *The Daily Pantagraph* had a bit of good-natured fun with a comic caricature and the following limerick:

Since to eat is a chief need of man,

And to wed is an excellent plan,

In preserving of food,

To be sure it keeps good,

He includes Wedding Rings in the can.[151]

The line about wedding rings referred to J.F. Humphreys' private label, an assortment of canned fruits, vegetables, and fish distributed as Wedding Ring brand products. Historically, grocers sold private labels and distributor brands were seen as cheap, low-quality products, but Humphreys marketed Wedding Ring canned goods as premium products, "put by" under the most scientific and hygienic methods.

McLean County's most famous trademark after J.F. Humphrey's Wedding Ring label was Campbell Holton and Company's Happy Hour brand foods. Holton's introduction to the grocery trade came in 1881, at age 16, when he went to work for C.E. Ross in Lincoln. Holton bought out Ross within a few years and soon caught the eye of Howard Humphreys. He brought Holton to Bloomington as general manager of J.F. Humphreys Wholesale Food Company in 1893.

By 1908, Holton was ready to take off on his own.[152] He opened a store in the 100 block of East Front Street, and began marketing a variety of canned goods bearing the Happy Hour trademark.[153] His products originally included canned fruits and vegetables, canned oysters, and canned milk. Soon there were Happy Hour pickles and olives, catsup and mustard, jams and jellies, spices and extracts, teas and coffees, syrups, dried fruits and nuts, macaroni and noodles, and various kinds of canned fish. A second label, "Red Mill," was launched in 1910. Yet another Campbell Holton trademark, "Camel," appeared in 1953 and was used to brand an economy line of canned goods. These additional labels allowed Happy Hour's quality to remain uncompromised.

> . . . all items under this brand are the best that their respective marts and climes can offer or produce. Mushrooms, olives and olive oil from France and Spain. Pineapples from Bahama and Hawaii. Fruit from California's Sun Kist Groves. Sweet potatoes from Jersey. Corn from Maine's stony hills. Salmon from Alaskan waters. Fig conserves from Texas orchards. Peas from Colorado's irrigated gardens. You may enjoy the world's best; they will come to you dressed in lavender labels under the Happy Hour mark.[154]

None of these foods were actually packed in Bloomington or by Campbell Holton. Early canners situated their industry on the coasts. They concentrated at first on high value products like oysters and salmon because cans had to be sealed by hand. Advances in mechanization reduced costs, much to the benefit of fruit and vegetable growers in California. Canneries started moving into the Midwest, including Illinois, in the 1920s.[155] McLean County's biggest canner, Lutz Greenhouse and Cannery of Normal, specialized in tomatoes.[156] Happy Hour products were packed in distant canneries, some of them thousands of miles away. Still, the company carefully monitored the quality of its products and took pride in selling them.

Bloomington's wholesalers became known for their coffees, and between 1910 and the mid '30s the city was the center of coffee roasting in downstate Illinois. Humphreys began roasting its own coffee in 1910, and shortly afterwards Campbell Holton and McAtee-Newell started doing the same. By 1932, the three firms together were importing more than 170 carloads of green coffee per year and selling over four million pounds.[157]   McAtee-Newell sold four brand names at different price points. There was Mainstay, the discount label; Inca Maiden; Rosy Morn; and Pal-O-Mine, the very best coffee McAtee-Newell blended.[158] The company sold the popular-priced Rosy Morn – ballyhooed to be as "Cheerful as the Morning Sun" – in one-pound tins and four-pound pails. These were commonly used by coffee roasters and were appreciated by consumers because they could re-use them for anything from slopping the pigs to washing the car. Campbell Holton's Campbell brand coffee was packed in bright yellow cans imprinted with a desert scene populated with three camels and the inscription, "combination of rare old coffees."[159]

As the years passed and independent grocers came under increasing pressure to reduce their costs, wholesalers like Campbell Holton organized them into networks. Eventually, 102 independent grocers gathered under the Holton's Happy Hour banner. By joining networks, associations, and cooperatives, local stores essentially leveled the playing field by taking advantage of purchasing power and expertise equivalent to the corporate chains'.[160] IGA (Independent Grocers Association), started in 1926, grew to become the largest organization of independent grocers in the country, but Campbell Holton and the Happy Hour stores remained the biggest group in Central Illinois. Operations had moved from Front Street to Gridley and Moulton Streets in 1912. In 1954, they moved into the Center Street property that previously housed Bunn Capitol. General Grocer of Illinois, a Bloomington-based division of General Grocer of St. Louis, moved in and bought out Campbell Holton in 1965. Organized as a cooperative, General Grocer supplied member stores with wholesale meats, vegetables, and packaged goods, as well as the kind of up-to-date accounting, advertising, and consulting that independents could no longer afford on their own.[161] General Grocer moved into a new 125,000-square-foot warehouse on Bloomington's General Electric Road in 1967. It went out of business in 1981.

G.C. HEBERLING COMPANY

Heberling Medicine and Extract Company, later the G.C. Heberling Company, opened around 1902 and continued in business for 55 years. It carried certain grocery products such as extracts (e.g, vanilla, root beer), flavorings, (e.g., strawberry, banana), spices (e.g., cinnamon, mustard), cocoa, chocolate dessert, chewing gum, and Japanese tea.[162] These products arrived at its downtown Bloomington warehouse from around the world. As a 1926 advertisement bragged:

> Our Tellicherry pepper comes from far off Java, Siam, and the Malay Peninsula; our cloves from the Indian Archipelago, Zanzibar, and Madagascar; our cinnamon from the sunny isles of Ceylon and ginger from Jamaica and Africa; our allspice from the West Indies and Mexico; our mustard from Holland and California; our essential oils and perfumes from Italy, France, Austria, Bulgaria and other small principalities in Southern Europe. 'The sun never sets on our sources of supply.'[163]

But, Heberling never pretended to be a full service grocer. Rather, it was a kind of specialized general store for farm families – specialized in the sense that it carried things that farmers were unlikely to find for sale in a small town. This, of course, included a vast number of goods, allowing Heberling to claim at one point that it stocked "a product for every need." In addition to food items, the company offered patent medicines, toilet articles, cosmetics, soaps, stock and poultry preparations, livestock minerals, and insecticides, everything sold door to door by catalog and shipped parcel post. Heberling at its peak employed more than 500 salesmen and did business in 28 states.[164] Sales declined as automobile ownership increased. The company went out of business in 1958.

CHAPTER 5 – FROM WARTIME RATIONING TO TOOLIN' THE GAG

The Second World War pulled the United States out of the Great Depression but soon plunged the country into another crisis by creating excess demand for agricultural products. Shortages developed. Federal authorities responded by setting up rationing programs and initiating educational campaigns to prevent malnutrition. These interventions had the lasting effect of increasing nutritional awareness among Americans. A far more radical effect came with the post-war automotive revolution. Everything changed. Cars and trucks in vast numbers propagated supermarkets, drive-ins, and profoundly affected practically every food-related industry in the country.

The number of supermarkets in the United States mushroomed after the war. Chain stores abandoned the older parts of the city, moved to the outskirts, and built spacious structures with sprawling parking lots. Facilities grew larger as the years passed and the number of products lining the aisles increased. The typical supermarket carried 3,000 items in 1940. By 1950, it was 5,000 items; by 1970, 10,000. Many of these products had been the stock-in-trade of local dairies, butcher shops, fruit and vegetable markets, neighborhood bakeries, sweet shops, and other specialty stores.[1] Other products, such as frozen foods and tomatoes that ripened on the road instead of on the vine, were new to the market.[2] Road construction, particularly the construction of interstate highways, benefited supermarkets by providing more efficient supply avenues than the nation's railroads. Corporate buyers and distribution centers bypassed terminal markets and rendered local wholesale houses marginal concerns.[3]

Highway construction prior to the war encouraged the development of roadhouses, truck stops, and drive-ins. Truck stops stood out as "oases of respectability" compared to the generally crude roadhouses that served traveling men.[4] At the same time, coffee-shop chains such as Howard Johnson's and Denny's prospered by catering to women travelers.[5] The drive-in restaurant of the Depression years, an incubator for quick service, introduced innovations along that line, including the electronic intercom systems of the 1960s and the drive-up window.[6] Drive-ins attracted young customers with a lot of time on their hands, and indeed by the '60s teenagers essentially took over many of these establishments and made them centers of youth culture.

WORLD WAR II

World War II took a great number of men out of McLean County and sent them abroad. Those who remained behind were left with an enormous amount of work to do. Railroad men worked overtime. Factories became defense plants and employed second and third shifts. Bloomington's Paul F. Beich Company implored anyone unemployed to report to its facility to help make Whiz Bars, Pecan Petes, and Dipsy Doodles, candies the armed services were buying in ever-increasing quantities.[7] People volunteered to serve in Civil Defense. They joined the Red Cross and practiced what to do in case of attack.[8] Authorities harangued everyone to conserve and save, just as they had during World War I. Conservation was voluntary the first time around. People had no choice in the matter during World War II.

RATIONING

The need to regulate the sale of certain foods became evident the Monday morning following Pearl Harbor when people hurried to stores and emptied their shelves of sugar.[9] Prices immediately shot upward and officials worried about inflation. Economists proposed rationing as a preventive measure. Heeding their advice, the federal Office of Price Administration (OPA) issued a "Sugar Book." It contained coupons that beginning in May 1942 had to be presented to a retailer by anyone intending to purchase that commodity.[10] The system, referred to as "Uniform Coupon Rationing," accorded everyone the same number of vouchers, each initially valued at one-half pound of sugar per week. Values changed from time to time as supplies fluctuated, but consumers had to use a particular coupon for whatever it was worth within a specified number of days. As a result, shoppers needed timely reminders like the notice Sprengel's Fine Foods of Bloomington placed in *The Daily Pantagraph* urging customers to "Use your No. 11 Sugar Stamp Not Later Than March 15th."[11]

Federal officials introduced a second method of rationing involving open-ended entitlements to commodities in various categories. This scheme, referred to as "Point Rationing," assigned everyone a fixed number of credits, but required more of them to buy items in high demand than to purchase items fewer people wanted.[12] Every member of a household under this system received Red Stamps and Blue Stamps, each worth a specified number of points. To purchase cheeses, butter and other fats, and nearly all meats and fish required a certain quantity of Red Stamps. Consumers needed Blue Stamps to purchase canned, bottled, and frozen fruits and vegetables; juices; dried beans; and processed foods such as soups, baby food, and catsup.

Some folks just did not get it. Coupons, points, Red Stamps, Blue Stamps – it was all too confusing. Retailers, including Bloomington's Happy Hour and Piggly Wiggly stores, listed the number of points required to buy particular products, but to some extent the stores may have inadvertently abetted confusion by urging customers to "spend" ration points on this or that item.[13] This apparently gave some people the impression that ration stamps amounted to a form of currency. Well into the war, Piggly Wiggly still found it necessary to remind shoppers ". . . That You Still Have to Pay for Merchandise in Money . . . ."[14]

For some goods all a purchaser needed was money, no stamps. Indeed, most of the items on the grocer's shelves were not rationed. Bloomington's Piggly Wiggly helped shoppers keep things straight by placing ads in *The Daily Pantagraph* with products conveniently arranged in two columns, one for rationed foods, the other for items not rationed. One such ad placed in 1943 listed Del Monte Canned Peaches, University Vacuum Packed Corn, Libby's Baked Beans, Widmer's Grape Juice, Camp   bell's Tomato Soup, Gerber's Baby Foods, and Birdseye Fresh Frosted Strawberries in the rationed column.[15] Although sugar was rationed, alternative sweeteners, including molasses, honey, maple syrup, and corn syrup, were listed as unrationed. Candy bars, condensed milk, pudding mixes, and sodas also escaped rationing.

Piggly Wiggly's advertisement directed special attention to Sunset Gold Bread. "You can buy all you want," the ad declared. The copy went on to emphasize, "Now It's Sliced Again," because for the previous two months, sliced bread had been banned owing to an anticipated dearth of waxed paper. Baking companies complained loudly about the ban, and Washington lifted it immediately once it became clear the shortage was not about to materialize. Bloomington's Purity Baking Company celebrated. It took out a newspaper ad addressed "To our friends on the quartermaster front in the National Nutritional Program." No more grumbling; "We're With You All The Way," the company announced.[16]

Still, there were other problems. In the case of Uniform Coupon Rationing, dissention arose concerning sugar. Most Americans good naturedly struggled with brown sugar and other substitutes when using recipes calling for white sugar, but it was not long before the public became aware that bakers had relatively little trouble procuring the genuine article. Consumers protested the inequity, and many complained bitterly about being in effect forced to purchase commercial bakery products.[17] Generally speaking, people took Red Stamp rationing much harder than Blue Stamp because of the importance of animal products in the American diet. The production of Red-Stamp foods increased by as much as half during the war years, but added demand always outstripped improved supplies. There was never enough butter.[18] Fat from bacon and other meats could be substituted as a cooking fat, but the vast majority of Americans had no fondness for margarine. Manufacturers tried to change that. Delrich, for example, pitched its product using a caricature of a pretty young housewife who proclaimed, "Rationing has its good points, too! It started me on delicious Delrich, the new margarine sensation."[19] Illinois, unlike many other states, did not disallow coloring margarine yellow to make it resemble butter, but in states that banned the practice the substance looked like a greasy lump of lard and was exceeding difficult to sell as a table spread. McLean County restaurant owners tried to relieve some of the demand on meat by agreeing to observe meatless Fridays, but less than half of the proprietors invited showed up at a meeting intended to seek their endorsements.[20]

With regard to meat, there was no shortage of suggestions about how to prepare meals using less. As during the First World War, there was plenty of advice about how to use unfamiliar cuts of meat, and various other products that promised to enliven meals and improve life on the home front. The federal government issued meal-planning guides, recipes, and daily menus. The State of Illinois published *Home Budgets . . . for Victory*.[21] *Good Housekeeping Magazine's* 1943 cookbook featured a special section for rationed foods, and companies throughout the country publicized recipes for economical dishes featuring their products.[22] Armour and Company of Chicago, for example, produced *69 Ration Recipes for Meat from Marie Gifford's Kitchen* (circa 1943), a booklet distributed free of charge to its customers. Gifford, Director of the Department of Food Economics at Armour, served the company as a kind of real-life Betty Crocker, the fictional kitchen advisor created by General Mills in 1921.

Clara Brian, still McLean County's Home Adviser and by this time something of a Betty Crocker figure herself, dusted off her notes from World War I and returned to the topic of wartime cooking. She contributed a set of nutritionally well-balanced menus to *The Daily Pantagraph* once a week, and every day she provided a new recipe. For example:

Macaroni and Cheese Cutlets

INGREDIENTS – 4 tablespoons fat, 5 tablespoons flour, ¾ teaspoon salt, ⅛ teaspoon paprika, 1 cup milk, 1 cup grated cheese, 1 cup cooked and drained macaroni, 1 pimiento cut in small pieces, 1 tablespoon chopped parsley, 1 teaspoon minced onion. PREPARATION – Melt fat in top of double boiler; add flour, salt, and paprika; add milk and cook until smooth and thick, stirring occasionally; add macaroni, pimiento, parsley, and onion and mix; spread mixture in shallow pan and chill until stiff; cut into cutlets with cookie cutter; roll in crumb, then in beaten egg, then in crumbs again; fry in hot fat 1 inch deep in heavy frying pan until brown; drain on absorbent paper. Serves six to eight.[23]

Macaroni and cheese, generally regarded as a Southern specialty before the war, became nationally popular as a stand-in for meat. The dish dates back to the early nineteenth century, but its ascent to major American comfort food did not begin until Kraft introduced a boxed version called "Kraft Dinner" in 1937. Kraft Dinner was advertised relentlessly during the war as a terrific bargain – two boxes for but one coupon. The campaign resulted in unprecedented sales, totaling 80 million boxes nationwide in 1943. Cottage cheese, promoted by dairy groups as a substitute for meat, also acquired a newfound popularity, going from less than 200 million pounds sold per year in the 1930s to 500 million pounds in 1944. Still, in spite of enormous efforts to pry Americans away from prime cuts and to convince them to eat less beef, pork, and poultry, more black market activity revolved around these products than any of the other rationed foods.[24]

In the restaurant industry, rationing and shortages spelled an end to *a la carte* dinners in many places. Restaurateurs offered two or three fixed menus as a way to control waste and cope with government allowances.[25] Fresh vegetables replaced hard-to-get canned goods. In addition, meals were subject to price controls administered by the OPA. These kept eating places out of the black markets by limiting how much owners could charge for meals. As a 1944 dinner menu for the Hotel Rogers' Fiesta Room noted,

> All prices are our ceiling prices or below. By OPA regulation our ceiling prices are based on our highest prices from April 4 to 10, 1943. Our price lists for that week are available for your inspection.[26]

This was to assure patrons that the 65 cents they were asked to pay for "Spaghetti with meatballs; head lettuce and French dressing; home made pecan rolls; coffee, tea or milk; choice of dessert" was no more than the amount guests paid the year before.

GARDENING, CANNING, AND COOKING

Victory Gardens became very popular during World War II. They had been tried during World War I, and the idea was the same. For a small investment in seeds and time, families could enjoy fresh fruits and vegetables for months. Many households had continued to garden after World War I and through the Great Depression out of economic necessity, so horticultural skills were widespread. The National Victory Garden Program, announced in December 1941, officially enlisted those skills, and every spring throughout the war local grocers displayed onion sets, seed potatoes, and other starter plants in their produce sections.

Shortages of commercially canned fruits and vegetables reinvigorated America's interest in home canning. Canning garden crops at home, however, entailed considerably more trouble than raising them because canning equipment was hard to come by. To cope with the equipment shortage, officials urged home canners to work in groups and to share pressure cookers and other tools. Some towns set up canning centers, but millions of novice canners working with questionable equipment risked tragic results. Writers flooded newspapers and magazines with safe-canning instructions, and for the most part, explosions and poisonings were avoided.[27]

Americans cultivated 20 million Victory Gardens during the summer of 1943 and raised nearly one-third of all vegetables consumed in the United States. Pantries and fruit cellars bulged with the largest supply of home-canned foods in history. By 1945, Victory Gardens were producing approximately 40 percent of the nation's vegetables. This sent the sale of commercially canned products into a tailspin and caused the official line out of Washington to change. Suddenly Americans were too sparing in their use of canned goods, and authorities launched anti-hoarding campaigns aimed at increasing consumption.[28]

RECOMMENDED DIETS

Nutritionists became major players in the area of food policy, thanks to President Roosevelt's decision to rely on the National Research Council for advice.[29] Responding to executive concerns regarding the nutritional needs of soldiers and defense workers, its Food and Nutrition Board (FNB) created a set of Recommended Dietary Allowances (RDAs). These stipulated the daily quantities of energy, protein, and eight essential vitamins and minerals the average adult needed to maintain good health. Survey data viewed in light of the committee's RDAs led to the conclusion that as many as one-third of the nation's families consumed less than adequate diets. As rationing threatened to make matters worse, "Vitamins Vital for Victory" and other diet-related war cries began emanating from Washington.[30] Policy makers responded by calling on manufacturers to fortify and enrich common foods.[31]

Fortification and enrichment were already commonplace in certain sectors of the food industry. Fortification was first undertaken in 1924 with the commercial development and sale of iodized salt in Michigan. A nationwide demand developed quickly, and within a decade iodine deficiency no longer existed as a health issue in United States. Subsequent programs were pursued as public health measures. Successes included the addition of vitamin D to milk in the 1930s, a move largely responsible for eliminating rickets from big city slums, and the enrichment of cornmeal and other cereal products with niacin, an intervention that effectively eradicated pellagra from regions of the South. Broader efforts to enrich flour and bread received a boost in 1942 when the Army decided to purchase enriched products exclusively.[32] One hundred percent enrichment was finally achieved in 1943 after the War Foods Administration put its foot down and required the addition of B vitamins and iron to flour.[33]

Americans required more than food fortification and enrichment programs to prompt them to eat a diet that would fulfill the RDAs. People had to consume a variety of foods, but as a practical matter they could hardly be expected to measure their daily intakes consistently and accurately. To solve this problem, the FNB came up with the idea of dividing food into eight groups. A person would concentrate on eating foods from each group everyday or over the course of a week. Instructions appeared in newspaper editorials and in advertisements entitled "Our Government Recommends" or "Uncle Sam's Food Rules."[34] Within a few months, Uncle Sam's eight groups shrank to the "Basic Seven" for the sake of simplicity. The seven food groups consisted of green and yellow vegetables; oranges, grapefruits, and tomatoes; raw cabbage or salad greens; potatoes and other vegetables or fruits; milk and milk products; meat, poultry, fish, and eggs or dried beans, peas, nuts, and peanut butter; bread, flour, and cereals; and butter or fortified margarine.[35] Some food companies concocted nutrition education schemes of their own. A&P, for instance, rated foods by vitamin content. Newspaper ads scored fresh head lettuce A+ B1+ C++ G+, meaning a good source of vitamins A, B1, and G (the original name for riboflavin) and an especially good source of vitamin C. Florida celery rated A++ C+, and Texas grapefruit earned a " B1+ C++."[36] Administration officials addressed public concern by funding programs in nutritional education. In Bloomington, Mrs. Fred Wollrab taught classes about nutrients and the dos and don'ts of proper nutrition at Withers Public Library every Monday night.[37]

Nutrition education became big business after the war. The USDA tried at first to simplify things by paring the number of food groups down to the "Basic Four" (meats, dairy products, grains, and fruits and vegetables). However, beginning in the 1950s, the matter of what to eat and how much became the business of an increasing number of government departments, agencies, public interest groups, and private enterprises. Research generated a flood of new information and ideas. Conceptual confusion, plus the welter of information flowing from various agencies and interest groups, has been of considerable benefit to the country's unregulated, 30 billion-dollars-a-year diet industry, a collection of firms in the business of telling people what and what not to eat, usually because they want to lose weight (see Chapter 7).

AUTOMOTIVE FOODWAYS

America's automotive revolution began prior to World War II, but it did not reach crisis proportions until mid-century. In 1945, the final year of the conflict, U.S. car sales totaled 69,500 units. One year later, sales amounted to over two million vehicles. By the mid-1960s, automakers were building around six million vehicles a year.[38] In the meantime, streetcars, interurban railroads, and other forms of public transportation succumbed to neglect and were dismantled. Soon there was no turning back; America pegged its future on the automobile and investment concentrated on compatible facilities. Supermarkets, motels, and shopping malls became commonplace. Drive-in restaurants and teenagers cruising around in the family car from one to another were by-products of the revolution and had little to do with the practical necessities of getting from here to there.[39]

RISE OF THE SUPERMARKET

Supermarkets hastened the downfall of the neighborhood grocery. They also lowered the boom on independent milk providers, meat markets, produce dealers, and bakeries. Why deal with all of these different businesses when everything they carried could be found under one roof?

Supermarkets actually originated prior to the automotive revolution, but initially they were little more than oversized, conventional food stores. Ralph's, an established Los Angeles chain, developed a prototype with 5,000 square feet of floor space back in the 1920s. In 1932, Michael Cullen built King Kullen, a 10,000 square-foot facility in Jamaica, New York. He added what would prove to be an essential feature, a big parking lot.[40] Soon large chains throughout the United States were doing the same. About the time the word "supermarket" entered the lexicon in 1936, there were 1,200 such stores scattered among 84 American cities.[41] A&P committed to supermarkets in 1935, and over the next five years the company opened 1,400 of them. By 1940, just 4,100 conventional A&Ps remained open. There had been 15,000 such facilities 10 years earlier.[42]

The supermarket did not begin to dominate the industry until the post-war boom in automobile ownership enabled a significant number of Americans to drive out of their neighborhoods and away from the built-up areas of town so they could "shop the modern way." This meant being able to select from a large assortment of products in different departments, including health-care items, cosmetics, and other things having little or nothing to do with food. Managers began stocking non-food items as a way to keep their shelves full despite wartime food shortages. The practice continued after the war because supermarket customers had come to expect an aisle of sundry goods.[43]

Nothing, however, attracted customers like exceptional values, and to create them post-war supermarkets instituted "predatory pricing."[44] This involved publicizing so-called "loss leaders," products offered at prices below cost. These enticed customers into the store and ginned up the sale of other products. The plan was to settle for a very modest profit per item but to make up for it by selling huge quantities. This concept put stores unable to sell in volume at a distinct disadvantage.

The industry became sensitive to volume and undertook serious campaigns to boost it beginning in the 1930s. Lierman's, a food store at Lee and Oakland in Bloomington, was typical in that it never let a week pass without at least one major sales event. The third week of January 1938, for example, was all about a visit from Aunt Jemima, a fictitious black woman "famous for her pancakes and syrup." Lierman's announced she would be visiting the store on Saturday and preparing free pancakes for everyone who stopped by.[45] Her cakes, the newspaper ads promised, would be covered with Log Cabin syrup, and they would be served with Lierman's Pure Pork Sausage, a product "seasoned to satisfy, and made to perfection." And, of course, Aunt Jemima Pancake Mix, the syrup, the sausage – all would be available to purchase at special low prices. Shoppers would also find Lierman's Blue Ribbon Meats, Armour's Star beef shoulder roasts, Cudahy's Puritan hams, "Genuine Young Baby beef liver," and various "Economy meats" on sale. Florida oranges in 10-pound bags, ripe strawberries, new potatoes, Purity Ann Twist Bread, and fancy mixed sandwich cookies also were going to be specially priced.

Lierman's offered free delivery and advertised "accessible parking," but as the large chains converted to supermarkets, independent companies found it difficult to muster sufficient capital to do the same.[46] Payne's, an established Bloomington grocer, proved an exception. In 1939, just months before Kroger debuted a supermarket in the 1100 block of North Main, Payne's opened its third store, a 4,000-square-foot facility at East and Locust Streets. It offered 11,000 square feet of parking on crushed stone within a few blocks of the downtown area. Farmers, many of whom came downtown to trade on Saturday and among whom car ownership was nearly universal, must have found Payne's a particularly convenient place to buy groceries.

THE DAIRY CASE

Payne's, Kroger, and other early supermarkets stocked bottled milk and other dairy products, but most families preferred to purchase them from a "milkman" who delivered right to the door. Milk left on the doorstep in the early morning hours now strikes most people as quaint, but Americans continue to consume dairy foods in immense quantities. Average consumption currently totals more than 500 pounds per person per year. This makes dairy the largest food group by weight in the American diet, and it supports a level of milk production unsurpassed anywhere in the world.[47]

Most of the milk produced in the United States today is made into cheese, but until about the middle of the twentieth century, most of it was churned into butter to be used in cooking or to spread on bread.[48] At Clover Lawn, the cows were milked to make butter for the David Davis family. The same held true throughout the county, where so many families owned cows that some towns employed a municipal herdsman. Of course, people drank buttermilk and even whole milk on occasion, but the primary object was butter. When William Snavely of Hudson established one of the county's earliest dedicated dairies it was first and foremost a butter operation. Snavely began about 1890 with a dozen Jersey cows, a steam-powered separator, and a butter churn hooked up to a dog wheel.[49] His mutts ran the wheel once a week, churning butter for Gray Brothers' Grocery in Bloomington where it was sold under the brand name "Edgewood Farm."

Milk drinking as a food habit originated around the middle of the nineteenth century when women unable or unwilling to nurse their babies turned to cow's milk as a substitute for breast milk.[50] This was risky, especially in urban areas where residents bought milk by the ladle from street vendors. Bacteria flourished in the buckets and other containers sellers used, and as daytime temperatures climbed the chances of bacterial contamination increased. The upshot was "summer complaint" or "summer diarrhea," a disease that often proved lethal among children. Poor parents who diluted their children's milk to make it go farther, frequently made things worse by unwittingly using polluted water. Gastrointestinal diseases accounted for up to 25 percent of infant mortality in the United States as late as 1900.[51]

To reduce mortality, cities stepped in and made certain sanitary procedures mandatory. Bloomington was slow to act because the purity issues troubling major urban centers such as Chicago and New York were not nearly so urgent. This can be explained by the relatively small size of McLean County's dairy operations and the immediacy of the relationship between producers and their customers. Frank Laesch and his wife, Sophie, opened East Side Dairy in 1907 serving just seven customers by personally delivering milk to each seven days a week.[52] Within a month, the Laesches were selling the rich yellow milk produced by their little herd of Guernseys to 10 times that number of households. Frank continued to deliver door to door by horse and wagon, and kept his milk in 10-gallon canisters of ice water. Customers called out the quantity of milk they wanted as Frank pulled up to the door and brought their own containers out to his wagon. Frank measured orders using a two-gallon spout. Kids loved it when he gave them a chunk of ice as a treat.

Local regulations went into effect four years after the Laesches began selling milk. Bloomington began with an ordinance making it illegal to sell milk directly from cans. This necessitated bottling and forced the Laesches to purchase glass containers in pint and quart sizes, plus the equipment to fill them. In addition, running water systems had to be installed to cool the milk. Home delivery continued, but Laesch and other dairymen moved deliveries to the early morning hours before the sun was up. This lowered cooling costs but made door-to-door delivery a bit dangerous since street lighting barely existed.[53] A milkman could be garroted by a clothesline, or he might step into a fishpond. He had to be careful during the heat of the summer not to trip over people sleeping outside on the lawn or on a porch.

Delivery by horse and wagon continued in Bloomington into the 1940s. This provided blacksmiths with work that otherwise was becoming difficult to find. Charlie Simmons, the blacksmith for Leman Dairy, often would be called out on winter nights to outfit the horses with sharp shoes so they would not fall on icy streets.[54] Leman's also kept William Ulbrich's Harness and Leather Shop on call in case of emergency. When the National Labor Relations Act was passed in 1935 it entitled milkmen to a six-day work week. To cover their days off, companies hired substitutes and supplied them with customer lists. Sometimes errors were made, but before they were replaced by trucks, delivery horses knew their routes well enough to stop at customers' houses whether or not their names appeared on the milkman's list.[55]

Pasteurization, a huge step forward in assuring the safety of milk products, was introduced to the world in 1895. In 1908, Chicago became the first city in the world to require pasteurization. Most big cities followed suit during the next decade. In Bloomington, the Snow and Palmer Dairy took the bull by the horns in 1922 and was the first to introduce pasteurization to its customers.[56] The company, which at the time processed approximately 1,800 gallons of milk and cream per day, sent a letter to its customers explaining the process and its advantages.[57] Snow and Palmer's customers may not have been clamoring beforehand for purer milk, but given the company's subsequent aggressiveness with respect to milk safety, it must have been heartened by the response its pasteurization program received.

The Snow and Palmer story began in 1870 when 14-year-old Willis Snow began selling milk in McLean.[58] He and Harry Palmer, a neighboring farmer, formed a partnership in 1897, intending to sell milk, cream, butter, and ice cream to the residents of Bloomington and Normal.[59] Palmer remained in McLean and took charge of milk production. Snow opened a plant in Bloomington and assumed responsibility for processing, sales, and distribution. Charles Snow, Willis's son, took over in 1925. He merged Snow and Palmer with Beatrice Creamery (later Beatrice Foods) and began selling milk products under the Meadow Gold banner. As Meadow Gold, Snow and Palmer employed leading-edge technology. The company introduced "Silver Seal" aluminum bottle caps, and it was quick to purchase homogenizing equipment.[60] In 1934, it became one of the first dairies in the country to market milk with no cream line. This involved considerable risk and a large measure of faith in customers' goodwill because nobody really knew if Meadow Gold's customers would remain so once they could no longer tell about the richness of its milk from the depth of the cream in the bottle.[61]

As milk consumption became more popular and the dairy industry grew, creamery owners had to do business with dairy farmers they did not know personally. By the 1930s, trucks were traveling up and down country roads to pick up milk containers at a considerable distance from Bloomington. Haulers working its milk shed area converged on the Shamrock Inn, a restaurant and bar on Route 150 a few miles east of the city.[62] The Shamrock served as an ad hoc transfer terminal and marketplace every day as milk haulers passed off their cargos to trucks from Bloomington-Normal's dairies. In addition to Snow and Palmer, Bevan, Leman, Normal Sanitary Dairy, and other creameries conducted business at the Shamrock. Snow and Palmer was the first to become concerned about the integrity of its milk and employ a field man charged with monitoring suppliers' practices.

Perry Piper, the company's first inspector, uncovered both honest mistakes and dishonest dealings. He once noted that a farmer and milk hauler named "Bill" always had three full cans of milk ostensibly from his own farm, but from day to day the milk varied in fat content, from seven percent or higher to a low of two percent. His milk also showed poor cooling. Otherwise, he seemed to be a fine producer, and he never complained, but Piper decided to go out to Bill's farm and check his operation.

> Course I knew he would be on the milk route but I figured his wife could show me around. When I got there and asked her to see the cows and the milk cooler, she looked a bit puzzled. It seemed that they only had one cow and she was dry.

'Oh, Oh.' Sez I, 'I wonder where those three cans per day were coming from.' Then I found out, Old Bill was stopping along the road under a friendly shade tree and dipping a never to be missed half gallon of milk out of every can on the truck and using it to fill three cans under his name. A neat little racket and one not likely to be caught . . . . The barn yard pump has sometimes been called the best cow on the farm but (Bill's scam) was an even better one.[63]

Laesch's was the last milk business in the area to remain independent and make home deliveries. Others, like Snow and Palmer, were absorbed by larger firms. Steege's Western Dairy, founded in the early 1890s by German immigrant Henry Steege, became Leman's Dairy in 1926.[64] When Elmer Rehker took the helm in 1929, he expanded the company's offerings and among other things began making sweet butter and sour cream to meet the demands of Bloomington-Normal's Jewish residents. The company's slogan, "You can beat our cream but you can't beat our milk," became a national catchphrase when cartoonist Sidney Smith began using it in his syndicated "Andy Gump" comic strip. When Rehker retired around 1940 Leman's became part of Normal Sanitary Dairy. It in turn became a unit of the Pure Milk Association, which wound up being acquired by Prairie Farms Dairy, a producers' cooperative headquartered in Carlinville, Illinois. Most of the other milk companies in the area simply went out of business, including Bonnett's in McLean; Allen's, Fletcher's and Little Boss in Normal; and Bevan's, Highland, and Zwick's in Bloomington.[65]

Frank Laesch himself temporarily bailed out of the dairy business in 1919 when his landlord raised the rent on his pasture.[66] Frank refused to pay and sold his herd. He and his wife bought 54 acres near Bloomington with the proceeds and were back in the dairy business the next year. Their two eldest sons, Daniel and Otto, took over in 1940. In 1943, Otto sold Daniel his half of the business, which at that point included two trucks serving approximately 600 customers.

Daniel Laesch began modernizing as quickly as possible after the war. He implemented pasteurization in 1947, expanded facilities, and added another truck to the company's little fleet. Ten years later Laesch had 3,500 home-delivery customers and decided to undertake another expansion of the processing facilities. In 1961, the company opened the first of four Dairy Barns in the Bloomington-Normal area. These were essentially convenience stores featuring the company's products as well as various ice cream specialties. Product lines included whole and skimmed milk, buttermilk, half-and-half, whipping cream, ice cream (15 flavors), sherbet (5 flavors), ice milk, cottage cheese, sour cream, French onion dip, and later on frozen pizza. Laesch manufactured its ice cream to premium specifications

(12 percent butterfat), and as a testament to its quality it won three Governor's Trophies at the Illinois State Fair. However, by the mid-1980s too few customers were willing to pay a premium price for a local product, making it necessary to retreat from previous standards.[67] Business at the Dairy Barns nevertheless remained brisk. Dairy Barn specialties included ice cream cones, ice cream sandwiches, "soft-serve home-paks," sundaes, shakes and malts, "polar punch" floats, and freezes. Laesch's Brownie Supreme Sundae stood out as a local favorite.

Laesch's Brownie Supreme Sundae
Select small banana boat (dish), draw 5.5 oz soft-serve ball into center of dish and finish with a curl, place one pecan fudge brownie on each side of the soft-serve, pump or ladle 1.5 oz hot fudge over soft-serve, dispense 3 stars of whipped dessert topping around product front and back, garnish with maraschino cherry.[68]

Laesch's diversification into retail stores proved timely as home-delivery peaked at 7,000 customers in the early '70s. The company at that time acquired milk from 21 farms. It had 46 employees, serviced 18 home-delivery routes, and maintained a fleet of 24 trucks. However, business declined as per capita milk consumption decreased. This occurred in part because of an increased use of soda water, particularly among children.[69] In addition, a growing number of shoppers decided it was more convenient and less costly to purchase dairy products where they purchased their groceries. Home delivery suffered as women increasingly took outside jobs, leaving nobody at home to put the milk in the refrigerator.[70] Laesch shut down its Dairy Barns in 1994 and turned to wholesaling. Milk bottling and ice cream production continued for another year or so until the company finally called it quits.

Currently, there are less than 1,000 milk handlers in the entire nation. The terrific attrition experienced in the industry has been blamed on the high costs imposed by health regulations, and the many federal and state programs meant to keep milk prices low and within reach of the poor. Still, as the twentieth century came to a close, the bottom line – just seven companies, three of them owned by grocery chains, were in control of 75 percent of the milk produced in the United States – was really no different in dairy than it was in other branches of the food industry.[71]

THE MEAT DEPARTMENT

Payne's Supermarket boasted of a "modern meat market with cuts conveniently and attractively displayed," but the practice of selling meat alongside groceries pre-dated the supermarket and its distinct departments by many years. In Bloomington, butcher Amasa "A.C." Washburn and grocer Elijah Horr joined forces in 1855.[72] Not much is known about Horr, but Washburn made a name for himself as Blooming Grove's first schoolmaster. Around 1843 he exchanged his hickory stick for a butcher's knife and went into the meat business.[73] Washburn and Horr teamed up later and erected a stand on Front Street next to the American Hotel. They traded meat and groceries, both wholesale and retail, from that location for several years.

Most grocers steered clear of perishables. Fresh pork spoiled quickly, and until the 1870s when Armour began butchering under refrigeration in Chicago it was strictly a seasonal product.[74] Fresh beef was available most of the year, particularly in cities, but slaughter took place one or two animals at a time, usually in basements and small sheds. This raised health concerns in congested neighborhoods, and in many places citizens effectively banished butchery to the edge of town.[75]

Bloomington addressed health concerns with an ordinance forcing local butchers out of their dank and often grubby shops and requiring them to conduct business in a new central facility called "City Market."[76] The building, constructed by B.F. Hoopes upon his return from the Civil War, featured a refrigeration system and was a model of sanitation.

City Market was most likely cooled by a mechanical refrigerator. The first machine capable of freezing water was conceived by John Gorrie, an American physician, in 1842.[77] His system used compressed air but did not achieve commercial success. Alexander Twining, who experimented with vapor-compression refrigeration, had commercial units up and running in the United States by 1856. Hoopes, who appears to have become acquainted with refrigeration during the war, may have learned the mechanics through the work of Thaddeus Lowe, a Union Army aeronaut (balloonist).[78] Lowe had experimented with the properties of gases for years and had taken out numerous patents on cooling devices.[79] How Hoopes became familiar with Lowe's work is anybody's guess, but within months of re-establishing himself in Bloomington, Hoopes built his state-of-the-art facility on the northeast corner of Monroe and Center.

Six of Bloomington's most prominent meat purveyors opened stalls in the new building. Tenants included A.C. Washburn, at this point in business by himself, and Charles Radbourn, a man regarded by many as the finest butcher in town.[80] An Englishman by birth, Radbourn opened his first shop on West Chestnut Street around 1856. His son, Charles, Jr., otherwise known as "Old Hoss" (see Chapter 3) may have acquired the terrific arm strength and endurance he displayed as a major league pitcher helping his dad in that shop. In any event,

Charles Sr. achieved a reputation for excellence. An obituary penned in 1909 praised his display cases as containing the "finest exhibit of meats ever seen in Bloomington" and recalled Radbourn's as the best place in the city to shop for bison, deer, bear, and other species of wild flesh.[81]

As for Benjamin Hoopes's City Market, it did not last long. Radbourn and his fellow butchers objected to being compelled to rent space there, sued the city over it, and won. Hoopes gave up on the scheme in 1870 when it became obvious to him it would never turn a profit. Besides, the facility distracted him from his latest enterprise, "The Fruit House," a store that featured both fresh and canned fruits as well as a complete line of groceries.[82]

Hoopes's crack at artificial refrigeration notwithstanding, it was cheaper in many places to cool commodities using natural ice. Ice houses in his day were extraordinarily efficient, losing little more than 10 percent of their coolant over the course of a summer. Refrigerated transportation was not nearly so efficient, but freight cars stocked with ice began to carry milk and butter to cities in the 1840s. By the 1860s, railroads had rolling stock capable of delivering fruit and seafood long distances in marketable condition.

Advances in refrigeration allowed Chicago packer Gustavus Swift to introduce a new system for marketing beef in 1879.[83] Previously, buyers shipped live cattle to local markets for slaughter. With improved refrigerator cars, Swift and Company fattened and slaughtered the animals in Chicago, dressed the beef, and delivered it fresh to wholesalers. This radically separated animal slaughter from consumption. It also laid the foundation for national companies like Armour and Swift to establish branch plants to supply local butcher shops. By the time the First World War broke out, Chicago packers had a presence in 25,000 American communities.[84] Consumers barely noticed because, unlike cured pork, cuts of red meat did not carry brand names. Central packinghouses sent entire quarters of beef weighing 200 pounds or more to branch facilities where meat cutters reduced them to wholesale specifications.[85] Retail butchers then cut family-sized portions and wrapped them in brown paper.

The Utesch family's grocery and meat market in Bloomington was typical. Utesch's had a large walk-in cooler refrigerated by big blocks of ice shelved overhead. Meat orders received from customers by telephone were wrapped and labeled inside the cooler every day. Saturday night was especially busy with everyone who worked at the store filling orders for roasts intended for Sunday dinner. Seeing as very few homes had refrigerators or any other means for keeping meat in palatable condition through a hot summer's night, George Utesch and Richard Fulkerson were out about five o'clock on Sunday morning making deliveries by horse and wagon.[86]

Home refrigerators became nearly universal after the Second World War and negated the need to buy meat in small quantities nearly every day. Consequently, independent butcher shops began to disappear.[87] Cellophane manufacturers adapted packaging invented for cured products to wrapping fresh meats, allowing stores to install self-serve meat departments. Cutting operations previously carried out in-house migrated up the distribution chain and into the packinghouses where low-paid immigrants were hired to do a small piece of the skilled butchery over and over again throughout the day. By the end of the century, skilled meat cutters still could be found in a few independent shops, but supermarket customers could no longer obtain a special cut of meat or watch a steak being cut from a primal quarter.[88]

THE LOCAL ICE INDUSTRY

The U.S. ice industry at the beginning of the twentieth century utilized nearly every body of water subject to freezing in the country. To satisfy local demands, McLean County's residents cut ice from the Mackinaw River and numerous small ponds. Haushalter's Meat Market in Lexington, which depended on the Mackinaw, housed a cooler that during the summer needed to be bunkered with two-and-a-half tons of ice every third or fourth day. Crews kept busy cutting ice for the store nearly every day throughout the winter. John Wagner, owner of Jack's Ice House in McLean, harvested Dode's Lake, a little reservoir built by the Funks years earlier to conserve water from a sulfur spring. Wagner employed four men. Two of them, Senator Wade and George Carlin, sawed blocks of ice, sometimes as thick as nine inches. The other two, "Greaser" Yates and Hart Wilcox, carried the blocks to the ice house and packed them in saw dust.[89]

The ice harvest was a matter of public concern, and the residents of McLean kept abreast of it through their local newspaper. In 1901, good quality ice was reported at the beginning of February.[90] Readers learned that Leach and Son, a food store, had just finished packing 175 tons. Others, including H.H. Fasig, R.S. Adkins, and William Welch had harvested all the ice they needed for their own households. National interest in the ice supply increased as sources of pure water became more difficult to find. The natural ice harvest peaked at 25 million tons in 1886.[91] By then, dairymen, meat packers, produce houses, and others were hearing increasingly from customers about pollution, and as a result companies began to turn more and more to mechanical refrigeration and manufactured ice.

PRODUCE

Fruits and vegetables made their way from producers to consumers in several ways back in pioneer days. People sold produce off the back of wagons and traded at a scattering of farmers' markets. Eliza Farnham in the late 1830s wrote about visiting an orchard not far from Tremont where a widow, famous for her apples, sold directly to customers.[92] Later on, dealers started combing the countryside for produce and buying it for resale in town.[93] These traffickers appear to have concerned themselves primarily with poultry, eggs, and butter and only secondarily with fruits and vegetables. The Patton Brothers of Bloomington and Colfax continued the practice of buying poultry and eggs at the farmyard gate after the turn of the century. N.E. Patton mailed a postcard to farmers in 1903 on which he wrote,

> We will from this time on run a poultry wagon through the country regularly and will at all times pay the Highest Market Price for all kinds of Poultry and Produce. We kindly solicit your patronage and guarantee you the same price at your door that you can get by delivering your stock. Also guarantee good honest weights and fair treatment. Yours truly, N. E. Patton, Per Wm. E. Goudy, Manager.[94]

Many farmers, of course, brought their own produce to town and traded directly with grocers, but growers generally did not show much interest in so-called "farmers' markets." Sarah Davis made passing reference in 1864 to a Saturday market – presumably a farmers' market – in Bloomington, but there appears to be no further reference to one until the 1930s.[95] The previously mentioned City Market, the municipal facility built by B.F. Hoopes, probably superseded the market mentioned by Davis. Unlike meat sellers, fruit and vegetable dealers were not compelled to do business in City Market, but locating there must have been attractive so long as nearly everyone in town shopping for a piece of meat would have to stop by the building. City Market from its inception housed four fruit and vegetable vendors – P. D. Burke, William Carruthers, B. F. Davis, and James Graham. Outside of the market, Bloomington residents could find fruits and vegetables taken in trade from farmers at a number of grocery stores, including C.M. Camp's, Ryan and Engelken's ("very popular among farmers"), and W.M. Reeves's Headquarters. The Headquarters on the corner of Main and Jefferson acquired sufficient quantities of berries and other fruits to offer them wholesale.

Once City Market closed, several new shops specializing in fruit opened for business.[96] One of them was the previously mentioned Fruit House established by

B.F. Hoopes. Another was John Dougherty's, which opened around 1875. During the 1880s, Albert B. Eastman set up a fruit stand at Main and Washington Streets, and Benjamin Riser opened a store a block north at Main and Jefferson. Other fruit vendors included Isaac Hopping and Richard Fanson. Fruits could also be purchased in tobacco shops and confectionaries. As the century drew to a close, the connection between fruit and tobacco disappeared, but the association with confections persisted. Bloomington confectioner William F. Kleinau, for example, sold fresh fruit in addition to candy and ice cream in his store on North Center.

Italians began taking over the business of buying and selling fruit in the 1890s. D. Baldwin and Company in Bloomington, operated by Dominic and Castantino Baldwin and John Bertoni, opened on West Front about 1890. Leonardo Costa opened a shop on North Main around the same time. These and other Italian immigrants traded fruits and vegetables for much the same reason German-Americans brewed beer and baked cakes. Catering to Old World tastes presented economic opportunities, but to take advantage very often required some sort of apprenticeship, knowledge of a particular language, and personal connections. Few of America's earliest fruit peddlers were Italian, but they sold their products in the streets or door to door much the same way they were sold in Italy. Their quality and freshness, however, fell short of Italian expectations, opening the door to immigrants with an abundance of hustle and an appetite for long hours – qualities that enabled them to be on the spot with the best produce on the market whenever a customer appeared. The promise of upward mobility provided strong motivation. Some Italian peddlers began with no more than a backpack, moved up to a cart, and sooner or later acquired a horse and wagon or perhaps a street-corner stand. After that, it was a truck or a shop, maybe even a produce house. Driven by such visions, the number of Italian-American fruit and vegetable vendors increased.[97] In Bloomington, Charles Bova opened a fruit store on North Main in 1911. Thomas Lombardo took over Costa's stand in 1922, and George Ventura started retailing fruits and vegetables on North Madison Street. Bova by then had shifted his business to wholesale.

CAPODICE AND SONS

Mariano Capodice, who eventually became Central Illinois's largest fruit and vegetable wholesaler, arrived in Bloomington a couple of years earlier.[98] His destitute parents had sent him to America from Sicily as a little boy in 1875. He managed to find his way to Cleveland and his uncle's front doorstep with little more than an address tag around his neck. Mariano's uncle saw to it that he received four or five years of schooling before he put him to work on a produce dock. As a child laborer, he received no pay other than an occasional box of oranges or case of lemons, which his boss expected him to sell for pocket money.

In time, Mariano's uncle arranged a marriage, and after a few years the new couple moved to Chicago. There Mariano found a job on South Water Street, the location of a large terminal market where carloads of fruits and vegetables arrived by train from all over the country. At the terminal, shipments were unloaded, broken into smaller lots, and sold to vendors throughout the region. Since Mariano already knew the ropes, it did not take long for him to accumulate some savings, buy a couple of train tickets to Pontiac, and open his own little produce house near the center of town. Business was good at first. His family grew – eight children within a decade or so, but future prospects turned dim. Three other Italian families showed up in Pontiac, and all of them began dealing in produce.

In 1919, Mariano decided to remove to Bloomington. As he saw it, its situation as a railway hub midway between the Chicago and St. Louis markets looked promising. Family and furniture were split between a horse-drawn wagon and an old Ford truck. Both headed south to their new home located on the third floor of the very building that once housed City Market.

Capodice & Son occupied the first and second floors and was an instant success. Jack Capodice, Mariano's youngest son, attributes this in part to location. The business was situated just one block from the Courthouse Square and near all of the grocery stores and restaurants that surrounded it. Proprietors frequently walked by, saw great looking fruits and vegetables, and bought them on the spot. Mariano's stock was actually no different from other dealers' when it came to locally in-season items. He and everyone else purchased nearly everything they sold from nearby farmers. But, when it came to non-local foodstuffs Capodice surpassed the competition by taking a train to Chicago and personally picking out the best items available on South Water Street. He then rode home with them in a boxcar, keeping everything warm enough or sufficiently cool to arrive in Bloomington in prime condition. This level of care and effort resulted in a reputation for superior quality.

Mariano's Chicago contacts and his insider's knowledge about procurement and pricing gave him a substantial edge over rivals such as J.F. Humphreys and Campbell Holton. Years later when General Grocer moved to Bloomington, the Capodices worried about being driven out of business. However, as it turned out General Grocer was no savvier than previous competitors. Capodice and Sons (two name changes later) became one of General Grocers' best accounts by buying items the Capodices knew to be priced below the current market and selling them to their own customers. The Capodices also sold fruits and vegetables to General Grocer, particularly when General's member stores were calling for something its buyers could not locate through regular channels.

There were always surprises. Jack Capodice recalls when Sunday brunches became popular during the early 1980s, and food writers declared the pineapple an essential component. The company, which had previously been supplying its accounts with about 12 per week, suddenly found itself with orders for around 180 pineapples. Effective contacts were essential to keeping up with consumer demands.

By the 1950s, Capodice had customers throughout Central Illinois and was buying fruits and vegetables by the carload. The expanding business relocated in 1952 to Bloomington's old interurban depot on South Madison Street. The building had a New York Central Railroad siding and an ice house out back. During the warm months, cars arrived on the siding loaded with lettuce or other vegetables packed in ice. A weekend arrival often occasioned a call to cousins and nieces and nephews throughout the city. Ed Ulbrich, a grandson of Mariano, remembers:

> We'd go down there on Saturdays and they would give us a pair of gloves . . . . And then we'd clean the ice off (the lettuce or other vegetables) and unload and put them in the cooler. It would be cold down there. We'd go to work at 7 o'clock in the morning. I loved it. And they would bring us home at noon and they'd give us 50 cents or a dollar, and they'd say, here, give this to your mom and dad. There would be a basketful of fruit and lettuce and just everything, you know. But that was how you grew up.[99]

New highways and trucks equipped with butane heating and cooling units expanded Capodice's territory and eliminated the company's need for the ice house. Once Interstates 74 and 55 were completed, sales covered a radius of 60 miles, and most produce was arriving at Capodice's own facility by tractor-trailer. Big regional wholesalers took advantage of the interstates, extended their reach into Central Illinois, and began to siphon off business. In an industry where a buyer never hesitated to drop a supplier for a difference of five cents a pound, Capodice stressed delivery speed to remain competitive.[100] A distributor from Iowa or Northern Illinois could not ship bananas to a Bloomington store in one hour, so Capodice – at this point headed by sons, Jack and Tony, and his nephew, Steve – promised customers exactly that kind of service. Orders went out to stores throughout the night and on Saturdays as well. Still, the company lost business as the number of grocery stores in the region declined and the proportion of food stores and restaurants belonging to chains grew. The chain supermarkets called on Capodice when they found themselves in a pinch, but under normal circumstances Jewel, Kroger, and the rest relied on their own buyers. Facing a bleak future, the Capodice family shut down their operation in 1995.

CASEY'S MARKET BASKET

Eldon "Casey" Casebeer had a passion for buying and selling fruits and vegetables.[101] When he moved to Bloomington from Horton, Kansas in 1941 with his wife Alice and daughter Alice Jane, it was at the behest of his employer, Swift and Company, one of the nation's largest meat packers. Casey changed jobs over the next several years, switching from meat salesman, to seed salesman, to grocery store manager. In the evenings, however, he always enjoyed moonlighting at Glen Langford's open-air fruit stand on the corner of North Main and East Kelsey. When Langford decided to retire in 1949, Casebeer purchased his business. Alice Jane remembers her mother cried and cried because the family had no savings, but her father insisted he could make something out of the little stand, particularly if it stayed open 24 hours a day, seven days a week.[102] The local banks disagreed and turned down Casebeer's loan applications.

Casey, however, knew the city and staked everything on its late-night potential. He enclosed part of the produce stand, renamed it "Casey's Market Basket," and began selling bread and milk in addition to fruits and vegetables. Gradually the store expanded, adding more and more grocery items until it carried a full line. Then came packaged meats, including hamburger brought over from Weberg's butcher shop in Normal.

By this time, it was evident that Casebeer's gamble paid off. With every other grocer in town closed by nine o'clock at night, Casey's had the uncontested patronage of the scores of railroad men and factory hands who knocked off work late at night or early in the morning and needed "something from the store." In addition, there were plenty of transients. Main Street carried Routes 66 and 51 and steady traffic throughout the night right by the store's front door. As a kind of bonus, the town's college students soon made Casey's an after-hours haunt.

Casey's Market Basket thrived on novelty. It introduced rotisserie chicken and soft-serve ice cream to the community. It sold "pop" (bottled sodas) and newspapers, items that in the '50s were not ordinarily found in grocery stores. Casey's became the first store in the area to sell Spudnuts, doughnuts made of potato flour and delivered to the store by the local franchisee. Casebeer also ventured into new territory with "gourmet foods," primarily S&W products, a line of premium canned goods from California. They did not sell very well, but Alice

Jane remembers her father was always trying something different, always looking for a little niche the big grocers had missed.

The backbone of Casey's business remained fresh fruits and vegetables. When Kroger opened a supermarket almost directly across the street and customers lamented it, Casebeer simply said, "You keep your nose to the grindstone, and you don't look across the street, and just do your thing." To him, that meant taking to the road frequently to pick up produce in St. Louis. Casebeer fired up his truck and also drove north to Michigan and as far south as Arkansas to buy apples, blueberries, peaches, strawberries, and other fruits as they ripened. Particularly well known and eagerly anticipated each year were Casey's watermelons, which were kept cold at the front of the store in big tanks intended to water livestock. Many Bloomington-Normal residents also looked forward to Casey's Christmas fruit baskets. These were big wicker baskets filled with red and white grapefruit, oranges, red and golden apples, bananas, grapes, nuts, and candy; everything wrapped in colored cellophane and finished with a big, hand-tied bow. Giving and receiving Casey's fruit baskets became something of a holiday tradition in Bloomington-Normal, so as Christmas approached store employees spent many days in the backroom making hundreds of them in assembly line fashion.

Casebeer added a garden shop to his grocery store in 1961. The garden shop still exists, owned and operated by Casebeer's daughter, Alice, her husband, Ray Lartz, and their son, named Casey after his grandfather. The Lartzes sold the grocery store in 1968, and it went defunct a few years later, but not the fruit baskets. As Ray recalls, 10 years after the grocery closed people were still talking about them. Casey suggested bringing the baskets back, and ever since they have been a big part of the garden shop's holiday business.

BAKED GOODS

Commercial bakers, faced with a growing number of complaints about dirty bread, began putting wrappers on individual loaves in the 1890s.[103] Bread slicers came on the market in 1928, and sliced bread became the proverbial benchmark for "the greatest thing." This gave added impetus to wrapping since unwrapped sliced bread had a shelf life next to nil.[104] Still, many bakers refused to sell sliced bread until sometime after 1930 when the required machinery became sufficiently reliable to warrant the investment.

As families increasingly turned to commercial bread, the number of bakers in Bloomington-Normal swelled. The City Directory for 1922 named 58 individuals involved in the business.[105] Gerken's continued as before with fresh competition from B & M Bread, located in the 300 block of East Front, and

Buttell's, operating out of a new facility on North Street in Normal. By today's standards, these were small shops (six employees at B & M, three at Buttell's), but the industrial attitude associated with modern baking was becoming apparent. Schneider's still employed less than 10 people in the early '20s, but instead of identifying itself as a bakery, the company called itself a "manufacturer" of breads, cakes, and pies.

For their part, craft bakers began gravitating toward department stores and food markets. My Store and Livingston's in downtown Bloomington installed in-house bakeries. Charles Utesch's grocery added ovens and two bakers. About 1932, Nierstheimer's grocery became the new home of Dierkes's, formerly a free-standing bakery. The Jefferson Bake Shop, opened in 1924 and originally located on East Jefferson Street in downtown Bloomington, expanded to five locations by 1940, including three Piggly Wiggly stores.[106]

On the eve of America's entry into World War II, Bloomington was down to a handful of independent ovens. William Gronemeier's, which took over Gerken's in 1927, employed less than half a dozen bakers.[107] While not exactly a mom-and-pop operation, it remained committed to producing baked goods by traditional methods. Gronemeier sold retail and wholesale to a variety of restaurants and grocery stores. By the time his son, Franklin, took over the business in 1940, it was apparent that a major infusion of capital was needed to compete with the bigger baking companies. Franklin decided against the investment and call it quits in 1948.[108]

Gronemeier Bakery sold half-loaves of bread during World War II.
Courtesy of *The Pantagraph*.

Other than a few places like Gronemeier's and the Jefferson Bake Shops, Bloomington entered the '40s with three industrial bread manufacturers – Bloomington Baking Company, B & M, and Purity Baking Company – all three manufacturing products typical of the "Wonder Bread Period" of American baking.[109] Wonder Bread was invented by the Taggart Baking Company of Indianapolis and first sold sliced in 1930.[110] In 1941, it was marketed as enriched with vitamins and minerals. Otherwise, Wonder Bread and its imitators consisted of sub-standard bleached flour and substances to enhance fermentation. Additives included chemicals to retard spoilage, emulsifiers, flavor enhancers, dough conditioners, yeast stimulants, stiffeners, and more. The last local bakeries to bake this type of bread were Banner Baking of Normal and the Purity Baking Company of Bloomington. The last store in Bloomington to host an entirely-from-scratch craft baker was Mike's Market on East Empire at Park Streets, where Jack Cable plied his trade until proprietor Dan Kniery closed the store in 1993.[111]

SUPERSTORES

Today, superstores, such as Wal-Mart and Meijer threaten the supermarkets. Wal-Mart, a store in which food items constitute a subset of a much larger inventory of manufactured products, is currently the nation's biggest grocer.[112]

The first superstore to open in McLean County was K-Mart (known today as Kmart), a division of S.S. Kresge, formerly a chain of dime stores.[113] It arrived in Bloomington in September of 1962 heralded by a series of items in *The Daily Pantagraph*. The first, an article published in late March, marveled at the size of project. The store, located at the junction of Illinois Route 9 and U.S. Route 66, would take up 26 acres of land and consist of 38 departments, including "discount food."[114] A pre-opening advertising blitz began on September 17 with a large display featuring an American flag splashed with the phrase "K-Mart is Coming." Underneath the flag, the copy informed readers, "You won't need cash at K-Mart – you can charge it."[115] The next day's paper contained an artist's rendition of the building and advertised an opening-day carnival, featuring free pony rides, refreshments, and prizes. "K-Mart's huge discounts give you cash savings on everything you buy – week in and week out," blared the advertisement, citing prices for turkeys, beef roasts, Oscar Meyer skinless all-meat franks, and a host of other products. On opening day, an article, reading very much like a company press release, portrayed K-Mart's snack bar as a place to savor "satisfying refreshments at economical prices."[116] The piece assured readers that K-Mart employed a full-time dietitian to ensure healthful menus.

THE DRIVE-IN

As in the case of supermarkets, drive-your-car-in restaurants existed prior to the automotive revolution. The very first, the Pig Stand, opened in 1921 as the brainchild J.G. Kirby of Dallas, Texas and featured pork barbeque sandwiches.[117] Kirby enjoyed phenomenal success. He quickly cloned the original Pig Stand to create a chain, and within a couple of years there were various copycats. One of the earliest was A&W Root Beer headquartered in Sacramento, California. It originated in 1919 as a walk-up soda stand in Lodi, California. J. Willard Marriott and a partner purchased an A&W franchise for the Washington-Baltimore region for $1,000 and went on to forge the largest food and hospitality business in the world.[118] Marriott and other pioneer drive-in operators stayed out of the big cities and away from the white boxes (See Chapter Three).[119] They preferred the suburbs and smaller cities and towns where there was a higher percentage of automobile ownership than in urban centers. By avoiding city centers and industrial areas, drive-ins also succeeded in disassociating themselves from the world of work, leaving them free to cultivate a clean-cut, playful image.

STEAK 'N SHAKE

Gus Belt, founder of Steak 'n Shake, essentially turned a white box into a drive-in. His early career revolved around cars and food.[120] He began as a General Tire distributor, and after that venture failed he tried running a steakhouse. It did not do well, so Gus went back to automobiles and acquired a Shell service station on South Main Street, U.S. Routes 51 and 66, in Normal. When the gas station began to stumble, Belt and his wife, Edith, added a restaurant. She would fix meals for customers while he took care of their cars. The restaurant also stood to profit from several thousand perpetually hungry Illinois State Normal University (ISNU, the predecessor of Illinois State University) students who resided just a few blocks away.

The Belts situated their restaurant in an old house adjacent to the service station and called it the "Shell Inn" after the brand of gasoline they sold. The restaurant opened in 1932 specializing in chicken and fish dinners.[121] Fried chicken with French fries, and coleslaw – all you could eat – sold for 45 cents. A glass of beer with dinner was an additional nine cents. The menu also offered fancy hamburgers accompanied by elaborate assurances of quality. These began with "Just a word about hamburgers" printed in the menu. The passage explained that the hamburger ". . . originated in Hamburg, Germany, and is defined by Webster as ground choice beef, properly seasoned." The menu offered customers a choice between a "Steak Hamburger" (choice ground steak, butter grilled, served on large toasted bun along with home-baked beans and potatoes) and a "Steak Bar-B-Cue" (ground sirloin steak, butter grilled, covered with Southern barbecue sauce and served with baked beans and potatoes). Both sandwiches, the Belts promised, were made with ". . . premium meats bought with extreme care and ground in sight, through our own grinders."

This pledge, which anticipated Steak 'n Shake's later catch-phrase, "In sight it must be right," appealed to a public that generally did not trust roadside restaurants, and with good reason. Not a single establishment just down the street in the City of Bloomington was clean enough as late as 1947 to receive an "A" rating from the county health department. Inspectors found most restaurants did not wash their dishes properly, and most had dirty restrooms. Indicative of the prevailing outlook, operators opposed stricter health department oversight.[122] The Belts' "in-sight" message represented a contrasting attitude and invited prospective patrons to look around and judge for themselves. At the Shell Inn, even the chili recipe was printed right there in the menu.

Shell Inn Chili

INGREDIENTS – 1 pound young beef suet (kidney); 2½ pounds ground choice beef; 1 pound onion, chopped fine; 2 tablespoons genuine chili powder; 1 tablespoon paprika, 2 tablespoons ground Spanish cumin seed; 1 (and an illegible fraction) tablespoon salt. PREPARATION – Grind suet coarse and render to a brown. Add meat and fry in suet 1 hour. Add the balance of ingredients and cook slowly 1½ hours. Add a Number 5 can of red kidney beans after cooking. Use highest price seasonings and meats.

The Shell Inn met with such success that in1934 Gus decided to close the service station. He and Edith dropped chicken from their menu and made hamburgers the specialty of the house. An improved parking lot and a remodeling in the art deco style of a White Castle made the old Shell Inn look like a new restaurant. Gus named it the "White House Steak 'n Shake." Customers, however, called it simply "Steak 'n Shake," and so it was renamed.

As Steak 'n Shake prospered, Belt opened additional stores. He built two in Bloomington and one further south in Decatur. Each of these was somewhat different than the others. Belt's original restaurant had an inside counter and several booths, but catered primarily to customers in cars parked outside. In this respect, it emulated another Route 66 hamburger parlor, the Park View Inn, which had opened around 1930 across the road from Miller Park on Bloomington's southwest side.[123] Gus's second Steak 'n Shake was nevertheless strictly sit-down. Committing to curb service exclusively came after he and Edith purchased the Goal Post Inns, a drive-in chain with locations in Champaign and Peoria.

Once he decided to focus on drive-in customers, Belt developed a training program for curb service employees. "Curbies," as they were called, were instructed to move no slower than a trot. The mantra was "Get going," and managers were to see to it. The idea was to create a dramatic and exciting effect called "running the curb." Servers learned to carry trays high, above eye level both for safety and for added show.

Running the curb was part of a bigger selling effort that featured a bright, festive atmosphere. At a Steak 'n Shake, 4,000 little 11 watt bulbs were turned on each evening. These bulbs blinked on and off in sequence, giving the effect of constant movement, and along with a variety of brightly-colored neon signs, suggested a carnival with lots of activity. If business was slow, employees had to park their cars in front of the store so it looked like things were popping. Belt believed that nothing had greater appeal than a pretty girl or a bright lad, neatly dressed, hurrying out to a customer's car with a cheery greeting and order pad in hand, and then trotting back with a hot burger and fizzing Coke. Steak 'n Shake served its food on real china and drinks in glasses rather than in paper or plastic cups.[124] Customers appreciated the hustle and glitz because, according to one of Gus's lieutenants, they "brought a little happiness into the dark Depression time."[125]

To keep them coming back, Belt wanted Steak 'n Shake customers to feel they were purchasing something superior to a greasy-spoon hamburger. He purchased high-quality meat from Pfaelzer Brothers in Chicago and had it ground out front for all to see, just as he had done at the Shell Inn. Sirloins, T-bones, and strip steaks all went into the grinder and Gus coached his managers to maximize the effect by waiting for a full house to witness it. Frying and mixing took place in plain view. When other burger restaurants went to automation, Steak 'n Shake demurred because of Belt's conviction that customers wanted to see what was going on.

To some extent Steak 'n Shake avoided being seen as a typical fast food restaurant, but from the perspective of its employees preparing and serving a meal was a race against the clock. The company's model was the fast-paced automobile manufacturing plant.[126] Gus and his managers wanted customers in and out in 20 minutes, and just as curbies were obliged to run, not walk, speed behind the counter was of utmost importance. High temperature grilling was part of the plan. Belt instructed his cooks to slap "pucks" (pre-shaped clumps) of meat on the grill and then flatten them to sear in the juices. The grill's temperature had to be exactly 350 degrees F. Any higher, the burger tended to dry out. Any lower, the puck took too long to cook. From the grill, a steakburger went to the "dressing table" where lettuce and other condiments were added. Once plated, a server whisked it to the customer's table. All of this had to take place in under five minutes.[127]

Belt imposed other measures in the interest of speed. He had his servers place customers' bills on their trays or tables moments after their food was delivered. When Gus complained that the cast-iron grills manufactured locally by Servrite did not reheat quickly enough, the company came up with a revolutionary new aluminum alloy stove equipped with thermostats to retain its Steak 'n Shake account.

Belt began to move Steak 'n Shake's offices from Central Illinois to St. Louis in the late 1940s. By the time he died in 1954, his company owned 27 stores. St. Louis had become its largest market. The chain extended eastward as far as Indianapolis and even included a handful of restaurants in Florida. Gus's widow, Edith, added more stores, but for 15 years she did nothing to change Steak 'n Shake's business model.

As times changed, curb service, which accounted for 80 percent of Steak 'n Shake's revenue, became increasingly difficult to sustain. Neighbors complained about the music and other noise coming from cars in Steak 'n Shake's parking lots. People objected to the traffic – the habitual "cruising" that took place to and from drive-ins. Parents protested about the pace at which Steak 'n Shake managers forced their children to work. Edith gave up in 1969 and sold controlling interest to Longchamps, a New York restaurant chain. It ran Steak 'n Shake for a couple of years, made some changes, and lost a considerable amount of money. Franklin Corporation purchased the chain in 1971 and moved its headquarters to Indianapolis. The move included the office of Steak 'n Shake's treasurer, the company's last remaining administrative center in Bloomington. Robert Cronin, the organization's new CEO reinstated some of the core ideas that had distinguished Steak 'n Shake from its competition. Hitting a higher note than McDonald's and the other "speedburger" joints became a strategic focus. The company rallied, and in 1981 was sold to Kelley and Partners. Under Kelley, the business thrived and the number of stores expanded. After his death in 2003, the company underwent a shake-up, which resulted in its absorption by Biglari Holdings of San Antonio, Texas. Consolidated Products of Indianapolis, the current owner, continues to position the chain a bit above the typical fast-food restaurant.

TOOLIN' THE GAG

From the late 1940s through the early 1970s, Bloomington's youth re-enacted a nightly ritual known as "Toolin' the Gag(s)." Toolin' (tooling) meant driving. Race car drivers tooled around the track. Cool guys did not drive; they tooled their vehicles down the road. The term "Gag" was used in different ways. Some intended it to refer to a Steak 'n Shake. Where were you last night? I was at the Gag in Normal. A person thus tooled the Gags, meaning that he or she drove drove back and forth between the original store located at Main and Virginia in Normal and the one situated at Hannah and Morrissey in Bloomington. Alternatively, Gag could be used to refer to the route everyone drove between the two locations. In this way, a person might say that the Dog 'n Suds, a drive-in situated a few doors south of Steak 'n Shake on Morrissey, was also a part of the Gag. Toolin the Gag amounted to a kind of unsupervised paseo. Young people drove their own cars or a family automobile back and forth to see and to be seen, particularly by members of the opposite sex. The drive-ins provided rendezvous points.

Tony Robbins, who was 18 years old in 1974, said it was still "a big deal" to tool the Gag when he was in high school.[128] You had to be in a nice car, he explained, "not a beater or a Volkswagen." Tony never drove his own 1963 Impala because he preferred to be seen in his friend's much newer Camaro. When he and his friend tooled the Gag, they started out from the Normal Steak 'n Shake and headed south on Main to Oakland. They turned and proceeded east on Oakland to Hannah. At Hannah, they turned right, tooled a short distance south onto Morrissey, and then turned into and drove through the Steak 'n Shake parking lot. They then continued south a few doors to the Dog 'n Suds, drove through its parking lot, and turned back up Morrissey and Hannah to Oakland. Turning left, they retraced their route to Normal and the Steak 'n Shake parking lot at Main and Virginia. There they turned around and began another lap.

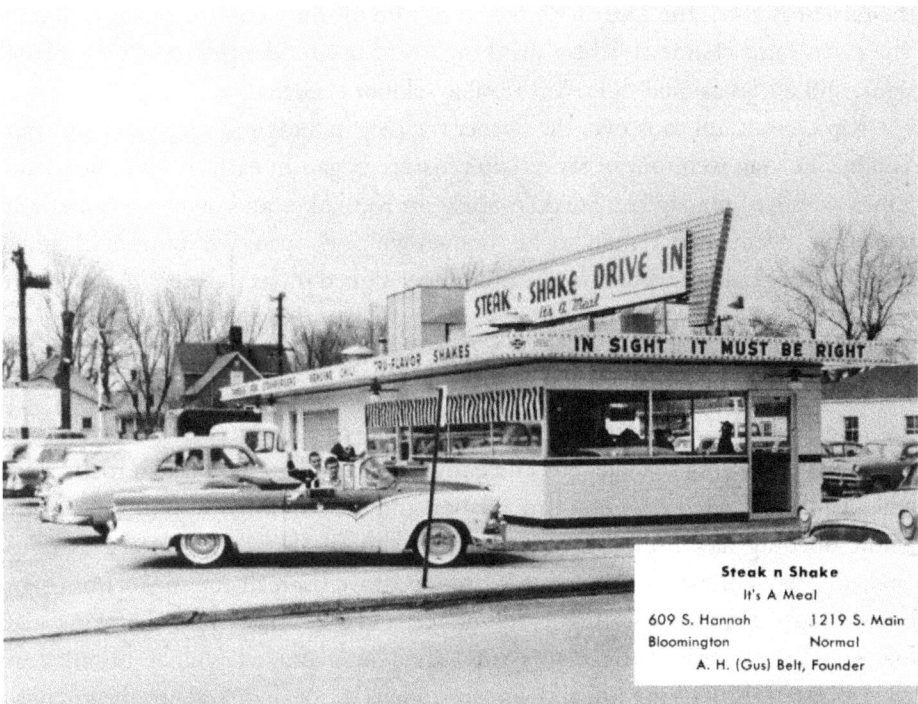

The Steak 'n Shake Drive-In on Morrissey Dr. in Bloomington was part of the tradition called "Toolin' the Gag." Photo from the mid-1950s.

Nancy Steele Brokaw, who grew up in Bloomington, recalled that when Toolin' the Gag she and her girlfriends occasionally stopped to eat.[129] This, however, was never for long unless some "cool boys" were at the restaurant. High school kids did not have much money, she explained, so they did not buy much food. They might split a coke, a shake, or an order of French fries. Brokaw remembered that the cheap hot dogs at the Dog 'n Suds were an attraction, but business there was often brisk and finding a place to park could be difficult. She once had trouble trying to back her mother's Buick Electra into a parking space and wound up demolishing a tray of food hanging from the window ledge on a neighboring car in the process. Like Tony Robbins, she preferred Toolin' the Gag in her best friend's car, a 1966 Mustang convertible, which Nancy thought was as cool as you could get.

For Normal resident Sally Pyne, stopping to eat at one of the Gags was essential.[130] You did not just drive around and go home. You stopped, even if all you ordered was a soda. Whatever you had, Sally reminisced, you never ate it inside the restaurant. A person had to be in the parking lot to watch others drive through.

The police monitored the Gag route closely. Friday and Saturday nights were the busiest nights. The Dog 'n Suds had to hire off-duty cops to direct traffic.[131] There was some clandestine beer drinking, some hot-rodder tire squealing at stop signs, and an occasional fight, but trouble seldom occurred.

Kip's restaurant took over the former the Dog 'n Suds and survived long after Toolin' the Gag went out of style. Kip's history began in early 1960s when Paul Kiper, who had managed a Steak 'n Shake in Kankakee and owned a restaurant in Peoria, decided to return to his hometown and open a restaurant there.[132] His brother Harley and his cousin Bob Kiper signed on as partners. As the men worked on their plan, two franchises came on the market, a McDonald's costing $35,000 and a Dog 'n Suds for just $5,000. The men purchased the more affordable Dog 'n Suds franchise.

The Kipers' Dog 'n Suds reigned as one of the busiest restaurants in Bloomington during the late '60s and early '70s. It had gotten off to a rocky start when Paul contracted with non-union labor, and the building was bombed shortly before opening day. Still, a unique ordering system, installed after the drive-in opened, drew crowds. Previously, a customer drove in, read the menu from sign boards, flashed the car's headlights for service, and a server on roller skates scooted out to take the order. The new system used intercom telephones installed at 28 stations in the parking lot, allowing customers to speak directly to the kitchen.

Harley Kiper left the business during the '70s, and the remaining partners decided they no longer needed the Dog 'n Suds name. They surrendered their franchise, added a dining room, but kept everything else pretty much the same. Greta Tallon, who began working for the Kipers at 16 and stayed with them for 40 years, blended fresh root beer and made Coney sauce for the hot dogs from scratch just as she had before. The Kipers' signature sandwich, the Texasburger, a double-decker hamburger with melted cheese, Coney sauce, lettuce, and another "special sauce," stayed on the menu. Wholesale prices rose over the years, and as Kipers raised their prices in response, they saw their business fade away. To make matters worse, the county health department kept insisting on the installation of expensive new equipment. Bob and Paul's son Steve, his successor, decided to shut down in 2003. Greta Tallon, who had not looked for another job since her first day with the Kipers, was heartbroken. Many in the community experienced a sense of loss as well. In its last week of business, shortly after the release of a closing announcement, Kip's was inundated with customers. Many had tooled the Gag but had not visited Kip's for years. All week lines of nostalgic customers extended out the front door until at last Bob Kiper closed for good.

ROUTE 66 EATERIES

It has been said that someday Route 66 will rank alongside the Oregon and Santa Fe Trails in American history.[133] If that happens, then Historic Route 66 may once again host a vibrant collection of drive-ins and cafés, much as it did back in its glory days.

Back when Route 66 was a busy roadway, as motorists drove two hours or so south of Chicago and approached the junction of Routes 66 and 24, they entered Chenoa's "gasoline alley," a string of service stations interspersed with barbecue stands and sit-down restaurants.[134] Burt Winter ran one of the latter. It included a small motel to accommodate bus and train passengers awaiting connections and primarily served barbeque pork sandwiches and chocolate malts. Burt, however, was most famous for his pies, especially his Dutch Apple Pie topped with a big slice of cheddar cheese.[135]

Thanks to long-haul truckers and other motorists who lived on pie and coffee, Chenoa nurtured great pie-makers. Edna Sherrington was regarded by many as "the best of the best" and baked pies for Steve's Café, the most popular gasoline alley restaurant.[136] Steve's began in 1924 as a garage, gas station, and lunchroom built by Tom and Charles Elliott. A couple of owners and name changes later, the business became Zirkle Brothers Café and remained so during the Great Depression. Tom and Clint Zirkle, both skilled cooks, baked delicious pies. Sometime later the Whal brothers leased the place, and it became known as Steve's Café, named for the Whals' chef, Steve Wilcox.[137]

Steve acquired a great reputation, especially for his steaks.[138] His cube steak, served with sliced bread, French fries, and a wedge of lettuce covered with Thousand Island dressing, became equated with good eating up and down the highway. Wilcox made the salad dressing, and, in addition to serving it in the restaurant, he bottled it and sold it to tourists. Trouble was it made them sick. Acting on complaints, the Illinois Department of Public Health discovered Steve used mineral oil, a powerful laxative, as an ingredient in his Thousand Island dressing. Despite that episode, and Steve's terrible temper—which he occasionally vented on customers—his reputation for serving "the finest steaks between Chicago and St. Louis" remained intact and "big shots" continued to stop in. Perhaps part of the attraction was the air conditioning. Steve's was the first restaurant in Illinois outside of Chicago to install a system. Time caught up with the place in the late 1940s when the new four-lane construction bypassed it. Patronage dropped off, and Steve quit. Eventually the kitchen closed, and the building became an antique shop.

Following World War II and modernization, traffic picked up, and the economic opportunities Route 66 presented made "the Mother Road" a veritable "mother lode." Locally-owned restaurants flourished, and travelers continuing south from Chenoa to Lexington came upon such places as The Filling Station Café and The Mesa, a 24 hour dining spot attached to a Skelly Service Station.[139] The Oasis, Lexington's first drive-in, opened in 1960, serving "on the go" fried foods, but by then chains had entered the picture. Stuckey's, a company headquartered in Eastman, Georgia established a store in Lexington in 1958. It consisted of a gasoline station, coffee shop, pecan counter, and candy store. A customer who purchased at least 10 gallons of gasoline received a free box of sweets. Down the pike at McLean, Horne's Candy Shoppe, a similar kind of operation, served up short orders and sold novelty confections, honey, and tropical fruit jellies. Both businesses shut down when Interstate 55 realigned the traffic patterns, taking most drivers a considerable distance from the familiar businesses along Route 66.

FOSTER'S PURE CAFÉ

Several McLean County Route 66 eateries bent over backwards to court truckers. One of them, Foster's Pure Café and Station Shop, began life as a Marathon service facility with a 100 seat dining room.[140] When Pure Oil took over and leased the place to Don Foster, he quickly recognized that truck drivers were his best customers and it was good business to treat them preferentially. A statement on Foster's menu informed customers, "This is primarily a truck stop, and we reserve the right to serve truck drivers first." Truckers had their own place to eat marked by a card that read, "This table reserved for truck drivers, their friends and family."[141] A lazy Susan on the truckers' table held a container of low-calorie sweetener, a "non-fattening" salad dressing, a selection of condiments, a cigarette lighter, and a can of lighter fluid. The kitchen prepared breakfast any time day or night and offered a variety of quick lunches. Foster's truckers' table was busiest between 10:00 p.m. and 4:00 a.m. The restaurant's "truckers first" service policy drew few complaints from other customers.

BRANDTVILLE

Veterans Parkway, originally called "The Belt Line," originated shortly before World War II as a Route 66 bypass to take through traffic east of Bloomington-Normal's built-up areas. The road included two long, sweeping curves designed to carry traffic at speeds up to 100 miles per hour – a prototype of what the U.S. military planned as an answer to Germany's autobahns. The Belt Line's success as a bypass proved fleeting, however. After State Farm Insurance relocated its corporate headquarters just off the highway in the early '70s, the area became choked with fast-food joints and other businesses.

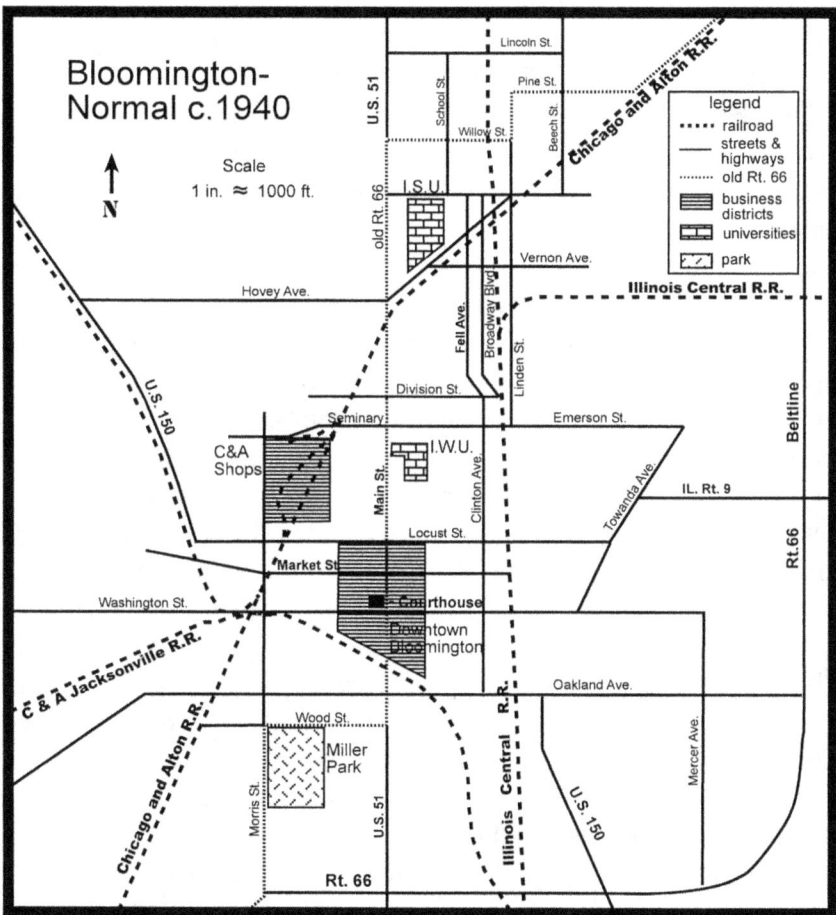

Note: Current Rt. 66 Belt Line is currently Veterans Parkway mini mall strip
Source: *Bloomington's C & A Shops*, Matejka, Koos, Wyman; MCHS, 1987
Cartography by: Rachael Kramp

Bloomington-Normal c. 1940. Many of Bloomington-Normal's food stores and restaurants were located on Route 66. It took traffic through the urban area until just before World War II when an east-side bypass was built. It later became Veteran's Parkway, a six-mile strip of shopping centers and chain restaurants.]

Prior to that, one of the few places to stop and eat was Bob Johnson's Brandtville Café, a place that originated as a truck stop on property owned by Arthur Brandt. A trucker himself, Brandt opened a restaurant on U.S. Route 150 in the late 1930s. A few years later he decided the food business did not suit him, so he turned it over to Jim Malloy. Bob Johnson purchased it from Malloy about 1955. In the meantime, the Beltline had arrived, and Brandtville found itself agreeably situated adjacent to the bypass's intersection with 150.

Bob Knapp, who eventually bought the place from Johnson, came there to work as a 13- year-old busboy in 1956.[142] Knapp recalls that back then Streid's, a locally popular steakhouse, and a Shell service station stood on opposite corners across the Belt Line. Two or three miles north, a General Electric factory and the Prairie Traveler Motel bracketed the highway. A mile or so south at the intersection with U.S. Route 51, motorists passed the Phil-Kron (later renamed The Sinorak) restaurant and drive-in movie complex and a little custard stand. Otherwise, drivers saw nothing but farmers' fields, except of course at night when everything just beyond the glare of the headlights was pitch black. Bob Johnson's materialized out of the darkness like Las Vegas. To create the effect, Johnson commissioned Bloomington's All Brite Sign Company to construct a marquee with letters six feet tall, studded with lights, practically shouting "CHICKEN DINNERS." In case that was not enough to capture drivers' attention, Johnson topped his sign with a gigantic plastic chicken, a great white hen standing 10 feet tall and awash in lights from the moment the sun set until it rose again in the morning.

Johnson's personality was as big as his chicken. He kept his place open "25 hours a day." At the start, the dining area seated about 100 customers. Over the years, its capacity more than doubled, but still, when the bars closed in Bloomington, Brandtville had a line out the door. The same was true on Friday and Saturday nights and Sunday afternoons when families drove out from the city for "Broasted chicken," a product Johnson acquired from the Broaster Company of Beloit, Wisconsin and put on the menu in the early '60s. Broaster sold restaurant operators pressure fryers capable of cooking any item in a flash. Bob Knapp remembers that in the 1970s a fry cook in Johnson's kitchen said he could turn out 40 pieces of chicken every 10 minutes from a single Broaster. The company offered clients several different flours and breadings and a variety of cooking oils. Johnson experimented and developed a combination that Bob Knapp still remembers as producing the best fried chicken he has ever tasted.

When Knapp took over the business, he stuck with Bob Johnson's menu of "basic Midwestern sandwiches and plate lunches." However, behind the scenes Bob and his wife, Sandy, began catering parties and various events and moving decisively upscale. They brought in European chef, Ron Klerk DeRuse, who brought cruise-ship experience and a phenomenal body of culinary knowledge to the business. Sandy had a real passion for cooking, and as a caterer found ample opportunity to exercise her considerable kitchen skills. Bob, who confessed to having little interest in food preparation, reveled in doing what he really enjoyed, organizing and conducting big, festive events.[143] The two walked away from the business in 1990 to answer a spiritual calling to become missionaries and ministers for their church. Since then, a succession of specialty restaurants belonging to small or aspiring chains has set up shop in Brandtville.

DIXIE TRUCKERS HOME

Truckers hauling past Bloomington around the Belt Line had Brandtville, and for a brief time during the1960s, a place called the "Five Star Truck Stop." However, just a few miles south awaited one of the greatest of all American truck stops, the Dixie Truckers Home (now called The Dixie Travel Plaza). This legendary refueling station, located where Historic Route 66, I-55, and U.S. Route 136 come together just outside of McLean, is one of the oldest continuously operating truck stops in the nation and one of the most revered tourist stops on Old Route 66.[144]

The Dixie was started in 1928 by J.P. Walters; his daughter, Viola; and her husband, John Geske as a midway stopping point for truckers driving between Chicago and St. Louis. The concept was new. Service stations had begun catering to truckers in the early 1920s, but it was not until around 1925 that truck havens with showers, bunkhouses, lounges, and mechanical facilities began to appear. The Dixie was the first in Illinois. The name was chosen to suggest Southern hospitality.[145] To begin with, there were two employees, 10 counter stools, and a couple of gas pumps.

Walters, who owned a grocery store in nearby Shirley, had flair. He buried the keys to the Dixie in the fresh concrete being poured around the newly constructed building, declaring the place would be open and serving 24 hours a day. Livestock headed to market could have a final feed in the Dixie's corral while drivers took in a free movie in the parking lot and something to eat during intermission.

After J.P. died in 1950, Viola's brother Dan joined the company. It thrived until 1965 when the building was leveled by fire. Rebuilding began immediately and was finished in 1967, just in time for the opening of I-55. Dixie's driveways now adjoined Route 66 passing to the west and the new interstate just to its east via exit ramps to U.S. Route 136 on the north. Other exits up and down the interstate led to roads that disappeared into the cornfields, but at McLean truckers and other motorists found everything they needed. When the Dixie reopened, its service area contained 20 double fuel pumps. Inside, drivers had access to a coin-operated laundry, showers, games, gift shop, and TV lounge furnished with overstuffed chairs and provisioned with free popcorn and soft drinks. A new restaurant seated 250 people, contained four "trucker only" booths, and offered "some of the finest and honest-to-goodness 'home-cooked' foods available anywhere."[146] Truckers' favorite dishes included Broasted chicken, fried cornmeal mush, and biscuits and gravy. *The All American Truck Stop Cookbook* published recipes for the Dixie's chili and its signature dish of ham and beans.

McLean Ham and Beans
INGREDIENTS – 1½ gallon Great Northern beans, 2 pounds onions diced, 2 cans (46 ounces) of ham shank meat, 3 gallons water, 1 tablespoon ground garlic. PREPARATION –Clean and soak beans; pour off soak water. Place beans, onions, meat, water, and garlic in soup pot; cook until tender; add water as needed. Place in 6-inch deep pans and serve hot.[147]

PHIL-KRON

Perhaps the most unique product of the automobile-age restaurants in McLean County was the Phil-Kron Outdoor Theater and Grill on far South Main (U.S. Route 51) at the Route 66 Bypass in Bloomington.[148] It opened in 1947, featuring the movie *Two Guys from Milwaukee*, and advertising itself as the only establishment of its kind in the world.[149] The idea, developed by co-owners Ken Phillips and Peter Karonis, was to sell people on seeing a movie "under the stars, in the comforts of your own car" and on being able after the show to stroll over to the restaurant for a bite to eat. Karonis was an experienced Bloomington restaurateur. His Servrite Steak House had been a very popular Front Street gathering spot for young people during the Depression.[150] The Phil-Kron debuted early on in the auto age, and not many people had cars, but no matter; the Greyhound stopped regularly, and the complex boasted city bus service to the door with "ample seating capacity for those without cars." For patrons with cars, the theater had 700 parking "terraces" spread over 15 acres, each terrace equipped with its own speaker for piping soundtracks into the vehicle.

The Phil-Krons' restaurant had parking spaces for another 200 vehicles. It featured an "Air-Conditioned Dining Room," but for those who preferred to remain seated in their automobile there was a special "gastronomical treat" – the "Original Chicken in the Basket On the Curb, Fried especially for you." Alternatively, the menu listed chicken salad sandwiches, made fresh daily, or "delicious baked ham."[151] This made the Phil-Kron, at least in its own management's estimation, the "'Coolest Curb in Town...'"

In 1957, 10 years after its opening, Phillips and Karonis announced a face-lift for the Phil-Kron. The facility grew to include an amusement park for kiddies, a miniature golf course, a small train circling the grounds, and a lagoon for scenic interest. Phillips and Karonis remodeled the restaurant and installed a self-service, cafeteria-style snack bar to serve movie goers.[152] A year later George Kerasotes, owner of a chain of movie houses, purchased the theater. The restaurant, then known as the Phil-Kron Country Kitchen, became the Sinorak (Karonis spelled backwards, as Harry Caray would relate to bored Cubs fans). The new restaurant and lounge served food smorgasbord style: "Eat as much as you like for $1.65 – lunch 95 cents."[153]

The theater-restaurant complex was dealt a serious but not fatal blow by a $200,000 fire March 19, 1963. Both were rebuilt, the restaurant at nearly twice its original size. Following Karonis' death in 1973, Mr. and Mrs. Don Reynolds took over the restaurant and continued to operate it until 1980 when declining business forced them to close.

CHAPTER 6 – FAST FOOD FASTER

The Second World War closed the curtain on horse-drawn farming and set the stage for monumental changes in the American diet. Mechanization begun during the war compelled specialization in one or two crops. Combined with hybrid species, inorganic fertilizers, herbicides, pesticides, and advances in veterinary medicine, machines enabled farmers to increase their productivity while decreasing the number of hours they worked. Many took jobs in town, an action forced by declining commodity prices and the need to earn additional income. Together these changes effectively severed the connection between production and consumption on the family farm and turned rural households into consumers essentially no different than their urban counterparts. Americans of every stripe subscribed to a post-war consumer culture that measured individual worth by material possessions. Striving to "keep up with the Joneses," homemakers by the millions took jobs in factories, stores, and offices. The idea of quick and easy meals propagated during the war became all the more appealing and laid the foundation for the development of the convenience kitchen. Instead of being regarded as a pleasurable experience, sitting down to eat came to be viewed increasingly as a distraction from more important activities. People "grabbed snacks," and a restaurant-industry catch phrase, "fast food," became the name of America's most popular cuisine.

The food industry aimed to make every product "quick and convenient" to use. Their objective was to prepare foods that the most distracted homemakers could throw together to create an outstanding meal with little or no trouble.[1] Quick-cooking items like steaks, chops, hamburgers, ready-to-eat hams, and canned and frozen vegetables filled the bill. Prepared sauces, soups, stews, and pastas became the standbys of "can-opener cookery," and light-weight, quick-to-heat aluminum pots and pans assumed the mantle of preferred cookware.[2] Artificial foods appeared on the market, including drinks like an ersatz orange juice called "Awake" and a fake whipped cream named "Dream Whip."[3] During the 1950s, television ads promoted salty snacks with great success. Lipton promoted use of its onion soup mix by showing how to blend it with sour cream and how to scoop it out of a bowl with a potato chip. Chips and dips – soon to include salsas and various cheese mixtures – became all but indispensable party dishes. These and other so-called "junk foods" – items such as salty snacks, candies, doughnuts, and sodas – grew to be salient components of the American diet during the 1920s. However, it was not until after junk foods began appearing in television commercials, many of them pitched directly to children, that consumption started crowding out other foods. Items classified as junk amounted to 30 percent of the average American diet by the 1970s.[4] This in large part explains the epidemic of obesity, Type II diabetes, heart disease, and decreased life expectancy observed by medical authorities through the remainder of the century and beyond.

THE WORKFORCE AND EATING OUT

Speed and convenience became regarded as culinary virtues among Americans due largely to a redefinition of homemaker as a part-time occupation. This was forced upon the nation during World War II owing to a critical shortage of labor in nearly every sector of the economy. By the time the war was over, women made up approximately 50 percent of the workforce. When men returned from military service the percentage of women in business and industry dropped, but by the end of the century over 60 percent were once more gainfully employed outside the home.[5]

Because of women's need to earn income, the traditional role of the wife, spending her day at housework and preparing meals for her family, has become no more than memory.[6] Eating meals away from home, remembered as a big deal by many elderly Americans, has become commonplace. People ate an average of one meal in four outside of the home in 1965. By 1973, one meal in three was eaten out.[7] Nowadays, many Americans eat more meals away from home or carried in from a restaurant than they make in their own kitchens.[8] In addition, meals taken at home are much less likely to be family meals than they were in days gone by.[9]

The extent to which individuals and families eat meals prepared and served outside their own homes varies with income, age, size of household, and region of the country. The National Restaurant Association found that consumers nationwide spent an average of $679 per person on food consumed away from home in 1994.[10] How much families spent on restaurant food rose with income. For households with incomes of $70,000 or more, nearly half the total food dollars spent went for eating out. Households headed by persons 55-64 years old posted the highest per capita expenditure on restaurant meals ($826). As household size increased, total spending on food consumed away from home increased, but per capita spending and proportion of food dollars spent decreased. From a regional perspective, the Midwest topped all other parts of the country in proportional spending for restaurant food (39.6 percent).

EATING OUT IN BLOOMINGTON-NORMAL

For 20 years or more, the residents of Bloomington-Normal and the surrounding area have supported an exceptionally large number of restaurants relative to population size. This came to light in the 1987 *Census of Retail Trade*, a publication in which an array of data for restaurants, lunchrooms, cafeterias, and refreshment places (limited menu or fast-food restaurants) were reported.[11] Information in the report included population per establishment (a good indication of market saturation) with everything broken down by average check size.

The data showed Bloomington-Normal Metropolitan Statistical Area (MSA) to be exceptionally saturated with eating places that collected comparatively little money per transaction. Among MSAs in the East North Central Region of the country, Bloomington-Normal ranked second in population per establishment with an average check size of less than seven dollars (the smallest average check size reported). The study counted one such establishment for every 1,590 persons in the area, a market saturation second only to LaCrosse, Wisconsin.

Tables reporting the top 50 MSAs in the United States by population per establishment confirmed Bloomington-Normal's apparent penchant for low-end restaurants. For establishments ringing up checks of less than $7 on average, Bloomington-Normal ranked seventeenth nationally. For check sizes from $7-14.99, $15-29.99, and $30 or more, Bloomington-Normal failed to make the top 50.[12] Did Bloomington-Normal's relatively large number of low-ticket establishments reflect the influence and perhaps limited means of its sizable student population? Probably not. Comparable numbers for other college towns in the region – Champaign-Urbana-Rantoul, Illinois (2,403), Bloomington, Indiana (2,971), Ann Arbor, Michigan (3,116), Lansing-East Lansing, Michigan (2,229), and Madison, Wisconsin (1,917) – all indicate less saturation by a considerable margin. This suggests the explanation for Bloomington-Normal's plethora of small-check eateries resided in its homes rather than in its dormitories.

CHAIN ALLEY AND FAST FOOD

Bloomington-Normal is an outpost of Chain Alley, one of six major U.S. restaurant regions delineated by geographer Richard Pillsbury.[13] Each region takes its name from the distinctive style of eating place that tends to dominate the landscape. Thus, Pillsbury characterizes the Northeastern seaboard as "Dinerland." The Midwestern Dairy Belt and a portion of the Corn Belt comprise "Taverntown." A region Pillsbury calls "The Barbecue Pit" extends across the South. The "Beefhouse" encompasses much of the West, but yields in the Southwest to "The Taco Stand."

Chain Alley covers a discontinuous urban constituency composed of twentieth century growth cities.[14] Giants such as Atlanta, Dallas-Fort Worth, Denver, and much smaller examples like Bloomington, were little more than regional

hubs at mid-century. These places subsequently grew quickly and became important business centers populated largely by corporate transfers and other newcomers with little sentimental investment in the community, and little regard for
local history or tradition. Outside elite circles, the arts excite little interest, and
in terms of culinary arts, the idea that someone might start a restaurant because
of interest in cuisine, traditional or modern, never enters most peoples' heads.
In Chain Alley, a hurry-up mentality attends eating as people skitter from one
activity to another with little real leisure or considered notion of how to enjoy it.

Eating as rapidly as possible has never been viewed as strange in McLean
County. It was as much a cultural trait of the Upland Southerners who first
settled Central Illinois as leisurely meals were the habit of the French.[15] Hurry-up
meals became a characteristic of twentieth century American life because of corporate demands and overcrowded schedules. When State Farm Insurance cut
its employees' lunch period from 45 to 30 minutes in 1972, employees praised
management for allowing them to leave the office and go home 15 minutes earlier
in the afternoon. With children waiting, evening activities, weekend sports, and
various other obligations, many have come to view meals as a waste of time rather
than something to look forward to and savor.

Fast food accommodates America's haste. The cuisine originated in commercial kitchens. Indeed, all the items on a typical fast-food menu have been invented
or reinvented in McDonaldized environments, and all required the invention of
new equipment.[16] Three precepts rule the fast-food menu: Serve things almost no
one finds objectionable; serve dishes that have a good profit margin; serve fare so
simple to make even the most inexperienced cook can prepare it. The hamburger,
Chain Alley's foundational food, fulfills these criteria in spades. It appears to have
had multiple origins, but the McDonaldized version began in 1916 as a ground
beef patty prepared on the iron griddle of a sandwich shop in Wichita, Kansas,
the very restaurant in which the White Castle concept developed. The hamburger
was probably prepared in some homes as early as the 1930s, but the 1942 edition
of *Joy of Cooking* contains what is probably the first hamburger sandwich recipe
published for the domestic kitchen.[17]

Although the hamburger already had become America's favorite sandwich
by the 1950s, McDonald's took it and other fast-foods to another level the following decade. By 1967, the chain consisted of nearly 1,000 restaurants. The
company surpassed the U.S. Army in 1972 as the biggest purveyor of food in the
nation, and by 1974 the number of outlets reached 3,000 with a new one opening every day. Nationwide the number of fast-food or quick-service restaurants
doubled between 1967 and 1974, but McDonald's was the big story. As *Time*
told it, McDonald's took ". . . a familiar American institution, the greasy-spoon

hamburger joint, and transformed it into a totally different though no less quint-essential American operation: a computerized, standardized, premeasured, super-clean, production machine."[18] The machine prided itself on getting diners in and out of the restaurant in a blink, and lest anyone doubt it, its first corporate symbol was a character named "Speedee." Bloomington and Normal also had Mr. Quick, not to mention Steak 'n Shake and numerous other fast-food outlets representing all of the major chains. Indicative of the area's taste for fast food, per-capita sales in 1998 ranked well within the nation's top third.[19]

BLOOMINGTON-NORMAL'S RESTAURANT GEOGRAPHY

Restaurateurs do not locate their businesses willy-nilly. They like to cluster in areas frequented by potential customers and around attractive landscapes like lakes, historic sites, and beautiful residential neighborhoods.[20] Restaurants cluster in and around entertainment districts such as Navy Pier in Chicago and tourist village environments like Galena, Illinois. They collect as well in hotel and convention zones, upscale shopping districts, and ethnic neighborhoods.

The Bloomington-Normal area has four major restaurant clusters and several minor ones. Besides downtown Bloomington, the majors consist of Veterans Parkway, a long strip of retail stores and chain restaurants; Main Street adjacent to Illinois State University; and Normal's central business district, essentially a village cluster engulfed by urban development. Newer clusters have sprouted up at interstate highway exits (Interstates 55 and 74 at West Market in Bloomington and Interstate 55 at North Main in Normal) and in and around shopping malls (The Shoppes at College Hills [originally called College Hills Mall] and Eastland). In addition, several "country inns" have historically drawn clientele from the Bloomington-Normal.

VETERANS PARKWAY

The cluster of restaurants along Veterans Parkway developed in a fashion typical of suburbia. Restaurateurs determined to locate on the outskirts of town but faced with the daunting task of snaring customers whizzing past in automobiles at 50 miles per hour, situate their businesses close by one another. A strip develops, often many miles long, nourished by the prospect that hungry motorists will be tempted to apply the brakes and patronize one of them. Such clusters may include a smattering of upscale places near expensive housing, but the strip consists primarily of fast-food joints interspersed with relatively inexpensive sit-down establishments.[21] Over the years, Veterans Parkway has hosted specialty restaurants such as Bennigan's, Olive Garden, and Ruby Tuesday; coffee shop franchises like Denny's, Bakers' Square, and International House of Pancakes; and inexpensive steakhouse outlets such as Bonanza, Lone Star, and Ponderosa. High volume seafood joints, including Red Lobster and Long John Silver's were also to be found, as well as barbecue chains, including Damon's and Famous Dave's; and pizza chains like Chuck E. Cheese's, Monical's, and Shakey's. Carlos O'Kelly's, Chevy's Fresh Mex, Chili's and other Mexican and Southwestern-themed restaurants sprang up, along with sandwich shops like Panera Bread, Potbelly Sandwich Works, and Schlotzsky's Deli, not to mention a swarm of fried chicken, hamburger, and Asian specialty shops.

Amidst this gaggle, two restaurants, Biaggi's Ristorante Italiano and Le Radis Rouge, both somewhat upscale, stand out as having significant ties to the local community. Biaggi's, a 19-unit, white-tablecloth chain, got its start on Veterans Parkway in 1998. Four years later financial experts valued the chain at $70 million. Biaggi's menu lists antipasti, soups, salads, pizzas, pastas, and grilled meats prepared in a style decidedly more Italian than traditionally Italian-American. However, what captured industry attention and weighed heavily in favor of Biaggi's success was a "press-the-envelope" approach toward assuring attentive customer service.[22] Restaurant professionals showered particular applause on a system of compensation that rewards servers on the basis of their average tip. Biaggi's system challenged its wait staff to maintain or improve their average tip percentage year to year. Rewarding staff members for improvement apparently encourages exceptional attention to detail.

Le Radis Rouge, a hotel dining room, distinguished itself from every other place on Veterans Parkway by virtue of its French provincial specialties and décor. The restaurant opened in 1988 as part of Jumer's Chateau, a first-class hotel built with the help of public money. The construction of the Diamond Star Motors (later renamed Mitsubishi Motors North America) automobile assembly plant in Normal created an immediate need for accommodations attuned to international standards. Bloomington officials selected Jim Jumer, CEO of a small hotel chain based in Peoria, to create the new facility.[23] Recognized as an expert in design, Jumer built or remodeled his hotels to look romantically Old World and furnished their interiors with antiques purchased wholesale in Europe. While in Europe, Jumer acquired chefs wholesale as well, at one point having at least 30 German cooks preparing food for guests at his properties. Jumer designed his Bloomington hotel to resemble a French chateau. Critics claimed the food never lived up to the dining room's décor, but Le Radis Rouge soldiered on and developed a following of locals. Jumer disposed of the property in 2000 and opened a casino in Rock Island. The hotel name was changed to The Chateau and Le Radis Rouge remained in operation.

A few independent restaurants persisted as members of the Veterans Parkway cluster. The Garden of Paradise, Grady's Pizza, and Jim's Steakhouse, all located a block or so off Veterans, existed before the highway became engulfed in a maze of access roads and strip malls, and over the years they have come to be regarded as "local institutions" or "old standbys." Indeed, they appear remarkably unchanged.

The Garden of Paradise, located just one shopping mall west of Veterans Parkway, has managed this in spite of several changes in ownership. This may be because the person at the cash register has always been a Greek-American or of some other Eastern Mediterranean ancestry and because the place has steadfastly remained a typical Midwestern café – accented with a smattering of Greek specialty dishes on the menu.

Jim's Steak House originated in Peoria in 1963 and has stuck by a big-steak, big-martini formula from the day founder Jim Comfort served his first guests. His son, Greg, opened the Bloomington restaurant in 1980, just off Veterans Parkway in a building previously occupied by the Brittany, a well-regarded specialty restaurant with a modern exterior and an oak-paneled interior. He soon found himself hosting what a reviewer characterized as an "extended boardroom" for executives from nearby corporations.[24] This depiction may have been only half serious, but as much as business customers and others appreciated Jim's big steaks and big martinis they also took pleasure in starting off their meal with a salad doused with "Brittany House Dressing."

Brittany House Dressing
INGREDIENTS – 8 strips bacon, 5 tablespoons sugar, 3 tablespoons cider vinegar, 16 ounces (2 cups) sour cream, chopped iceberg lettuce. PREPARATION – One half-hour before serving, combine sugar and vinegar; stir into sour cream. Refrigerate. Fry bacon until crispy, then cool and crumble. Pour desired amount of bacon grease over lettuce. Toss. Serve salad topped with dressing and crumbled bacon. Serves 6-8.[25]

Grady's Pizza opened one block north of Brandtville in 1959 when pizza was still new to Bloomington. Founder Jim Grady made his pies with a wafer-thin crust, covered it with a sweet tomato sauce, and developed an appreciative following. Years later his grandson, Chris, ran into the same problem encountered by Ike Chiu at the Grand Café; the slightest change and the regulars become upset (see Chapter 3). Some of Grady's regulars have eaten there since they were children, and should the onions have a bit more bite than usual or the sauce a little more acidity, the kitchen is quick to hear about it. The result is a concern with the predictable that rivals the dogged pursuit of uniformity typical of a fully McDonaldized kitchen. At Tobin's Pizza on the other side of town, Kelly Tobin embraced the motto: "Take good care of all your customers and don't change anything." Kelly told a *Daily Pantagraph* writer that some of his guests could detect a difference in pizza sauce if he used canned tomatoes harvested at different times during the season. Because customers objected to such slight variations, Tobin has felt compelled to make little adjustments so that the taste of his sauce transcends the inconsistencies of nature.

MAIN STREET NORMAL

Main Street skirts the west side of the Illinois State University campus. From downtown Bloomington to College Avenue in Normal, it has been a one-way thoroughfare north for many years. Kingsley Street, one block to the west, carries traffic south and onto Center Street for the trip downtown. Motorists headed north on Main Street pass a mish-mash of school buildings and dormitories, business properties that are vacant or in need of remodeling, parking lots, off-the-shelf commercial buildings, fast-food outlets, and sandwich shops. For a number of years, parts of that stretch of road looked dilapidated, although in recent years, an effort has been made to improve the look of the area. Main Street has been good for restaurants owing to thousands of university students within a radius of three or four blocks, not to mention visiting families on weekends, two nearby high schools (one later became a junior high school), and a continuous round of sports and cultural events at nearby venues.

Oddly enough, the area never became a typical Campus Town. This may be because previously it was a Route 66, motorist-oriented strip. During the 1940s and '50s, The Huddle, the Midget Inn, Bob's Drive Inn, Sleevar's Restaurant, and Weed's Drive In clustered along it. The first pizzas sold in Normal were baked at Casella's Pizza Palace on Main Street across from the university campus. The area, however, remained a kind of bastion of old Normal, representative perhaps of town over gown and boundaries that existed before the legalization of alcohol sales in 1973. Student bars have been fixtures among the eating spots on the east side of campus since then, but on the Main Street side no place serving drinks has remained for long. The White Horse Inn tried for a period in the '80s and Spanky's in the '90s, but for years the Main Street Cluster consisted of fast-food and sandwich places. These include the area's first McDonald's, which opened in 1959, the original Mr. Quick, which opened the same year, and two local stalwarts, Golden West Steak House and Avanti's Italian Restaurant.

Mr. Quick opened as the brainchild of Marcel Comte of Harding's Corned Beef fame (see Chapter 2). Comte worked for a time for Steak 'n Shake and understood the fast-food revolution. He set Mr. Quick apart from McDonald's and its imitators by cooking up charbroiled hamburgers and serving them with fried onion rings called "Golden O's." The latter turned out to be a particularly big hit, and by 1965 Comte had 13 Mr. Quicks in Illinois, Indiana, Arizona and Texas. Comte's chain introduced heated and air conditioned dining rooms to the hamburger industry. Mr. Quick opened a flagship store in 1966 at Washington and Clinton in Bloomington that sat 64 customers inside and had parking for 35 cars.[26]

Hamburgers being grilled at Mr. Quick on E. Washington Street in 1961.
Courtesy of the *Pantagraph*.

The Golden West, situated one block west of Main on South Kingsley, opened in 1969 as a kind of Bonanza or Ponderosa Steakhouse with full table service.[27] Booths upholstered in bright yellow vinyl and walls decorated with fanciful representations of cowboys and Indians made it clear to first timers not to expect Morton's or Lowery's. Kids received "Indian hats" from their servers and the menu featured sandwiches with names like "The Cowpuncher" and "The Mustang." Such things made the Golden West a favorite among families with children. The area's elderly stopped in at times in even greater numbers. For many seniors on fixed incomes, the Golden West served good food, and special deals. January's cup of soup at a price matching the outside temperature seemed just too good to pass up.

Avanti's Italian Restaurant opened shortly after the Golden West Steak House, but unlike the Golden West, which closed in 2003, it is still going strong.[28] Indeed, it has been a favorite of children and students for close to 40 years, and many adults who enjoyed Avanti's in their younger years have retained a steadfast allegiance. A particularly strong following exists for Avanti's trademarked Gondola, a sparse little submarine sandwich, made with remarkably soft and *very* sweet bread. During the 1990s, Avanti's baked 3,000 loaves of it a day, and sent many hundreds out the door as sandwiches destined for various get-togethers throughout Bloomington-Normal. At school events and children's parties, kids swarm to Gondolas like bees to nectar. A couple of Gondola parties and a few visits to Avanti's as a kid, and the rest may be no more than classic conditioning.

Guido Zeller and his brother Leo share credit for making Avanti's the popular restaurant it has become. A native of Switzerland, Guido came to Illinois in 1961 to work for the Walnut Cheese Company (Walnut, Illinois). He spent three years making cheese and seven years out on the road selling it. His brother, Albert, who also sold cheese for Walnut, found his way into the frozen pizza business, and opened the first Avanti's in Peoria in 1966. He and Guido opened the Normal store in 1971. After a couple of years, Albert sold his share to Guido and concentrated exclusively on Peoria. Leo Zeller joined Guido in 1976. Guido's sons, Marcus and Richard, currently operate the restaurant, and they take pride in the support their restaurant has received over the years from the students and faculty across the street at ISU. They also continue to welcome budget-minded diners willing to enjoy their meals without a glass of Chianti Classico alongside that plate of lasagna and red sauce.

UPTOWN NORMAL

The Normal business district just east of the ISU campus is an example of what Pillsbury calls "an engulfed village." Typically, an engulfed village originates in a small town. As the years pass and nearby metropolitan areas expand, they swallow up the town and its businesses, leaving behind a neighborhood that looks like a suburban shopping area. As a shopping area, downtown Normal retained a kind of sleepy college-town atmosphere for years, though of late promoters began to call it "Uptown Normal" in an attempt to gentrify its image and add some panache.

A previous effort to reinvigorate the area took place in the early 1970s when the town lifted its prohibition against the sale of alcohol, a ban that went all the way back to its incorporation in 1865. Prior to that, the area had been known as North Bloomington. After the students and faculty of Illinois State Normal University moved into the brand new facility (Old Main) that had been built for them north of the city, the area around the new university was founded as a town named after the school. Its citizens elected five trustees who immediately outlawed the sale of intoxicating drinks.

Following its establishment, Normal did not have a restaurant for about 15 years. During that time, students and unmarried faculty had to dine in private lodgings or club together for meals because neither Illinois State nor any other university had any idea that it ought to be in the business of feeding people. Student clubs were self-organized and segregated by sex.[29] A group of students and unmarried faculty got together and decided how much they could afford to spend on meals for the term. On that basis, they assessed dues, nominated a member as club steward, rented facilities, and hired a cook. The steward, or stewardess, collected dues and purchased groceries. Many clubs rotated such tasks as waiting tables and busing dishes rather than incur the expense of additional help.

Public eating places appeared around 1880. The Normal Hotel opened a dining room about that time, followed by Sweeting's Hotel in the early 1890s. Around 1902 the town acquired its first restaurant, a place on North Street under the proprietorship of James Veach. Directory listings for 1922 identified two central business district establishments, the Broadway Inn and the Normal Cafeteria. Ten years later there were a number of other restaurants serving the downtown area including The Alamo, the Campus Inn Tea Room, the English Kitchen, and Hall's Coffee Shop. Northeast of campus and the business district, along Pine and Linden Streets, was another cluster of restaurants. Snedaker's, The Blue Lantern, Sprague's Super Service, and Manning's Lunch Room and Service Station catered to motorists following Route 66 in and out of town. Other popular places to eat over the years have been the Pilgrim Restaurant on School Street; the Barrel Inn and Riordan Stanley Sandwich Shop on Beaufort Street; and the Coop Blue Grill, the Ko-Ko Shop, and Cline's Coffee Shop on North Street. These and more recent places like the Welcome Inn, Kosher Chuck's Deli (run by Chuck Peterson, a gentile who loved corned beef on rye), and The Galery (a later incarnation of this popular bar/restaurant added an "l" to the name) contributed to Normal's collegiate atmosphere. The Pub II and The Coffeehouse and Deli have continued in that tradition.

Fast-food joints and the national chains steered clear of downtown Normal until ISU created a food court and leased space to a bunch of them in Watterson Towers, a 28-story dormitory on Fell Avenue between North and Beaufort. Early tenants included Sbarro, Eleanore's Kitchen, Starbucks, Panda Express, Chick-Fil-A, Freshens, Ben and Jerry's, and Pepe's Mexican Restaurant. Burger King, Pizza Hut, and McDonald's have been ensconced in ISU's Bone Student Center at various times over the past several decades.

Prior to ISU launching its own chain alley, Normal had a couple of chains that hardly seemed like chains. One of them was the Velvet Freeze, a St. Louis-based soft-serve ice cream franchise that occupied a prominent place on North Street through the '70s and '80s. It had the look and feel of a typical small-town sweet shop. Normal native Sally Pyne tells of going there as a high schooler for Cokes spiked with cherry, chocolate, or vanilla syrup and thinking they were quite a treat. The manager, known to the kids simply as "Smitty," had an imposing sign on the wall declaring "Teen Time Limit 15 Minutes. " It showed a big clock with just a quarter hour on its face, but as Sally remembers, nobody paid attention.

> We used to sit there for hours, but if anybody acted up, then they had the sign to point to. Sometimes kids would take salt and pepper shakers and loosen them up for the next person and swoosh! That's why they had signs like that.[30]

Garcia's, a pizza chain started in 1971 by two University of Illinois students, Ralph Senn and Joe Ream, opened a store on Fell Avenue directly across the street from Watterson Towers. It had an interior of light wood with marble countertops that made it seem rather fancy. Ralph and Joe, who called themselves "the Flying Tomato Brothers," opened a second store on Dale Street just off Main on the other side of campus. By 1992, they had 18 stores in four states. They declared bankruptcy in 1998, largely because their architecturally engaging stores cost so much to build they could not price their pizzas as cheaply as their competitors.

COUNTRY PLACES

City dwellers everywhere usually have a number of restaurants beyond suburbia they enjoy "discovering" and revisiting from time to time.[31] These are spiritual destinations in the sense that people do not go to them because they are hungry. The trip is an excursion, a planned event filled with an excitement not experienced closer to home – a vacation in miniature, perhaps.

Bloomington-Normal's favorite out-of-town spots have been remarkably diverse from the standpoints of both food and atmosphere. Near Goodfield, Conklin's Barn II Dinner Theater experienced a remarkably long run. For many years, it sold a buffet dinner followed by a comedic melodrama enacted by cast members who doubled as the wait staff. Since 1991, the Bayern Stube has enticed folks to drive out Route 9 to Gibson City for a dinner of expertly prepared German specialties. Charlie's Place in Kappa once drew especially large crowds from McLean County on Sunday until voters decided selling alcohol on the Lord's Day was not as morally reprehensible as some preached. Charlie's steaks were good but his location, just over the Woodford County line, was prime. Minier's Village Inn, once described as comfortable as a farmhouse kitchen, lifted many of its recipes from fundraiser cookbooks.[32] Favorite items on the salad bar included Pickled Chicken Gizzards (the Village Inn sold 40 pounds a week), Scroddle Noodle Salad (broccoli, rotini noodles and Italian dressing), Spaghetti Salad (spaghetti noodles, apples and pineapple in a sweet, whipped cream dressing), and Cookie Salad (fudge-striped cookies broken up and combined with instant vanilla pudding, canned crushed pineapple, canned mandarin oranges, and whipped topping).

At Gil's Country Inn outside of Minier, it was chicken dinner on Wednesday night.[33] The crowd, often nearly 1,000 people, began arriving around five o'clock for "supper." For the best cheeseburger in the county, people drove out to the Green Gables adjacent to Lake Bloomington.[34] Those in the mood for Italian food and up for a longer drive went to Mona's or Capponi's, two nearly identical restaurants in Toluca some 50 miles north, just off Highway 51. At both places, the ravioli and the sausages were spiced with tales of Al Capone and the days when Toluca was a good place to go for drinking and gambling, as well as a big plate of spaghetti.

PROCESSED FOODS

Many foodstuffs require milling, boiling, or some other process to render them safe, increase their nutritional value, or extend their shelf life. Some are processed a second time to save consumers time. Others – so-called "convenience foods" – undergo further processing so they are ready to heat and eat or to consume directly from the package.

Primary processing is as old as the human species, but prior to the nineteenth century secondary processing rarely occurred. The products of secondary processing, often referred to as "prepared foods," first became a major component of the American diet during World War II when millions of women began working outside the home and were willing to give anything that saved time in the kitchen a fair trial. Some of the things they tried – for example, brown-and-serve rolls – were new to grocer's shelves. Other things, however, like cake mixes and canned soups, had been around for years.

CANNED SOUP

Soup, a dish that usually takes a long time to cook, was a perfect candidate for sale in a prepared form. John Dorance of the Joseph Campbell Preserve Company thought up the idea, and working with a chemist he invented a soup that could be prepared in a commercial kitchen, then condensed and packed in cans. Dorance's first soups – tomato, vegetable, chicken, consommé, and oxtail – arrived in markets in 1896. By 1904, the company had 21 varieties on grocers' shelves and was selling 16 million cans a year. The firm changed its name to the Campbell Soup Company in 1921.

Persuading homemakers to use convenience products was not easy. The problem was the natural connection between feeding and love and its emblematic relationship to home cooking.[35] How loving was opening a can of soup? Campbell's advertising department answered by representing the company's products as not only loving but progressive. The women who appeared in Campbell's ads made it clear their families were better off eating Campbell's soup than they would be if mother spent hours at the stove. Besides, as Campbell's would have it, its soups were healthier, less expensive, and better tasting than homemade.

As prepared foods inundated the market, Campbell's Soup published a little booklet called *"Cooking with Condensed Soups"* (1952). It was supposed to sell canned soup. No one anticipated the deep and lasting impression it made on American cooking. A number of its recipes became American standards, including Heavenly Ham Loaf, Green Bean Bake, and Perfect Tuna Casserole.[36] In addition, it helped popularize the use of commercially prepared foods as ingredients in familiar home-cooked dishes, in effect greatly simplifying standard cookery. By the end of the decade, prepared foods existed in such variety that a homemaker could prepare three meals a day and yet be completely ignorant of traditional kitchen skills. Erika Endrijonas argues that with the advent of "the cream-of-mushroom-soup school of cookery" fixing meals in American households underwent a major "de-skilling."[37]

DE-SKILLED RECIPES IN LOCAL COOKBOOKS

The rise of the cream-of-mushroom-soup tradition can be detected paging through the McLean County Museum of History's local cookbook collection.

It consists primarily of fund-raiser cookbooks put together by schools, church groups, and other volunteer organizations. Members typically jot down a favorite recipe, and the group has them all printed up. The result, aside from a few new ideas about what to prepare for dinner, is a record of taste – a testimony to what some segment of the community considered good eats at the time. Reading through a collection of dozens of these cookbooks going back many years creates a panorama of popular eating habits. For McLean County, this picture begins in 1877 with *The Bloomington Library Cookbook* and continues through the beginning of the twenty-first century.

At the start, the only processed ingredients found in local fund-raiser cookbooks were such primary items as cured meats and milled grains. Aunt Jemima Pancake Mix, one of the first prepared flour products on the American market, did not appear in grocery stores until 1889.[38] Ads for Swans Down Prepared Cake Flour published in *The Daily Pantagraph* in 1910 appear to be the first for a pre-mixed flour product in the Bloomington market.[39] Some of the earliest prepared foods were ready-to-eat products. Battle Creek Sanitarium Foods, later to become Kellogg's, took out advertisements in *The Daily Pantagraph* in 1901 for two products, Granut and Granola. The company touted these as suitable for instant use, morning, noon, or night and as an especially good food for children. Charles Post, once a patient at Battle Creek Sanitarium, produced Grape Nuts, a rival product. Post also invented Postum Cereal Food Coffee, later sold as "Instant Postum," a food simply prepared by adding hot water. Battle Creek publicized a competing brand, "Caramel Cereal," an odd name for an instant beverage that was marketed as the "successor to coffee."

The first prepared food to appear as an ingredient in a local cookbook was unflavored gelatin (see Chapter 4). Jell-O brand gelatin added the sugar and the fruit flavoring to the package, making it a fully prepared instant food. Its inventor, Pearle Wait, struck upon the idea in 1897. Waite was a patent medicine man who knew a thing or two about disguising unsavory substances with bright colors and appealing flavors.[40] He conceived of his creation as a dessert mix, but he met with little success selling it. Consequently, he sold his recipes to Orator Woodward, another creator of patent medicines, who likewise failed to do well with the product until it dawned on him that the problem with Jell-O was that nobody knew what to do with a food that was almost ready to serve. Homemakers at the time were accustomed to preparing dishes involving several steps from raw food to finished item. They needed recipes, so Woodward supplied them.[41] In 1902, he printed Jell-O recipe books, thousands of them, which he distributed door-to-door. Follow-up ads bragged about how much children loved Jell-O and how easy it was to make. As a result, Jell-O experienced tremendous sales and numerous rivals entered the market. By 1910, The Tea and Coffee Store in down-town Bloomington could merely advertise two packages of "jelly dessert" for just 15 cents, suggesting that consumers were totally familiar with the product.

The earliest use of the term "easy" in the Museum's cookbook collection can be found in a 1910 booklet entitled *Normal Community Cookbook: Simple Recipes*. In this economy-minded little volume, "easy" meant uncomplicated, not unskilled. The recipes generally involved few steps but resulted in elegant little dishes – for instance, an "Easy Dessert" consisting of sliced bananas sprinkled with sugar and a mixture of lemon juice and water and served in sherbet cups. The cooking-out-of-a-can concept made its first noteworthy appearance in the *McLean County Home Bureau Cook Book* of 1948, but clearly the style had yet to gain currency. Only two of the 20 recipes for "One Dish Meals," called for canned soups. A meat chapter, composed of 78 recipes, contained just three list-ing canned soup as an ingredient. Suggesting ambivalence, the Home Bureau published two Italian Spaghetti recipes, one calling for canned tomato sauce, the other calling for whole tomatoes.[42] *Kitchen Kapers*, published two years later by St. Matthew's Episcopal Church in Bloomington, showed considerably more commitment to prepared food products. Of the 35 recipes it offered for meat dishes, 11 listed canned soup as a main ingredient. Remarkably, however, the collection's recipe for tuna casserole did not involve opening a can of cream of mushroom soup.

By 1960, it was canned cream of mushroom soup and other prepared products from beginning to end. That year *A Collection of Recipes from WJBC*, a radio station fond of referring to itself as "the voice of McLean County," featured a compilation of listeners' favorites. It led off with instructions for preparing Spamburgers and a dish called "Chili Burger Supper" that combined ground beef, elbow macaroni, canned tomato soup, canned chili-beef soup, and processed cheese. Subsequent pages served up additional "hamburger specials." The first called for pouring a can of cream-style corn into the frying pan, and the second a can of chicken gumbo soup. The collection continued with Beef Stroganoff prepared with canned cream of chicken soup, steak smothered in cans of cream of mushroom or cream of cel-ery soup, and other concoctions prepared in a similar manner.

Beef Stroganoff WJBC Style

INGREDIENTS – ½ cup minced onion; ¼ cup butter; 1 clove garlic, minced; 1 pound hamburger; 2 tablespoons flour; 2 teaspoons salt; ¼ teaspoon salt; 8 ounce can sliced mushrooms; 1 cup sour cream; 2 tablespoons minced parsley; 10½ ounce can cream of chicken soup. PREPARATION – Sauté onion and garlic in butter over medium heat. Add meat and brown. Add flour to thicken. Add salt, mushrooms, and pepper. Cook 5 minutes. Add soup. Simmer uncovered 10 minutes. Stir in sour cream. Heat through. Sprinkle with parsley.[43]

If homemakers who cooked from the can felt a little hesitant about it, all they needed to do was read Peg Bracken's *The I Hate to Cook Book*.[44] Published in 1960, well before feminist literature became popular, it essentially absolved women from taking shortcuts and spending as little time in the kitchen as possible. Bracken viewed canned goods and instant mixes as standard ingredients. Her recipe for Sweep Steak, one of the most popular dishes of the '60s, called for covering a pot roast with a package of onion soup mix, wrapping it in aluminum foil, and baking it in the oven. Fixing Sweep Steak required almost no effort and represented the kind of triumph homemakers could only dream about during the era of the scientific kitchen.

With food quality very much a back-burner issue and the door now wide open to a kind of McDonaldization of the family kitchen, convenience cooking in McLean County became standard. *Cooking Time: A Book of Favorite Recipes*, first published by members of the Ellsworth United Methodist Church in 1973 and reprinted in 1980, tendered main dish recipes consisting mostly of casseroles, two-thirds of them based on canned soups. *Recipes from the Kitchens of Home Sweet Home Mission Auxiliary Members and Friends*, a collection that came out in 1985, included the iconic "Fix and Forget Dinner," a combination of ground chuck, dry rice, frozen vegetables, onion soup mix, and cans of beef consommé and cream of celery soup. Another mélange entitled "Casserole for an Electric Skillet," consisted of ground beef mixed with olives, celery, canned tomatoes, wide noodles, and American cheese. The Museum's collection of local cookbooks testifies to the continued popularity of this approach through the emergence of microwave cookery in the mid-1980s. Abetted by the emergence of frozen main dishes, convenience cooking continued as a popular style of cookery through the end of the century.

THE CONVENIENCE KITCHEN

When American Vice-President Richard Nixon got into an argument with Soviet Premier Nikita Khrushchev in 1959 at a trade show in Russia, a bone of contention was consumer satisfaction in the U.S. as opposed to the Soviet Union. In the exchange, referred to as the "Kitchen Debate" because it took place in the kitchen of a model American home, Nixon cited statistics about appliance ownership in the United States as evidence of capitalism's success in satisfying peoples' needs. Khrushchev dismissed Nixon's numbers as nothing more than evidence of America's fascination with gadgets.[45]

NEW STOVES AND REFRIGERATORS

Nearly every kitchen in the United States needed to be rewired in years following World War II to accommodate the new stoves, refrigerators, dishwashers, garbage disposals, microwaves, and other appliances now regarded as part and parcel of the standard kitchen The electric stove made its American debut in Chicago at the World's Columbia Exposition in 1893. However, owing to the cost of electricity it took more than 30 years for electric cooking even to be considered as a replacement for gas in middle-income households. The same was true for electric refrigerators. The Domelre (Domestic Electric Refrigerator), a Chicago brand, arrived on the market in 1900. Kelvinator initiated mass production in 1916. General Motors acquired the Guardian Frigerator brand shortly afterward and changed the name to Frigidaire.[46] "Fridges" grew in popularity as prices dropped. Retail prices in 1921 were beyond ordinary means; hence, only 5,000 electric refrigerators were produced for home use. In 1926, a total of 200,000 units were sold. In 1930, refrigerators began to outsell iceboxes, and by 1950 over 80 percent of American farm kitchens and approximately 90 percent of urban households had a fridge.[47] Stand-alone freezers became commonplace about the same time, especially among farm families still producing much of their own food.

FROZEN FOODS AND MICROWAVE OVENS

Freezing as a domestic food preparation technique predated commercial freezing by more than a century. Recipes for making ice cream appeared in American cookbooks in the 1820s. Consumers could purchase ice cream makers by 1846, and by the 1880s homemakers were using them to make many sorts of frozen desserts, including custards, mousses, puddings, and sorbets.[48]

The commercial frozen food industry began with the work of Clarence Birdseye in 1925. His purpose was to sell fish, but the problem was that almost nobody had facilities in which to keep frozen food.[49] Birdseye persisted and developed a line of frozen meats and vegetables. Still, by 1933 only 500 stores in the United States had retail freezer space. Heavy advertising and better quality products helped increase that figure to 10,000 stores in 1940.[50]

Keeping frozen foods in the home presented a challenge. The typical refrigerator manufactured before the Second World War contained a freezer unit barely big enough to hold ice cubes.[51] Still, the war gave frozen food a tremendous boost. As industry guru E.W. Wilson explained it, "Tin went to war; frozen foods stayed home."[52] The military's need for tin rendered canned goods scarce, but frozen foods could be packaged in almost anything. Frozen prepared items avoided rationing, and after the war frozen meats and vegetables generally became available more than a year before their canned counterparts.[53] Availability and quality improvements boosted freezer cabinet installations in retail stores and led consumers to demand larger freezer compartments in domestic refrigerators.

The most popular frozen food at first was orange juice. For the grocery, this served as a kind of tune up for the arrival of Swanson's "TV Dinner," which created a veritable craze for frozen convenience foods. Swanson, a division of Campbell Soup Company, had originally been a huge butter and egg concern. It came out with a line of frozen chickens during the war and later introduced a variety of frozen pot pies. Complete frozen dinners consisting of turkey or roast beef, mashed potatoes and gravy, and green peas followed in 1954. Swanson sold them in a foil-coved aluminum tray with separate compartments for the meat, potatoes, and peas. The idea came from Pan American World Airways' foil-covered dinners meant to be warmed in convection ovens aboard overseas flights. The public, however, assumed that TV Dinners were supposed to be eaten in front of the television set, and some companies began manufacturing light-weight metal folding tables so people could eat in the living room while watching their favorite shows.[54] Inventor Gerry Thomas actually meant the name to do no more than associate the product with the newest and most modern electronic device and thereby make the food seem very contemporary and cool.[55] He did succeed because TV dinners soon represented the ultimate in convenience and a leisurely new postwar lifestyle.[56]

What happened to the idea of frozen fish, the product that led Clarence Birdseye to explore freezing in the first place? It bears mention that before World War II almost all of the fish recipes collected in McLean County's cookbooks called for canned varieties.[57] Such was no longer the case after the war. The *McLean County Home Bureau Cook Book* (1948) by then, contained recipes for baked, broiled, fried, and steamed seafood, all available in supermarket freezers.[58]

Frozen foods, especially convenience products, experienced a second surge in popularity with the introduction of the microwave oven. The first microwave, the Radarange, was sold in 1947 for commercial use and was as big as a refrigerator. Amana introduced the first countertop model in 1967. By mid-'70s, sales surpassed those of gas ranges. Nearly 52 million American households (approximately 60 percent) had a microwave in 1976 – more than the number of homes equipped with dishwashers. Still, McLean County's fund-raiser cookbooks had no recipes for microwave dishes prior to 1984, suggesting that until then the device was used primarily as a food warmer and defroster, which continues to be the case in many kitchens.

SWEETS AND SNACKS

Historically, the only foods prepared in Bloomington that went on to become national brands have been candies and snacks. Candy, as the term is used in North America, refers to a great variety of sweets, including sugar candies, chocolates, candy bars, marshmallows, and more. A snack usually refers to a bite between meals. The label "snack food" applies specifically to fare designed to be portable and non-perishable. Ingredients commonly include substantial amounts of sweeteners, preservatives, and flavorings. Collectively, candies, snack foods, and the like qualify as "junk food," a category invented to describe foodstuffs exceedingly rich in energy but notably deficient in nutrients other than carbohydrates and fats.

CANDY AND CHOCOLATES

The concept of candy as a distinct type of food began to take shape about the time settlers started arriving in McLean County in appreciable numbers. Prior to that time there was "rock candy," a product people regarded as a form of sugar. When they thought of sweets, Americans imagined candied fruits and nuts, puddings, cakes, and preserves, which they generally spoke of as "sweetmeats."[59]

Candy as we think of it today emerged as the work of confectioners inspired by druggists. For years, they had been encasing medicines in sugar coatings to make the active ingredients more palatable. Confectioners created a non-medicinal lozenge with mint or some other herb instead of medicines. Such lozenges became known as "treats" by turning what previously had been a verb into a noun.[60] By the 1850s, a variety of inexpensive hard candies had developed from the lozenge, and their sales quickly surpassed those of nougats, pralines, and other more expensive confections.

FRESHLY MADE SWEETS

Early candy factories and sweet shops were called "confectionaries." One of the first in Bloomington, Bender and Owens, advertised itself in 1854 as a "New Confectionary," offering candy, ice cream, and soda water.[61] Three years later Denison and Mitchell advertised ". . . the largest and best assortment of fancy and stick candy ever before offered in the market."[62] Fancy candy meant chocolates and other sweets normally given as gifts. Stick candy, sugar cooked to a hard-crack stage, was intended mainly for children.

A decade or so later a new set of faces appeared and the industry started to grow by leaps and bounds. Newcomers included the Mrs. Sophia Osborn,

Bloomington's first female candy maker, W.G. Cochrane, recently arrived from Chicago, and J.L. Green and J.L. Timmerman, founders of Bloomington Steam Candy Works.[63] Cochrane set up shop in the Ashley House Block on Jefferson Street, where in addition to cooking up various sweets, he made ice cream and dispensed soda in an elegant new "saloon." Green and Timmerman made candy in large batches and sold them wholesale. Other late nineteenth century manufacturers included Isaiah and Fred Wilmeth (formerly in the baking business), Kitchell and Peacock, Wood and Bird, Chisholm-Gray, and Paul F. Beich. From the beginning of the twentieth century through the Great Depression, there were some 15 or 20 confectioners at a time supplying area consumers' demand for sweets. Among the most popular were August Fissel, Zier Brothers, W.F. Kleinau and Sons, Bertoni and Baldwin, A.M. Kitchell (successor to Kitchell and Peacock), Normal Kandy Kitchen (successor to August Fissel), Baldwin's Confections (successor to Bertoni and Baldwin), Goodie Candy, Cat n' Fiddle Confections, and Phillis Pure Candies.

The market for locally made candies contracted sharply after the Second World War due to competition from soft drinks and the advent of modern packaging and preservatives. Prior to the war, many sweets had a short shelf life, and products shipped from afar often arrived in poor condition. This favored local confectioners, and explains why local firms frequently used the phrase "freshly made" in their advertising.[64]

For local confectioners "made fresh daily" may have been as much a matter of economic necessity as an assurance of quality – at least during the Great Depression. Candy-maker Martin Pease, Jr., otherwise known as "Noonie," once said he had to make two candy sales each day. The first would buy the ingredients for tomorrow's production; the second would put food on the family table that night.[65]

Noonie's dad, Martin Pease, Sr., ventured into the candy business as a sideline. He first sold candies out of his home in Canton, Ohio and later in Elgin, Illinois from a shop located on the second floor above a funeral parlor. After his employer, the Eureka Vacuum Cleaner Company, transferred him to its home office in Bloomington in 1917, Martin and his sons opened a candy store at 206 North East Street.[66] As his expertise grew, Martin wrote a series of four books about candymaking.[67] When the Great Depression and hard times descended on Bloomington, Martin's sons looked for outside work. Noonie moved to Springfield, opened a store, and founded the company that bears the Pease name today.[68]

PIGGING OUT AT BOYLANS

Boylan's, another Bloomington candy-maker, was also conceived during the Depression. It began in 1920 as a food store started by brothers John and George Boylan on West Market Street. When the business began to falter in the 1930s, the Boylans converted half the store into a confectionary. Their hand-made candies proved a hit. Groceries were phased out, and ice cream was phased in, particularly for the summer months when candy sales petered out.[69] Soon there was a menu of short orders and fancy ice cream creations, a second location on North Main, and a late night crowd of Illinois Wesleyan University students. The Main Street location had the confectionary up front and pine booths and a jukebox in the back. One of the students' favorite dishes was called "The Pig's Dinner," – essentially a double banana split served in a little wooden replica of a hog's trough. Those who ate one received a button proclaiming, "I was a pig at Boylan's."[70] The most popular item at Boylan's was the Funny Sundae. It consisted of a parfait glass layered with vanilla ice cream at the bottom, then milk chocolate, followed by chocolate ice cream, marshmallow, pecans, whipped cream, and a cherry.

The nearby Caramel Crisp Shop adhered to essentially the same formula as Boylan's. Caramel Crisp, where one day Beer Nuts would be developed, offered hand-made caramel apples, caramel popcorn, and peanut brittle.[71] The shop also offered a selection of sandwiches, including boiled ham on a bun, "hamburger on a bun," "frizzled" ham, pork tenderloin, "chip steak," and toasted cheese. The menu listed several salads – cottage cheese, banana-nut, pear salad, perfection salad, pineapple-cottage cheese, and head lettuce with mayonnaise or French dressing. The menu offered a number of canned Heinz Soups (cream of mushroom, cream of tomato, old-fashioned bean, etc.) as well as French fries, "Pie Alamode," and all sorts of shakes and sundaes. Beverages included "Our Orange Drink," and a long list of bottled sodas – Coca Cola, Seven-Up, Pepsi-Cola, Hires Root Beer, Barq's Root Beer, Dr. Pepper, and Fruit Bowl.

As for Boylan's, it almost disappeared when Michael "George" and James Boylan took over in 1962. The Main Street store had closed during the war due to commodity shortages, and George turned the old store on Market Street into a bar. James got himself elected McLean County Treasurer and had no time for confections. Still, old customers kept showing up looking for Boylan's Candy. Eventually, James reopened the store on the second floor above the bar and returned to making the caramel apples, peanut brittle, and other candies that had made Boylan's a household name in the community. Pat Boylan, James's son, took over the business in 1998 and remained true to tradition. He adhered as closely as possible the Boylan brothers' original recipes (which they had recorded in shorthand to deter would-be thieves), deviating here and there only after it became apparent that certain modern flavoring agents were not nearly as strong as those used in the '20s. Pat later sold the confectionary to Dan and Sally Flynn who have carried on the Boylan name and continue to use the old recipes.[72]

PAUL F. BEICH AND THE WHIZ BAR

The story of Paul F. Beich is an account of a local candy-maker succeeding in becoming a major brand name only to be swallowed up by a giant multi-national corporation. The company's beginnings can be traced back to 1854.[73] That year J. L. Green opened a variety store in Bloomington, and after awhile he began supplementing his usual stock with homemade candy. Soon it became the most popular item in his shop. Green brought J.L. Timmerman on board in 1867 and created J.L. Green and Company. He called his shop a "fancy goods" store, and moved it to 104 North Main. The characterization of his shop as an outlet for fancy goods suggests that Green was venturing into the world of choco-lates. Candies made of chocolate had first appeared on the market in 1847 when Joseph Fry and Son, an English company, invented a way to mix cocoa powder, sugar, and cocoa butter with water to make a paste that could be molded into various shapes. Henri Nestlé produced the first chocolate bar from this paste, and Rudolphe Lindt found a way to reduce its grittiness and improve texture.[74] Chocolates subsequently proved very popular in the United States. At first, they were either produced by skilled French immigrants or imported from Europe. Either way, they were usually hand wrapped and sold in expensive containers to suggest European refinement. Their supposed elegance made chocolates a popu-lar gift item – hence, their sale in fancy goods establishments.[75] Soon it became fashionable for a man to present a box of chocolates to a woman as a token of love.[76] However, by the 1870s women were purchasing a considerable volume of chocolates and other candies on their own.

Green and Timmerman caught the wave. In 1871, they moved to 118 South Main, renamed their company Bloomington Steam Candy Works, and started selling their products wholesale. In December of that year, they received one order for a ton of candy, and within a short time they were making every candy known to the trade, including the finest creams and brandy pieces. When Bloomington Steam Candy Works was running at full capacity in the weeks leading up to Christmas, it employed 13 people, including four skilled candy makers. It also employed three salesmen charged with covering all of Illinois and parts of Missouri.

Over the next 20 years, Bloomington Steam Candy was bought, sold, and renamed several times. Green sold his half of the business to Timmerman in

1877, and the firm became known as the "J.L. Timmerman Company." In 1885, Everett Page Brown of Bruce and Brown, Timmerman's chief competitor, bought him out and merged the two organizations. Within a year, John W. Gray, co-owner of Gray Brothers' Grocery of Bloomington, purchased the business. Gray formed a company called Chisholm-Gray in 1888 with fellow grocer John Chisholm, formerly of Chisholm Brothers'. Shortly thereafter the company moved to the Chisholm Building on East Front.

Paul F. Beich, a former employee of Bruce and Brown, purchased the company in 1892. Beich's personal history began in Whelau, East Prussia, where he was born in 1864. He attended school in Clum, West Prussia and apprenticed with a friend of his father who manufactured food flavorings. Beich immigrated to the United States at age 16 and moved immediately to Bloomington. He worked briefly at a number of occupations before joining Bruce and Brown as a salesman. From that time on, Beich remained in the candy business, but in 1884 he moved to St. Louis and the Peckham Candy Company. He stayed with Peckham until 1888, all the while growing increasingly adroit in the business of confections. His next step was to partner with another expert in the field, Otto Buffe. Together Beich and Buffe quickly built a substantial business as jobbers and must have made out very well when, after a few years, they sold their business to National Candy, a much larger firm.[77]

Beich used his share of the proceeds to acquire Chisholm-Gray, which he promptly renamed Paul F. Beich. He continued to operate for awhile out of the Chisholm-Gray facility, but expanded operations in 1894 into a three-story facility in the 100 block of East Front Street. The new building allowed Beich to make use of gravity in his manufacturing procedures and thereby speed up production. This was essential because the market for sweets was growing rapidly. To keep up, the Beich Company employed 40 people in its kitchens. To build market share, it had eight salesmen on the road, covering large areas of the East and Midwest and peddling a diverse line of products. These included caramels, bon bons, chocolates, and Pansy Brand Fine Candies. In Bloomington, where the company maintained a downtown candy store, it solicited orders for the Waukesha Water Company, maker of Waukesha-Hygeia Ginger Ale and Boro-Lithia, and jobbed fruits, nuts, and cigars to stores throughout the area.

Mr. PAUL F. BEICH, Manufacturing Confectioner,
109-111 E. Front.

The Paul F. Beich Manufacturing Confectioner on E. Front Street in
Bloomington, c. 1896.

Paul F. Beich by 1908 was one of the biggest candy companies in the
United States, shipping its products throughout North America, providing area
farmers with a ready market for milk and cream, and employing more than
200 people.[78] The company's products included Beich chocolates, Bride-Elect
caramels, jellybeans, and Jordan almonds. Beich's downtown plant churned
out many of the company's most popular lines. A second factory located on
Lumber Street on Bloomington's west side produced chocolates and a variety
of other fine candies.

The Lumber Street plant originally belonged to Milton Hershey who later became America's premier chocolate maker. As an active member of the National Confectioners' Association, Paul Beich became acquainted with Hershey and persuaded him to locate a branch of his Lancaster Caramel Company in Bloomington. Hershey found an excellent building originally constructed as carriage factory in which to install his kitchens. Lancaster Caramel immediately proceeded to build its own dairy facilities and create a large number of jobs for young women. A couple of years later, however, Hershey decided to quit caramels and focus exclusively on chocolates. Beich and his former partner, Otto Buffe, reunited and purchased Hershey's Bloomington facility in 1900. The company established a presence in Chicago about 1907. It consisted at first of a sales and distribution headquarters, but in 1912 Beich purchased the William Hagley Company and began manufacturing in its plant.

Beich's market early on consisted primarily of women. *The New York Times* reported in 1899 that women made up three-quarters of the candy consumers in the United States.[79] *Candy*, a popular play in 1892, depicted Kitty, the young daughter of a millionaire, as a girl much too fond of candy.[80] Her father proclaimed he would give away half of his fortune to any man who convinced her to stop eating it. "Kisses . . . sweeter than candy" and a marriage proposal cured Kitty of her addiction by the end of the play. However, the conception of candy eating as a kind of vice, forced confectioners like Lowney's Chocolate Bonbons to inundate the public with messages of purity.[81] This was during the Progressive Era and at a time of great public concern about the cleanliness of food. Beich brand names like Saint Regis and Pansy were advertised with insistent declarations that candy was virtuous – clean, fresh, and pure.[82]

The legitimization of candy as a food men could enjoy began around 1910.[83] To begin with, candy was represented as an alcohol substitute. Women and children became addicted to candy. Men became addicted to alcohol, but a craving for sweets did far less social damage than a craving for liquor.[84] Candy was also trumpeted as a source of energy and strength. Indeed, when women started to worry about becoming fat in the 1920s, Beich responded with an ad featuring actress Pauline Frederick. Frederick described eating six pieces of candy every night she performed in the play, *The Scarlet Woman*.[85] Candy did not make her fat, Frederick testified. Rather, it prevented fatigue. Salesmen originated the get-up-and-go pitch during the First World War and promoted candy as essential to soldiers' well being. Immediately after the war, the candy bar became popular.[86] Beich introduced the Whiz Bar in 1926, and instantly it became a best-seller.[87] The company closed its Chicago kitchens in 1939 to concentrate on its Lumber Street factory in Bloomington where the Whiz Bar was made.

The Whiz Bar and other confections brought carloads of commodities from around the world to a facility viewed as a center of technological innovation in candy-making.[88] Beich's Lumber Street factory received approximately 70 farm products, including sugar, corn syrup, dextrose, various starches, molasses, honey, maple syrup, almonds, pecans, peanuts, and soybean derivatives. Cocoa beans came directly from the African Gold Coast and Brazil. In 1954, the plant had storage capacity for 23 carloads of corn syrup, making it one of the largest users in the Midwest. The factory housed the most advanced candy casting, coating, and wrapping machines available in the world. Chocolate beans were roasted on site and ground to exacting standards. Justin Alikonis, the company's leading technician, perfected pulverization with patented units capable of reducing dry ingredients to particle sizes so fine as to be undetectable by the human tongue.[89] Temperature-controlled chocolate storage was developed on site, allowing confection workers to pump properly heated chocolate through 250 feet of circulating lines. Alikonis modified stainless steel cookers and beaters to improve sanitation and increase production. He invented the whimsically named "Whizolator" to create higher quality aerated fillings such as marshmallow and nougat. The machine turned out 1,400 gallons of marshmallow per hour. It made Whiz Bar one of America's most popular confections by creating a fine-textured marshmallow with extended shelf life. By 1964, Lumber Street housed two cooking kettles with a capacity of 2,300 pounds of chocolate. Its marshmallow cooker could churn out 3,600 pounds of the gooey substance per hour, and it possessed equipment capable of automatically wrapping 10,000 pieces of caramel per day.

Paul Beich died in 1937, leaving the business to his sons and their heirs. They sold the firm in 1984 to Nestlé USA Inc., a part of Nestlé S.A. of Vevey, Switzerland, the largest food company in the world. Under Nestlé, Paul F. Beich became Kathryn Beich, Inc., one of the leading fundraising businesses in the country. The business was named for Kathryn McNulta Beich who in 1950 first thought of selling chocolates through schools and churches. Beich's Bloomington plant, located since 1967 in a windowless steel-clad factory building on the far southern edge of city, continues to make candy for Nestle, including Nestle Treasurers, Laffy Taffy, Flips Pretzels, and Kathryn Beich specialty candy.[90]

BEER NUTS

Americans have purchased roasted nuts from street vendors or have roasted and salted nuts at home since colonial days. Grocery store sales began early in the twentieth century after a technique for making salt stick to roasted nuts was invented.[91] Since then, the almond, the pecan, and the walnut have each had a turn as the nation's favorite, but from the 1920s on, the peanut has held sway.

The peanut, which in truth is a legume, originated in South America. It diffused to Africa and Asia, and then as a result of the slave trade it traveled back across the Atlantic to North America. Vendors began peddling them on city streets after the Civil War. Amedeo Obici, a Wilkes-Barre, Pennsylvania street vendor, formed the Planters Peanut Company in 1906.[92] His packaging and creative advertising made Planters America's premier snack in less than two decades. Beer Nuts, a peanut product that found a national market in the 1950s, has one foot in the tradition of such sugar-coated treats as Cracker Jack (first sold in 1893 by W.F. Rueckheim) and Goobers (a chocolate-covered peanut), the other in the tradition of salty foods like potato chips and pretzels.

Beer Nuts originated as "Redskins," a hand-made product cooked up by members of the Shirk family in the basement of their Caramel Crisp Shop in Bloomington. Arlo Shirk, assisted by his father, Edward, purchased the shop in 1937 and received an early version of the recipe as part of the deal. It called for mixing peanuts, their skins intact, with a sweet glaze and a dash of salt. Edward and his son Russell, who joined the business in 1940 after Arlo's death, fiddled around with proportions a bit and sold their version of Redskins over the counter at 25 cents a pound. Sometimes they offered samples free of charge to persuade customers to buy more homemade orange drink.

Redskins found a wider market in 1950, thanks to Tom Keefe and Alan Sycle, proprietors of National Liquor Stores in Bloomington. After hearing that Russell Shirk was interested in wholesaling, they asked him to package Redskins for resale through their chain.[93] Russell agreed and packed them in 1½ ounce bags under the name "Shirk's Peanuts (Glazed)" (later called "Shirk's Glazed Peanuts").

They sold remarkably well and caught the attention of local Blue Star Potato Chip distributor Eldredge Brewster. In 1952, he made a deal with Shirk. They renamed the product "Beer Nuts," and Brewster began marketing them on his potato chip route.[94] Soon Brewster was selling all the Beer Nuts he could get to bars in Chicago, St. Louis, Milwaukee, and Indianapolis.[95]

This convinced Russell to sell his shop and manufacture Beer Nuts full time. He began in 1953 with a 2,000-square-foot facility in downtown Bloomington. The operation outgrew this plant by 1955, and production moved to a 7,000-square-foot facility on North Prairie Street. A new 100,000-square-foot factory had to be built in 1974 to meet ever-increasing demand.

Consumers' taste for Beer Nuts peaked in 1985. That year the company sold 15 million pounds of product, but it faced major difficulties. For one thing, it had come to be perceived as an "old fogy snack."[96] With Russell Shirk and Eldredge Brewster both retired, Jim Shirk, Russell's son, took charge and sought to modernize Beer Nuts' image. He deployed fresh graphics and new packaging, but another set of concerns related to the snack's high caloric value and its fat and sodium contents proved more difficult to dispel. A big increase in the number of snack products, including several Beer Nuts knock-offs, all competing for grocery store shelf space, was another troublesome issue. To remain competitive, the company has expanded its product line to include Beer Nuts Golden Cashews, Beer Nuts Choice Almonds, and Beer Nuts Old Fashioned Peanuts.

DOUGHNUTS

The doughnut rates as one of America's most popular confections as indicated by the sustained success of Dunkin' Donuts, Krispy Kreme, and similar chains. Many of these businesses are open 24-7, often selling several, if not a dozen, or more doughnuts per customer. As readily available as doughnuts are today, it is difficult to imagine they originated as a special occasion food introduced to these shores early on by the Dutch, French, and other immigrant groups. The Dutch made *oliekoecken* (oil cakes) for the Christmas holidays. The French made *beignets* for Shrove Tuesday. In the United States, however, the doughnut – essentially fried bread coated with sugar or frosting – became a virtual staple by the middle of the nineteenth century.[97] Many homemakers fried doughnuts weekly, using either yeast dough or a dough leavened with baking powder and lard. Doughnut-making began to turn commercial in the 1920s with the introduction of automation. Soon mom-and-pop shops sprang up around the country, followed a decade or so later by various chains.

Locally owned shops in McLean County have existed alongside the national chains and supermarket bakeries for decades and have proved quite adept at keeping their names and their products in the public eye. Jeff Prochnow, who entered the business at age 19 by purchasing a Mr. Donut store, gave up his franchise in 1987 and opened The Bakery Banc – a doughnuts, cake, and muffin shop – on North Main Street in Bloomington. Being independent left Prochnow free to purchase ingredient mixes for his products from a variety of manufacturers, but it also meant he had to purchase advertising directly out of pocket. To preserve the bottom line, Prochnow began pulling stunts right and left.[98] For example, when Skylab, a Soviet satellite, was about to disintegrate, he painted a sign offering $1,000 to any person who brought a piece of the satellite into his store. The offer attracted more than $1,000 worth of free TV and radio attention. When a Minneapolis firm asked Prochnow to test market a bran muffin mix, he went to the radio stations with some nutritional facts supplied by the manufacturer and talked one manager into free airtime. He had to order two additional bags of mix thanks to the publicity.

Denny Marquardt, another "boy wonder" in the local doughnut business, began working at age 14 for Fred's Spudnuts, a doughnut franchise so named because the chief ingredient was potato flour.[99] Marquardt purchased the business, which was located on South Main in Bloomington, in 1974 at age 19. In just seven months the shop went from one of the least profitable in the Spudnuts organization to fourth in sales nationwide. A year and a half later, the company folded and the young franchisee was on his own. This proved no deterrent to Marquardt's success. Denny's Doughnuts eventually became Denny's Doughnuts and Bakery, a chain of four Bloomington-area coffee shops that offered breakfast, lunch, and a line of cakes in addition to a variety of potato-flour doughnuts.

Denny's potato-flour doughnuts represented a comeback of sorts. After Spudnuts' collapse, Marquardt abandoned potato flour because he could buy wheat flour for considerably less. However, after Wal-Mart and Sam's Club showed up in the local market and began selling doughnuts for half the price at which Denny's could break even, the necessity to differentiate became imperative, and Marquardt returned to potato flour. When Kroger and Jewel opened in-store bakeries and began selling doughnuts, Marquardt took his products out to the small, family-owned stores still selling groceries in LeRoy, Heyworth, and other places in Central Illinois. Wholesaling to small groceries led to a relationship with Convenient Food Marts, a chain of convenience stores headquartered in Louisville, Kentucky. Denny's contracted with Convenient in 1981 to supply doughnuts to 34 of its Illinois stores. When Convenient went out of business in the late '80s, Marquardt picked up the slack with sales to independent stores. He diversified his business by acquiring the local franchise for Bagelmen's sandwich shops and expanded by developing a catering business. This would appear prudent in light of a quarter century of attacks against the doughnut industry by health authorities worried about rising obesity rates. Doughnuts remain central to the eating habits of many Americans, and as of the end of the twentieth century, the expansion of the doughnut industry continues unabated.

SODA FOUNTAINS, VENDING MACHINES, AND THE PEPSI GENERATION

Soda water, a label that applies to all non-alcoholic, carbonated beverages, first appeared as various fizzy mineral waters thought to have medicinal value.[100] Artificial carbonation became technically possible during the eighteenth century.

By the early nineteenth century, carbonated water was being manufactured and sold for therapeutic purposes throughout the United States.[101] People did not have to be sick to enjoy carbonated water, and by 1820 soda makers were adding flavored syrups to non-medicinal seltzers. Soda makers sold their products by "dispensing" them at a soda fountain.[102] Fountains, often housed in drug stores, were quite simple at first. The apparatus used in the early 1800s consisted of a spigot or faucet fastened to a simple counter set against the wall. Tubing connected the dispenser to carbonating equipment and an icebox under the counter. The soda was poured into a glass and mixed with flavoring if so desired. Soda water production in McLean County began with Bloomington Soda Water Manufactory about 1858.[103] In 1871, W.G. Cochrane drew crowds to his new venue in downtown Bloomington with a beautiful, new-fangled fountain, the like of which local residents had never seen before.

Shortly after the turn of the century, customers could sit at the soda fountain and watch their drinks being made. Year after year fountains and counters became increasingly ornate structures, out-and-out "architectural fantasies made of marble and mirrors," surmounted with pumps for drawing various syrups.[104] Soon, soda fountains grew into important social gathering places, so popular that temperance advocates envisioned them supplanting the saloon as America's favorite drinking place. Initially, this posed a dilemma because certain sodas and shakes contained alcohol. Trade journals, however, urged their elimination and suggested instead malted milks, a beverage which men especially seemed to enjoy.

Making sodas behind a well-equipped fountain looked easy. After all, they usually contained nothing more than carbonated water and a syrup extracted from a push pump – mix and serve, or so it would seem. Behind the scenes, though, soda making involved a great deal of trouble, mainly because the syrup usually fermented and went bad in just a day or two.[105] This meant fountain operators had to prepare fresh batches nearly every day, and it explains why operators, typically less interested in making syrups than selling sodas, eagerly purchased ready-made products with extended shelf lives. Hires Root Beer syrup was one of the first. Charles Hires originally sold it as a home mix, but by the 1880s soda fountains were his best customers. *Daily Pantagraph* advertisements promoted Hires as a healthful alternative to beer and whiskey.[106]

Rose Remschner remembers Edward Gabriel's drug store in Towanda where syrups freshly prepared on premises were still used to prepare mix sodas well into the 1920s. Gabriel and his successor, Lewis Michael, bought concentrated fruit flavorings and kept them on the fountain in porcelain jars. The flavorings were mixed as needed with simple syrup, which the men made by bringing equal parts of sugar and water to boil. The drug store's fountain had to be recharged about once a week. This involved filling the reservoir with water and attaching it to a tank of gas. To mix the water with the gas, an employee had to push the reservoir back and forth on a wooden rocker for a full 30 minutes before reinstalling it under the fountain. Edward Biasi of Bloomington, who purchased the store in 1926, tore out the old fountain and installed a modern, electrically equipped one in its place.[107]

By this point, fountain drinks had evolved. Milk and ice cream had become popular ingredients, and preparing a proper soda was demanding.[108] A top-notch fountain attended by a so-called "soda jerk" offered patrons a variety of malted milk drinks, milk shakes, flips, fizzes, phosphates, ice cream floats, sundaes, banana splits, and more. Soda jerks made good money, but acquiring the skills required years of practice. Journals provided professionals with recipes and tips regarding showmanship, which increasingly became an important aspect of the job.[109]

As an institution, the fountain reached its zenith during the Great Depression when Biasi's, Boylan's, and Hildebrandt's drug stores, and soda shops like Gus Schrolle's and The Oasis, were THE places in the Bloomington area to go for ice cream and ice cream drinks. Prohibition triggered an ice cream boom, pushing consumption in the United States upward by some 100 million gallons.[110] After World War II, ice cream drinks migrated to the drive-in, and grocery stores began selling ice cream for home consumption. Bottled soda grew increasingly popular. As a result, soda fountains disappeared.

Bottled soda first appeared in Bloomington at Peter Kreis's bottling works on the corner of Madison and Mulberry Streets in 1880. At that time, bottling carbonated water was tricky. Sufficiently strong bottles and sure-sealing caps had yet to be invented. Bottles exploded now and then, and the wired corks that secured their contents sometimes leaked.[111] These problems disappeared and soda water bottling took hold as an industry after 1890 when strong, inexpensive glass bottles and the crown metal bottle cap were introduced. Bloomington had three soda water bottlers by 1893 – Excelsior Bottling Works owned by Frank Abbott, the Herman Quosick Bottling Company, and Bloomington Bottling works belonging to Edward and John Holland. Quosick and Bloomington Bottling Works continued into the 1920s, but the Depression changed everything. In place of the old names, the 1932 City Directory listed Chero-Cola Bottling, Watkins Beverage, Evergreen Beverage, and Bloomington Coca-Cola Bottling Company.

Coca-Cola, invented by Atlanta pharmacist John Pemberton, began as wine drink laced with cocaine and sold as a nerve tonic. After Atlanta went dry in 1886, Pemberton changed his formula to sugar, coca leaf (his source of cocaine), kola nut (a source of caffeine), an assortment of flavorings, and caramel for color.[112] He cooked these ingredients down to a syrup which he mixed on demand with carbonated water. Headache and hangover sufferers swore by a glass of Coca-Cola, and by the end of the nineteenth century it was available at drug stores throughout the country.[113] Another pharmacist, Caleb Bradham from New Bern, North Carolina, tinkered with various blends of fruit flavors and other extracts and came up with one that scored a big hit with his customers. They called it "Brad's drink" after Bradham. He renamed it "Pepsi-Cola" after it became more popular. "Pepsi" referred (if somewhat obliquely) to pepsin, an aid to digestion. "Cola" was meant to evoke the feeling of refreshment imparted by existing cola drinks.[114] Pepsi began its ascendance toward national recognition in 1934 when trademark owner, Loft Candies of New York City, began selling it in twelve-ounce bottles at the same price (five cents) Coca-Cola sold for in eight-ounce bottles.[115]

Pepsi became immensely popular throughout McLean County in spite of a lower-class image which stereotyped it as the poor man's alternative to Coke. Indeed, Pepsi so dominated the local market that residents had difficulty finding Coca-Cola and other competing brands. Pepsi's domination of the Bloomington market was engineered by Evergreen Beverage Company, a shoestring enterprise that would eventually become Irvin Brothers Pepsi-Cola Bottling Co. The Irvin brothers – Lawrence, Leo, and Maurice – founded Evergreen in 1930 after their father, Pat, learned about a derelict bottling plant for sale and urged his sons to buy it.[116] They scraped together a $300 down payment, set up shop in the back of a building on West Washington Street, and went into business. Bottles were washed by hand in a wooden tub and soda was delivered out of the back of a Model T. The car could carry no more than eight cases at a time, but since the Irvins had just three steady customers, that was not an immediate issue. Lawrence, who looked after the business at first, turned it over to Leo and Maurice after they lost their day jobs. The two men struggled, but they were able to support their families by making root beer, ginger ale, and a variety of fruit-flavored sodas and placing their products in shops and stores throughout the Bloomington area.

Evergreen Beverage began selling Pepsi-Cola in 1936. By 1938, sales volume outstripped Evergreen's existing capacity, forcing the Irvins to move to a larger facility across the street and upgrade their equipment. Even so, the bottle washing machine leaked so badly that the operator needed to wear a raincoat and boots.

Meanwhile, Coca-Cola modernized its Bloomington bottling plant and began selling its soda from vending machines. A reporter for *The Daily Pantagraph* marveled at the company's new facility (described as conservatively modernistic) and was especially impressed by its huge plate glass window where passersby could watch gleaming stainless steel bottling machines filling

110 Coke bottles per minute automatically.[117] Coca-Cola's automatic vending machine, which debuted in 1935, was placed on the first floor of State Farms' downtown headquarters about the time the new bottling plant opened. When he first saw the machine, George Mecherle, the insurance company's president, became upset, thinking that a soda dispenser would detract from the business-like atmosphere of the building. Alarmed employees summoned Mecherle's son, Ernie, head of the personnel department. The younger Mecherle ran downstairs to explain to his father that employees who used the machine and drank a Coke on their breaks went back to work with a little extra pep. This argument, taken directly from Coca-Cola's advertising copy, saved the day for hallway vending at State Farm.

The extra-pep rationale for drinking soda originated with Pepsi during the Great Depression. From about the time the Irvins first bottled it through the 1950s, Pepsi promoted itself as a quick energy food. Coca-Cola, on the other hand, represented itself, if somewhat vaguely, as medicinal. As far back as 1910, an ad placed in *The Daily Pantagraph* spoke of "weather weariness" and offered Coca-Cola as a cure for exhaustion during the hot summer months. Owen Bush, "snappy" shortstop for the 1909 American League baseball champion Detroit Tigers, endorsed Coke as "beneficial." By the 1940s, Coca-Cola was promising "the pause that refreshes," and from World War II into the '50s, ads claimed increased worker productivity and contentment. Pepsi's message primarily revolved around the idea that customers got more for their money. That changed about 1960. Pepsi's formula now included less sugar, and instead of an energy drink, it became "the light refreshment," a life-style beverage, marketed with catch the phrases "be sociable" and "join the Pepsi generation." Coca-Cola also remodeled its image with King-Size Coke, Diet Coke, and messages centered on the notion of sharing.

Evergreen Beverage had become Irvin Brothers Pepsi-Cola Bottling Company, and the watchword was expansion. After the Second World War, the brothers moved their bottling equipment into an old welding shop situated on two acres of land on Greenwood Avenue. In 1968, they bought City Bottling Corp., adding Squirt and Dr. Pepper to their product line. This made them Bloomington's largest bottler. Machinery and labor costs soon led to centralization and the closure of other bottlers, leaving Irvin Brothers the only locally-owned and operated bottler in the area. The Irvins discontinued bottling in the mid 1970s, but continued to distribute Pepsi and other products. By the 1980s, the territory served by Irvin Brothers was one of the leading per-capita markets for Pepsi-Cola in country. The Greenwood Avenue facility had been expanded 13 times. The company had 40 full-time employees, maintained a fleet of

30 vehicles, and delivered soda across a broad swath of Central Illinois. Pepsi-Cola envisioned even greater centralization and made Irvin Brothers an offer the company owners could not refuse. As a result, the sales territory the Irvin Brothers built up became part of the domain of Pepsi-Cola General Bottlers, the largest bottler of Pepsi products in the country.

CHAPTER 7 – SLOW FOOD CODA

Slow foods, the antitheses of fast foods, are irrational in the sense that they are raised, prepared, and consumed with concern for the sake of tradition, well-being, and enjoyment rather than economy.[1] Some of the best examples have been handed down as family traditions or involve community celebrations in which participants happily go to some lengths to prepare special dishes, share them with neighbors, and indulge in the pleasures of a well-populated table. Other examples have arisen as relatively recent reactions to McDonaldization.

American food and drink underwent some serious rethinking beginning around 1960 when natural foods, vegetarian, and back-to-the-land movements either emerged or re-emerged and steadily gained strength. Early natural food advocates were mostly "hippies" or ephemeral figures who haunted peculiar shops frequented by "health food nuts." However, devotees who once baked their own bread, made yoghurt, and grew sprouts on the kitchen counter soon found themselves in the company of legions of fellow believers. As the cohort aged, members became obsessed with bran and dietary fiber and learned about the virtues of olive oil and the Mediterranean diet. Then there was canola oil and fish oil, and by the end of the century, the health food market had grown so large that every grocery chain in the nation felt compelled to create its own lines of "healthy alternative" and organic products. Similarly, vegetarians, once viewed as members of a strange cult, swelled in number and became impossible for food manufacturers and restaurateurs to ignore. The back-to-the-land movement of the late '60s matured and inspired "locavores," yet another slow-food species to be reckoned with.

In the meantime, American eating habits became a matter of fad and fancy. With people spending less time in the kitchen on a daily basis, cooking in many households became a hobby. Cooks experimented in the '60s with flamed dishes like Crepes Suzette and Cherries Jubilee. After that, it was cheese fondue. The quiche acquired immense popularity in the '70s when it was apt to be served for brunch, a meal freshly elevated to the weekend's most eminent social repast. Restaurant fashion latched onto Northern Italian, regional Chinese, and Japanese foods. A reformed French cuisine called French *nouvelle* helped inspire a "new American cuisine." A succession of suddenly popular styles and hot "new foods" followed in the 1980s and '90s: Tex-Mex, Cajun, pesto, chocolate, hot chilies and salsas, and Caribbean to name just a few.

FAMILY AND COMMUNITY

Food and drink are essential to family and community life. People coming together and sharing things to eat and drink invariably enjoy a special familiarity. This is why groups all over the world celebrate meaningful occasions with dinners, banquets, feasts, parties, and other get-togethers involving food and drink. The Christian communion revolves around the concerted acts of sharing bread and wine, and congregations regard these substances as emblematic of their spiritual community. The Thanksgiving dinner draws on American history and tradition to enact a kind of national communion in which families and friends feast on special foods symbolic of their gratitude to god and country. At family reunions and holiday gatherings, traditional foods are often mandatory – part of the liturgy, so to speak.

An unwillingness to sit down at the same table and share food has indicated estrangement in every society throughout human history. People everywhere are loath to eat with those they fear or regard as grossly inferior. That aversion made the lunch counter such a flashpoint during the Civil Rights movement and created the dramatic tension in the movie, "Guess Who's Coming to Dinner." From the standpoint of interracial commensality, Bloomington-Normal was little different from cities in the Deep South into the mid-1950s. A survey conducted in advance of a State Human Relations Conference to be held at Illinois State Normal University in 1955 found only nine of the more than 60 eating places in the area willing to "welcome Negroes as cordially as whites."[2]

FAMILY TRADITIONS

Convenience foods and McDonaldized meals are not entirely compatible with traditional ideas about family life. Family, after all, is not all about convenience and efficiency, nor is it as much about eating cheaply as it is about eating well. This is why on the occasions when families celebrate, time-consuming preparations, traditional dishes, large servings, and expensive foods are usually the order of the day.

Christmas illustrates the quintessential relationship between foods and celebrations. For generations, foods have been presented as gifts, kitchens have bustled with candy making and cookie baking, and homemakers have strived to prepare splendid dinners. Older McLean County folks fondly remember Christmas stockings and the oranges and other fruits and nuts they found inside. Monica Berry recalled making a lot of peanut brittle every year to give as gifts.[3] Caroline Hamlow made chocolate-covered cherries.[4] Special meals were nearly universal.

Farmers did little or no work between Christmas and New Year as relatives and friends came to visit over richly laden tables. Christmas Eve and Christmas Day were for close family. For many years, Vera Dornaus's family visited her mother on Christmas Eve and ate Oyster Stew accompanied by salad of chopped apples, pineapple, miniature marshmallows, nuts, and whipped cream. The kids did not like oysters, so Vera's mother fixed them potato soup with wieners.[5] Margaret Laesch remembered that after the cows were milked on Christmas morning, it was off to Grandma's house with hopes that she had prepared noodles with browned cracker crumbs on top. Grandma also had *Stollen* (a loaf-shaped fruit-cake), nut breads, and homemade strawberry preserves as well as various cookies sprinkled with red and green sugar.[6] At Betty Hopkins's Christmas Day brought turkey and noodles. Family members came to dinner toting a favorite dish, and once assembled they all had eggnog to toast the occasion.[7]

In the same way noodles for Christmas indicated Pennsylvania Dutch roots, other dishes also told of a particular heritage. In keeping with its Irish legacy, the Reedy family's holiday favorites included roast goose and mashed potatoes and gravy.[8] Bloomington's German Americans made *Stollen* for Christmas. They also baked Spritz cookies (*Spritzgebäck*), *Springerle*, and *Lebkuchen*, a cookie something like soft gingerbread. Eileen Walters and her family clung to the German tradition of having wilted endive for dinner, even after it became difficult to find endive in local stores.[9] Swedish-American families baked *Pepparkakor*, a kind of ginger snap. Marguerite Fryer remembers as a little girl going to midnight services at the Swedish Lutheran Church at the corner of Allin and Olive Streets in Bloomington with her dad on Christmas Eve. Afterward they had a *Lutefisk* Supper with his brothers and their families.[10] A Swedish tradition Bernice Gilchrist tenaciously upheld was making Season's Greeting Punch for guests to drink while the Christmas smorgasbord was being laid out.

Season's Greetings Punch
INGREDIENTS – 1 quart of orange juice squeezed fresh or made from concentrate; ¾ cup of Grenadine syrup; club soda; 2 fresh oranges (segmented). PREPARATION – combine orange juice, 2 cups club soda (poured down side of bowl to retain bubbles), and Grenadine in punch bowl; in the mixture float a small block of frozen club soda, and decorate with oranges and cherries.[11]

Bernice made sure she was squeezing the last orange when her company arrived and always served the punch in a large crystal bowl made by a cousin in Sweden.

Some families invented their own traditions. LaVonne Cunningham and her husband had romantic dinners together on Christmas Eve during the early years of their marriage. As children arrived, this developed into a special family dinner in the dining room with the good china, silver, the works. The menu was decided by general agreement, and as the years went by the Cunninghams feasted on everything from steak to pancakes. Deborah Giannoni and her husband traveled between families during the Christmas holidays, but one year they decided to set Christmas Eve aside just for themselves. Eventually they developed their own set of customs which began with mass at nine that evening, followed by a drive around town to look at the Christmas lights, and a little feast of smoked sausage, cheese, German rye bread, and wine. Next they watched a video of "A Christmas Carol," starring Alistair Sim as Scrooge. Then, they exchanged gifts, had a last glass of wine, and went to bed.[12]

For some McLean County folks, family gatherings at Christmas have become annual reunions, particularly in those instances where a set of relatives has grown so large that none of the families can accommodate the gathering at home. Such parties become "potluck" meals typically held in a church hall or community center, usually a week or more before Christmas.[13] Doris Builta found the idea of a holiday potluck appealing after she and her husband inherited the daunting task of assembling 53 family members spread far and wide across several states. Her mid-December potlucks succeeded in bringing together an average of 35 family members every year.[14] Jeanne Wagner attended two reunions annually.[15] A day or so before Christmas, her dad's mother's kindred got together, and in 1987 members shared candies and cookies, and cracked nuts with hammers and bricks for the one hundredth year in a row. Jeanne's other big reunion came on the Fourth of July when the folks on her dad's father's side of the family got together for their annual picnic, an event that marked its 85th year in 1991. Alma Galloway also attended a big reunion on the Fourth of July. It originated as a birthday party organized by her grandmother for her mother's brother in 1903.[16]

McLean County seniors have warm memories of birthdays as occasions for enjoying special meals and favorite foods. A child celebrating a birthday received his or her favorite cake topped with candles representing the recipient's age and accompanied by a rendition of "Happy Birthday." The child then made a wish and tried to blow out all of the candles on the cake so the wish would come true. Typically, elders remember birthdays as family celebrations with everyone in the household present. Occasionally, mother would organize a birthday party and invite the child's playmates. Such parties eventually became common and migrated to commercial facilities. During the 1980s, Chuck E. Cheese's, a family pizza chain that integrated food with animated entertainment and indoor games, sold parents on the idea that they could host a child's birthday party "without lifting a finger." Grady's Pizza in Bloomington sweetened that prospect by adding miniature golf and other outdoor activities to the list of amusements.

No discussion of family food traditions would be complete without mentioning Sunday dinner. Sunday in many McLean County households was the only day the family ate in the dining room, and company was customarily invited for the occasion. Lois Spaulding recollects that such meals were planned well ahead.[17] The table was always decked out in linen and set with the good silver and more delicate china. When Lois's family got home from church, it was sometimes necessary to set extra places because the children would invite friends. Nina Necessary remembers the guests, but she also recalls that Sunday was homemade ice cream day when she was a little girl.

COMMUNITIES, GROUPS, AND FOOD EVENTS

Food is rarely absent from festivals and other sorts of community and group celebrations. These events bring individuals and their families together and create feelings of camaraderie not normally felt in everyday situations. Sharing food is part of the experience.

In McLean County, as throughout the United States, non-commercial festivals and celebrations are commonly organized as fund-raisers. Fund-raising events became a part of American culture during the nineteenth century in places where increasing secularism diminished church revenues.[18] This prompted women to step forward and use their cooking skills to raise money. The practice spread to educational institutions and groups involved in various reform movements. Oyster suppers raised large sums for wounded soldiers and hospitals during the Civil War. A short time later ice cream socials and church suppers became immensely popular. Indeed, communities responded so positively to food-related events that many congregations felt they needed to install a church kitchen. Today it is rare for a church in Central Illinois not to have a kitchen and periodically convene a pancake breakfast, hold a bake sale, or prepare lunch for a group of mourners just returned from the cemetery. No less rare is the school or volunteer organization that does not hold a bake sale, ask neighbors to buy candy, or sell tickets to a banquet. During the late 1990s, *The Pantagraph's* community calendar listed on average nearly seven food-related fund-raising activities per week.

THE HUNGARIAN CLUB

The oldest food-related fund-raiser in Bloomington is the Hungarian Club's twice-annual Sausage Fry. Formally known as The American Hungarian Family Society (AHFS), the club convened its first meeting in 1919.[19] The membership of 27 men consisted mostly of Chicago & Alton Railroad employees. For years, they got together at one another's homes, rolled up the rugs, and danced to the Hungarian and gypsy music they had grown up with in their native country, but occasionally large crowds made clean up a nasty chore. The group considered renting a house for their dances. Instead, they pooled their money, bought two acres of land on North Calhoun Street, and built a clubhouse. At its 60th anniversary in 1979, the AHFS numbered 108 families, all of them descendants of the original 27 members.

Over the years the AHFS has remained true to its beginnings. It has never hired full-time employees. Each month a committee of three handles building care and member services. Nobody can refuse or neglect his duties on pain of excommunication. Most of the founders – all of them natives of the southeastern corner of the Austro-Hungarian Empire – spoke German. Some spoke Hungarian as well, and a few knew Romanian. By the end of the twentieth century, only a few members understood any language other than English and knowledge of Hungarian traditions had faded. Today the AHFS deliberately works to preserve the customs and dances and celebrates the foods their grandparents enjoyed together.[20]

The society inaugurated its sausage fries, which regularly attract around 700 guests, in 1951. The name, however, is misleading because from the beginning the sausages have been baked, never fried. Club members grind the pork, season it mildly, and stuff it into the casings themselves. Accompaniments traditionally include mashed potatoes, green beans, applesauce, bread, and coffee. The following recipe for Hungarian sausage, or *kolbas*, comes from a short memoir written in 1974 by Paul Abraham. It describes how when Paul was a child a family in Bloomington's Forty Acres neighborhood prepared 100 pounds of sausage in the fall for use the following spring. [21]

Forty Acres Magar *Kolbas*

INGREDIENTS – 100 pounds fresh picnic ham or pork shoulder ground very coarse; 1 pound paprika, crushed garlic aged 2 days in a jar of water (1-3 buds according to taste); salt and pepper. PREPARATION – The man of the house places 50 pounds of meat in his tub and 50 pounds in the kids' tubs. He and the kids mix the meat while adding ½ pound of paprika to their respective tubs. They divide garlic water and add it to the mixtures. They then add salt and pepper to taste and continue mixing thoroughly, being careful not to allow the sausage to become mushy. Once the mixing is finished, the old man removes approximately 1 pound of sausage from the tubs. This is flattened and fried while he goes to the basement and draws wine. Everyone waits for the meat to cook through. The woman of the house divides the fried sausage and takes the first bite. Others sample the sausage. If the woman pronounces it good, stuffing begins. If not, additional salt and pepper are added. The well-seasoned sausage is stuffed into pork casings. These are twisted into 18-inch lengths and hung to smoke slowly over wild cherry, apple, or other fruit-tree wood.[22]

Once the mess was cleaned up and smoke came rolling out of the smoke house, the household sat down to eat. The menu typically consisted of roasted *kolbas*, paprika potatoes, coffee, and *bor* (wine). Sometimes there were noodles with cream cheese and *pobasca* (biscuits with cracklins). When the feast was over and everyone pushed back their chairs, Abraham remembers the old man always paused to wonder if there would be enough sausage to last until next butchering season.[23]

MENNONITE RELIEF SALE

The Illinois Mennonite Relief Sale has its roots in the traditional way local congregations met their churches' mortgage obligations. To raise money for payments, the women would prepare a dinner and charge admission. In addition, congregations organized ice cream socials, potlucks, and bake sales to help meet their financial obligations.[24] Aside from their financial utility and in spite of all the work involved, church members greatly enjoyed these events and looked forward to them as important social occasions.

The Illinois Mennonite Relief Sale has been held annually at the Interstate Center in Bloomington since 1998. Its spiritual inspiration comes from church teachings and the example of Jesus, whose life has inspired compassion among the faithful for those suffering throughout the world from disease, hatred, and war. To alleviate suffering, every year approximately 1,500 volunteers contribute their time and money in support of the Mennonite Central Committee (MCC) and its projects around the world.[25]

The Illinois sale, one of several held throughout the country, traditionally takes place on the third Friday and Saturday in March and is a huge undertaking that now raises in excess of $6.5 million annually through raffles and the sale of arts, crafts, and various commercial goods.[26] Foods, including a pancake and sausage breakfast, a fish and barbecue chicken dinner, strawberry pies and cheesecakes, and a great variety of Pennsylvania Dutch specialty foods prepared and donated by both homemakers and commercial manufacturers, comprise a major part of the event. Beginning a week or so before it takes place, church members grind and stuff 4,000 pounds of whole-hog pork sausage. One congregation alone makes 200 cherry pies. Another congregation bakes 500 mincemeat pies. Donations come from more than 30 Anabaptist churches, including Apostolic Christian, as well as Mennonite.

The first Illinois Mennonite Relief Sale took place in 1959 and was organized by John Roth, a resident of Morton. Current and longtime co-chairman Don Roth remembers that "Uncle John" got the idea from a Mennonite newspaper story about a relief sale held in Pennsylvania.[27] Uncle John recruited Don and a number of other church members, and together they put on a sale at Congerville Angus Barn, a livestock auction house. The event earned $5,000. It moved to Peoria in 1966 and to the Interstate Center in Bloomington in 1998.

Don Roth and his wife, Ruthie, pour an incredible amount of energy into the project. Don, who, very much like Bob Knapp, delights in organizing, served on the Morton Village Board and for eight years as mayor. He and Ruthie miss the politics, but now they have the efforts of 35 congregations to organize and a multimillion-dollar event to produce. All this is in addition to Don managing a farm and Ruthie teaching school.

Volunteers served up pork chops at the 2007 Mennonite Relief Sale at Bloomington's Interstate Center. Photo by Jose Sacaridiz.

The Roths live directly across the street from Morton's Mennonite Church which specializes in producing strawberry pies and cheesecakes for the sale. The Roths and a group of volunteers start making the cheesecakes on the Wednesday before the big event. Their first step is to mix 30 five-gallon buckets of red gel. On Thursday, they deal with graham cracker crumbs and pack them down in disposable aluminum pans. These shells then spend two minutes in the church's convection ovens. Their church kitchen, which would be the envy of most restaurants in the area, contains no less than three ovens, each with sufficient capacity to hold 30 or more pies or cakes. About ten o'clock in the morning, the group begins mixing the cheesecake batter. The baking occurs through late afternoon and sometimes into the evening. As the cakes come out of the oven, they are cooled on rack using three large fans. The cakes, some 700 of them, are then glazed with gel. At one time, the cheesecakes were left overnight on tables in the church hall. Health authorities objected and said the cakes had to be placed in a cooler. "Well, where are you going to put them in a cooler?" asked Don. The answer was to acquire a refrigerated truck. The pies now spend the night in the trailer, the volunteers show up at dawn to bring them out, cover them with strawberries and another layer of gel, and then truck them fresh for sale in Bloomington. Similar scenes are enacted in Mennonite churches throughout Central Illinois.

For a great many, the jewel of the Illinois Mennonite Relief sale is the Dutch Kitchen and its traditional products. Visitors have freshly ground breakfast sausage and traditional cured sausages such as Lebanon Bologna and Sweet Summer Sausage to choose from. There are tables full of jarred beef and chicken and various soft cheeses. People arrive at the checkout counter carrying bags and boxes of small-batch noodles, pretzels, potato chips, apple butter, chow-chow, various pickled vegetables, and fruit jams. Patrons also find many, many kinds of pastry for sale, including Shoo Fly Pie, a pioneer variety rarely tasted these days outside the Mennonite community.

JEWISH FOOD FAIR

The food-focused fund-raising event in Bloomington that comes closest to having the level of recognition accorded the Girl Scout cookie sale is the Moses Montefiore Temple's Jewish Food Fair, a day-long celebration of Jewish-American specialties. Bloomington's first and only congregation of Jews dedicated their first temple in 1889. By 1957, membership had outgrown this facility and two years later Moses Montefiore Temple, the congregation's current home, was completed. It currently serves approximately 100 families.

Since 1960, the congregation's major fund-raiser has been its food fair.[28] It began as a sit-down dinner, but owing to overwhelming popularity it morphed into a carryout lunch and specialty food sale. The event traditionally takes place in late October, but preparations usually begin in September when volunteers assemble to make cabbage rolls. A week or so later, the schedule calls for a chicken soup cook-in, followed the next week by the making of blintzes for the sale. In the meantime, members solicit orders for the centerpiece of the food fair, a sack lunch consisting of a Kosher-style corned beef sandwich, a big dill pickle, a bag of potato chips and a piece of homemade *raiglach*. This rich Ashkenazic cookie is made from a pareve (no dairy ingredients) dough which is rolled and filled with an assortment of goodies, including raisins, walnuts, cinnamon, chocolate, marzipan, poppy seed, and apricot preserves.[29] The *raiglach* has developed a considerable number of fans, so the Temple also takes orders for nine-piece trays.

Food Fair *Raiglach*

INGREDIENTS for Dough– ½ pound cold butter, 2½ cup unsifted flour, 1 package yeast, ¼ cup milk, 2 tablespoons sugar, 3 beaten egg yolks, ¾ teaspoon vanilla, grated rind of 1 orange (optional). PREPARATION – Sift flour and salt together. Cut in butter until crumbly. Scald milk. Let cool until lukewarm. Add sugar to milk. Dissolve yeast in milk mixture. Add flour, egg yolks, vanilla, and orange rind. Mix thoroughly. Divide into 3 equal parts and wrap in waxed paper. Place in refrigerator overnight.

INGREDIENTS for filling – 3 eggs white, ¾ cup sugar, 1 cup white raisins, 1 cup chopped nuts, cinnamon, sugar, powdered sugar. PREPARATION – Beat egg whites until stiff. Gradually beat in sugar. Roll each piece of dough on a well-floured pastry cloth or board, using a rolling pin covered with a floured pastry sleeve. Dough should be rolled into rectangle, approximately 12x16 inches. Spread with one-third of filling. Sprinkle with cinnamon, sugar, nuts, and raisins. Roll as for jelly roll and cut the roll into 8-10 pieces, about 2 inches each. Repeat with remaining pieces of dough. Place pieces on ungreased cookie sheet and bake at 350 for 20 minutes or until lightly tanned. Sprinkle heavily with powdered sugar while still warm. Can be frozen; makes 25-30 pieces.[30]

Temple members deliver trays of *raiglach* and sack lunches to homes and offices, and staff a deli and bake sale unlike any other held in the community. No brownies, chocolate chip cookies, or Rice Krispie treats here. Each member of the congregation is asked to prepare a Jewish specialty incorporating at least $30 worth of ingredients, or to contribute at least $60 for the purchase of specialty items. The local community has a big appetite for baked sweets, and bake sales are always well patronized, but the Jewish Food Fair's sale has a line waiting to buy from the moment it opens.

Preparing well over 4,000 corned beef sandwiches and packing up the lunches has provided the members of Moses Montefiore Temple with memorable moments. One year, volunteers showed up at the appointed time, but the truck hauling the corned beef and rye bread from Chicago failed to show. Someone had forgotten to contact the trucking company that for years had donated the transport. Following some harried calls, a truck was dispatched, finally arriving with the sandwich fixings about midnight. Another year the sandwich crew ran out of rye bread. Because there was no Jewish or even Jewish-style rye bread in the town, a member called her daughter in Peoria who visited every store in that area, found 55 loaves, and at last got them delivered in the middle of the night. There have been trials due to oversized pickles, too few pickles, and a death in the family of the Food Fair chairperson's family on the eve of the event. The mystique of a food event lies as much in the working together and preparing as in the sitting down together and eating. Hence, setbacks have become "war stories" and part of the sense of community that engages the congregation.

THE APPLE AND PORK FESTIVAL

The Apple and Pork Festival (also referred to as Apple N' Pork Festival) held every September in Clinton, about 25 miles south of Bloomington, originated to raise money to support the DeWitt County Museum Association. At first the festivities involved little more than a friendly get-together around a kettle of soup and a stack of sandwiches. By the 1990s, however, the festival had burgeoned into a major weekend event staged on the grounds of the C. H. Moore Homestead, a large Victorian house and barn preserved as a farm museum. The buildings provide a picturesque backdrop for a crafting area where artisans demonstrate time-honored skills. Country bands, musicians in regimental uniforms playing Civil War instruments, strolling balladeers, and a huge flea market have been part of the event for years.

As its name implies, the Apple N' Pork Festival was intended to celebrate two of the region's most historically important foods, and with certain liberties it has remained true to that goal. Booths manned by church and civic groups provide visitors with a chance to taste apples as cider and to enjoy them in fritters and pies. Vendors sell taffy apples, apple butter, apple butter tarts, apple crisp, and applesauce. Pork can be had either cured or fresh. The bill of fare typically includes BBQ ribs, a butterfly pork sandwich, bratwurst, a ham sandwich, pig ears, pork rinds, and pork chili. The star of the show, however, has always been a bowl of ham and beans. Virgil Gibson, who was involved with the festival from its inception, always oversaw the cooking. He labored away with a big wooden paddle, stirring great kettles of ham and beans suspended over crackling fires as a line of festival-goers patiently waited. Cooking the 30 pounds of ham hocks and 50 pounds of beans, seasoned with Virgil's "secret ingredients," commenced at sunrise, and by the time the grounds were empty Sunday evening, some 20 volunteers had usually dished out around 6,000 servings. [31]

OLD SETTLERS' PICNIC

The Apple N' Pork Festival recalls the old settler reunions that became fashionable throughout the Midwest in the late 1800s. Although thematically these had nothing to do with food, as day-long, outdoor gatherings they became community picnics and in many places developed into something like oversized family reunions.

The first Old Settlers' Picnic held in McLean County took place in July 1885. The idea originated with a committee in Ellsworth that wanted to honor the area's early settlers by presenting them with badges commemorating their accomplishments. The committee erected a log cabin in Ellsworth's Christina Park and advertised a commemorative picnic. Cost of admission was to be 50 cents, and to keep away the riff-raff there would be no gambling or other "immoral practices" and no intoxicating liquors.[32] Within a few years, the committee found itself hosting thousands of people from all over the county. With as many as eight to 10 thousand people showing up, the event moved to Betzer Park outside of town. Long excursion trains chugged out of Bloomington. Passengers got off at Ellsworth and walked or took a carriage to the park.[33] Others drove their own carriages. The traffic filled the air with so much dust that the first order of business upon arrival was visit a nearby farm where water and towels were available for cleaning up.

People attending the Old Settlers' Picnic might hear the Lexington Crescent Glee Club and the Ellsworth Band, see a circus act or two, and listen to various speakers, and for the price of admission everyone also received a big dinner basket, usually containing fried chicken and two or three accompaniments. These were savored picnic-style with a blanket spread on the grass. Charles Kimler, owner of the Silver Moon Restaurant, sold additional food, and nearly every year he scooped out more than 125 gallons of ice cream. Concession stands sold brick popcorn wrapped in bright paper. Concessionaires had Cracker Jack and ladled lemonade out of a tub at a nickel a glass. For a dime, a customer could have her lemonade shaken with sugar. Farmers sold apples and cider by the barrel. Some vendors had honey; others wanted people to buy sorghum molasses. There was also a wagon selling bananas by the dozen for 20 cents. The price in the afternoon dropped to 15 cents.

BOOSTER FESTIVALS

The last Old Settlers' Picnic took place in the fall of 1915, and since then chambers of commerce and other business associations throughout the area have organized weekends of celebration with hopes of attracting crowds to their own hometowns. Some of these events have been promoted as food festivals and have themes particularly pertinent to the community.

Morton's annual Pumpkin Festival, for example, celebrates its status as "The Pumpkin Capital of the World." Exactly how the Pumpkin Festival got started no one knows for sure, but the event itself can be seen as a kind of tribute to the importance of the pumpkin in the local farm economy and a salute to the city's pumpkin packing plant where over 80 percent of the world's canned pumpkin is processed.[34] The celebration occurs on a September weekend during the canning season and features the usual carnival rides, foot races, merchants' tents, bands nobody has heard of, craft exhibits, and car shows. For a wacky event, something a town festival almost has to have, Morton staged a pumpkin chucking contest. Competing teams used catapults, trebuchets, air cannons, or maybe even a ballista to see which of them can throw a pumpkin the greatest distance. The sport attracted a big following and now has its own weekend in October. As for the festival proper, eats include butterfly pork chop sandwiches and funnel cakes. Vendors are also prepared to cater to anyone with a yen for pumpkin pie, pumpkin ice cream, pumpkin pancakes, or pumpkin fudge.

Corn festivals seem to be everywhere in Central Illinois. Chatham, El Paso, Hoopeston, Mendota, Morris, Normal, and Urbana all host such events, but only Hoopeston's seems to be genuinely related to local history. The town, which calls itself the "Sweet Corn Capital of the World" and has made the cornjerker its high school mascot, was once an important canning center.[35] El Paso's corn festival relates to Pfister Hybrid Corn Co., a local seed corn producer. El Paso, along with all the other corn-fest towns (and nearly every town in Central Illinois), is immersed in a landscape dominated by corn varieties unsuited for direct human consumption. This explains why Normal's annual Cornfest (known lately as the Sweet Corn Blues Festival) ignores locally grown corn. Organizers have always trucked in up to 50,000 ears of sweet corn from neighboring states. The corn is dumped in a great heap near the center of town and either bagged for take-home sale, or boiled in the effluent of an antique steam tractor for immediate consumption. Sweet corn has a wholesome reputation and looks like the commodity grown just outside of town, but in fact sweet corn is essentially foreign to McLean County. More likely to have local provenance is the coating on the corn dogs sold across the street or perhaps the oil in which they are cooked.

OFFICE FOOD DAYS

Work groups may not always be the "one big happy family" employers like to talk about, but like family, they do periodically get together around a table full of food. State Farm Insurance Company, for instance, has a tradition of special "food days." These began with an annual celebration of Founder's Day on June 7 – the birthday of company president G.J. Mecherle.[36] Employees in the 1920s began observing his birthday by gathering outside the building and presenting him with a bouquet of roses. This continued until 1944. The company instituted an anniversary party that year. In addition, management began presenting a rose and a greeting card to each employee on his or her birthday. Within a few years, the presentation evolved into a "Coke party." Nobody knows quite how it started, but for birthdays and five-year anniversaries with the company, managers would initiate a few minutes of celebration by unlocking the Coke machine for a "drink on the house." Later on it became customary to roll in a coffee cart for anniversary celebrations and leave it in place stocked with sodas and juices all day. Birthdays continue to be celebrated officially with a rose and a card. Employees in some departments embellished the occasion by bringing food to work on their birthdays as a treat for co-workers. As departments grew bigger the birthday spreads became larger and more elaborate. The employee newsletter published a list of birthdays for the week, and workers marked them on their calendars so they could set aside some time that day to a call at the desk of a celebrant and have a bite to eat from the food table. The individual being feted received a card signed by co-workers and festooned with coins. Mary Meadows remembers that when she began with the company in 1997 it was customary for everyone in the work area to tape two quarters to the card, the price of a cup of coffee at the vending machine. Some said that the money was to help the birthday person pay for the food that he or she brought to the office that day to share.

THE REVITALIZATION OF MCLEAN COUNTY'S FOODWAYS

Dissatisfaction with McDonaldized foods and eating habits has arisen from various quarters. Nutrition and health issues have played a part. A growing

artificial sweeteners, caused bladder cancer in rats. Scientists assembled a list of approximately 3,000 additives in American foods. There were milkshakes devoid of dairy content, chocolate bars that seemed to contain everything except chocolate, and meats and vegetables saturated with unidentified chemicals.[47] Political pressure intensified in favor of stricter labeling requirements. The FDA finally stepped up in 1973 and demanded standardized nutritional information on food labels.[48]

FOOD AND HEALTH CONCERNS IN THE MCLEAN COUNTY AREA

None of the disclosures that shook public confidence in America's food supply came as a surprise to followers of Jerome Rodale, a Pennsylvania farmer, who since the 1940s had been advocating organic farming. Rodale broadened his scope and in 1950 began publishing *Prevention*, a magazine dedicated to healthy eating. His concerns about nutrition were elaborated by Adele Davis whose books, *Let's Cook It Right* (1947) and *Let's Eat Right to Keep Fit* (1954), launched the health food movement in the United States. The counterculture movement of the '60s latched onto Davis, and later found in Frances Moore Lappe's *Diet for Small Planet* (1971) ecological justification for vegetarian ideas derived from various Oriental philosophies.[49]

The first person in the McLean County area to frankly reject chemical agriculture, Willis Wiegand, was neither a counterculturalist nor a disciple of Rodale. Wiegand grew up in Woodford County and began farming before World War II. Just like everybody else at the time, he farmed organically. He had no choice because back then, chemical agriculture had yet to be invented. Following the war, herbicides and pesticides came on the market and seemed like useful tools, so Wiegand and his neighbors began using them. After awhile, however, he noticed disturbing changes in the soil. Then, the wife of a close friend on a nearby farm died of cancer, and Willis wondered if the chemicals they used caused her death. To play it safe and avoid the same thing happening to members of his family, Willis returned to pre-war methods and organic farming.

Wiegand subsequently became a kind of role model to young grain and livestock producers in the area. They read about organic farming, saw Willis making a living at it, and went to him to learn what they could about his methods. Among the earliest were Dennis and Emily Wettstein, who farmed near Carlock and who received organic certification in 1988. Others in the Eureka, Goodfield, and Congerville areas, which are hilly and not especially well suited for heavy farm machinery, followed suit.[50]

Common Ground, the earliest privately-owned organic food store in Bloomington, opened in 1977 and remains in business. Mary Munson, Common Ground's founder, had worked as a journalist for the Champaign *News-Gazette* and was teaching at Bloomington High School. Her interest in natural foods led Munson to purchase a building in the 500 block of North Main Street and stock it with various unrefined and organic products, including dairy goods, honey, apple cider, tofu, fruits, vegetables, dried beans, nuts, and herbs. Her initial inventory included a few packaged foods and nutrition books, but it excluded vitamins, minerals, and food supplements. As her business increased, Munson added products and services, including organic flours, pastas, and coffees. She maintained a filing cabinet full of nutrition literature so customers could learn about food allergies and natural remedies, and she kept her clientele abreast of the latest news in popular nutrition. Common Ground's club-like ambiance no doubt helped when Grand Central Grain Company, a whole foods chain, arrived in town in the late '70s and went after Mary's customers.[51] In response, she cut costs, including her own salary, and sold memberships entitling shoppers to a discount. Grand Central Grain gave up after five years and left town. Munson sold her store a few years latter to her co-manager, Katha Koenes. She continues at the same location and persists in a business philosophy that regards minimally processed, locally produced, environmentally responsible, and fairly traded as more important than price.

When Common Ground first opened it was called a "health food store" because the concept of organic food had yet to gain currency. Today, even the retail giant Wal-Mart and Bloomington's Kroger stores carry products labeled "organic." Kroger doubled its sales of organic products from 2005 to 2006 while selling up to $1,800 a week in organic produce. Its Nature's Market department, which included organic and other natural health food products, grossed as much as $10,000 a week. Cathy Smith, a Kroger employee who has worked in Nature's Market for 14 years, recalls that when she started, her inventory consisted of just three rows of cereal, pasta, and other dry foods. Now the department includes freezer and refrigerator space as well as sauces, soups and even baby food.[52] Brian Steffen, general manager at Dave's Supermarket in Fairbury, remembers when the store tried to carry organic milk several years ago. It would not sell and ended up going bad. Dave's reintroduced organic milk in 2006 after a couple of customers requested it, and sales took off immediately. Is the public's taste for organic foods a passing fancy? Steffen wonders about that and worries that organic, like America's many fad diets, is just another craze.

Fad diets have been part of what Michael Pollan has called "America's national eating disorder" from the days of Sylvester Graham and other nineteenth-century dietary reformers.[53] Perhaps the first fad to be noted in McLean County's public record was the Hay diet, an eating plan that in the late 1930s advocated natural foods.[54] Upper-class women were subscribing to various gimmick diets in order to control their weight as early as the '20s.[55] Women in the 1950s generally became obsessed with slimming, inspired in no small part by magazines filled with beautiful fashion layouts featuring extraordinarily skinny mannequins and an endless stream of weight-loss plans. A skeletally-thin look represented by the model "Twiggy," came into fashion in the 1960s. Dieting by then had developed into a national obsession. Weight Watchers, a company founded in 1961, applied a group therapy approach. Other dieting schemes came and went, but Americans generally continued to gain weight. By 1978, the national average was 14 pounds heavier than it was in 1963.[56] Bloomington's first commercial weight control clinic, Nutri-System Weight Loss Medical Center, began soliciting its first clients in 1982. In 1984, *The Eureka Employees Cookbook* became the first locally produced recipe book to include a section of "low calorie" dishes.

THE JOY OF COOKING LOST AND REDISCOVERED

I-hate-to-cook cookery and the de-skilling of American cooking was made possible by moving much of the work involved out of household kitchens and into centralized venues. These industrial kitchens, churning out Chicken McNuggets, Hamburger Helper, and other prepared foods imposed culinary uniformity on the American foodscape, and left a generation of children largely ignorant of the possibilities of cooking and profoundly limited in their tastes.[57] But, even as factories were churning out prepared foods and parents were setting a "kids table" of hot dogs or Spaghetti-Os instead of introducing their children to hand-made foods, others were rediscovering the joy of cooking and the variety of tastes and flavors the world has to offer, thanks to television, foreign travel, and ethnic and gourmet stores and restaurants. These outlets have reawakened interest in the kitchen and helped redefine its place in society.

TELEVISION CHEFS AND POPULAR COOKS

Television created the celebrity chef, a person made famous by cooking in public, long before newspapers and magazines began using the label. Nowadays the term applies to well-known chefs from the past as well as the present. The key idea is entertainment; celebrity chefs are at once cooks and entertainers. Fans pay dearly to dine at their restaurants, and some are willing to shell out even more to sit in their kitchens or experience working there for a night. Similarly, so-called "foodies" might travel to such epicurious meccas as the Greenbrier resort in West Virginia, California's Napa Valley, perhaps Tuscany or Bangkok, to take lessons from famous cooks.[58]

Cooking in public in an entertaining way started with Julia Child and her popular television series, "The French Chef." It debuted on PBS in 1962 and became a national sensation, so much so that in 1966, *Time Magazine* featured Child on its cover.[59] Sandy Knapp, a veteran cooking instructor and a bit of a local celebrity herself, remembers Martha Stewart as especially admired in the Bloomington-Normal area.[60] Other early public television cooking stars included Joyce Chen, Margaret and Franco Romagnoli, and Graham Kerr, "The Galloping Gourmet."

These and dozens of other celebrities made cooking look like anything but a chore. They rekindled the realization in a nation that had passed through two generations of struggle in the kitchen, either from shortages or insufficient time to cook, that cooking was an art. They inspired many to try their hand at creating unique and memorable dishes for their families and friends.

McLean County has never produced a nationally famous kitchen personality, but several residents have acquired reputations for good cooking and have attracted publicity. Laurent Torno, former conductor of the Bloomington-Normal Symphony Orchestra and an avocational cook, inspired orchestra supporters. In 1964, the Bloomington-Normal Symphony Guild published a cookbook as a fund-raising project. *Symphony in Food* celebrated Torno as a person, ". . . whose interest in harmony, both orchestral and gastronomic, has inspired the Guild in all its endeavors." The volume contained several of the maestro's own recipes, including his guidelines for preparing Beef Tenderloin Medici, Salad of *Auvergne*, and Ice Cream Pie.

Laurent Torno's Beef Tenderloin Medici

INGREDIENTS – 4 slices of beef tenderloin ¾ inch thick; butter; salt; freshly ground pepper; 4 rounds of French bread skillet toasted in butter until golden in color; ½ cup port wine (tawny port preferred); 8 fresh mushrooms sliced and sautéed in butter; 2 tablespoons heavy cream . PREPARATION – Sauté tenderloins in butter for about 3 minutes per side. Season and keep warm. In the same skillet used to sauté beef, stir in port. Add the cooked mushrooms and cream and simmer for about 2 minutes. Pour sauce over meat and serve on toasted bread.[61]

Guild members, determined to live up to maestro's standards, contributed recipes for *Asopao a la Biatriz* (beef and tomato soup), *Boolkoki* (marinated broiled beef), *Tagliarnini* (noodle casserole), Gourmet Spaghetti, *Pollo Con Naranjas*, Gourmet Rice (made with Uncle Ben's Rice, mushrooms, onion, and canned consommé).

Restaurant owner Rebecca Hawkins-Valadez published a collection of recipes in 1996. Her restaurant, Bec's Far East Texas Grill, opened in 1992 adjacent to the ISU campus in Normal. Bec's only remained open for about four years, but her cooking, a creative blend of Thai, Caribbean, and Mexican styles, represented Central Illinois's first exposure to fusion dishes and filled the tables. Her book, *You Asked for It: A Collection of Favorite Recipes from Bec's Far East Texas Grill*, represented a kind of farewell to the community and contained instructions for preparing some of her best-selling dishes at home, including *Picadillo*, Thai Curry Sausage, and Peanut Curry Chicken[62]

Bec's Peanut Curry Chicken

INGREDIENTS – 3 pounds boneless chicken thigh or breast meat or combination of the two cut in chunks, 10¾ ounces canned chicken broth, 2 tablespoons ground ginger, 1 tablespoon garlic powder, 1 cup peanut curry sauce (see below), ½ cup Thai chili sauce, ½ cup dried whole chili peppers, 1 tablespoon oil, 1 cup chopped peanuts, ½ cup chopped scallions, ½ cup fresh cilantro. PREPARATION – Place chicken chunks in stock pot and add broth and enough water to cover. Add ginger and garlic and cook slowly until chicken is done (about 40 minutes). Scrape off any foam and discard. Add peanut curry sauce and chili sauce. Simmer for about 15 minutes – mixture should be almost thick. Remove from heat. In a skillet, heat oil and sauté whole chili peppers until almost brown. Serve chicken over hot rice garnished with chopped scallions, cilantro, and roasted chili peppers.

Bec's Peanut Curry Sauce

INGREDIENTS – 10-ounce can coconut milk, ¼ cup peanut butter (smooth or crunchy), 2 tablespoons curry powder. PREPARATION – Mix and heat slowly. If mixture is too thick, add a little water; if it is too thin, add a lot more peanut butter. Makes 12 ounces of sauce. Keep refrigerated until ready to use, then heat slowly before using.

Marian Harris may be the only McLean County Cook to have gained national publicity. Born Marian Wilhelm, she grew up on a dairy farm near Edwardsville during the Great Depression. That experience—particularly her mother's warnings against waste—made her very economy minded. Years later as an Extension volunteer living about halfway between Colfax and Cooksville, she shared her concern about the demise of home cooking and the immense popularity of bread and cake mixes with Extension Adviser Margaret Esposito. When cookbook author Jean Anderson was researching grassroots American cooking and visiting county Extension advisers throughout the country, she met with Margaret Esposito, who passed on Marian's name. As a result, several of Marian's favorite old recipes wound up in Anderson's book, *The Grass Roots Cookbook*.[63] Anderson also wrote about Marian and her recipes as part of a series for *Family Circle* magazine. The article, "America's Great Grassroots Cooks: Delicious Dishes from Central Illinois Farm Country," presented Marian's instructions for preparing Apricot-Pecan Tea Ring, Basic Sweet Dough, and Open-Face Dutch Apple Pie.[64] In addition, it reported Marian's recipe for *Mustcohola* and German Coleslaw, a dish Marian learned from a Bohemian lady she worked for while attending high school in Edwardsville. The recipe provided here does not include the ¼ cup of vegetable oil that Anderson inserted into it because Marian did not approve of the addition.

Marian Harris's Coleslaw

INGREDIENTS – 8 cups finely shredded cabbage, ½ medium-sized green pepper cored, seeded, and minced, 1 medium-sized yellow onion finely chopped; for the dressing: 3 tablespoons sugar, 3 tablespoons hot water, 3 tablespoons cider vinegar, ½ teaspoon celery seed, ½ teaspoon salt, pinch of pepper. PREPARATION – Place cabbage, green pepper, and onion in large bowl and toss well to mix. For the dressing, combine sugar and hot water, stirring until the sugar dissolves; stir in vinegar, celery seed, salt, and pepper. Pour over slaw and toss well again. Cover and let marinate in the refrigerator for 2 to 3 hours before serving. Toss well once more before serving.[65]

FOREIGN TRAVEL

Many of America's TV chefs exposed their audiences to foreign foods. Julia Child renewed an interest in French foods that had died out two generations previous. The Romagnolis and cookbook author Marcella Hazan – *The Classic Italian Cookbook: The Art of Italian Cooking and the Italian Art of Eating* (1973) – expanded notions about Italian cooking. Diane Kennedy did the same for Mexican cooking. Others pushed culinary consciousness even further afield. The Time-Life Series, *Foods of the World*, for example, captured a vast readership.

At the same time, foreign travel had a big effect. Leisure travel boomed in the 1960s, but well before then many of the hundreds of thousands of American soldiers and sailors sent abroad during and after World War II took a liking to the strange foods they encountered. This had a perceptible effect back home. In McLean County, benefit cookbooks published before the Second World War usually contained no more than a few clichéd foreign dishes (e.g., Swedish Meatballs, Spanish Rice, Italian Spaghetti). That changed about 1950. That year, *Kitchen Kapers*, a collection of recipes compiled by members of Saint Matthews Episcopal Church in Bloomington, contained instructions for preparing French Hot Chocolate, English Cookies, and Yorkshire Pudding. The collection also described how to prepare a complete Swedish smorgasbord (a pre-Prohibition favorite in Bloomington), including pickled herring, chilled baked fish, fish salad, pickled beets, coleslaw, and rice pudding. A 1968 title, the *Bloomington-Normal Junior Women's Club Cook Book, 40th Anniversary*, contained the usual recipes for hamburger and tuna casseroles, but readers were also guided through the steps involved in making Armenian Eggplant and Mediterranean Olive-Crab Bake.

NEW ETHNIC FOOD STORES AND EATING PLACES

Eating in an ethnic restaurant can be very much like eating abroad, provided a considerable number of recently arrived immigrants dine there and give the cooks good reason to remain true to native palates. After World War I, McLean County ceased to draw many new immigrants. The tastes of second-generation German Americans, Swedish Americans, and other ethnic groups changed, and with that the experience of eating abroad without leaving town eluded residents. Happenstance occasionally intervened, as it did in the 1980s when a French bakery opened near the Illinois Wesleyan University campus in Bloomington. The baker regularly sold out before closing his shop for the day, but within a year or so, he and his wife moved away. When America attracted a new wave of Chinese immigration in the 1960s, and Chinese and other Asian restaurants began sprouting up all over the country, the few that opened in Bloomington-Normal quickly found that a healthy bottom line depended on preparing Americanized dishes rather than trying to be too authentic.

The construction of a Japanese automobile plant in Normal and a significant influx of Mexican immigrants changed things. Mexicans began arriving in Central Illinois in substantial numbers in the 1990s, and at first they were so badly underserved by local grocers that many drove to Chicago to purchase favorite foods. Chicagoans Daniel Sanchez, a cheese maker, and Oscar Flores, a baker, got wind of this and opened *La Carniceria Mexicana*, a meat market and grocery store in 2001.[66] As the only place in Central Illinois selling meats cut and prepared Mexican style, *La Carniceria Mexicana* almost immediately began attracting shoppers from Champaign, Decatur, and Peoria. Japanese eateries, aside from the Benihana-type steakhouses deliberately invented for the American market, have not normally served small Midwestern cities like Bloomington because of their distance from the sea and the absence of any significant Japanese community. However, the construction of the Diamond Star (now Mitsubishi) factory on Normal's far west side brought the Akemiya restaurant and genuine Japanese cuisine to the city. The restaurant began in a small room at the back of Akemi Navarro's store at the behest of customers impressed with the food samples she often prepared for them to taste.[67] Over time, patrons requested more space, private rooms, and karaoke. Her business grew, but her food remained true to its national character because Akemiya's clientele continued to be primarily Japanese.

GOURMET DINING

Inspired by celebrity chefs, foreign travel, and tantalizing encounters with exotic cuisines, America's middle class began snapping up copies of *Gourmet* magazine and organizing gourmet clubs. These began popping up in the late '50s when fancy cooking to most people meant preparing French dishes like Beef *Bourguignon, Coq au Vin*, and Duck *á l'Orange*.[68] These continued to be popular through the 1970s and beyond.

In Bloomington, the first restaurant to exude a gourmet ambiance was Jan Loeseke's Terrace (see Chapter 3). However, local foodies are more inclined to think of Arden Nowers, proprietor of the Brack Shop and co-founder of Central Station, as the entrepreneur who introduced gourmet food to the city.

The venue was the Brack Shop, a little place Nowers started on North Main Street shortly after he moved to Bloomington in 1960. Arden was just 23 years old, and he recalls that back then "You could buy anything you wanted in Bloomington as well as you could in a big city."[69] Downtown was an exciting place to shop and the Brack Shop was meant to add to the adventure. Arden filled his store with unusual gift items and furnishings. He added dried herbs. Then a salesman from New York showed up with coffee beans and a line of coffee grinders and coffee makers. The beans included flavored varieties like those now sold in grocery stores. Arden thought he could sell them, but when he pitched his gourmet coffees to shoppers his talk fell on deaf ears. His clientele knew whole-bean coffee; a nearby A & P sold it, but nobody could accept paying more for it than they paid for the supermarket's Eight O'Clock brand. Similar things happened with other Brack Shop items. When Arden first put fondue pots on his shelves in the 1960s, he could not give them away. Five years later stores could not keep them in stock.

Nowers and a partner, Danny Doyle, opened Central Station, a restaurant in downtown Bloomington in 1976, a late date for the gourmet food movement but one Arden feels may have been ten years too early for Bloomington.[70] In any event, a proposal to city officials to locate the restaurant on East Front Street in an abandoned fire station saved a landmark structure from impending demolition and infused it with new life, thanks in no small measure to the new owners' imaginative use of existing features. Again, the idea was to do something different by bringing a gourmet dining experience to Bloomington. The menu included nothing prepared off site, not even the bread. Arden had no formal training in cooking or experience running a dining room, but he set about developing menus and training staff. Most of the baking he did himself. His first menu listed a choice of entrées including pork chop, beef filet, red snapper, and chicken breast. A few months later it became more elaborate. For appetizers, guests had a choice of Mushrooms Sautéed in Garlic Butter, Mushroom *Piroshki*, Quiche Lorraine, and Swedish Meatballs. The menu listed a Cornish Pasty as the specialty, with "Shish-ke-bob," Chicken Breast Veronique, Quail and Filet of Beef, and Baked Rainbow Trout as alternative entrées. Central Station's wine list contained nothing other than a few Christian Brothers varieties, but since almost no one in the area knew any better the matter was overlooked.

Nowers and Doyle managed to keep Central Station open for 10 years. They experimented with dinner theater and musical groups to fill the tables, but eventually they stopped making money. Bob and Cindy Anet purchased the place in 1986, redid the interior, and restored profitability.[71]

KITCHEN GADGETS AND THE GARLIC PRESS

The American kitchen changed considerably in the years following World War II. The kitchen once again became a social gathering place, a room for visiting and "koffee klatching."[72] By the 1970s, the kitchen in newly built homes had moved part way into the living room and assumed a more decorated look with woods, built-in appliances, and Formica and vinyl countertops. Some homeowners purchased restaurant stoves, convection ovens, and other professional cooking equipment, though often these were barely used or used only on weekends.[73] The kitchen by this time was meant to be seen, and it soon became a place to be seen in. No longer did men shy away from cooking. Hobby cooks became common, lured perhaps by all the nifty machines that lined the kitchen counters of TV chefs. Well-equipped cooks had blenders, food processors, electric woks, electric rice cookers, slow cookers, toaster ovens, electric grillers, pasta-makers, bread machines, and more at their disposal. Many of these were real time-savers, and do-it-yourself entertainment cookbooks such as Julee Russo and Sheila Lukins's *The Silver Palate Cookbook* (1985) and Martha Stewart's *Entertaining* (1982) encouraged the use of such devices as food processors.

America's first food processor debuted at a house wares show in Chicago in 1973. Of all the modern countertop appliances used today, it still rates as the most revolutionary, drawing praise as the single most labor-saving device in the kitchen, and one that allows home cooks to prepare complex meals with the speed and ease of a professional. Still, when it was first introduced, the machine was dismissed as an oversized, overly expensive blender.[74] Not discouraged, inventor Carl Sontheimer personally contacted influential food writers, gave them personal demonstrations, and proved his point – the food processor was a versatile appliance that eliminated tedium and provided a shortcut to preparing labor-intensive dishes such as coleslaw and hash brown potatoes. After that, the machine got plenty of publicity and untold millions were sold.[75]

No business in McLean County has been more closely associated with Cuisinart than the Garlic Press, a cookware specialty shop located on North Street in Normal. Frankie Hipp, whose husband headed the Music School at Illinois Wesleyan University, established the shop in 1974. At the time, little cookware stores were popping up all over the country. Frankie sensed an opportunity in the buzz about Cuisinart, and this prompted her take an additional step. She banked on customers being willing to part with $200 for a countertop appliance, and became one of the first in Illinois to sell the food processor. When the Hipps moved to Texas in 1976 and Dorothy Bushnell purchased the store, sales were modest, but it was not long before owning a Cuisinart became a craze. Dorothy remembered one Christmas when production could not keep pace with demand, and Cuisinart began selling empty boxes.[76]

> We had stacks of empty boxes with a certificate inside . . . . I think it was the only company that ever got away with selling empty boxes for Christmas. I mean stacks of empty boxes! It was just amazing!

Dorothy, who had worked as a teacher and "raised a bunch of kids," credits time spent living abroad and her efforts to cook internationally at home with prompting her into the cookware business. Dorothy poured over a catalogue from *Bazaar Français*, learning about knives, au gratin pans, duck presses, and all the other special utensils deployed in European kitchens. During the early years, there were always new gadgets coming out, and people stopping by to see the latest. After a while, few new implements appeared, but as Dorothy jokes, manufacturers continued to oblige buyers by putting new handles on old items.

The variety of cooking appliances, however, always seemed to be growing. After the Cuisinart, the wok became another huge item. According to Dorothy, most people understood little about Chinese cooking and stir-frying.

> We did tons of classes on the techniques of stir-frying. That went on . . . for years. Carol Hiebert, my niece, she just kept doing it because there was a demand – the basics of stir-fry. She had lived in the Philippines for a while. So, woks were a big part of what we were selling . . . . We had a whole section in the back there of woks of every shape and form – round bottoms, black bottom, sets, 12-inch, 14-inch, separate lids – I mean it really got out of hand, but we just had this huge section of woks and we sold them!

After countless demonstrations of Cuisinart and wok cookery for church groups and clubs, along came the pasta machine and pasta-making lessons.

With a succession of new products, the store ran out of space, and in 1981 it moved down the street and into larger quarters. The move tripled Dorothy's floor space and allowed her to add whole bean coffee and a small section of gourmet foods to her inventory. Over the years, more has been added, including dinnerware, handcrafted jewelry, and a line of women's clothing. Dorothy brought three partners – Sarah Bushnell McManus, Pam Locsin, and Jackie Pope-Ganser – into the business in 2001. Since then, the store has added the "Market Café," for casual dining and sales of take-home entrées, fancy sandwiches, and artisan cheeses in an adjoining space.

COOKING CLASSES

Cooking classes, conducted as adult education in public schools or as auxiliary sources of income for restaurants and cookware shops, became popular in the second half of the twentieth century largely because celebrity chefs made cookery seem like fun. Hobbyist cooks wanted to perfect their skills, yet sometimes Julia Child and James Beard were difficult to follow. Jacques Pepin's *La Technique: The Fundamental Techniques of Cooking, an Illustrated Guide* offered guidance, but an in-person, hands-on experience proved more effective and far more entertaining.[77]

The Garlic Press started to offer cooking classes in 1977. The first classes met in the kitchen of First Presbyterian Church in Normal and were taught by Leslie Lash, the owner of a local framing shop. Leslie was skilled in French cooking, and she impressed Dorothy as a superb "stand-in" for Julia Child. For the next 20 years, other instructors brought additional cuisines to the curriculum and attracted a growing number of students. To accommodate a five-night-a-week class schedule and to facilitate product demonstrations, a demonstration kitchen was added to the store in 1996.

Garlic Press cooking classes typically attracted 30- to 50-year-old women in the beginning, but as the years passed, enrollments became more diverse. Newly married couples started signing up for sessions because they planned to share responsibilities in the kitchen. College students began registering, particularly as sassy young chefs began showing up on television. Men generally began enrolling in significant numbers in the '70s. This appears to have been related to the development of a competitive attitude toward cooking, when the old-fashioned and genteel competitions to win the blue ribbon for the best apple pie at the fair morphed into contests with all the attributes of professional sports.[78] In some households, men took over the kitchen. Food pages gravitated from the women's to the life-style section of newspapers, indicating a major shift in attitude toward food preparation.[79]

Male or female, many of the students served by the Garlic Press in the recent past have been what Dorothy calls, "chocolate chip cookie kids," because the only thing their mothers taught them about cookery was how to bake cookies. Michael Pullin, a local resident who frequently teaches classes at "the Press," accuses a whole generation of women – the "TV dinner generation," he calls them – for being remiss when it came to imparting kitchen skills.[80] Jackie Pope-Ganser cites her mother-in-law's cookbook collection as an example of the previous generation's disengagement.[81] It consisted of booklets from the electric company and the gas company and a Home Extension volume, all of them mostly about how to use prepared foods. "They were horrible recipes," Jackie complains.

> They were totally, open this can and open this box and mix together and magic happens, and people were so thrilled at having convenience foods because when it had been your local produce that you had to grow in your garden . . . it was so much work.[82]

Curiously, a certain ambivalence exists among Garlic Press staff about cooking out of cans, boxes, and other containers. Michael Pullin, for instance, talks about the excesses of cooking with prepared foods, but he neither sees an end to it nor thinks it particularly desirable. He finds his students especially receptive to be shown how to fix quick dishes. As Michael puts it, "You know, it can taste great, but if it is going to take you all day long to make a sauce, it's not going to happen." As someone who takes teaching healthy cooking as an important mission, Pullin wants to keep it quick and simple. Otherwise, he feels his students are not going to apply what they are taught at the Garlic Press to how they cook at home. Pullin professes an appreciation for companies that "do the gourmet for you." You come home, boil some pasta or a couple of cups of rice, and pour a bottled sauce over it. In that vein, he occasionally teaches a class entitled "Taste of the Garlic Press" that promotes products Dorothy and her colleagues have labeled "secret weapons." These have included various lines of bottled goods bearing the names of such celebrity chefs as the Barefoot Countessa, Bobby Flay, Charlie Trotter, Emeril Lagasse, Rachael Ray, and Rick Bayless. Pullin has found no difficulty incorporating such products into his recipes. He describes his job as showing people how to fix great tasting meals without having to melt half a pound of butter.

PUTTING A FACE ON FOOD

The rise of the supermarket entailed more than the closure of countless mom-and-pop grocery stores. Many of the local producers who supplied them had to find other buyers or switch to commodity crops. Home-grown produce stands and farmers' markets all but disappeared. As local farmer, Henry Brockman observes,

> There weren't really any alternatives for a vegetable grower except for the wholesale market. There weren't farmers markets – unless you were close to a major city as big as Chicago, New York or Washington D.C. There was no farmer's market in Springfield or Champaign or Bloomington-Normal 20 years ago. Restaurants weren't really buying directly from the farmers. Grocery stores certainly weren't buying directly from the farmer. If you were going to be a vegetable farmer, you were going to raise one or two or three major crops. And they were going to be shipped off to who knows where though the wholesale distribution system. That was the only model. That was just 20 years ago.[83]

Alternative models had been tried. In Bloomington, a group of workers organized a cooperative store as early as 1917. Members wanted inexpensive groceries, but more than that, they saw their effort as part of a movement through which the working class could control certain industries.[84] In addition, there were student coops in the 1960s and '70s.

By the '90s the issue was alienation. Few consumers knew who produced their food or how it was handled. This made some people uneasy, particularly in the wake of reports of the meat of diseased animals and contaminated fruits and vegetables being sold to a naïve public that mistakenly believed their government carefully watched out for such things. The increasingly promiscuous and obviously deceptive uses of the terms "natural" and "organic" on product labels, and the deliberate underfunding and political subversion of government regulatory agencies only made matters worse. When Henry Brockman began growing vegetables, he figured the time was ripe to develop local markets. The gap between consumer and grower had gotten so wide and the difference between real foods and artificial foods so great, that the pendulum just had to swing back.[85]

"Locavores," the term coined to refer to people committed to eating food grown close to home, had and continue to have a number of reasons for seeking out nearby growers. For some consumers, the primary reason had to do with safety. Farmers and processors situated nearby and known personally seemed infinitely more trustworthy than distant and unfamiliar companies. For other people, the key concerns were economy and ecology – the costs of packaging and transportation, plus the positive community effects that spring from supporting local businesses. In addition, there was the matter of taste and the conviction that local foods are so much more flavorful that they were worth seeking out, regardless of the extra time or expense that may be involved.

The fact that locally produced foods often cost consumers more than supermarket products has in part, been a consequence of government policy. Bill Davidson, owner of Blue Schoolhouse Farm in Congerville, blames federal subsidies to large-scale growers.[86] He argues that, thanks to subsidies, the typical grocery store's produce is under-priced while the prices he charges have to reflect the true cost of growing vegetables. Davidson has sold produce to the Garlic Press Market Café in Normal, Common Ground Grocery in Bloomington, and at Bloomington's and Normal's farmers' markets. He has written letters, dropped off food samples, and talked with restaurateurs to try and spur sales, but to no avail. Henry Brockman's price comparisons with local supermarkets show his customers save money. Mollie Bradle, co-owner of Rosie's, a downtown Bloomington restaurant, has arranged to receive a weekly case of tomatoes, peppers, lettuce, squash, and various herbs from a Secor grower because she finds them of superior quality and often less costly than the produce she can obtain from her wholesaler.[87] The problem has been getting enough of the locally grown stuff exactly when she needs it.

The customers of produce dealers and supermarkets never have to think about dry spells or the change of seasons. Dealing with local growers, on the other hand, brings buyers face to face with nature. As Mollie Bradle explained,

At the start of the summer, (growers) have a plethora of cucumbers.

Then cucumbers die off. Then they have tons of tomatoes. Now tomatoes are dying out.[88]

For locavore promoters like Bill Davidson and Elaine Sebald, coordinator of Bloomington's farmers' market, the quandary is how to persuade cooks to continually adjust their menus, prepare dishes in harmony with the seasons, and to get consumers to accept as their ancestors did, that the same dishes may not be available every time they sit down to eat.

DIRTY STORIES AND THE LAND CONNECTION

Elaine Sebald, with Bloomington's Downtown Farmers' Market, is passionate about local foods.[89] She would not even consider eating a peach shipped from out of state or an egg bought at the supermarket. Elaine feels sorry for people who have never tasted really fresh food. Marty Travis of Spence Farm in Fairbury thinks much the same way and believes that consumers need to be re-educated. Once they come to know local foods, Marty feels certain they will never again settle for anything else.

There is evidence supporting Travis's view from parts of Europe where place-based food habits are deliberately taught. In the Loire Valley of France, for example, parents and teachers take children to meet farmers and other local food producers to taste and learn firsthand about their products.[90] Through this exposure, children grow up to be "situated consumers" and inclined to reject products that fail to measure up to local standards.

In Illinois, Terra Brockman has educated consumers by writing "dirty stories." The phrase appeared in 2006 as a catchy headline for a story about her written by Barbara Mahany for the *Chicago Tribune*.[91] Mahany wrote about how Brockman had captivated readers in the Chicago area. Terra's weekly e-mailed stories about the daily struggles to raise vegetables on her brother Henry's organic farm inspired, according to Mahany, feelings of connectedness with the bucolic rhythms of agrarian life.[92] Terra's epistles recounted the routines, worries, successes, and misadventures of farming. Occasionally they introduced a little science or philosophy to help make sense of things, and almost always explained how to turn the vegetables currently coming in from the fields into an elegant dish or two. Terra's essays continue to connect farmer to consumer and field to kitchen. The fact that many hundreds of shoppers troop to Evanston's Farmers' Market to seek out Henry, ask him about the farm, and embrace Terra like an old friend, attests to their success. The Brockmans may live and work 150 miles away, but to their customers, they are neighbors from just down the road.

Terra Brockman and several other Central Illinois residents conceive of their work as community development. In this connection, Terra founded The Land Connection, an organization devoted to promoting locally viable food systems throughout the Midwest.[93] The Land Connection aims to give every farmer in the region an opportunity to grow food in a sustainable manner, and every consumer a chance to purchase locally grown crops. To achieve these ends, the Land Connection has worked to situate and train farmers interested in sustainable agriculture and to help food buyers locate such farmers in their neighborhood. Stewards of the Land, another organization involved in developing local food systems, has helped growers get their produce into supermarkets. After Marty Travis and his wife, Kris, founders of Stewards, introduced Janet Jablonski of Eden's Harvest Farm near Blackstone to the folks at Dave's Supermarket in Fairbury and County Market in Pontiac, she was pleasantly surprised to find a demand for her squash, jalapeño peppers, beets, and Swiss chard she never thought existed.[94] Marty and Kris Travis maintain there is no reason to ship locally produced crops clear across the country. "Our mission," as Marty puts it, "is to put a face on food."[95]

COMMUNITY-SUPPORTED AGRICULTURE

Over the past decade or so, a handful of McLean County residents, both farmers and consumers, have gotten together as members of small, face-to-face groups committed to sharing the risks and benefits of producing food locally. The model for these little organizations originated in Japan when a group of 200 homemakers got together and asked a local dairyman to supply them with milk at a reduced price in return for advanced payment.[96] Massachusetts farmer Robyn Van En started the first such collective in the United States and dubbed it a "CSA" (for community-supported agriculture).

CSA members know the man or woman producing their food and generally pay less for fruits and vegetables than they would in the supermarket. This, however, requires paying for a share of the harvest in advance so the farmer can cover anticipated costs. Money in hand, the grower then goes to work to provide members with their share of the harvest as the season progresses. There are risks, of course. In return for absolutely fresh produce, members may not receive all of the tomatoes or eggplants they would like should the weather not cooperate. Or, they may have turnips or apples coming out of their ears for several weeks. CSA members eat with the seasons – lots of lettuce in May and June, none in July and August.

Several CSAs exist in and around McLean County. Henry Brockman, who introduced the concept to Central Illinois, became familiar with it while living in Japan. As residents of Tokyo, he and his wife, Heriko, actually belonged to an organic vegetable CSA.

> A box of produce from a nationwide group of organic farmers would be delivered to our door each week. So even before I started farming I was thinking about . . . loading up a truck each week and going on a delivery route in Bloomington-Normal. I was thinking along the lines of the way the milk trucks used to deliver milk door to door. I liked the idea of directly selling to the consumer and also selling directly to the consumer in my own community.[97]

When Henry returned home and began farming near Congerville, he at first trucked his produce to farmers' markets. When Grand Prairie, an organic food distributor, came along, he began selling vegetables through that company. By the time it went out of business in 2000, Henry had learned more about CSAs, and he decided to start his own. It made particularly good sense because many vegetables had to be picked twice weekly. On Saturday, Henry had Evanston's farmers' market. A CSA based in Bloomington-Normal provided him with a committed group of mid-week customers eager to pick up their shares truck-side on the Unitarian Church parking lot.[98]

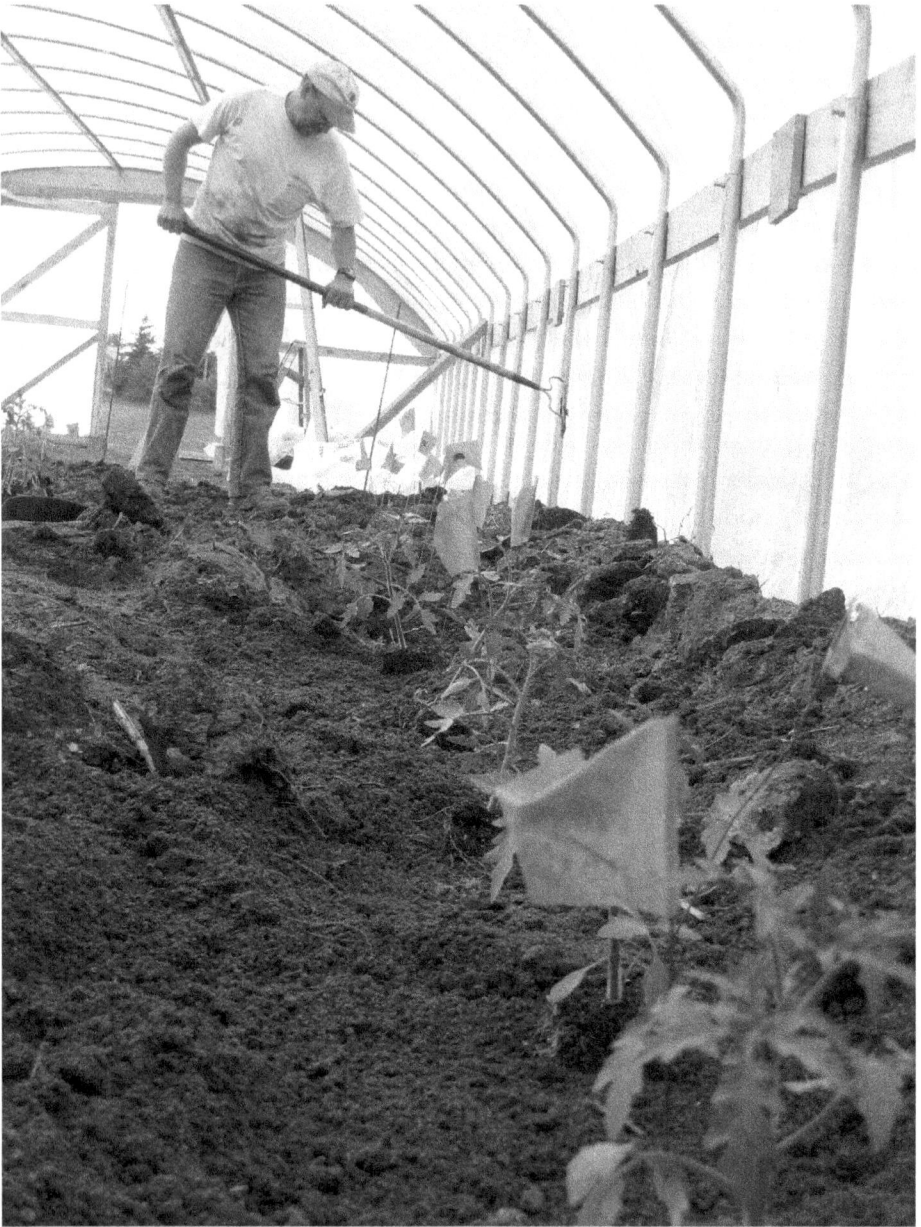

Organic farmer and local foods entrepreneur Henry Brockman in his
greenhouse, 2009. Courtesy of Terra Brockman.

The parking lot became considerably busier the next year after Brockman
approached his neighbors, Larry and Marilyn Wettstein, and suggested they start
a beef and poultry CSA to work in tandem with his vegetable group.[99] Larry and

Marilyn were the third generation Wettsteins to farm their land. Over time, the soil had deteriorated, so after Larry's father died in 1990, the couple decided they would be doing themselves and their children a great favor by swearing off chemicals. Ten years later that decision and a lot of hard work found fruition in 250 tillable acres sown in corn, soybeans, oats, rye, wheat, flax, alfalfa, and clover, plus 250 acres of pasture and timber supporting dairy and beef cattle, pigs, sheep, turkeys, and chickens, all certified organic.

The Wettsteins climbed on board with Henry, but to meet their long-term marketing goal they needed a USDA-certified organic label. To obtain that, they required a compliant butcher and sufficient know-how to work their way through the maze of federal certification requirements. The Land Connection helped out by putting Larry and Marilyn in touch with Midwest Organic Services Association. The organization guided them and their meat processor, Scott Bittner, through the steps necessary to obtain USDA certification. With the certified-organic label came a considerable bump in demand and the ability to command premium prices. The Wettsteins now supply beef to several high-end Chicago restaurants, including Blackbird, North Pond, and 312 Chicago.[100] As for the members of Larry and Marilyn's CSA, they continue to take pleasure in once a month bringing home a bundle of beef from animals that never spent a moment in the muck of a Nebraska feedlot, fattening on chemically produced corn.

CONCLUDING THOUGHTS

This book began with the idea that culinary habits change when novel foods and foodways gain traction and create a kind of crisis. Many people feel conflicted between the new and the old and search for a new comfort zone. Such is the situation in America today. Hard-pressed men and women feel compelled to feed their families as cheaply as and as effortlessly as possible, yet they worry about the safety of food from wherever processed by God knows whom. What to do? Perhaps those meats and vegetables labeled "organic" at Walmart are the answer.

Millions of consumers toy with the same idea. Walmart and other giant retailers sense the market and push their suppliers to provide foods produced and processed in safer and more environmentally friendly ways. Alternative growers feel optimistic and believe the system is tilting their way. Conventional growers and suppliers on the other hand turn defensive. They argue that their job is to feed the world and to produce foods that everyone can afford. Spokesmen lash out at the editors of *Time Magazine*, the producers of *60 Minutes*, Oprah Winfrey, Michelle Obama, or whoever appears to be bad-mouthing the industry or advocating change. Some Farm Bureau members in McLean County consider proponents of sustainable agriculture and local foods as misguided souls, unrealistic people who want to reconstitute the farm of yesteryear and recreate an economy similar to what existed around the beginning of the last century. But the opponents of the unconventional miss the point. The alternative farmer, the celebrity activist, the media; none of them drive change. At best they have been struggling to stay out front of ideas that surfaced decades ago, ways of thinking that made more and more sense as McDonaldization became increasingly extreme.

Is the country's food system approaching a tipping point; or has it already tipped? What lies ahead? There are no certain answers, but no doubt the next decade will be full of developments. McLean County's heavy investment in agro-industrial production likely means that any changes in the landscape will not be marked by bright lines. Consumers, however, could be in for a wild ride as the corporate food sellers that line Veterans Parkway strive to keep up with the changing culture.

[20] See http://www.floriculture.net/spencefarm/history.cfm.

[21] *Marty Travis Interview*, Come & Get It! Exhibit Collection, MCMH.

[22] *Bon Appétit* Test Kitchen 2009.

[23] Duis 1968:641-642.

[24] Hendrix and Dawsons, MCMH.

[25] *Ibid.*

[26] See Davis 1998:29.

[27] Oliver 1843:77-80. William Oliver, an Englishman, set out for Illinois from New York City in 1841. His book was written for peasants and common laborers back home in need of information about emigrating. Oliver spent eight months in Illinois writing mainly about farmers and their communities.

[28] See Davis 1998:130.

[29] *The Daily Pantagraph* 20 February 1938; other accounts of butchering day can be found in Yoder 2005 and Zehr and Zehr 2006.

[30] Zehr and Zehr 2006.

[31] Oliver 1843:85-86.

[32] Edwin Samuel Burtis, 1955, The Ancestry of a Certain Burtis Family. Xerox of typescript. El Paso, TX. p 58, MCMH.

[33] Duis 1968:199, 673.

[34] *Ibid.*, 457-458.

[35] *Ibid.*, 159.

[36] Prince nd(a).

[37] Stubblefield, John and George, MCMH.

[38] Prince nd(a).

[39] See Arnold, W.C. – Moore's Mill, MCMH; Brigham, Wm. – Millstone, MCMH; Moore's Mill, MCMH.

[40] Duis 1968:622.

[41] Sahlins 1972:186.

[42] Duis 1968:579.

[43] Oliver 1843:74-77

[44] Farragher 1986:151.

[45] Stubblefield, John and George, MCMH.

[46] Farragher 1986:152.

[47] Oliver 1843:120,124.

[48] Pond 1938:4, Clara Brian Collection, MCMH.

[49] Farragher 1986:81-82.

[50] Farnham 1846:217.

[51] Oliver 1843:181.

[52] Stubblefield, John and George, MCMH.

[53] Leinicke 1983.

[54] Men of Affairs in Early Bloomington, Amasa Washburn, MCMH.

[55] Greenman, Ezekiel E., Papers 1830-1890, MCMH.

[56] Duis 1968:159.

[57] See Mazrim 2003.

[58] Duis 1968:755.

[59] *Ibid.*, 723.

[60] Gregory, Mary Ann Henline, MCMH.

[61] An Old Letter in Possession of Mrs. Mary Handbury – Written 84 Years Ago, Pekin & Peoria: Taken from *Peoria Journal*, June 21, 1910, MCMH.

[62] In the fall when parts of the Illinois River were apt to be too shallow for steam ships, teamsters carted commodities overland along narrow and rutted roads all the way to St. Louis (Duis 1968:311).

[63] Duis 1968:503.

[64] In addition to seven general stores, Bloomington circa 1838 had a brick courthouse, a jail house built of logs, two meeting houses, two steam mills, two taverns, and two grog shops (low-class bar rooms); see *Hayes, Samuel J.*, MCMH.

[65] Hayes, Samuel J., MCMH.

[66] Greenman, Ezekiel E., Papers 1830-1890, MCMH.

[67] Duis 1968:416.

[68] *Ibid.*, 127-131.

[69] *Ibid.*, 764. The war was fought in 1832.

[70] *Ibid.*, 479.

[71] Frink, Dwight E. – Ewing, MCMH.

[72] Pillsbury 1998:33.

[73] Duis 1968:632.

[74] Gregory, Mary Ann Henline, MCMH.

[75] Pond 1938, Clara Brian Collection, MCMH.

[76] Dirks nd.

[77] Stubblefield, George and John, MCMH.

[78] Farragher 1986:68.

[79] See http://www.burgoo.org/.

[80] See http://www.lthforum.com/bb/viewtopic.php?t=15469

[81] Dawson-Paist, Maria, MCMH.

[82] Stubblefield, Geoge and John, MCMH.

[83] *Ibid.*

[84] Mazrim 2003:44.

[85] Mazrim and Walthall 2002.

[86] Farnham 1846:30.

[87] Babcock 1864:103.

[88] Farragher 1986:52.

[89] Farnham 1846:88.

[90] *Ibid.*, 87.

[91] Holloware (or hollowware) refers to table service items such as sugar bowls, teapots, water pitchers, platters, and other metal pieces that accompanied china on the table. Typically, it is thick walled, silver plated, and meant to be durable (http://en.wikipedia.org/wiki/Holloware).

NOTES TO CHAPTER 2

Pages 37-75

[1] Friedman 2004:627.

[2] The phrase is J.M. Peck's (1837:121).

[3] See Koos and Wyckoff 1982.

[4] Garrett 1990:95.

[5] *Ibid.*, 96-106.

[6] Farnham 1846:93.

[7] Brewer 2000:29-30.

[8] *Ibid.*, 30.

[9] *Ibid.*, 28.

[10] Transcribed in *Ibid.*, 68.

[11] Boggs, Amelia Louise, Memoir, MCMH.

[12] Edwin Samuel Burtis, 1955, The Ancestry of a Certain Burtis Family. Xerox of typescript. El Paso, TX. p 58, MCMH.

[13] *The Weekly Pantagraph* 18 August 1849.

[14] *Ibid.,* 20 August 1851.

[15] *Ibid.*

[16] Groft 2005.

[17] *The Weekly Pantagraph* 6 February 1856.

[18] Brewer 2000:156.

[19] Seward, Maurice D. – Cooking Stove Patent, MCMH.

[20] Bloomington Stove Works specialized in simple, coal-burning models (Lawrence 1871:62). These were popular in places like Bloomington where bituminous (high-energy, high-sulphur) coal was cheaper to buy than wood.

[21] Cooperative Stove ceased production about 1912.

[22] *The Daily Pantagraph* 12 January 1940.

[23] Hayes-Custer employed 275 workers that year and deployed a sales force of 35 nationwide (*Hayes-Custer Stove Co. – 1887-1937*, MCMH).

[24] Brewer 2000:86-88.

[25] Pillsbury 1998:54.

[26] Brewer 2000:86-88.

[27] *Ibid.*, 151.

[28] *The Bloomington Daily Leader* 7 May 1860.

[29] Levenstein 1988:12-13.

[30] *Ibid.*, 13.

[31] Tower 1901.

[32] Duncan 1979.

[33] *The Weekly National Flag* 27 June 1856.

[34] *The Bloomington Daily Leader* 27 April 1893.

[35] Beecher 1841; Beecher and Beecher Stowe 1869.

[36] See Ross 2004.

[37] My depiction draws on *The David Davis Mansion Volunteer Manual* and Landau nd.

[38] Strasser 1982:19.

[39] David Davis Mansion research collection.

[40] Collections of Sarah Davis's letters are housed in the Abraham Lincoln Presidential Library, Springfield, Illinois; the Illinois State Historical Library, Springfield, Illinois; and the Williams College Library Archives, Williamstown, Massachusetts. The David Davis Mansion State Historical Site in Bloomington has photocopies of the letters in these collections.

[41] Beeton 1861.

[42] *Ibid.*, 1655.

[43] *Ibid.*, 1654.

[44] The Bloomington area produced and consumed a lot of pears. Herman Schroeder and Son as late as the 1898 harvest claimed to be selling as many as 120 bushels daily from their orchard east of the city (*The Daily Pantagraph* 30 September 1898).

[45] Beecher 1850:156.

[46] *Ibid.*, 153.

[47] *The Daily Pantagraph* 2 March 1876; also Dirks, Hawkins, Shulman, *et al.*, 2007.

[48] *Ibid.*, 21 November 1890.

[49] from *McLean Businesses*, an album of newspaper clippings compiled in 2004 by Henrietta Crain and deposited with Mt. Hope-Funk's Grove Townships Public Library. The clipping has no attribution.

[50] Sinclair 1906; *Good Housekeeping Magazine* quoted in Levenstein 1985:7.

[51] See http://en.wikipedia.org/wiki/Meat_Inspection_Act.

[52] See http://en.wikipedia.org/wiki/Pure_Food_and_Drug_Act.

[53] Wyman 2000:2-3.

[54] Burke 2000:22.

[55] Census of McLean County Citizens Born in Ireland, Plus Their Families, MCMH.

[56] Burke 2000:22.

[57] Dirks nd.

[58] McCormack 1988.

[59] Vales (2005) provides recipes for some of the dishes that the residents of Clover Lawn may have eaten. However, the book is meant primarily as a guide to the life of Sarah Davis.

[60] Late nineteenth and early twentieth century dietary studies conducted in 326 American households by the United States Department of Agriculture found just 31 instances in which spareribs were encountered. Of these, only one household was considered to be in comfortable economic circumstances. The others were poor and working class. See Dirks nd.

[61] Matejka nd(a). http://www.bntrades.org/news.php?id=25.

[62] For a brief history of corned beef in Irish tradition, see Dirks 2007.

[63] From the 1858 edition of Catharine Beecher's *Miss Beecher's Domestic Receipt-Book*, quoted in Vales 2005:28.

[64] *The Daily Pantagraph* 16 March 1957.

[65] *Ibid.*

[66] See Baer 2000.

[67] See Dirks nd.

[68] Prince nd(b).

[69] See Dirks, Hawkins, Shulman, *et al.*, 2007.

[70] *Ibid.*

[71] Ross 2004(d).

[72] *Ibid.*

[73] See Dirks and Duran 1998. This paper includes references to several early dietary studies of boarding establishments.

[74] Grindley 1900.

[75] Chicken, fish, and cheese amounted to no more than peripheral foods (*ibid*).

[76] Other vegetables (listed in descending order by weight) included string beans, beets, tomatoes, cucumber pickles, fresh cucumbers, onions, and canned beans (see i*bid*).

[77] Other fruits (listed in descending order by weight) consisted of raspberries, pears, lemons, and huckleberries (*ibid*).

[78] Pillsbury 1990:27.

[79]Reardon 2004.

[80] *The Weekly Pantagraph* 7 December 1853.

[81] *The Daily Pantagraph* 12 June 1858.

[82]*Ibid.*, 18 March 1858.

[83]*Ibid.*, 12 June1858, 29 September 1858.

[84] *The Bloomington Daily Leader* 25 October 1870.

[85] *The Daily Pantagraph* 15 December 1862.

[86] Pillsbury 1990 and Davis 2004 provide fine overviews of restaurant history.

[87] Pillsbury 1990:31.

[88] *The Weekly Pantagraph* 4 Dec 1867.

[89] *The Weekly National Flag* 21 January 1857.

[90] *The Weekly Pantagraph* 11 January 1856.

[91] *Ibid.,* 17 January 1879.

[92] Hallett's opened a second location at the corner of Washington and Madison. It advertised a lunch or a warm meal at "any hour," and for those in the mood for oysters, they too were available done up in any style (*The Bloomington Daily Leader* 23 February 1870).

[93] *Bloomington Daily Leader,* 13 October 1897.

[94] *Ibid.,* 27 August 1893.

[95] *Ibid.,* 13 October 1897.

[96] Bateman's European Restaurant, MCMH.

[97] See Dirks, Hawkins, Shulman, *et al.,* 2007.

[98] The term originally referred to restaurants located in the basement of a city hall or *Rathaus* (German for "council cellar"). In contemporary usage, the word refers to eating and drinking places below street level.

[99] *The Daily Pantagraph* 22 October 1871.

[100] Kadgihn, Karen Kadgihn Letter and Recipes, MCMH.

[101] *Ibid.*

[102] Kaufman 2004(a).

[103] Pillsbury 1998:68.

[104] Carlock 0000:202.

[105] *The Weekly Pantagraph* 18 March 1858.

[106] See Dirks, Hawkins, Shulman, *et al.,* 2007.

[107] *The Daily Pantagraph* 10 August 1889.

[108] Hungarian Roller Mill, MCMH. Also see, Dirks, Hawkins, Shulman, *et al.*, 2007.

[109] Kossuth brand was named for the Hungarian patriot and statesman, Lajos Kossuth, who tried unsuccessfully to establish an independent Hungarian republic in the middle of the nineteenth century.

[110] Smith, Andrew 2004(a).

[111] *The Weekly Pantagraph*, 7 December 1853.

[112] *Ibid.,* 12 July 1854

[113] *Ibid.,* 11 January 1856.

[114] *Ibid.,* 12 June 1858.

[115] Gerkin's employed eleven bakers. Schneider's employed seven. For W.A. Gerkin, see Dirks, Hawkins, Shulman, *et al.*, 2007.

[116] Charles Kammerman, MCMH.

[117] See Dirks, Hawkins, Shulman, *et al.*, 2007.

NOTES TO CHAPTER 3

Pages 77-118

[1] Gabaccia 1998:126-127.

[2] http://en.wikipedia.org/wiki/Temperance_movement.

[3] http://en.wikipedia.org/wiki/Prohibition_in_the_United_States.

[4] See Earles and Earles 2006:89.

[5] Yoder 2005.

[6] I rely on Estes (1982) for the history of Mennonite and other Anabaptist congregations throughout this chapter.

[7] Art and Verna Nafziger in Gunden 1987.

[8] *Ibid.*

[9] *Ibid.*

[10] Earles and Earles 2006:87.

[11] For an overview of Pennsylvania Dutch, see Weaver 1983 and http://en.wikipedia.org/wiki/Pennsylvania_Dutch_cuisine#.

[12] Showalter 1950:79.

[13] *Ibid.*, 52.

[14] Weaver 1983:151-156.

[15] Showalter 1950:392.

[16] Martin 1904.

[17] Weaver 1983:152.

[18] Art and Verna Nafziger in Gunden 1987.

[19] Dirks, Hawkins, Shulman, *et al.*, 2007.

[20] Koos nd.

[21] Yoder 2005.

[22] Anon. 1881:35.

[23] *Weekly National Flag*, 19 November 1856.

[24] *Ibid.*

[25] *Weekly Pantagraph*, 23 January 1874.

[26] See Dirks, Hawkins, Shulman, *et al.*, 2007.

[27] *The Daily Pantagraph* 3 February 1894.

[28] *Ibid.*

[29] *The Daily Pantagraph* 19 March 1904. Also, see *Bloomington Pickle Company*, MCMH. Gehlert sold the business to Charles Pearce in 1897.

[30] Pay Tribute to German Citizens from Historians Pen. First meeting of McLean County Historical Society in Court House, MCMH.

[31] Pay Tribute to German Citizens from Historians Pen. First meeting of McLean County Historical Society in Court House, MCMH.

[32] *Bloomington Daily Bulletin* 20 February 1899.

[33] *Ibid.*

[82] *The Daily Pantagraph* 6 April 1864.

[83] *The Daily Pantagraph* 3 June 1938; Anon. 1976; Brokaw 2000.

[84] The group consisted of *Mesdames* Haterman, Baylor, Pennell, Laney, Dadson, Bishop, Russell, McMullen, and Cary (Roberts and Winter 1976).

[85] Brokaw 2000.

[86] Smith, Johnathan 1988:55; Summers 2005:6-7.

[87] Summers 2005:6.

[88] *The Weekly Pantagraph* 12 April 1889.

[89] *The Daily Pantagraph* 8 May 1914.

[90] See Kyvig 2002:15-17.

[91] *The Daily Pantagraph* 21 July 1896.

[92] Home brewing flourished, or at least so it would seem judging from the many newspaper ads for malt extract published during Prohibition.

[93] For information about local speakeasies, see Irvin, Maurice - Prohibition in McLean County, MCMH.

[97] Kemp 2009(b).

[95] See, for instance, advertisements in the *The Weekly Pantagraph* 10 May 1881 and *The Trades Weekly* 30 August 1895.

[96] *Bloomington Daily Bulletin* 18 July 1904, 29 June 1910.

[97] See Samson 1911.

[98] "Chatterton Opera House Program" in *Swedes*, MCMH.

[99] Ojakangas 2004:409-411.

[100] Yoder 2005.

[101] Munson and Koos 1991:51-54.

[102] *The Daily Pantagraph* 5 June 1918.

[103] Zehr and Zehr 2006.

[104] Pillsbury 1990:37-42.

[105] Samson 1917.

[106] See *Federal Café*, Come & Get it! Exhibit Collection, MCMH.

[107] *Arden Nowers Interview*, Come & Get it! Exhibit Collection, MCMH.

[108] Lexington Township Library and Historical Society, Come & Get it! Exhibit Collection, MCMH.

[109] *Nancy Steele Brokaw Interview*, Come & Get it! Exhibit Collection, MCMH.

[110] Davis 2004.

[111] See *Roland's Tea Room*, Come & Get it! Exhibit Collection, MCMH.

[112] *The Daily Pantagraph* 10 June 1922.

[113] *Ibid* 19 March 1939.

[114] *Ibid*.

[115] Kraig 2004.

[116] Ebel 1891.

[117] Ebel 1893.

[118] Tony Robbins (*Interview*, Come & Get It! Exhibit Collection, MCMH) recalls eating at Kresge's and Woolworth's lunch counters in downtown Bloomington as a kid. In the 1960s, he ate a lot of BLTs with French fries at both, and he also liked their open-faced "horseshoe" sandwiches. The original horseshoe sandwich was invented in the 1920s at the Leland Hotel in Springfield by Chef Joe Schweska (http://whatscookingamerica. net/History/Sandwiches). To make a horseshoe, he placed two slices of toasted bread on a sizzling metal plate (known as the anvil). He covered the toast with a thick slice of ham cut in the shape of a horseshoe and on top of that ladled a Welsh rarebit cheese sauce made of sharp white cheddar cheese seasoned with Cayenne pepper and Worcestershire Sauce. Freshly-made French fries (the nails) were heaped over the sandwich. By the end of the 1960s, the horseshoe had largely disappeared from Central Illinois menus outside of the Springfield area.

[119] Kyvig 2002:97.

[120] Kraig 2004.

[121] The Goodie Garden – Menu, MCMH

[122] Robert Gaston, *Transcription of Oral History – Tape 1, Bloomington-Normal Black History Project, MCMH;* Lue Anna Brown Sanders Clark & Ike Sanders, *Transcription of Oral History – Tape 1, Bloomington-Normal Black History Project, MCMH.*

[123] Lue Anna Brown Sanders Clark & Ike Sanders, *Transcription of Oral History – Tape 1, Bloomington-Normal Black History Project, MCMH.*

[124] *Dan Barringer Interview*, Come & Get it! Exhibit Collection, MCMH.

[125] *Ibid.*

[126] Tobias 2004.

[127] Graybill 1995.

[128] *Nancy Steele Brokaw Interview*, Come & Get it! Exhibit Collection, MCMH.

[129] Pillsbury 1998:95.

[130] Pillsbury 1990:58-59.

[131] Pillsbury 1998:175.

[132] Pillsbury 1990:68; 1998:175.

[133] Kyvig 2002:98.

[134] See *Quality Café, Rathskeller, Jan's Grill*, Loeseke / Quality Café Collection, MCMH.

[135] Linneman 2008.

[136] *The Daily Pantagraph* 30 September 1954, Loeseke / Quality Café Collection, MCMH.

[137] http://en.wikipedia.org/wiki/Pork_tenderloin_sandwich.

[138] Lovegren 2004(a):655-656.

[139] *Here's a gourmet coup: 2 Loeseke dressings, The Daily Pantagraph* 30 October 1974, Quality Cafe, Rathskeller, Jan's Grill (Folder 4), Carl William Loeseke / Quality Café Collection, MCMH.

[140] See *Green Mill Café*, Come & Get It! Exhibit Collection, MCMH; also *Green Mill Café*, MCMH. Greeks had a special affinity for restaurant industry, and many of them moved into smaller Midwestern communities. It was estimated in 1950 that a Greek man was 30 times more likely to be a restaurant manager or cook than were the men of other ethnic groups. Greek owned restaurants rarely served Greek food. Cuisine generally reflected the preferences of the clientele, not the ownership (Pillsbury 1990:125).

[141] The history of the Grand Café is sketched in Swiech, 1996; Grand Café, *Nancy Steele Brokaw's Restaurant Reviews*, Come & Get It! Exhibit Collection, MCMH; and *Ike Chiu Interview*, Come & Get It! Exhibit Collection, MCMH.

[142] *Mabel Wu Interview*, Come & Get it! Exhibit Collection, MCMH.

[143] *Ibid.*

[144] *Ibid.*

[145] Grand Café, *Nancy Steele Brokaw's Restaurant Reviews*, Come & Get It! Exhibit Collection, MCMH.

[146] See Chinese Community, MCMH.

[147] Newman, Jacqueline M. 2004.

[148] *The Daily Pantagraph* 6 June 1896.

[149] Sirota, *et al.* 1996.

[150] Newman 2004; Sirota, *et al.* 1996.

[151] *Ike Chiu Interview*, Come & Get it! Exhibit Collection, MCMH.

[152] Adams nd., and Adams and Williams, nd.

[153] Lucca Grill, *Nancy Steele Brokaw's Restaurant Reviews*, Come & Get It! Exhibit Collection, MCMH.

[154] Zanger 2004.

[155] Adams nd.

NOTES TO CHAPTER 4

Pages 121-162

[1] Newman, Kara 204:640.

[2] Goldstein 2004:679.

[3] *Ibid.*, 678, 680.

[4] *Ibid.*, 681.

[5] Kyvig 2002:162.

[6] *Ibid.*

[7] Pierson and Hasbrouck 1921:165.

[8] *Ibid.*

[9] *Ibid.*, 166.

[10] *The Daily Pantagraph* 4 June 1918.

[11] Pierson and Hasbrouck 1921:166.

[12] *Ibid.*

[13] Department of Household Science 1918:20.

[14] People were also asked to cut bread at the table as required to eliminate waste and to use stale bread in cooking and as toast (Pierson and Hasbrouck 1921:169).

[15] Illinois State Council of Defense 1918.

[16] Department of Household Science 1918:3.

[17] Pierson and Hasbrouck 1921:169.

[18] *Ibid.*, 166-169.

[19] *Ibid.*, 169.

[20] Esposito 1989:4-6.

[21] Brian 1950:2.

[22] Esposito 1989:8-14.

[23] Illinois State Council of Defense 1918:61.

[24] Esposito 1989:6.

[25] Pierson and Hasbrouck 1921:167.

[26] *Ibid.*

[27] Brian 1950:4.

[28] Goldstein 2004:677-678.

[29] As Thomas Parran, Surgeon General of the United States, explained "the great preponderance of boys who were rejected for the draft were found to be boys who in earlier school life had poor nutrition" (quoted in Levine 2008:56).

[30] Preparation of Foods, Home Economics Extension Service, University of Illinois, Vegetables, Everybody Needs Them – Eat Them Year Around - Rosemary Laughlin, Home Bureau, Box 2, MCHM Archives.

[31] The study polled 3,139 children (see Food Project 1938 - December – 1939, Reports 1939, Home Bureau Box 9, MCMH).

[32] Annual Narrative and Statistical Report of McLean County Home Bureau Illinois December, 1929 – December 1, 1930, Home Bureau Box 8 MCMH.

[33] Food Project 1938 – December – 1939 Reports 1939, Home Bureau Box 9, MCMH.

[34] Narrative and Statistical Report McLean County Home Bureau 1930 December 1931, Home Bureau Box 8, MCMH.

[35] Brian collected this information exclusively from members present at Home Bureau meetings.

[36] Annual Narrative and Statistical Report of McLean County Home Bureau Illinois December, 1929 - December 1, 1930, Home Bureau Box 8, MCMH.

[37] Esposito 1989:14.

[38] Brewer 2000:180.

[39] *Ibid.*, 180-181.

[40] Wajda and Uber 2001.

[41] Esposito 1989:15.

[42] Brewer 2000:218.

[43] Nor, declared Brian, should any homemaker fail to provide in writing a schedule of meals (Esposito 1989:15).

[44] Esposito 1989:15.

[45] *Ibid.*

[46] The fireless cooker is a contraption consisting of an insulated box into which one or more wells were set, each of sufficient size to hold a cooking pot. A thick disk of preheated soapstone was placed under the pot, and heat radiating from it slowly cooked whatever food the vessel contained (Mooney-Getoff 2004).

[47] Brian nd.

[48] Revere Copper & Brass, the manufacturer of Revere Ware, opened a factory in Clinton, Illinois some 30 miles south of Bloomington in 1950. The company, renamed "Revere Ware Incorporated," made Clinton its headquarters in 1986. The corporation shut down the facility and moved production to Indonesia in 1999.

[49] Brewer 2000:220.

[94] *Ekstam, Florence, Folder 6*, Great Depression Exhibit Collection, MCMH.

[95] *Ensign, Preston, Folder 7*, Great Depression Exhibit Collection, MCMH.

[96] *Ekstam, Florence, Folder 6*, Great Depression Exhibit Collection, MCMH.

[97] *Penn, Paul, Folder 17*, Great Depression Exhibit Collection, MCMH.

[98] *Bittner, Walt, Folder 1*, Great Depression Exhibit Collection, MCMH.

[99] *Steele, Ruth, Folder 19*, Great Depression Exhibit Collection, MCMH.

[100] *Ekstam, Florence, Folder 6*, Great Depression Exhibit Collection, MCMH.

[101] *Steele, Ruth, Folder 19*, Great Depression Exhibit Collection, MCMH.

[102] *Bittner, Walt, Folder 1*, Great Depression Exhibit Collection, MCMH.

[103] *Ensign, Preston, Folder 7*, Great Depression Exhibit Collection, MCMH.

[104] Dirks nd.

[105] Bloomington-Normal Black History Project, MCMH.

[106] *Wilbur Barton, Food and Daily Life*, Bloomington-Normal Black History Project Oral Interview, MCMH.

[107] Dirks 2010.

[108] Cobb 2007:41.

[109] *Ibid.*, 42.

[110] *The Daily Pantagraph* 4 March 1956.

[111] To break it down, there were seven A&Ps, 10 Piggly Wigglys, and three Krogers.

[112] Hasbrouck 1924:78-79.

[113] Leinicke 1983.

[114] *Ibid.*, 29 January 1850.

[115] *Ibid.*, 30 April 1851.

[116] *Ibid.*, 17 September 1851.

[117] *Ibid.*, 3 May 1854.

[118] *Ibid.*, 2 July 1862.

[119] As one resident put it, "There were times when it was pay time, and those were times when the bills got paid" (Caribel Washington, Bloomington-Normal Black History Project Oral Interview, MCMH).

[120] Crain 2004.

[121] Hamilton and Myers nd.; *Meltzer, Mauer's*, Marketing Class IWU, Illinois Wesleyan University Marketing Papers, MCMH.

[122] *Ibid.*

[123] Carlock's last grocery store went out of business in 1960 (Hamilton and Myers nd.).

[124] *McLean Businesses*, compiled in 2004 by Henrietta Crain

[125] My Store, MCMH; Schwartz, Steven – Biography of Oscar Mandel, MCMH; *Trades Review* 30 August 1895, MCMH.

[126] *The Daily Pantagraph* 21 April 1913.

[127] *The Weekly Pantagraph* 29 September 1869.

[128] *Ibid.*, 7 December 1853.

[129] *Ibid.*, 3 May 1854.

[130] Tea & Coffee Store, MCMH.

[131] *The Daily Pantagraph* 8 March 1920.

[132] Marton, Miss, MCMH.

[133] Pillsbury 1998:102; Smith, Andrew 2004(b):578

[134] Piggly Wiggly, MCMH.

[135] *The Weekly Pantagraph* 4 October 1865.

[136] See Husband and O'Laughlin 2004:154-155.

[137] Brower 2004:1.

[138] *Ibid.*, 1-2.

[139] Husband and O'Laughlin 2004:154-155.

[140] Most famously, Upton Sinclair's novel, *The Jungle* (1906).

[141] Krondl 2004:8.

[142] Pillsbury 1998:110.

[143] Krondl 2004:7.

[144] Pillsbury 1998:104.

[145] Second Christian Church 1902.

[146] *The Weekly Pantagraph* 21 Jan 1857.

[147] Anon. 1881:49.

[148] See Lawrence 1871:49.

[149] Hoopes & Son, Jobbers and Commission Merchants, Grinders of Corn Meal, etc., continued to operate for at least another decade.

[150] Four years later the company changed its name to Bunn-Capitol Grocery.

[151] *Daily Pantagraph* 11 March 1914; also, A Portfolio of Cartoons, MCMH.

[152] *The Daily Pantagraph* 23 August 1953; *The Daily Pantagraph* 13 February 1959.

[153] Campbell Holton Co. – Trademarks, MCMH.

[154] Campbell Holton & Co., MCMH.

[155] Pillsbury 1998:62-63.

[156] City Directory listings indicate Isadore Lutz ran a combination of fruit growing and canning enterprises beginning in 1924. Lutz Canning and Greenhouse appears between 1930 and 1953.

[157] *The Daily Pantagraph* 16 October 1932.

[158] Kemp 2010.

[159] Smedley 1998.

[160] Smith, Andrew 2004(b):579.

[161] *The Daily Pantagraph* Special Supplement 12 March 1967 (General Grocer, MCMH).

[162] Heberling Co., MCMH.

[163] *The Daily Pantagraph* 30 March 1926, in Heberling Co., MCMH.

[164] *Ibid.*, 3 March 1952 in *Heberling Co.*, MCMH.

NOTES TO CHAPTER 5

Pages 163-201

[1] Smith, Andrew 2004(b):581.

[2] Hawkes 2004:553.

[3] *Ibid.,* 554.

[4] Tobias 2004:367.

[5] *Ibid.,* 367-368.

[6] Witzel 2004:412.

[7] *The Daily Pantagraph* 6 September 1943.

[8] Munson, Wyckoff, and Koos 1982:346-350.

[9] Hayes 2000:3.

[10] *Ibid.,* 77.

[11] *The Daily Pantagraph* 8 March 1943.

[12] Hayes 2000:4.

[13] Kroger, for example, asked prospective purchasers of Country Club Canned Foods, "would you DARE spend your ration points for anything but the BEST" (*The Daily Pantagraph* 8 March 1943)?

[14] *The Daily Pantagraph* 8 March 1943.

[15] *Ibid.,* 8 March 1943.

[16] *Ibid.*

[17] Hayes 2000:77.

[18] *Ibid.,* 151.

[19] *The Daily Pantagraph* 17 June 1943.

[20] *Ibid.,* 11 May 1943.

[21] Pensinger 1942.

[22] Fisher and Marsh 1943.

[23] *The Daily Pantagraph* 9 March 1943, p. 7.

[24] Hayes 2000:101.

[25] *The Daily Pantagraph* 9 March 1943, p. 12.

[26] Hotel Rogers, MCMH.

[27] Hayes 2000:53-54.

[28] *Ibid.*, 54.

[29] Fisher and Marsh 1943.

[30] Hayes 2000:27.

[31] Fortification refers to the addition of a nutrient to a food in which that nutrient does not naturally exist. Enrichment means adding nutrients already there or supposed to be there in the first place.

[32] Bishai 2003.

[33] *Ibid.*, Carlin 2004(a):202.

[34] Hayes 2000:26-27.

[35] Bentley 2004:650.

[36] *The Daily Pantagraph* 8 March 1943.

[37] *Ibid.*

[38] Kaledin 2000:55.

[39] *Ibid.*

[40] Smith, Andrew 2004(b):580.

[41] Pillsbury 1998:104.

[42] Kyvig 2002: 101.

[43] Smith, Andrew 2004(b):581. A prospective owner in the 1940s needed a large block of land, a building with at least 400 square feet of floor space, and an inventory of approximately 3,000 items. A typical inventory consisted of over 10,000 items by the 1970s.

[44] Kyvig 2002:101.

[45] *The Daily Pantagraph* 21 January 1938.

[46] Smith, Andrew 2004(b):580.

[47] Berzok 2004:367.

[48] *Ibid.*, 368.

[49] See William Snavely, in Dirks, Hawkins, Shulman, *et al.*, 2007.

[50] Block 2004.

[51] Husband and O'Loughlin 2004:210.

[52] Laesch Dairy Company, MCMH.

[53] Ringo nd.

[54] *Ibid.*

[55] *Ibid.*

[56] See Snow and Palmer Co. in Dirks, Hawkins, Shulman, *et al.*, 2007.

[57] Snow and Palmer Company, MCMH.

[58] *Ibid.*

[59] Laesch Dairy Company, MCMH.

[60] Piper, Perry E., MCMH.

[61] *Ibid.*

[62] Ringo nd.

[63] Piper, Perry E., MCMH.

[64] Ringo nd.

[65] For a nearly complete list see *Laesch Dairy Company*, MCMH.

[66] Laesch Dairy Company, MCMH.

[67] Dennis Gieseke, former General Manager of Laesch Dairy Barns, personal communication.

[68] Laesch Dairy Company, MCMH.

[69] Block 2004:113.

[70] Some customers instructed their milkman to come into the house when no one was home and put their delivery into the refrigerator (Dennis Gieseke, personal communication).

[71] See Pillsbury 1998:75; also Berzok 2004.

[72] *The Daily Pantagraph* 21 September 1939.

[73] *Men of Affairs in Early Bloomington, Amasa C. Washburn*, MCMH. *Men of Affairs . . .* (taken from *The Sunday Bulletin* 7 January 1906) credits Washburn with running Bloomington's first regular provision store.

[74] Horowitz 2004.

[75] *Ibid.*

[76] Munson and Koos 1991:50-51.

[77] http://en.wikipedia.org/wiki/Refrigerator.

[78] http://en.wikipedia.org/wiki/Thaddeus_Lowe.

[79] Americans generally were not ready for artificial refrigeration. Lowe discovered this after he began shipping fruit from New York to the Gulf aboard a steamer outfitted with a refrigeration unit. The vessel took on fresh beef at Galveston for the return voyage, but the meat proved difficult to sell. Few New Yorkers would buy beef from a packinghouse more than a thousand miles away (http://en.wikipedia.org/wiki/Thaddeus_Lowe).

[80] Six shops moved into the new stalls, including Dabertz and Kack, S.W. Huber and Company, Kuntch Meyer, A.C. Washburn, Jacob Stautz and Company, and Radbourn and Hartry.

[81] *The Daily Pantagraph* 3 August 1909.

[82] See *B.F. Hoopes & Son*, Come & Get It! Exhibit Collection, MCMH.

[83] Tozzi 2004:635.

[84] Horowitz 2004.

[85] *Ibid.*

[86] Fulkerson, Richard – Utesch, MCMH.

[87] Horowitz 2004.

[88] Shelke 2004:142.

[89] *Jack's Ice House*, unidentified newspaper clippings in *McLean Businesses*, compiled in 2004 by Henrietta Crain, Mt. Hope Township Library. Wagner used most of his stored ice during the hot summer months when he was busy dispensing cool drinks from his drug store's soda fountain.

[90] From unidentified newspaper clipping, 1 February 1901 in *McLean Businesses*, compiled in 2004 by Henrietta Crain, Mt. Hope Township Library.

[91] Jenkins 2004:702.

[92] Farnham 1988:110.

[93] Oliver 1843:110.

[94] See Patton Bros. in Dirks, Hawkins, Shulman, *et al.*, 2007.

[95] Ruth Steele (*Folder 19*, Great Depression Exhibit Collection, MCMH) remembers her father buying produce at a Saturday farmers' market during the Great Depression.

[96] Peaches are plentiful at the fruit stores, wrote Sarah Davis in 1872.

[97] Eastwood 2004.

[98] Much of Mariano's story and history of Capodice and Sons comes from *Jack Capodice and Ed and Anna Marie Ulbrich Interview*, Come & Get It! Exhibit Collection, MCMH.

[99] Ed Ulbrich from *Jack Capodice and Ed and Anna Marie Ulbrich Interview*, Come & Get It! Exhibit Collection, MCMH.

[100] Hollie Walen, *Capodice Wholesaler*, Marketing Class IWU, Illinois Wesleyan University Marketing Papers, MCMH.

[101] See *Lartz Family Interview*, Come & Get it! Exhibit Collection, MCMH.

[102] Weidig 1984.

[103] Smith, Andrew 2004(a):121.

[104] The first mechanical bread-wrapping machine came on the market in 1911 (Martindale 2004:124-125).

[105] Leshnick's 1922.

[106] See advertisement in *The Daily Pantagraph* 28 June 1940.

[107] See W.A. Gerken in Dirks, Hawkins, Shulman, *et al.*, 2007.

[108] O'Malley, *History of the Gronemeier Family Business*, Marketing Class IWU, Illinois Wesleyan University Marketing Papers, MCMH.

[109] Purity advertised bread baked with unbleached flour in 1930 (see *The Daily Pantagraph* 13 June 1930).

Pages 203-236

[1] Lovegren 2004(b):659.

[2] Mendelson 2004:644.

[3] Lovegren 2004(b):659.

[4] Smith, Andrew 2004(c):449.

[5] Kaledin 2000:21.

[6] Pillsbury 1990:85.

[7] Marty 1997:37.

[8] Pillsbury 1990:85.

[9] Marty 1997:37.

[10] National Restaurant Association 1996.

[11] As reported by the National Restaurant Association (1991).

[12] Bloomington-Normal, however, did rank among the 10 most saturated MSAs in the East North Central Region in the $15-29.99 class. Still, with 24,800 residents per establishment, it was not even close to category leader, Madison, Wisconsin with 14,458 residents per eatery (National Restaurant Association 1991).

[13] Pillsbury 1990:186-187

[14] *Ibid.*

[15] Dirks nd.

[16] Pillsbury 1990:49.

[17] The hamburger, the essential fast-food sandwich, was rarely prepared and eaten at home before the Great Depression. In the 1920s, the hamburger was strictly restaurant food. The most popular sandwich in drive-in restaurants throughout the '30s and '40s was barbecued pork. The hamburger took over in the 1950s (Pillsbury 1998:176-177).

[18] Quoted in Marty 1997:129

[19] See Binkley and Eales 1998.

[20] Pillsbury1990:199.

[21] *Ibid.*, 215-217.

[22] Wilson 2006:14

[23] See Daviau, *Jumer's Hotel*, Marketing Class IWU, Illinois Wesleyan University Marketing Papers, MCMH.

[24] Jim's Steak House, Nancy Steele Brokaw's Restaurant Reviews, Come & Get It! Exhibit Collection, MCMH.

[25] The exact recipe actually remains a secret, but this one closely approximates the original. (*Jim's Steak House, Nancy Steele Brokaw's Restaurant Reviews*, Come & Get It! Exhibit Collection, MCMH).

[26] Swiech 1996. In 1965, Paul Womack replaced Comte as president of Mr. Quick, Inc. and shortly afterward the chain's headquarters moved to Moline. The chain's South Main Street store was closed and replaced by an Arby's.

[27] Golden West, Nancy Steele Brokaw's Restaurant Reviews, Come & Get It! Exhibit Collection, MCMH.

[28] Mavros, *Avanti's,* Marketing Class IWU, Illinois Wesleyan University Marketing Papers, MCMH.

[29] Dirks nd.

[30] *Sally Pyne Interview*, Come & Get It! Exhibit Collection, MCMH. William, W.C., Smith (Smitty) managed the Velvet Freeze from 1967 until his death in April 1986. His wife, Naoma, and their 14 children also worked at the popular shop. Mrs. Smith stepped into the management role after her husband's death, and retired in November 1988 (*The Pantagraph* 5 November 1988).

[31] Pillsbury 1990:221.

[32] Schmitgall and Schmitgall 2001.

[33] Gil's Country Inn, Nancy Steele Brokaw's Restaurant Reviews, Come & Get It! Exhibit Collection, MCMH.

[34] Harding; *Green Gables*, Marketing Class IWU, Illinois Wesleyan University Marketing Papers, MCMH; also see *Notes on Green Gables*, Come & Get It! Exhibit Collection, MCMH.

[35] Parkin 2001:52.

[36] Pillsbury 1998:90.

[37] Endrijonas 2001:158-159.

[38] Smith, Andrew 2004(d):606.

[39] *The Daily Pantagraph* 16 June 1910.

[40] Wyman, Carol 2004:732.

[41] *Ibid.*, 733.

[42] It is instructive to compare the Home Bureau's *Twentieth Anniversary Cook Book* (1938), published just before World War II, to its post-war collection published in 1948. The pre-war volume contained 73 meat and poultry recipes. To a few, one added catsup or prepared mustard. Just one called for canned soup and then only as an alternative to milk. Members provided 10 fish recipes, none of them requiring a prepared ingredient. A recipe for barbecue sauce to which one cup of tomato soup is added made no reference to a can. The donor of a beef casserole recipe stipulated fresh or canned tomatoes. The creamed beef recipes specified whole milk. With respect to reliance on the can, pre-war and post-war cookery compared like night and day.

[43] Newberg and WJBC nd.

[44] Haddix 2004 1:303.

[45] It remains an issue to this day whether all of the kitchen gadgets and small appliances sold in the United States really save time or actually encourage more work (Kaledin 2000:122-123).

[46] The term "fridge" stems from General Motors' brand name; see Lovegren 2004(c):351.

[47] *Ibid.*

[48] Smith, Andrew 2004(e):508.

[49] McMillan 2004:525.

[50] Pillsbury 1998:65.

[51] McMillan 2004:526.

[52] *Ibid.*

[53] *Ibid.*

[54] Pillsbury 1998:66.

[55] Thomas 2004:00.

[56] Smith, Christopher 2001:175.

[57] Recipes calling for fresh shellfish, however, were not uncommon.

[58] Jordan, et al. 1948.

[59] Woloson 2004:176.

[60] *Ibid.*

[61] *Ibid.*, 12 July 1854.

[62] *The Weekly Pantagraph* 5 December 1857.

[63] Lawrence 1871:50.

[64] See, for example, *Phillis Candy Co.*, MCMH.

[65] Pease's Candy nd.

[66] He had six sons and one daughter (*Ibid*).

[67] Pease 1903, 1908, 1913, 1923.

[68] The company currently has four retail outlets in the Springfield area, and its products can be found in many downstate gift shops.

[69] Vidas, *Boylan's Candy*, Marketing Class IWU, Illinois Wesleyan University Marketing Papers, MCMH.

[70] Graybill 1995

[71] See *Beer Nuts*, MCMH

[72] See Monti 2007.

[73] Paul F. Beich Company nd.

[74] Woloson 2004:178.

[75] As a Beich's chocolates advertisement stated, "The Giver is Known by His Gifts" (*The Daily Pantagraph*, 12 December 1910).

[76] Woloson 2004:178

[77] Jobbing is a type of wholesale mercantile business that buys goods and bulk products from importers, other wholesalers, or manufacturers, and then sells to retailers.

[78] See Paul F. Beich Company 1954, nd.

[79] Dusselier 2001:17.

[80] *Ibid.*

[81] *Ibid.*, 18

[82] *Ibid.*, 26.

[83] *Ibid.*, 29.

[84] *Ibid.*, 31.

[85] *The Daily Pantagraph* 23 April 1929, p. 5.

[86] Dusselier 2001:41.

[87] Paul F. Beich Company 1954, nd.

[88] See Paul F. Beich Company in Dirks, Hawkins, Shulman, *et al.*, 2007.

[89] Steinbacher-Kemp 2006(b).

[90] Kathryn Beich, Inc. was sold to Great American Opportunities in 2008 and no longer conducts business locally (*The Pantagraph,* 26 April 2008:A10).

[91] See Paul F. Beich Company in Dirks, Hawkins, Shulman, *et al.*, 2007.

[92] Smith, Andrew 2004(c):446.

[93] Parker, *The Beer Nuts Product Life Cycle*, Marketing Class IWU, Illinois Wesleyan University Marketing Papers, MCMH.

[94] The name was inspired by the product's success at National Liquor.

[95] Parker, *The Beer Nuts Product Life Cycle*, Marketing Class IWU, Illinois Wesleyan University Marketing Papers, MCMH.

[96] *Ibid.*

[97] Ross 2004b:408.

[98] Doyle, *The Bakery Banc*, Marketing Class IWU, Illinois Wesleyan University Marketing Papers, MCMH.

[99] See Olson, *Denny's Doughnuts & Bakery Inc.: A Business History*, Marketing Class IWU, Illinois Wesleyan University Marketing Papers, MCMH.

[100] Quinzio 2004.

[101] Coe 2004.

[102] Kelly 2004.

[103] *The Daily Pantagraph* 18 May 1859; Also see *Mueller & Stein*, Come & Get It! Exhibit Collection, MCMH.

[104] Quinzio 2004.

[105] Coe 2004:451.

[106] *The Daily Pantagraph* 16 June 1920. Other brands, including Cola-Cola and Moxie, were also sold as "temperance drinks" (Kelly 2004:454-455).

[107] Biasi 1950.

[108] Kelly 2004:454.

[109] *Ibid.*

[110] Quinzio 2004.

[111] Coe 2004:451.

[112] After cocaine became recognized as addictive substance in 1903 it was removed from the formula (Pendergast 2004:261)

[113] *Ibid.*, 260.

[114] Stoddard 2004:255.

[115] *Ibid.*, 256.

[116] See Irvin Brothers, Inc. in Dirks, Hawkins, Shulman, *et al.*, 2007; Schaefer, Irvin Brothers Pepsi-Cola Bottling Company, Marketing Class IWU, Illinois Wesleyan University Marketing Papers, MCMH.

[117] *The Daily Pantagraph* 16 May 1939, 27 June 1938.

NOTES TO CHAPTER 7

Pages 239-273

[1] The term "slow food" originated with Slow Food, a non-profit organization founded in 1989 to counteract fast food, the disappearance of local food traditions, and people's ignorance about the food they eat, where it comes from, and how individual food choices affect the rest of the world.

[2] *The Daily Pantagraph* 24 June 1955.

[3] Wolfe 1991:205.

[4] *Ibid.*, 214.

[5] *Ibid.*, 205.

[6] *Ibid.*, 209.

[7] *Ibid.*

[8] Zehr and Zehr 2006.

[9] Wolfe 1991:130.

[10] *Ibid.*, 208.

[11] *Ibid.*, 216.

[12] *Ibid.*, 207.

[13] *Ibid.*, 213.

[14] *Ibid.*, 212.

[15] *Ibid.*, 40.

[16] *Ibid.*, 39.

[17] *Ibid.*, 79.

[18] Ross 2004(c):538.

[19] See American – Hungarian Society, MCMH.

[20] Wolfe 2009.

[21] Abraham, *Butchering and Meat Preparation*, MCMH. Forty Acres was a northwest side Bloomington neighborhood populated around 1900 for the most part by Irish Americans and a variety of folks from Eastern Europe (see Abraham --- *40 Acres, MCMH*).

[22] Abraham's recipe has been extracted from a sometimes difficult-to-read narrative written as a memoir (Abraham, *Butchering and Meat Preparation*, MCMH).

[23] *Ibid.*

[24] Estes 1982:17.

[25] The MCC first undertook relief works in Russia and Ukraine in 1920. It serves today in 53 countries (http://en.wikipedia.org/wiki/Mennonite_Central_Committee).

[26] Coulter 2008. See also *Don and Ruthie Roth Interview*, Come & Get It! Exhibit Collection, MCMH; also, Illinois Mennonite Relief Sale, March 16-17, 2007, March 18-19, 2005, Come & Get It! Exhibit Collection, MCMH.

[27] *Don and Ruthie Roth Interview*, Come & Get It! Exhibit Collection, MCMH.

[28] See *Myra Gordon Interview*, Come & Get It! Exhibit Collection, MCMH.

[29] Numerous alternative spellings include *rugulach, rugalach, rogelach, rugalah,* and *rugala*.

[30] Moses Montefiore Sisterhood 1983.

[31] http://www.chmoorehomestead.org/apple-pork.htm

[32] Scrapbook: Old Settlers' Picnics 1885-1915, LeRoy Township Library.

[33] Munson and Koos 1991:6-7.

[34] Nestlé / Libby's owns the facility.

[35] Stokely-Van Camp and American Can had major facilities in town.

[36] *Dan Barringer Interview*, Come & Get It! Exhibit Collection, MCMH.

[37] Atwater and Woods 1895.

[38] Gerrior, Bente and Hiza 2004:19.

[39] *Ibid.,* 24.

[40] *Ibid.,* 25.

[41] Wiltsee 1998.

[42] Root and de Rochemont 1976:443.

[43] Marty 1997:37.

[44] *Ibid.*

[45] *Ibid.,* 128.

[46] *Ibid.,* 129.

[47] *Ibid.,* 128-9.

[48] *Ibid.,* 128.

[49] Smith, Andrew 2004(f):348.

[50] Dwight Wiegand, Willis's son, continues to organically farm his dad's property to this day.

[51] Haun, *Common Ground*, Marketing Class IWU, Illinois Wesleyan University Marketing Papers, MCMH

[52] *The Pantagraph* 27 February 2007.

[53] Pollan 2006:2.

[54] Food Project 1938 – December – 1939 Reports 1939, Home Bureau Box 9, MCMH Archive.

[55] Kyvig 2002:99.

[56] Marty 1997:38.

[57] See *Dorothy Bushnell and Company Interview*, Come & Get It! Exhibit Collection, MCMH.

[58] Kaufman 2004(b):330.

[59] Sampson 2004:196.

[60] See *Sandy Knapp Interview*, Come & Get It! Exhibit Collection, MCMH.

[61] Bloomington-Normal Symphony Guild 1964:5.

[62] Hawkins-Valadez 1996.

[63] Anderson 1977.

[64] Anderson 1978:82,157-158.

[65] *Ibid.*, 157.

[66] Beales, *La Carniceria Mexicana*, Marketing Class IWU, Illinois Wesleyan University Marketing Papers, MCMH.

[67] Onderisin, *Akemiya*, Marketing Class IWU, Illinois Wesleyan University Marketing Papers, MCMH.

[68] Lovegren 2004(b):655.

[69] *Arden Nowers Interview*, Come & Get It! Exhibit Collection, MCMH.

[70] *Ibid.*

[71] Wade, *Central Station Café*, Marketing Class IWU, Illinois Wesleyan University Marketing Papers, MCMH.

[72] Houston 2004:16.

[73] *Ibid.*, 17.

[74] Anderson 2004:503.

[75] *Ibid.*, 504.

[76] *Dorothy Bushnell and Company Interview*, Come & Get It! Exhibit Collection, MCMH.

[77] Kaufman 2004(b):329.

[78] Haddix 2004:304.

[79] Marty 1997:129.

[80] *Dorothy Bushnell and Company Interview*, Come & Get It! Exhibit Collection, MCMH.

[81] *Ibid.*

[82] The cookbook collection aside, Jackie called her mother-in-law a "great cook."

[83] *Henry Brockman Interview*, Come & Get It! Exhibit Collection, MCMH. In Bloomington, a farmers' market has existed off and on for more than 30 years, changing locations several times and managing to remain more or less invisible most of the time. Since 2000, however, the market has settled on the Courthouse Square, where it is conducted every Saturday morning from mid-May through October.

[84] Matejka nd(b).

[85] *Henry Brockman Interview*, Come & Get It! Exhibit Collection, MCMH.

[86] Koetters 2007.

[87] *Ibid.*

[88] *Ibid.*

[89] *Ibid.*

[90] Lynse 2006.

[91] *Chicago Tribune* 24 September 2006.

[92] Published as *Food & Farm Notes* (See http://www.henrysfarm.com/).

[93] *Terra Brockman Interview*, Come & Get It! Exhibit Collection, MCMH.

[94] Koetters 2007.

[95] *Ibid.*

[96] Jochnowitz 2004:281.

[97] *Henry Brockman Interview*, Come & Get It! Exhibit Collection, MCMH.

[98] *Ibid.*

[99] *Larry and Marilyn Wettstein Interview*, Come & Get It! Exhibit Collection, MCMH.

[100] *Ibid.*

REFERENCES CITED

Adams, Bill "Ace." nd. *40 Years at the Lucca*. Lucca Grill vertical file, MCMH.

Adams, Bill "Ace" and Chuck Williams. nd. *50 Years at the Lucca Grill*. Lucca Grill vertical file, MCMH.

Anderson, Jean. 1977. *The Grass Roots Cookbook*. New York: Times Books.

_____. 1978. America's Great Grass Root Cooks Number 8. *Family Circle*, February 3, 82-83, 157-158.

_____. 2004. Food processors. In *The Oxford Encyclopedia of Food and Drink in America*, ed. Andrew F. Smith, 1:503-504. New York: Oxford University Press.

Anon. 1868. *Holland's Bloomington City Directory for 1868-9*. Chicago: Western Publishing Company.

_____. 1881. *Historical and Descriptive Review of the Industries of Bloomington, Illinois*. Bloomington.

_____. 1991. Best Bakery / Best Meat Market Counter ... Mike's Market. *Business to Business*, December p. 27.

_____. 1998. Per-capita Fast Food Sales. *Restaurant Business* 97, no. 19: 73.

_____. 2004. Per-capita Fast Food Sales. *Restaurant Business* 103, no. 16: 44-44.

_____. nd. *American Hungarian Family Society*. Bloomington, IL: American Hungarian Family Society.

_____. nd. *The David Davis Mansion Volunteer Manual*. Bloomington, IL: David Davis Mansion State Historic Site.

Atwater, W. O. and C. D. Woods. 1895. Food Investigations and Publications. *Storrs Agricultural Experiment Station Bulletin* 15: 3-15.

Baer, Cynthia. 2000. The Labor of Irish Women in Nineteenth Century Bloomington-Normal: A Portrait Painted Through the Writings of Sarah Davis and Helen Ross Hall. In *Irish immigrants in McLean County, Illinois*, ed. Greg Koos :29-37. Bloomington: McLean County Historical Society.

Beck, Ken, Jim Clark, and Les Kerr. 2002. *The All-American Truck Stop Cookbook*. Nashville: Rutledge Hill Press.

Beecher, Catharine and Harriet Beecher Stowe. 1869. *The American Woman's Home*. New York: J. B. Ford and Company.

Beecher, Catharine E. 1841. *Treatise on Domestic Economy.*

_____. 1850. *Miss Beecher's Domestic Receipt-Book: Designed as a Supplement to Her Treatise on Domestic Economy.* Third edition. New York: Harper & Brothers.

Beeton, Isabella. 1861. *The Book of Household Management.* London: S.O. Beeton.

Bentley, Amy. 2004. Historical Overview: World War II. In *The Oxford Encyclopedia of Food and Drink in America*, ed. Andrew F. Smith, 1:647-652. New York: Oxford University Press.

Berzok, Linda Murray. 2004. Dairy. In *The Oxford Encyclopedia of Food and Drink in America*, ed. Andrew F. Smith, 1:367-372. New York: Oxford University Press.

Biasi, Edward C. 1950. The Inception and Growth of Biasi's Drug Stores, Inc. In *Home Town in the Corn Belt: A Source History of Bloomington, Illinois 1900-1950 in five volumes*, ed. Clara Louise Kessler, IV:244-249. Bloomington: Unpublished

Binkley, James K. and James Eales. 1998. Demand for Fast Food Across Metropolitan Areas. *Journal of Restaurant and Food Service Marketing* 3, no. 1: 37-50.

Bishai, David and Ritu Nalubola. 2003. History of Food Fortification in the United States: Its Relevance for Current Fortification Efforts in Developing Countries. *Economic Development and Cultural Change.*

Block, Daniel R. 2000. Milk. In *The Oxford Encyclopedia of Food and Drink in America*, ed. Andrew F. Smith, 2:109-114. New York: Oxford University Press.

Bloomington-Normal Symphony Guild, ed. 1964. *Symphony in Food.* Bloomington.

Bon Appétit Test Kitchen. 2009. Seared Salmon with Linguine and Ramp Pesto. *Condé Nast Digital.* Accessed 25 April 2010. Available from http://www.epicurious.com/recipes/food/views/Seared-Salmon-with-Linguine-and-Ramp-Pesto-352051.

Brian, Clara R. 1950. McLean County Home Bureau. In *Home Town in the Corn Belt: A Source History of Bloomington, Illinois 1900-1950 in five volumes*, ed. Clara Louise Kessler, IV:165-177. Bloomington: Unpublished.

_____. nd. Pageant of Cookery. typescript, MCMH.

Brokaw, Nancy Steele. 2000. Town Sought to Keep Dry in Two Ways. *The Pantagraph*, 17 April.

Burke, John J. 2000. *The Irish in McLean County*. In *The Irish immigrants in McLean County, Illinois*, ed. Greg Koos:21-27. Bloomington: McLean County Historical Society. Original edition, *The Daily Pantagraph*, 5 May 1900.

Carlin, Joseph M. 2004(a). Nutrition. In *The Oxford Encyclopedia of Food and Drink in America*, ed. Andrew F. Smith, 2:201-203. New York: Oxford University Press.

————. 2004(b). Saloons. In *The Oxford Encyclopedia of Food and Drink in America*, ed. Andrew F. Smith, 2:387-389. New York: Oxford University Press.

Carlock, W.B. nd. *Pioneers buried in Evergreen Cemetery*.

City-data.com. 2010. McLean County, Illinois (IL). Advameg, Inc. Accessed 26 July 2010. Available from http://www.city-data.com/County/McLean_County-IL.html.

Clark, Marian. 1993. *The Route 66 Cookbook*. Tulsa: Council Oaks Books.

Cobb, Ruth. 2007. *A Place We Called Home: A History of the Illinois Soldiers' Orphans' Home 1864-1931, Illinois Soldiers' & Sailors' Children's School 1931-1979*: Illinois Soldiers' & Sailors' Children's School Historical Preservation Society.

Coe, Andrew. 2004. Soda drinks. In *The Oxford Encyclopedia of Food and Drink in America*, ed. Andrew F. Smith, 2:451-452. New York: Oxford University Press.

Coulter, Phyllis. 2008. Mennonite sale offers food, crafts, grateful hearts. *The Pantagraph*, 15 March.

Craig, L. A., B. Goodwin, and T. Grennes. 2004. The Effect of Mechanical Refrigeration on Nutrition in the United States. *Social Science Nutrition* 28: 325-336.

Cronin, Robert P. 2000. *Selling Steakburgers: The Growth of a Corporate Culture*. Carmel, IN: Guild Press of Indiana.

Davis, James E. 1998. *Frontier Illinois*. Bloomington & Indianapolis: Indiana University Press.

Davis, Mitchell. 2004. Restaurants. In *The Oxford Encyclopedia of Food and Drink in America*, ed. Andrew F. Smith, 2:353-360. New York City: Oxford University Press.

Dawson-Paist, Maria. nd. Reminiscences. manuscript, MCMH.

Department of Household Science, Illinois Farmers' Institute. 1918. *Keep the War Foods Cooking*. Springfield, IL: Illinois Farmers' Institute.

Dietrich, Julius. 1893. *Bloomington's Deutsche in Wort und Bild*. Translated by Elsa Schmidt. Edited by Nola Marquardt. Bloomington: McLean County Genealogical Society.

Dirks, Robert. 2007. Irish Americans and corned beef, MCMH.

_____. 2010. What Early Dietary Studies of African Americans Tell Us about Soul Foods. *Repast*. Vol. XXVI, No. 2, Part 2, pp. 8-18 (2010).

_____. nd. American Diet and Nutrition at the Beginning of the 20th Century. manuscript, Bloomington.

Dirks, Robert and Nancy Duran. 1998. Experiment Station Dietary Studies Prior to World War II: A Bibliography for the Study of Changing American Food Habits and Diet Over Time. *Journal of Nutrition* 128, no. 8: 1253-1256.

Dirks, Robert, Meredith Marie Hawkins, Rachel Shulman, *et al*. 2007. *Food-related People and Businesses: Names from the McLean County Museum Archives* Come & Get It! Exhibit Collection, MCMH.

Duis, E. 1968. *The Good Old Times in McLean County, Illinois, Containing Two Hundred and Sixty-one Sketches of Old Settlers, and a Complete Historical Sketch of the Blackhawk War, and Descriptions of all Matters Relating to McLean County*. Bloomington: McKnight & McKnight. Original edition, Leader Publishing and Printing, 1874.

Duis, Perry R. 1983. *The Saloon: Public Drinking in Chicago and Boston 1880-1920*. Urbana and Chicago: University of Illinois Press.

Duncan, T. C. 1878. *How to be Plump or Talks on Physiological Feeding*. Chicago: Duncan Brothers.

Dusselier, Jane. 2001. Bonbons, Lemon Drops, and Oh Henry! Bars: Candy, Consumer Culture, and the Construction of Gender, 1895-1920. In *Kitchen Culture in America*, ed. Sherrie A Inness:13-49. Philadelphia: University of Pennsylvania.

Illinois State Council of Defense. 1918. *Official Recipe Book Containing All Demonstrations Given During Patriotic Food Show, Chicago, January 5 - 13, 1918*. Chicago: Illinois State Council of Defense.

Jarvis, Brooke. 2009. Can a Farm State Feed Itself?. In *Yes!* Positive Futures Network.

Jenkins, Virginia Scott. 2004. Ice. In *The Oxford Encyclopedia of Food and Drink in America*, ed. Andrew F. Smith, 1:700-702. New York: Oxford University Press.

Jochnowitz, Eve. 2004. Community-supported agriculture. In *The Oxford Encyclopedia of Food and Drink in America*, ed. Andrew F. Smith, 1:280-281. New York: Oxford University Press.

Jordan, Mrs. Walter, Mrs. Harry Johnson, and Mrs. Bert Matlock, eds. 1948. *McLean County Home Bureau Cook Book*. McLean County: McLean County Home Bureau.

Kaledin, Eugenia. 2000. *Daily Life in the United States, 1940-1959: Shifting Worlds*. Daily Life Through History. Westport, CT & London: Greenwood Press.

Kaufman, Cathy K. 2004(a). Bakeries. In *The Oxford Encyclopedia of Food and Drink in America*, ed. Andrew F. Smith, 1:61-62. New York: Oxford University Press.

_____. 2004(b). Cooking Schools:Twentieth Century. Edited by Andrew F. Smith. *The Oxford Encyclopedia of Food and Drink in America*. New York: Oxford University Press.

Kellogg, Ella Eaton. 1892. *Science in the Kitchen: A Scientific Treatise on Food Substances and Their Dietetic Properties Together with a Practical Explanation of the Principles of Healthful Cookery*. Battle Creek and London: Modern Medicine Publishing Company Limited.

Kelly, Patricia M. 2004. Soda fountains. In *The Oxford Encyclopedia of Food and Drink in America*, ed. Andrew F. Smith, 2:452-455. New York: Oxford University Press.

Kemp, Bill. 2007. Bloomington's German community was once sizeable and strong. *The Pantagraph*, 21 October.

_____. 2008. Famed 19th century ballplayer 'Old Hoss' came from Bloomington. *The Pantagraph*, 4 June.

_____. 2009(a). Local gambler 'broke the bank' at Monte Carlo. *The Pantagraph* / Pantagraph.com, 17 May.

_____. 2009(b). German pride reached its height with 1913 festival. *The Pantagraph*, 21 October.

_____. 2010. Bloomington once regional coffee roasting center. *The Pantagraph*, 18 April.

Koetters, Michelle. 2007. Central Illinois farmers put local food on shelves. *The Pantagraph*, 8 September.

Koos, Greg. nd. *The Heritage of Illinois Wine*. Bloomington: McLean County Museum of History.

Koos, Greg and Martin A. Wyckoff. 1982. *The Illustrated History of McLean County*. Bloomington: McLean County Historical Society.

Kraig, Bruce. 2004. Luncheonettes. In *The Oxford Encyclopedia of Food and Drink in America*, ed. Andrew F. Smith, 2:40-41. New York City: Oxford University Press.

Krondl, Michael. 2004. Advertising. In *The Oxford Encyclopedia of Food and Drink in America*, ed. Andrew F. Smith, 1:3-16. New York City: Oxford University Press.

Kyvig, David E. 2002. *Daily life in the United States 1920-1939*. Westport, CT and London: Greenwood Press.

Landau, Rebecca. nd. Clover Lawn. Word document manuscript, Bloomington.

Lawrence, R S. 1871. *The Evergreen City. Past, Present and Future of Bloomington, McLean County, Illinois*. Bloomington, IL: R. S. Lawrence.

Leinicke, Linda. 1983. *George Dietrich: Your Helpful Hardware Man*. Jackson: University of Mississippi.

Leshnick's. 1922. *Bloomington and Normal City Directory*. Peoria: Leshnick Directory Company.

Levenstein, H A. 1985. The American Response to Italian Food, 1880-1930. *Food and Foodways* 1: 1-24.

_____. 1988. *Revolution at the Table: The Transformation of the American Diet*. Oxford: Oxford University Press.

Levine, Susan. 2008. *School Lunch Politics: The Surprising History of America's Favorite Welfare Program*. Princeton: Princeton University Press.

Linneman, Bill. 2008. Chili, Chile, Chilly. *The Normalite Weekly Newspaper*, 6 November.

Lovegren, Sylvia. 1995. *Fashionable Food: Seven Decades of Food Fads*. Chicago: University of Chicago Press.

_____. 2004(a). Historical overview: From the 1960s to the present. In *The Oxford Encyclopedia of Food and Drink in America*, ed. Andrew F. Smith, 1:659-666. New York: Oxford University Press.

_____. 2004(b). Historical overview: From World War II to the early 1960s. In *The Oxford Encyclopedia of Food and Drink in America*, ed. Andrew F. Smith, 1:652-659. New York: Oxford University Press.

_____. 2004(c). Refrigerators. In *The Oxford Encyclopedia of Food and Drink in America*, ed. Andrew F. Smith, 2:351-352. New York: Oxford University Press.

Mahany, Barbara. 2006. Dirty stories. *Chicago Tribune*, September 24.

Martin, Helen Reimensnyder. 1904. *Tillie, a Mennonite Maid; a Story of the Pennsylvania Dutch*. New York: Grosset and Dunlap.

Marty, Myron A. 1997. *Daily Life in the United States, 1960-1990*. Daily Life Through History. Westport, CN & London: Greenwood Press.

Matejka, Mike. 2000. *Building a Railroad: 1850s Irish Immigrant Labor in Central Illinois*. In *Irish Immigrants in McLean County, Illinois*, ed. Greg Koos: 7-18. Bloomington, IL: McLean County Historical Society.

_____. nd(a). *Building a Railroad: 1850s Irish Immigrant Labor in Central Illinois*. Bloomington & Normal Trades & Labor Assembly. Accessed 1 April 2010. Available from http://www.bntrades.org/news.php?id=25.

_____. nd(b). Working Class Voice: Labor Unions in McLean County. In *"Mother" Jones & the 1917 Streetcar Strike:* Bloomington and Normal Trades and Labor Assembly. Accessed 1 April 2010. Available from http://www.bntrades.org/news.php?id=9.

Mazrim, Robert. 2002. "Now Quite Out of Society": Archaeology and Frontier Illinois. Illinois Transportation Archaeological Research Program, *Transportation Archaeological Bulletin* Number 1. Urbana, IL: Department of Anthropology, University of Illinois, Urbana-Champaign.

_____. 2003. The Earthenware of Cotton Hill. *Sangamo Archaeological Center Material Culture Bulletin* Number 1. Elkhart, IL: Sangamo Archaeological Center.

Mazrim, Robert and John Walthall. 2002. "Queensware by the Crate." Ceramic Products as Advertised in the St. Louis Marketplace. *Sangamo Archaeological Center Archival Studies Bulletin #2.* Elkhart, IL: Sangamo Archaeological Center.

McClure, Gordon T. 1987. *Carlock Centennial History, 1888-1988.* Heyworth: Heyworth Star.

McCormack, Malachi 1988. *Irish Country Cooking*: Equation.

McLean County Home Bureau, ed. 1938. *Twentieth Anniversary Cook Book.* Bloomington: Homemakers Extension Association.

McMillan, Matt. 2004. Frozen Food. In *The Oxford Encyclopedia of Food and Drink in America*, ed. Andrew F. Smith, 1:523-527. New York: Oxford University Press.

Mendelson, Anne. 2004. Historical Overview: From World War I to World War II. In *The Oxford Encyclopedia of Food and Drink in America*, ed. Andrew F. Smith, 1:642-647. New York: Oxford University Press.

Monti, Gretchen. 2007. Bloomington-made candy known internationally. *Images of McLean County*, Illinois. pp. 26-29.

Mooney-Getoff, Mary. 2004. Fireless Cookers. In *The Oxford Encyclopedia of Food and Drink in America*, ed. Andrew F. Smith, 1:468-469. New York: Oxford University Press.

Munson, Don. 1980. *Don Munson's WJBC Sesquicentennial Stories: Glimpses of McLean County's 150 Years*: pamphlet.

Munson, Don and Greg Koos. 1991. *History You Can See.* Bloomington, IL: McLean County Historical Society.

Munson, Don, Martin A. Wyckoff, and Greg Koos. 1982. *The Illustrated History of McLean County.* Transactions of the McLean County Historical Society. Bloomington, IL: McLean County Historical Society.

Murray, Marcee. 1998. *Cosmic Cooking on the Grand Prairie*: Grand Prairie.

National Restaurant Association Research Department. 1991. *Eating Places by Check Size.* Washington, D.C.: National Restaurant Association.

_____. 1996. *Restaurant Spending Consumer Expenditure Survey: 1994.* Washington, DC: National Restaurant Association.

Newberg, Don and WJBC, eds. nd. *A Collection of Recipes from WJBC Selected from Problems and Solutions.* Bloomington.

_____. 2004(d). Boardinghouses. In *The Oxford Encyclopedia of Food and Drink in America*, ed. Andrew F. Smith, 1:105-107. New York: Oxford University Press.

Ruschmann, Paul. 2004. Beer Halls. In *The Oxford Encyclopedia of Food and Drink in America*, ed. Andrew F. Smith, 1:86-87. New York: Oxford University Press.

Sahlins, Marshall. 1972. *Stone Age Economics*. Chicago: Aldine.

Sampson, Lynne. 2004. Celebrity Chefs. In *The Oxford Encyclopedia of Food and Drink in America*, ed. Andrew F. Smith, 1:195-197. New York: University of Oxford Press.

Samson, Charles M. 1911. *Bloomington and Normal City Directory 1911*. Bloomington: Pantagraph Printing and Stationery Company.

_____. 1917. *Bloomington and Normal Illinois City Directory 1917*. Bloomington: Pantagraph Printing and Stationery Company.

Schlosser, Eric. 2001. *Fast Food Nation: The Dark Side of the All-American Meal*. New York: Houghton Mifflin.

Schmitgall, Mike and Kate Schmitgall. 2001. *Meals and Memories*. Minier.

Second Christian Church. 1902. *Bloomington Cook Book*. Bloomington.

Shelke, Kantha. 2004. Butchering. In *The Oxford Encyclopedia of Food and Drink in America*, ed. Andrew F. Smith, 1:141-142. Oxford: Oxford University Press.

Showalter, Mary Emma. 1950. *Mennonite Community Recipes*. Philadelphia: John C. Winston Company.

Simeone, James. 2000. *Democracy and Slavery in Frontier Illinois: The Bottomland Republic*. DeKalb: Northern Illinois University Press.

Sinclair, Upton. 1906. *The Jungle*. New York: Doubleday, Page & Company

Smedley, Gene. 1998. Coffee craze perks up downtown. *The Pantagraph*, 31 May.

Smith, Andrew F. 2004(a). Bread. In *The Oxford Encyclopedia of Food and Drink in America*, ed. Andrew F. Smith, 1:116-124. New York: Oxford University Press.

_____. 2004(b). Grocery store. In *The Oxford Encyclopedia of Food and Drink in America*, ed. Andrew F. Smith, 1:578-582. New York: Oxford University Press.

_____. 2004(f). Counterculture, Food. In *The Oxford Encyclopedia of Food and Drink in America*, ed. Andrew F. Smith, 1:347-351. New York: Oxford University Press.

_____. 2004(e). Freezers and freezing. In *The Oxford Encyclopedia of Food and Drink in America*, ed. Andrew F. Smith, 1:508-510. New York: Oxford University Press.

_____. 2004(c). Snack Food. In *The Oxford Encyclopedia of Food and Drink in America*, ed. Andrew F. Smith, 2:446-450. New York: Oxford University Press.

_____. 2004(d). Wheat. In *The Oxford Encyclopedia of Food and Drink in America*, ed. Andrew F. Smith, 2: 603-607. New York: Oxford University Press.

Smith, Christopher Holmes. 2001. *Freeze Frames: Frozen Foods and Memories of the Postwar American family. In Kitchen Culture in America*, ed. Sherrie A. Inness:175-209. Philadelphia: University of Pennsylvania Press.

Smith, Johnathan F. 1988. *Cold Water on the Prairie: The Temperance Movement in Bloomington, Illinois 1830-1875*, Illinois State University.

Steinbacher-Kemp, Bill. 2006(a). A page from our past: Twin Cities' ties to New Deal run deep. *The Pantagraph*, October 22, B5.

_____. 2006(b). Bloomington's unconventional chemist and candy-maker. *The Pantagraph*, 14 May.

_____. 2007(a). Highland Park Golf Course site of old German brewery. *The Pantagraph*, 17 June.

_____.2007b. K-mart arrival hastened exodus of downtown retailers. *The Pantagraph*, 7 August.

Stewart, Martha. 1982. *Entertaining*. Clarkson Potter.

Stoddard, Bob. 2004. Pepsi-Cola. In *The Oxford Encyclopedia of Food and Drink in America*, ed. Andrew F. Smith, 2:255-256. New York: Oxford University Press.

Strasser, Susan. 1982. *Never Done: A History of American Housework*. New York: Pantheon.

Strickland, K. A. 1993. *Saloonkeepers in Fairbury, Illinois, 1860-1920: Traditional Business in an Evolving Modern Community*. research paper, Bloomington, IL.

Summers, Candace. 2005. *Wet or Dry? McLean County, Illinois During Prohibition, 1920-1933*. Normal: Department of History, Illinois State University.

Swiech, Paul. 1996. It's a Grand Cafe, all right. *The Pantagraph*, 6 June.

Thomas, Gerry. 2004. TV Dinners: A Firsthand Account. In *The Oxford Encyclopedia of Food and Drink in America*, ed. Andrew F. Smith, 1:524-525. New York: Oxford University Press.

Thompson, Christine. nd. *The Good Life in Bloomington-Normal: A Brief Look at Saloons and the Liquor Business*. research paper for History 289.33, Dr. Holsinger, Bloomington.

Tobias, Ruth. 2004. Cafeterias. In *The Oxford Encyclopedia of Food and Drink in America*, ed. Andrew F. Smith, 1:148-150. New York City: Oxford University Press.

Tower, O. F. 1901. *Dietary Studies at Western Reserve University*. Cleveland: Western Reserve University.

Tozzi, Allison. 2004. Historical overview: From Victorian America to Word War I. In *The Oxford Encyclopedia of Food and Drink in America*, ed. Andrew F. Smith, 1:633-640. New York: Oxford University Press.

Vales, Sarah. 2005. *Managing Clover Lawn from Ingredients to Enjoyment: A Guide to the Kitchen of Sarah Davis and the Life that Filled it*. Bloomington, IL: The David Davis Mansion Foundation.

Wajda, Shirley Teresa and Terrence L. Uber. 2001. *Designing Domesticity: Decorating the American Home Since 1876*. Broadbent Gallery, Kent State University Museum. Accessed 12 September 2008 2008. HTML document. Available from http://www.personal.kent.edu/~swajda/designing_domesticity1.htm.

Weaver, Williams Woys. 1983. *Sauerkraut Yankees*. Philadelphia: University of Pennsylvania Press.

Weidig, Barbara. 1984. Casey's Dream Lives on. *The Northwest Bloomington Neighborhood Association Newsletter*, Fall.

Welsh, S. O. and R. M. Marston. 1982. Review of Trends in Food Use in the United States, 1909 to 1980. *Journal of the American Dietetic Association* 81: 120-125.

Wilson, Sara. 2006. Motivational Metrics. *Restaurant Business* 105, no. 10: 14.

Wiltsee, George. 1998. *Waste Grease Resources in 30 U.S. Metropolitan Areas*. Valencia: Appel Consultants, Inc.

Wolfe, Marsha. 1991. *Family Traditions*. Illinois Homemakers Extension Federation.

Wolfe, Sharon K. 2009. Still dancing. *The Pantagraph*, 2 May.

Woloson, Wendy A. 2004. Candy Bars and Candy. In T*he Oxford Encyclopedia of Food and Drink in America*, ed. Andrew F. Smith, 1:176-184. New York: Oxford University Press.

Wyman, Carol. 2004. Jell-O. In *The Oxford Encyclopedia of Food and Drink in America*, ed. Andrew F. Smith, 1:733-734. New York: Oxford University Press.

Wyman, Mark. 2000. *The Irish as American Industrial Pioneers. In Irish immigrants in McLean County, Illinois*, ed. Greg Koos:1-6. Bloomington: McLean County Historical Society.

Yoder, Robert. 2005. *Milestones and Altars Along my Road of Faith*. Eureka, IL: self-published Xerox, spiral binder.

Zanger, Mark H. 2004. German American Food. In *The Oxford Encyclopedia of Food and Drink in America*, ed. Andrew F. Smith, 1:561-567. New York City: Oxford University Press.

_____. 2004. Italian American Food. In *The Oxford Encyclopedia of Food and Drink in America*, ed. Andrew F. Smith, 1:716-724. New York City: Oxford University Press.

Zehr, Bertha Mae Reedy and Loren Zehr. 2006. *Richly Blessed: The Life and Memories of Bertha Zehr as Told to Loren Zehr*. Harrisonburg, VA.

INDEX

*To find specific businesses, look
under the business type (i.e. restaurants)*

ABOUT THE AUTHOR

Robert Dirks is an Emeritus Professor of Anthropology at Illinois State University in Normal, Illinois. He has conducted research in the areas of food and nutrition for nearly 30 years. His publications include papers in: Annual Review of Nutrition, Journal of Nutrition, The Cambridge World History of Human Disease, African Food Systems in Crisis, American Anthropologist, Current Anthropology, Natural History, and World Cultures.

www.ingramcontent.com/pod-product-compliance
Lightning Source LLC
Chambersburg PA
CBHW060241100426
42742CB00011B/1601